NOVA SCOTIA MUSEUM
HALIFAX   1979

CLEMENT W. CROWELL

NOVASCOTIAMAN

© The Nova Scotia Museum 1979
ISBN 0-919680-11-9

Published by
The Nova Scotia Museum
as a part of
The Education Resource Services Program
of the
DEPARTMENT OF EDUCATION
Province of Nova Scotia

Hon. Terence R.B. Donahoe
Minister

Carmen F. Moir
Deputy Minister

Produced by the Nova Scotia
Communications and Information Centre

Printed in Canada

To my wife
ESTHER LEWIS CROWELL
who has shared with me a deep interest
in the days of the Yarmouth sailing ships

CONTENTS

ILLUSTRATIONS

ACKNOWLEDGEMENTS

This book has been published with the help of a grant from the Canadian Federation for the Humanities using funds provided by the Social Sciences and Humanities Research Council of Canada.

I should like to express my appreciation to the many persons who have assisted in various ways in the preparation of the book:

Mr. J. Lynton Martin, Director of Cultural Services, N.S. Dept. of Education and Mr. Raymond A. Simpson, Publication and Reference Services, N.S. Dept. of Education, for their encouragement and help.

Mr. Wilfred E. Finbow, Editor, Publication and Reference Services, N.S. Department of Education and Mrs. Barbara Shaw, Editor, N.S. Museum, for editorial assistance.

Mr. Niels Jannasch, Curator Marine History, N.S. Museum, for help and advice.

Dr. Lewis H. King, Bedford Institute of Oceanography, Dartmouth, N.S., for preparing maps.

Capt. I.C. MacInnis, Dept. of Transport, Yarmouth, N.S., for help with marine terminology.

Mr. C.L. Merritt, New Orleans Cotton Exchange, for assistance re cotton freight rates.

Mr. Kenneth Seaman, Yarmouth, N.S., for giving me his fine collection of Yarmouth newspaper clippings relating to the sailing ships of Yarmouth.

Mr. Michael Trask, Yarmouth, N.S., for assistance in the use of marine insurance terms.

Miss Alice Wetmore, Librarian Yarmouth County Museum, for help in researching items of local history.

And Dr. Ben. Gullison of Vancouver for information concerning the Gullison family; my son, C. William Crowell, my brothers in-law Lt. Col. J. Gordon Quigley and J. Galen Vickery, my sister Eileen Quigley and George Leslie Green for their suggestions regarding the preparation of the manuscript and the many other persons and institutions in Canada, England and the United States who have provided me with assistance in my search for information.

And my thanks to (Mrs.) Beverley Penny Melanson of Salmon River who so willingly typed at least three revisions of the manuscript before it was edited.

Excerpt from *The Down Easters* by Basil Lubbock reprinted by special permission of Brown, Son & Ferguson, Ltd., Glasgow.

As a boy in Yarmouth, before World War 1, I lived between the homes of Captain Henry Lewis and his son Harry Lewis, and alongside the former home of Nathan Lewis. In 1920 I married Esther Lewis, the grand-daughter of Captain Henry. About forty years later, quite by chance, we found the material which has made it possible to recreate this story of a Yarmouth ship.

About 1958 Douglas Wyman, a friend of ours in Lake Annis, where we have our home, told us that the furniture and effects of a deceased ship captain were being sold, and that included in the sale would be the painting of a ship, the *N.B. Lewis*. The location of the captain's house was in Beaver River on the Bay of Fundy shore, about ten miles west of Lake Annis. The name of the ship had been recognized as being that of Esther's great-uncle and it was thought that we might like to buy it.

Going to Beaver River the next day, we found that the furnishings of the house were indeed being sold, and we were able to buy the painting. On the frame there was a small wooden plaque with the inscription 'Ship N.B. LEWIS – Gullison Commander 1887' and on the lower right side of the painting was the signature of the artist, 'H. Versaille Dunkirk 1887'. On the way home with the painting, it occurred to me that when Captain Gullison retired from sea, he might have saved some of his ship's papers. Knowing that the ship had been managed and partly owned by the firm of H. & N.B. Lewis, I realized that if the papers had indeed been saved, they would be of great interest to us.

When I returned to the Gullison house the next day, the lady who was selling the furnishings said that there was a quantity of books and papers in the attic. If I wanted them, she would be glad to give them to me, as she planned to discard them before selling the house. Returning the next week, I found a collection of books and cartons of papers in the back porch. Looking over the material, we found that some had no historical interest, but all the papers and books relating to the ship were taken home to Lake Annis.

Examining the papers afterwards, I found that there were a hundred or more letters written by my wife's grandfather, Henry Lewis, and great-uncle, Nathan Lewis, to Captain Gullison when he was in command of ships managed by the firm of H. & N.B. Lewis. Other letters were from his family and friends, as well as from ships' agents in various ports such as New York, Liverpool and London. Most interesting of all was a tissue book containing copies of the captain's letters.[1] In addition to the correspondence there were logs of the ship *N.B. Lewis*, lists of ships' stores, wage account books, invoices and other records. The collection looked so interesting I decided that when I settled into my retirement I should try to organize the material into a connected narrative. For various reasons, this time did not arrive until the spring of 1970.

During the next few years the letters were typed and arranged chronologically. Some of the tissue copies were indecipherable (many were so faint that hours were spent on one letter), but in the end it was possible to make copies of most of the letters. Putting all the correspondence, papers, logs and accounts together, there emerged the story of a captain and firm engaged in the trade of international freighting during the closing years of the sailing ship era.

To supplement the information contained in the collected papers of Captain Gullison, there has been research in the Yarmouth newspapers of the period, shipping records, real estate records, the archives of the Yarmouth County Museum library, the Provincial Archives of Nova Scotia and The Maritime History Group of Memorial University, St. John's, Newfoundland. More intimate knowledge of the local history and geography of the area concerned was obtained through visits and talks with the older residents.

An attempt has been made to supply enough narration and notes to make the letters understood by the general reader. Without altering the structure of the letters, there have been, for clarification of meaning, a few changes in punctuation, spelling, sentence length and wording. Such changes have been kept to a minimum so as to alter as little as possible the characteristic style of each writer.

---

1 Captain Gullsion's letters were preserved in a tissue copying book. Before the advent of the typewriter and carbon paper, a book of this type was in common use in business offices.

   During the school vacation months of July and August in the year 1912, I worked in the Yarmouth office of the Boston and Yarmouth Steamship Company as office boy. One of the responsibilities of this job was each day, in the late afternoon, to copy the day's letters in the tissue copying book.

   A letter written in ink was placed in the book face up and over it was turned a blank tissue page. Then a cloth rag the same size as the page was dipped in water, wrung out and placed on top of the tissues. Over this was placed a piece of heavy blotting paper and a piece of cardboard, both page size, to separate the pages being used from the pages upon which copies had already been made. (The most important part of this operation was the amount of moisture left in the cloth. If it was too wet, the copy was ink blotted; if too dry, the copy was too faint to be read.)

   After the letters for the day had been placed in the book, it was then put in a press. When a heavy screw was turned, the leaves of the book were pressed together, thus making the copy. The book was then taken from the press, the letters were removed and the copies studied to see if good legibility had been obtained. If not, the job had to be re-done.

To provide sufficient information for the reader to appreciate the story, the Introduction contains a short history of the port of Yarmouth and the development of its shipping industry, a review of influences affecting shipping, information about the ship owners, H. & N.B. Lewis, and the Gullison family.

Clement W. Crowell
Lake Annis
Yarmouth County, N.S.
1976

FIG. 1. Letter press and copying book.

History of the Port of Yarmouth and Development of its Shipping Industry

EARLY SETTLEMENT

For the first fifteen years of its existence, Yarmouth, Nova Scotia, was, in fact, a little colony of Massachusetts. While a scattering of the first settlers came from all over New England, the majority were from the two Capes — Cape Cod and Cape Ann — which enclose Massachusetts Bay. Of the first one hundred families, about forty came from within fifteen miles of Marblehead and half of the remainder from Cape Cod and Plymouth. From June, 1761, when the first settlers arrived from Cape Cod, until the outbreak of hostilities between the American colonies and Great Britain in 1775 − 76, there was a constant flow of trade and people back and forth between the New England settlement and Massachusetts. The war years stopped this easy communication but after the end of the war the traffic resumed.

It is evident that from the earliest years of settlement, the men of Yarmouth turned to the sea for their livelihood. Progress was slow in the eighteenth century and the first quarter of the nineteenth. Money was always scarce and times were hard. In the early days, without charts and with few navigational aids such as buoys and lighthouses, the sea took a heavy toll of men and ships. A study of the chart (page 7) will show that during the period covered, one third of all vessels built were lost and other records state that over 100 vessels sailed from port to be lost with all hands.

A review of the vessels wrecked provides considerable information about the early activities of Yarmouth sailors. Between 1777 and 1812 sloops and schooners were trading over an area extending from Quebec to the West Indies, including the Magdalene Islands, around the shores of the Gulf of St. Lawrence, Newfoundland, and Nova Scotia. In Boston, New York and Philadelphia, dried cod was sold and the vessels were loaded with a general

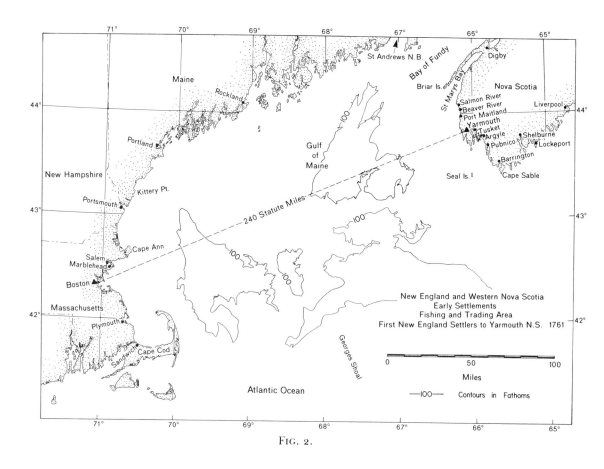

FIG. 2.

cargo for return to Yarmouth or Halifax. They were even venturing across the Atlantic, for in 1805 the schooner *Blanche*, 45 tons, owned by William Robertson and others, with Robert Robertson as master, sailed for England from Yarmouth in September and was not afterward heard from. These schooners had tonnages ranging from 12 to 103, with most being between 20 and 50 tons. Of many of them, particularly those on trading voyages, the master was also the owner or part owner.

In 1784, after the Revolutionary War had ended, there was another influx of settlers to Yarmouth County from the former American colonies – now the United States. These were United Empire Loyalists – people who had remained loyal to the British Crown during the war years and who now sought new homes under the British flag. The 'Loyalists' of Dutch and English descent came in greatest numbers from New York and New Jersey, with lesser numbers from Delaware, Virginia and the Carolinas. Many came of families which had been settled in North America for three to five generations. As Yarmouth County was first settled by French Acadians, more than one hundred years before the arrival of the New Englanders and Loyalists, it can be said that few parts of North America have inhabitants of European ancestry with a longer history on this continent than this part of western Nova Scotia.

Yarmouth opened as a port of Registry for Shipping in 1840. Previous to this time vessels were registered at Halifax (1787 – 1840) and at Shelburne (1787 – 1823).

Modern research has shown that it is difficult to obtain accurate shipping information from the records of the early 19th century. The figures compiled by Lawson are therefore not totally reliable. Despite this, the records can be accepted as providing information relating to the size, type and number of vessels built, used and lost by the Yarmouth shipowners during the period covered.

From the beginning to the end of the sailing ship era, the trading conditions which existed between Nova Scotia and the United States were very important to the prosperity of Yarmouth. There follows, therefore, a summarization of this particular relationship as well as other general conditions affecting the growth of the shipping industry of Yarmouth.

REVOLUTIONARY WAR

The Revolutionary War of 1775–83 had a deleterious effect on the development of the infant shipping industry of Yarmouth. Although Great Britain was the dominant sea power, there were a number of American privateers operating off the Nova Scotia coast, making raids on the little settlements. However, there continued to be some traffic between Yarmouth and the Marblehead area and Boston. Usually it was for the sale of dried cod and the purchase of the various necessities of life so scarce in Nova Scotia. At the same time some Yarmouth vessels were providing conveyance for Americans who had been captured by British warships and imprisoned in Halifax, but who had escaped and made their way down the Atlantic coast to Yarmouth. There were still many close family relationships between the people of Marblehead and western Nova Scotia, and considerable sympathy for the captured Americans seeking a way home to New England.

AMERICAN REVOLUTION, WAR OF 1812 AND SUBSEQUENT TRADE RESTRICTIONS

At the close of the American Revolution, the British Government, in July of 1783, passed an Order-in-Council which stated that hereafter trade with the British West Indies must be carried on in British ships owned and manned by British subjects. This was a move to prevent vessels of the newly-formed United States from trading *legally* with the West Indies and was an encouragement to the British ship owners of Nova Scotia. In retaliation against this restriction, the states of New York, Massachusetts, New Hampshire and Rhode Island imposed various restrictions on British vessels using their ports. Southern states such as Virginia and the Carolinas continued to allow Nova Scotian vessels to engage in trade through their ports.

Another restriction on the trade of Nova Scotian ships was an act proclaimed by the United States Congress on July 4, 1789, levying duties on goods imported into the country, with a ten per cent rebate on goods imported in vessels built and owned by American citizens. Also, a United States vessel entering a u.s. port paid a tonnage duty of six cents a ton, while British vessels were required to pay fifty cents a ton. Then in 1792 annual bounties were given on vessels amounting to $1.50 per ton between 20 and 30 tons, and $2.50 per ton for every ton over 30. Three-eights of this bounty was to be paid to the owner and five-eights to crews. The u.s. Tariff and Navigation Act was amended in 1794 providing for a ten per cent surtax on all duties on goods imported in a foreign vessel.

The war between Great Britain and the United States which commenced in 1812 and ended in 1814 certainly disturbed the peaceful trade and fishing operations in Yarmouth. The net effect on the port, however, is a little difficult to assess.

In 1812 a brig and at least three schooners were captured by u.s. privateers; in 1813 privateers captured three schooners, and 1814 saw the loss of a brigantine and a schooner. On the other hand, during the same years a number of American vessels were captured and are listed as prizes obtained by Yarmouth ship owners: 1812 – a schooner and two sloops; 1813 – a brig and five schooners; 1814 – one ship, one brigantine, eight schooners and two sloops. The fact that Yarmouth continued to build schooners in gradually increasing numbers (1812 – 12 schooners; 1813 – 13 schooners; 1814 – 19 schooners) would perhaps show that for the total war period more money was made than lost.

4

A Commercial Convention between the United States and Great Britain in 1815 bound these countries to impose no discriminatory duty on ships or trade between them, but Great Britain stipulated that she should continue to regulate the trade of her colonies in the West Indies and on the American continent. In this way Nova Scotian vessels were assisted somewhat in their trade with the West Indies.

In 1816 an export tax of twenty shillings a ton was laid on plaster shipped from Nova Scotia to the United States in a U.S. vessel. The United States Congress retaliated by forbidding a foreign vessel to bring plaster to the U.S. from a port from which American vessels could not carry it free of export tax.

All in all, between 1789 and 1828 the United States Congress passed fifty tariff and other laws protecting American shipping against foreign competition, which were bound to have a restricting effect on other than American shipping. Under the Reciprocity Act of 1828 the United States allowed British vessels to bring cargoes to U.S. ports in return for the same privilege for U.S. vessels in British ports. However, the Nova Scotian vessels still had certain preferences in trade with the West Indies. For instance, a cargo of lumber from St. Andrews, N.B., to the West Indies, carried in a Nova Scotian vessel, could, because of preferential import charges at the West Indies port, make more profit than the same cargo from Maine carried in a U.S. vessel. Yarmouth vessels engaged in this trade on a substantial scale.

In 1849, in recognition of terms more favourable to U.S. shipping incorporated in the revision of British navigation laws in 1849, British vessels were admitted to U.S. ports on the same terms as U.S. vessels, and in 1854, under a Reciprocity Treaty between Great Britain and the United States, fish from Nova Scotia entered the United States duty free. In 1858, however, the U.S. fishing bounties were repealed.

EFFECTS OF CRIMEAN WAR, CIVIL WAR AND OTHER FACTORS AFFECTING SHIPPING

The Crimean War, 1854-1856, was a time of prosperity in shipping because of the great demand for vessels to transport troops and supplies. During these years the number of barks built yearly for Yarmouth almost tripled over the average of previous years.

Oil was discovered in Pennsylvania in 1859. The freighting of oil from Philadelphia and New York to Europe and the Far East became an important source of income for Yarmouth ships during the latter part of the nineteenth century.

The greatest single impetus given to the building of ocean freight carriers by Yarmouth ship owners during the nineteenth century was provided by the Civil War in the United States. While the Confederate States were defeated on land, the war practically ruined the New York and New England shipping industry. Many United States ships were sold to Great Britain and thus there developed a great opportunity for British shipping. During the years 1862-65 Yarmouth ship owners built sixty-one barks and seventeen ships. Many of the fortunes of Yarmouth shipping families stemmed from this war.

After the Civil War, in 1866, the Reciprocity Treaty of 1854 was repealed by the United States Congress because of the sympathy in Great Britain and her American colonies for the Confederate cause. This situation lasted until 1871 when Canada was again given a free market for fish in the United States.

The United States continued to support its maritime commerce by prohibiting foreign registered vessels from engaging in coastal trade between U.S. ports. A Nova Scotian ship, for instance, could not carry grain from San Francisco to an eastern Atlantic port. However, the grain trade from California to Europe was for many years a source of revenue to Yarmouth ships. There was a considerable variation in freight rates. For example, in the years 1872-74 the rates were approximately between 75 and 80 shillings per ton. These were profitable rates as it was considered a vessel of 1,000 tons or over could operate on a rate of 40 shillings.[1]

Following the American Civil War the United States trade in ocean freighting declined rapidly. On the one hand Great Britain began to enter the trade on a scale and at rates with which the United States found it hard to compete. On the other hand, the money which had accumulated in Boston, New York and Philadelphia could be used more advantageously in the development of business interests within the U.S. In these cities money made from the sea was invested on land in the building of factories, railroads, banks and in real estate development.

TYPES OF VESSELS

The period after the close of the War of 1812-15 to the middle of the century was one of slow but steady growth in the number of vessels owned in Yarmouth and in the experience gained by the owners in the development of trade. The fishing schooners reached an average tonnage of between fifty and sixty tons in the decade of the 1830's and remained at that average size for fifty years. Over two hundred schooners were built, but eighty of these were lost.

At first the most favored type of vessel for freighting was the brig, which was built in steadily increasing numbers until 1840; but from 1840 onward the brigantine became more popular and exceeded the number of brigs. The brigantine was a little more manoeuvreable because of its large fore and aft mainsail, and a little cheaper to operate because of its smaller crew; the brig, however, was, on an average, larger and could thus carry more freight. The type chosen would depend on the expected use of the vessel. There was also a start in the building of barks and ships but no more than twenty were built before 1840 and none was reported lost.[2]

1   Ship *N.B. Lewis* in 1886 received 27 shillings and sixpence.
2   See Record of Shipping, p. 7.

Fig. 3 Record of Yarmouth Shipping 1787 – 1900

Years	Sloops			Schooners			Brigantines			Brigs			Barks			Ships			Barkentines		
	A	B	C	A	B	C	A	B	C	A	B	C	A	B	C	A	B	C	A	B	C
1787-99	3	53	2	98	33	18	1	53	1	2						1	290				
1800-09	4	37	2	87	46	12	3	140	1	3	56					1	300				
1810-19	8	51	1	128	54	30	2	119		14	202	3	7	302							
1820-29	1	13	2	95	45	27	7	116		22	174	3	6	226		4	298				
1830-39	1	36	1	101	46	28	36	120	10	25	202	8									
Total	17		8	509		115	49		12	66	163	14	13			6					
1840-49				106	55	21	54	120	22	43	209	20	26	362	11	1	559				
1850-59				117	51	31	44	139	26	37	260	24	56	499	17	3	483				
1860-69				174	55	66	36	128	27	17	278	20	104	528	38	37	854	10			
1870-79				141	56	66	31	183	21	2	248	4	72	881	48	79	1169	25			
1880-89				90	66	32	7	190	8	6	336	3	9	1134	36	21	1594	29	3	508	
1890-00				50	47	6	1	144		4	225	8	5	869	12	3	1680	12	11	545	6
Total				678		222	173		104	109		79	272		162	144		76	14		6
Grand Total				1187		337	222		116	175		93	285		162	150		76	14		6

Column A – Number of Vessels
Column B – Average Tonnage of Vessels
Column C – Number of Vessels Lost

Total Vessels Owned – 2050
Total Vessels Lost at Sea – 798

From records compiled by J. Murray Lawson long-time editor and owner of the weekly newspaper *The Yarmouth Herald*. Recorded in three volumes:

Record of Shipping of Yarmouth N.S. pub. 1876
Appendix to the Record of Shipping of Yarmouth N.S. pub. 1884
Yarmouth Reminiscences pub. 1902

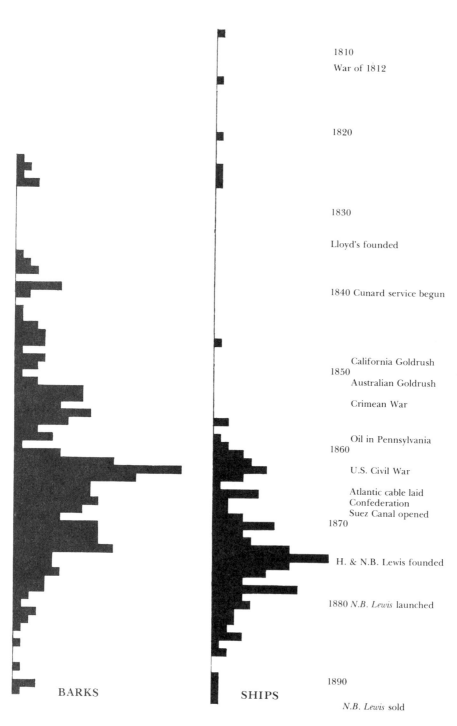

FIG. 4 Registry of Shipping,
Yarmouth, N.S., 1799 – 1892

1799
1800

1810
War of 1812

1820

1830

Lloyd's founded

1840 Cunard service begun

California Goldrush
1850
Australian Goldrush

Crimean War

Oil in Pennsylvania
1860
U.S. Civil War

Atlantic cable laid
Confederation
Suez Canal opened
1870

H. & N.B. Lewis founded

1880 *N.B. Lewis* launched

1890

N.B. Lewis sold

BARKS

SHIPS

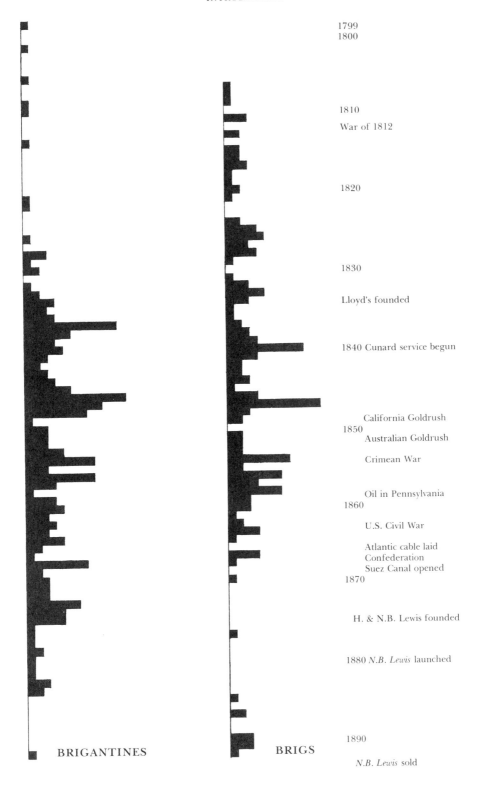

1799
1800

1810
War of 1812

1820

1830

Lloyd's founded

1840 Cunard service begun

California Goldrush
1850
Australian Goldrush

Crimean War

Oil in Pennsylvania
1860

U.S. Civil War

Atlantic cable laid
Confederation
Suez Canal opened
1870

H. & N.B. Lewis founded

1880 *N.B. Lewis* launched

1890

N.B. Lewis sold

BRIGANTINES   BRIGS

Schooners continued to be used for fishing and trading around the coasts of Nova Scotia, the Gulf of St. Lawrence and Newfoundland. The larger ones took cargoes of fish to the West Indies, the Mediterranean and markets in the United States.

During the period 1840-1865 schooners continued to be built in greater quantity than any other type, and the use of brigs and brigantine gradually declined, 1846 being the peak year for brigantines and 1847 for brigs.

By the middle of the century the expanding ocean freight trade made larger vessels more lucrative and the bark with three masts was preferred to the two-masted brigs and brigantines. The greatest number of barks was built in the decade 1860-69 with an average of 528 tons.

In 1868 and 1869, Donald McKay, the famous ship builder born in Jordan Falls, Nova Scotia, launched from his yards in Boston two ships, *Sovereign of the Seas* and *Glory of the Seas*, for the California grain trade. They were designed to have more speed than the old 'lumber-carriers' but more cargo capacity than the clippers, and they could be sailed by a crew half the size of a clipper's crew. Ships and barks of this type became popular in northern New England, particularly in Maine, during the latter part of the nineteenth century. They were known as 'Down Easters'. During this same period much the same type of vessel was being built in the Maritime provinces. Throughout the shipping circles of the world, the latter were known as 'Bluenosers' or 'Novascotiamen'. A substantial percentage of the vessels of this type built in Canada were owned in the port of Yarmouth.

The narrative of the Yarmouth ships *N.B.Lewis* and *Republic*, as told in the letters and records in this volume, is typical of the many similar vessels of this pattern engaged in the world shipping trade of the time.

The years 1870 to 1879 saw the full-rigged ship take over as the favourite type, although barks continued to be built in larger tonnages but fewer numbers. Between 1870 and 1879 seventy-nine full-rigged ships were built, with an average capacity of 1,169 tons. The peak year was 1879 when there were registered in the port of Yarmouth 59 ships of 681 to 1,680 tons, 80 barks of 390 to 1,192 tons, 13 brigs of 115 to 440 tons, and 121 schooners of 20 to 120 tons. The registered total was more than eleven per cent of the Canadian vessel tonnage for that year. Shipping intelligence of the time showed that there was seldom a day when a Yarmouth vessel was not entering or leaving an Atlantic port.

In summation, the most prosperous years for Yarmouth were from 1860 to 1880. Until 1879 there was a steady increase in the number of vessels launched and their average size. It will thus be noted that the great expansion in this port came as the clipper ship era drew to a close in both the United States and Great Britain.

TYPES OF CARGO

In the period 1815-1850 brigs and brigantines carried fish and lumber to the West Indies and brought back the produce of the islands. One of the most common routes was to St. Andrews, New Brunswick, for lumber, thence to the West Indies and back to Yarmouth or some other Nova Scotian port with produce or salt. Potatoes and apples were carried from the Annapolis Valley to Yarmouth and Halifax, plaster from Windsor, Nova Scotia, to the United States, and general cargoes from Boston and New York to Nova Scotia. There were such diverse cargoes as flour from Virginia to Halifax, cattle and hay from Yarmouth to Bermuda, oak staves and pitch pine from Norfolk, Virginia, to the West Indies, mahogany[3] from Yarmouth to England and raw hides from Barbados to Yarmouth.

During the middle and later years of the nineteenth century the nature of some of this cargo changed. Timber and deals went from Quebec and New Brunswick ports to Great Britain, with a return cargo of coal, rails, iron or manufactured goods to the United States. Grain and oil were shipped from Philadelphia and New York to Europe and, in later years, oil to the Far East.

Cotton was carried from New Orleans to Great Britain; pitch pine from a number of southern U.S. ports to South America and Europe; coal from Great Britain was transported to ports all over the world by Yarmouth ships over a period of many years. Guano was a return cargo to Great Britain from the Pacific coast of South America and, in later years, grain was a frequent cargo from San Francisco to Europe.

Toward the end of the nineteenth century many of the Yarmouth ships were in the lumber trade from the St. Lawrence River, and ports in New Brunswick and Nova Scotia and New England, to South America, particularly to Buenos Aires and the Rio de la Plata. Various cargoes were obtained for the return voyage from South America and the West Indies. Far too often, however, no return cargo was available and the return voyage was 'in ballast'.

REASONS FOR THE SUCCESS OF YARMOUTH SHIPPING

A number of factors might be cited to account for the success of Yarmouth ship owners in the world freighting trade:

Experience had been acquired. By the middle of the 19th century there had been accumulated a considerable amount of experience in the building and operation of vessels for general trading and freighting.

All along the Yarmouth waterfront were a succession of wharves with their docking facilities, warehouses, storage sheds and sail lofts. Interspersed between the wharves along the shore and to the north of the docks were several shipyards. Moreover, on the coast of Nova Scotia from Shelburne on the

3 Probably bought in the Caribbean as a speculative venture.

Atlantic to the Annapolis Basin on the Bay of Fundy were, at the height of the sailing ship era, perhaps 30 other shipyards from which Yarmouth owners could commission vessels to be built. The yards most commonly used were at Shelburne, Tusket, Yarmouth and along the Bay of Fundy coast from Port Maitland to Belliveau Cove.

Capital was available. Vessels were usually purchased or built by groups. The total cost was divided into 64 shares. Large firms or ship owners might subscribe for the majority of shares in any one transaction while other merchants or individuals would subscribe for one or more shares as their financial circumstances might allow. At the end of a successful voyage profits on a ship would be divided on a per share basis. Usually one of the local business firms acted as manager of the vessel. This included arranging for captain and crew, outfitting the ship, arranging for the purchase of supplies, obtaining charters for freight, the payment for ship's expenses and the distribution of profits to shareholders. In foreign ports the captain acted for the owners in many of the above capacities.

In the town and county of Yarmouth and throughout western Nova Scotia there were hundreds of individuals owning one or more shares in many different vessels. As returns were received from one vessel the proceeds were usually re-invested in a new vessel being launched. By investing smaller sums in a number of different vessels rather than a comparatively large amount in one, subscribers felt they were not 'putting all their eggs in one basket'.

At intervals, shares of individuals, firms, or estates would be auctioned off to the highest bidder. Values of the shares varied with the age of the vessel, her condition and the general business situation in the freighting trade.

Skilled labour and facilities for the building and repair of vessels was available. As Yarmouth continued to develop as a ship owning community it became almost self-sufficient as a center for shipbuilding needs. Within a range of about 10 to 15 miles from the sea coast there were good stands of timber suitable for ship building needs, including long straight sticks of black spruce for the masts and spars.

Specialists in all kinds of ship work developed. There were those skilled in constructing the hull with its great keel, heavy ribs and planking; others were mast and spar makers, or finish carpenters for fine detail and the interior finish of cabins. There were block makers for pulleys, pattern makers for the foundries, riggers for all the stays and running gear of a large full-rigged ship, sail makers, and perhaps last but not least, an artist who carved the figurehead.

Captain James F. Landers' reminiscences of the early 1870's, published during the nineteen thirties and forties in the Yarmouth newspapers, contain some interesting details of the waterfront of the period.[4]

4 Clippings from Yarmouth newspapers on file in the library of the Yarmouth County Museum with other papers concerning the ship *N.B. Lewis.*

... After mid-summer new ships built in yards in nearby villages would be towed here to be rigged and fitted out for sea. Their spars were ready and piled on a wharf, and their rigging and sails were in lofts all ready, because when the keel was laid the dimensions were known, and all would be ready when needed. All the Fall ships would be rigged here and as baseball was not much thought of then, boys would go to the wharves to watch things.

Many of our successful captains got their first idea of the sea there and many of the girls could talk ship and name sails. In 1935 I had proof of this. I had two cases of photos of old Yarmouth ships showing at the Fall Fair. An elderly lady with others came to look them over and turned to me and said "Mr. Landers, some of your ships carry skysis" [skysails]. I said, "Madame are you a Yarmouth girl?" She said "I am and well remember those days when ships were rigged at our wharves". I said "Do you remember the riggers singing their chanties?" She said "Indeed I do and what music; we girls would gather at the head of the wharf to listen".

Among other details remembered by Captain Landers was the Kinney Haley Woodworking factory making doors, sashes, tanks, skylights and interior cabin fittings; George F. Allen's five story cooperage and box factory making barrels and boxes of all sizes for the fish trade, and buckets, rakes and plows for farmers. Those factories employed one hundred or more men. In the large one-story sail loft of Zebina Goudey, the stoves hung from the roof leaving the floor clear for the making of the large mainsail. All the new ships took on extra sails and many were made to be sent abroad to Yarmouth ships in various ports. Owners kept a record of the size of sails their vessels needed.

Opposite the slip wharf was the six-forge blacksmith shop of W.H. Gridley,[5] a skillful iron worker and one of nature's gentlemen. His iron handiwork took first prize at the Fall Fair of Yarmouth County.

Near the Gridley[6] blacksmith shop was the Pendrigh Brass Foundry where three generations of the family worked. The grandfather, with a pronounced Scottish burr in his speech, was a pleasant old gentleman. Also named by Captain Landers were a salt works, a spar yard, a tannery and a grist mill. Other firms listed were Crowell's blacksmith shop, J.D. Horton's block shop and the foundry of Burrell-Johnson.

Communications had improved. The great improvement in communications after the middle of the 19th century made it possible for the ship owners of Yarmouth, in their small offices, to manage fleets of vessels engaged in freighting throughout the oceans of the world.

By 1850, Samuel Cunard, who commenced his shipping operations in Halifax, Nova Scotia, was operating a regular steamship service between Liver-

5 See note below.
6 There is now in the Yarmouth County Museum an iron steering tiller weighing approximately 700 pounds, with an inside diameter of 18 inches. It was constructed by W.H. Gridley and considered such a fine piece of iron work that it was displayed in 1900 at the Paris Exhibition.

pool, England, Halifax and Boston. Yarmouth ship owners had steamers in regular service to Boston and after 1879 the Western Counties Railway, organized by Yarmouth capitalists, was operating a daily passenger service to Digby, from where there was a steamer to Saint John, New Brunswick, and a ferry on the Annapolis Basin connected with a train for Halifax. After 1869 transcontinental trains were going from the Atlantic to the Pacific in the United States and after 1885 in Canada.

The Pacific Mail Steamship Company had a regular steamship service between San Francisco and Hong Kong after 1868.

A telegraph office was opened in Yarmouth in 1852 and the Atlantic cable was finished in 1866. After 1861, telegrams could be sent to San Francisco, and ten years later a cable was completed across the Pacific to China.

Reliable agents had established their businesses. These world-wide communication systems usually made it possible for the managing owners to arrange for their ships' cargoes through their agents in various ports in the United States and England.

Many of the owners had served their time at sea and had become personally acquainted with agents in the various ports. Some of the agents representing Yarmouth firms were: W.F.Hager & Co., 111 Walnut Street, Philadelphia; J.F.Whitney & Co., 16 State Street, New York; J.G.Hall & Co., Boston; John Black & Co., 19 Change Alley, Cornhill, London, E.C.; G.J.Soley & Co., 28 Brunswick Street, Liverpool; and T.C.Jones & Co., Liverpool and Antwerp.

These firms not only found cargoes but also acted as financial agents. They collected charges for freights and when necessary advanced sums for port expenses. Principals or agents of these and other firms frequently visited Yarmouth to keep in personal touch with the owners.

Banks facilitated business transactions. The first banking facility in Yarmouth was a branch of the Halifax-based Bank of Nova Scotia, which established an agency there in 1839. A sign of the increasing prosperity of Yarmouth was the establishment of two banks financed by local capitalists. In January, 1865, the Bank of Yarmouth began business with a subscribed capital of $400,000. Within four years another bank, the Exchange Bank of Yarmouth, was established with a similar capitalization of $400,000.

When the captain or an agent collected the freight due a ship, a banker's draft would customarily be purchased on a London bank, which would remit the funds to the Yarmouth owners through the local Yarmouth bank.

Insurance companies were established. Local histories state that the first marine insurance company in Yarmouth was organized in 1809, but that it only lasted until 1812, when it went 'out of business'. Probably the shareholders were not prepared to carry insurance risks during the War of 1812, when there were a number of American privateers cruising the waters between the Nova Scotian coast and the United States mainland. Between 1812 and 1838, the *Record of*

Yarmouth Shipping lists ninety-four vessels lost, with no mention of any insurance.

The next insurance company established in Yarmouth was the Marine Insurance Association, which was organized on January 30, 1837, a meeting having been held on that day of 'shipowners, merchants and others interested'. It was decided that the sum of £10,000 should be subscribed as a stock for the company, and a committee of nine gentlemen was appointed to prepare the necessary rules and regulations. On March 18, 1837, the Society put forth its first announcement as follows:

Yarmouth Marine Insurance Association

The above Association, being now formed, and all the Shares subscribed for, offer to take risks on Vessels, Merchandise, etc. belonging to the County of Yarmouth, against the perils and dangers of the seas and other usual risks (according to the form and tenor of their policies) to an estent not exceeding Fifteen Hundred Pounds on any one vessel or risk.

The Committee chosen at a Meeting of the Shareholders will meet on every Thursday in the week at 2 o'clock, p.m., at the office of the Subscriber, to decide upon the applications submitted to them, and for the transaction of ordinary business.

Blank forms of application, terms as to credit on premiums, etc. and all other necessary information can be obtained at the Office of the Broker.

All applications for Insurance will be addressed to the Broker, and letters per mail to him must be postpaid.

Yarmouth, March 18th, 1837   *Benjamin Barnard*, Broker.

There were originally 60 shareholders and 80 shares. The shares were subsequently increased by stages until in 1858 they numbered 200. The business of this company was brought to a close in 1883 with net proceeds of $206,171.00.

Between 1837 and 1870 five other marine insurance companies were established by local businessmen.[7] In 1882 the Boston Marine Insurance Company of Boston, Mass., established an agency in Yarmouth which was so successful that by 1886 the last of the local insurance companies had ceased to do business.

Decline of Shipping

As previously stated, the period from 1860 to 1880 was the most prosperous for Yarmouth ship owners, the year 1879 marking the peak for tonnage owned in the port. During the next twenty years, however, the decline was as pronounced as the previous increase. By the 1880's it was realized that the de-

---

7   Among these were the Pacific Insurance Company which began business in February, 1865, of which Nathan B. Lewis was a director, and the Oriental Insurance Company, established January 1, 1874, with Henry Lewis as one of the directors.

velopment of the iron and steel sailing vessels in Great Britain, the opening of the Suez canal and the use of tramp steamers for bulk cargo was giving the wooden ships of ports such as Yarmouth stiff competition.

As early as 1838 a small iron-hulled sailing vessel, the bark *Ironsides*, 271 tons, was built at Liverpool, England, for Jackson and Gordon. She proved satisfactory and from this start the building of iron hulls began to increase steadily and experience in this type of design continued to improve. By 1854 a special committee of Lloyd's Register was able to draw up the first general rules for the classification of iron vessels and by the later fifties they began to appear in large numbers. By 1860 the prices of high grade wooden vessels and the iron square riggers had become approximately equal in Great Britain. With the end of the sixties the iron sailing vessels of Great Britain were replacing the wooden square-riggers in the ocean freighting trade.

During the period of change in construction from wood to iron and steel there was, for a time, a type of vessel known as a *composite*. The frame of this type was fabricated of iron or steel and the hull planked of wood (usually teak). The famous *Cutty Sark*, now lying at the dock of the Greenwich Museum in England, is a vessel of this type.

During the period of rapid growth in the steel ship building industry of Great Britain the French shipyards found they could not compete in price with the British yards. The French Government therefore, desirous of encouraging the building up of the French merchant marine, began a policy of providing bounties for both the construction and operation of sailing ships. With bounties amounting to 65 francs ($12.55 U.S.) per ton for French built metal sailing vessels and a subsidy towards the operation, the owners were able to make profits of 20 to 25% on a voyage. This policy resulted in a heavy investment in French shipping and a decrease in the world freight rates, particularly on grain and other long-voyage trades such as oil and sugar.

Thus as the nineteenth century drew to a close the aging wooden ships of Yarmouth found it more and more difficult to obtain cargoes at favourable rates. At the end of the era the most common loads were lumber from North to South America and deals from the southern United States to Europe or South America.

As the demand for the wooden vessels declined and the steel sailing ship demonstrated its successful use, some Yarmouth ship owners, in the 1890's, purchased and operated a few iron and steel vessels. Eighteen vessels of this type were bought by Canadian owners of which nine were owned in Yarmouth. However, for Yarmouth owners, even the steel sailing ships were not found to be profitable, and none were purchased after 1900.

A Yarmouth syndicate of local businessmen also experimented in the ownership of a tramp steamer. The *Usher*, 2,350 tons, was bought in 1901. One of the owners, Harry Lewis, stated this vessel was not a profitable operation and she was sold at a loss.

Despite the increasing competition from the European shipyards, the Yarmouth ship owners found it difficult to concede defeat in an industry which had grown and flourished for over a century. Through the 1880's the shipyards of western Nova Scotia, while not as busy as in former years, were still launching vessels for the ocean freighting trade. However, as the ships and barks were wrecked, lost at sea or sold to foreign owners, they were seldom replaced with new launchings. By 1890 the number of ships owned was reduced to 36 and the number of barks to 37.

By the turn of the century, the shipyards were deserted spots and the days of prosperity were over. Most of the ship owners went out of business. The few that remained changed the direction of their interest from ocean freighting to other activities. Many decades of shipping records were regarded as old paper to be burnt or thrown off the wharf. Of the hundreds of Nova Scotian sea captains who commanded vessels in this interesting period of marine history, few left any extensive records. Some of the ship's logs have survived but, in most cases, the notations are short and terse with little to interest the student of the period.

The correspondence which forms the basis of this narrative can be considered as almost unique. In order that it may be better understood the reader is first introduced to the personalities involved: the Lewis brothers who were the managing owners of the ships, and the Gullison family which provided the captains to sail them.

Those Involved in the Correspondence Which Follows

THE LEWIS BROTHERS

Captain Henry Lewis, born in 1830, and his brother Nathan, two years younger, were descendants of Waitstill Lewis, an early settler of Yarmouth from Westerly, Rhode Island.

Henry went to sea as a boy of fifteen and by the time he was twenty-one had become captain of the brigantine *MicMac*, 104 tons, built in 1847 and owned by C. & G.W. Tooker. Four years later, in 1855, he is listed as owning eight shares in the brigantine *Avon*, built in Yarmouth the same year. His brother-in-law, William Rogers, was the principal owner, with twenty-four shares. The *Yarmouth Herald* records the *Avon*, Lewis, master, cleared from Yarmouth for Saint John in ballast October 21, 1855. The ship was probably bound for a load of lumber.

The passing of the Merchant Shipping Act in 1854 made it necessary for all captains of ships having British registry to pass an examination of competency as set by The Lords of the Committee of Privy Council for Trade, commonly known as the Board of Trade. Captain Lewis took this examination at Belfast, Ireland, on January 5, 1864, and received his certificate, number 30054, on January 11.

During the next ten years, until he retired from the sea, he was master of various Yarmouth ships engaged in the ocean freighting trade. In his later years, he was able to say he had never lost a vessel nor made an insurance claim.

In a short biography in *Wooden Ships and Iron Men* Frederick William Wallace states that Captain Lewis died in December, 1921, aged 91 years, an honoured citizen of his native town.

The writer, as a boy in his late teens, before World War 1, did not know Captain Henry Lewis well. He was a personage who lived nearby and was respected as such. Recollections of his grand-daughter, Esther Lewis Crowell, will provide a more intimate picture of him.

'I first remember my Grandfather at the turn of this century when he was in his early seventies, so he always seemed elderly to me. As a child, he struck me as being a big man, but on looking back, I rather think he was broad shouldered and of average height. His eyes, the colour of the Atlantic on a fair day, were set off by a sun-tanned and weathered skin and thus perhaps looked bluer than they actually were. He wore a beard, kept trimmed and neat, and had a vigorous shock of steel-gray hair. He was deliberate and slow of speech and had probably trained himself in this habit, so giving himself sufficient time to think, and leeway to consider the subject at hand before making any rash committments. He belonged to the breed amply educated for the time, whose chief source of reading was the Bible and the daily newspaper. He was not a laughing man, for his Puritan background kept a tight rein on his emotions, and though he was a strict disciplinarian, I never heard him raise his voice in anger or even irritation as we children ran through his house a dozen times a day. In fact, I am sure that he thoroughly enjoyed the life and colour that his grandchildren brought into the old home. As well as a love for children he had a great fondness for cats, and often allowed Tabby and her semi-annual batch of kittens to come into the house so that he might enjoy their playful antics.

Grandfather walked to the offices each day, and during the colder months of the year always wore a heavy navy blue reefer and a captain's cap with patent leather bill. Sunday was a different story when, as a family, we attended services at Providence Methodist Church. Then he was dressed in heavy, dark, Irish serge and wore a soft grey felt hat. After church, we gathered at our grandparents' home for our weekly noon-time Sunday dinners where we were served juicy roast beef topped off with desserts of apple or mincemeat pies. I also have memories of our Christmas dinners at Grandfather's when the whole family, including six grandchildren, gathered around a linen damask covered table, centered always with a rosy Christmas cactus and groaning with delicious food.

Another custom, during the summer months of my early years, was a Saturday drive behind one of the horses – 'Bess' or 'Scud'. My younger sister Adaline and I sat on a little brown, upholstered iron seat which Grandfather had had made by one of the black-smiths of the town. We were seated with our backs to the dashboard and facing our grandparents. I can remember driving up the Fundy shore road to visit one of the Gullison captains after he had retired from the sea or, as the saying went 'swallowed the anchor'.

I cannot remember either my great uncle Nathan Lewis or his wife Adaline, as they both died soon after I was born. I do remember their beautiful garden which lived long after them.

Henry's brother Nathan did not become a sailor. He was a merchant and the records show that for some years previous to the formation of the Lewis firm he was buying shares in Yarmouth vessels and thus accumulating experience in the shipping industry. His reputation as a leading businessman of the town was recognized when he was elected a member of the first Town Council.

The firm of H. & N.B. Lewis was founded in 1874. The business establishment, at the southern end of the Yarmouth waterfront, comprised wharves, warehouses, fish sheds, the 'lower store' and the 'upper store'. The lower store was a ships' chandlery near the wharves carrying all the various supplies needed by the vessels, fishermen and sailors. The upper store, about a block up the hill on the corner of Main Street, was a general merchandise emporium with its own office staff, clerks and delivery service. On top of the warehouses and sheds, and on the surrounding ground area, were drying flakes for the codfish brought in by the fishing vessels.

In the early years the firm was chiefly concerned with the management of barks and ships engaged in the world-wide freighting trade. As this business declined, they expanded their interests in the fishing fleet, and trade with the West Indies. As the latter declined, they entered the coal trade. A descriptive booklet about Yarmouth published in 1918 stated that 'H. & N.B. Lewis own a wharf of 60,000 square feet utilized for the unloading and storage of hard and soft coal, as well as fishing supplies'.

Esther Lewis Crowell remembers the Lewis office as it was at the turn of the century:

Back of the lower store was the office. It was a room snug and cosy with a pot-bellied stove in the corner on which there always seemed to be a black iron kettle with the soft sound of simmering water escaping through its swan-necked spout. The walls of the office were wainscoted three-quarters of the way to the ceiling, and where the wooden panels ended there were shelves which ringed the room and on which sat small oaken chests, each lettered in gold and black with the name of some vessel. Usually there was the wonderful frangrance of coffee beans which were ground in the big red coffee mill which stood in the outer store. Mingled with this splendid aroma was the smell of Barbados molasses, hemp, tamarinds, tar and all the odors of a ships' chandlery. Even to this day, after a lapse of more than 60 years, any one of those smells will occasionally waft me back in memory to my childhood days. The office of the lower store looked over the harbour, and by one small-paned window was Grandfather's swivel chair from which he watched the harbour's activities. Robert Ellenwood, the book-keeper, was perched on his high stool at his sloping desk, his black felt hat pushed towards the back of his head, while his snow-white locks fringed the collar of his frock-tailed coat. The heels of his

FIG. 5. Wharf buildings of H. & N.B. Lewis.

FIG. 6. "Upper" Store of H. & N.B. Lewis, Main St., Yarmouth, taken c. 1910.

high-laced boots were locked securely back of the worn rungs of the birch stool and behind an ear was the invariable handy pencil.

When I was a little thing I remember visiting the office and like any curious child I asked 'Mr. Ellenwood, what is really in the little trunks?' He was slow to answer but finally lifted his head, and with a sweeping motion of his arms said 'I guess they are your Grandfather's graveyard'.

How true; for in those little chests were contained the records of the vessels once owned and managed by the firm but now lost at sea or sold to foreign owners. Among these boxes were the records of:

The ship *Republic* 843 tons, built for William Rogers and associates, launched at Shelburne, 1871. On a voyage from Philadelphia to Dunkirk with a cargo of oil she went ashore one mile outside the latter port, December 1, 1886, and became a total wreck. Crew saved; partial insurance.

The bark *Mizpah* 898 tons, launched at Salmon River, 1873, Michael Dowley, master. Sailed from Philadelphia May 6, 1887, for Quebec with a cargo of hard coal, and went ashore off Gabarus Bay, Cape Breton Island, May 26. Total loss; crew landed safely, very little insurance.

The ship *Otago* 1,095 tons, built at Salmon River, 1874. Sailed from Philadelphia September 21, 1894, for Havana with a cargo of coal, encountered a terrific hurricane from the south east on the 27th, in lat. 31.36N., long. 74.05W., lasting twenty-four hours, during which the vessel laboured heavily and sprang a leak. The water gained so rapidly that the men were obliged to take to the boats and abandon the ship, which foundered a few hours after wards. On the 29th they fell in with the steamer *Empress*, which took them on board and landed them at Jamaica. The men saved nothing. Vessel and freight partially insured.

The bark *B. Hilton* 986 tons, built at Shelburne, 1874, Bradford R. Hilton, master. Sailed from Philadelphia on January 27, 1882, for Antwerp, with a cargo of oil, ran aground in the River Schelde on February 24 and was towed off and taken to Antwerp, where she was condemned and sold. Insured for $11,700. Freight insured for $800.00.

The ship *Equator* 1,273 tons, launched from the Salmon River shipyard July 1, 1878. About ninety years later she was found by scuba divers on the ocean floor off Brier Island, Digby County, in sixty feet of clear water. She was resting within twenty-five miles of the place of her birth and her name and port of registry, Yarmouth, could still be deciphered by the divers who found her.

When the *N.B. Lewis* sailed from Yarmouth on August 11, 1880, bound for Philadelphia, the above listed vessels were still sailing the seas in the ocean freighting trade under the management of the Lewis brothers.

In 1873, the year before the firm was founded, the brothers had built, at Salmon River, the bark *Mizpah* mentioned above, and during the next nine years two more barks and four ships were built for them as managing owners. At this time there were probably five shipyards on the Bay of Fundy shore north of Yarmouth, between Port Maitland and Salmon River. All had the same type of location, at the edge of a shelving beach just above the high tide limit and exposed to all the winds that blew. As this is being written, one hundred years later, it is hard to find any evidence of the activity which once went on at these spots. A careful observer may find the end of a log jutting out from a bank of sand to mark a site, but there is little else. Working in these yards during a Nova Scotian winter and spring would not be as arduous as reefing a heavy sail during a winter gale on the North Atlantic, but the men who built the vessels, like the seamen who sailed them, had to be tough.

The shipyard used by H. & N.B. Lewis was at the top of the beach just south of the mouth of the Salmon River. The vessels were built at this yard under the same general conditions. The Lewis firm made the financial arrangements and Jacob S. Allen was the master-builder. Local carpenters and other skilled artisans, often French Acadians, built the vessels. The timber needed was obtained from within a 10 to 15 mile radius extending back from the Bay of Fundy shore.

The *N.B. Lewis* was built in this yard in the winter and spring of 1880 and two years later the *Euphemia*, almost an exact duplicate, was launched from the same yard. A barkentine, the *Maggie Thompson*, was built at Meteghan River in 1889 by John C. Blackadar, in which Nathan B. Lewis owned 38 shares and George C. Lewis, son of Henry, had four shares. Capt. Henry Lewis was not one of the owners. This vessel was operated until February, 1893, when she sailed from Cuba for Delaware Breakwater and was not afterwards heard from.

By 1890 the Lewis firm was enlarging its interest in fishing and in trade with the West Indies. The last vessel to be built for the Lewis brothers by Jacob S. Allen was the brigantine *Harry*, registered tonnage[8] 144.33, designed for the trade between Yarmouth and the West Indies.

Details concerning the building and launching of the *Harry* were recalled by Commander G.R. Parry, who was born at Beaver River. Commander Parry went to sea as a boy of seventeen on a sailing ship and rose by sheer ability to the command of the Canadian Pacific steamship *Empress of Britain*. He retired to Yarmouth County and published in the Yarmouth papers a number of his reminiscences. The following hand-written account was found among his papers after he died and is now in the library of the Yarmouth County Museum:

The *Harry* was built at Beaver River on the left bank of the river immediately to seaward of the bridge and on the edge of a strip of sandy land that is now my property; her builder was Jacob Allen, known to all as 'Skipper' Allen, our next-door neighbor on the Digby side of the county-line road. I spent many happy hours playing around the small shipyard and watched the vessel grow from the day her keel was laid until her launching. Oh, the delight of watching a fresh plank being taken from the steam box and fitted in its

8   Registered tonnage: see Appendix D.

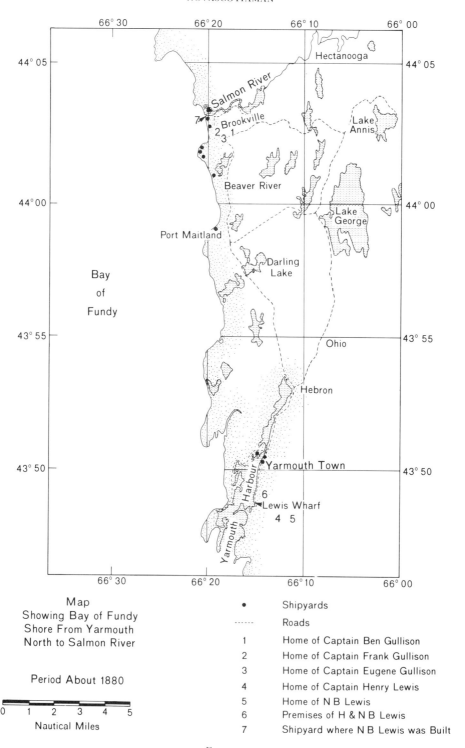

Map
Showing Bay of Fundy
Shore From Yarmouth
North to Salmon River

Period About 1880

0 1 2 3 4 5
Nautical Miles

•   Shipyards
......   Roads
1   Home of Captain Ben Gullison
2   Home of Captain Frank Gullison
3   Home of Captain Eugene Gullison
4   Home of Captain Henry Lewis
5   Home of N B Lewis
6   Premises of H & N B Lewis
7   Shipyard where N B Lewis was Built

FIG. 7.

FIG. 8. Brigantine *Harry*.

appointed place, the sweet music to my boyish ears of the caulking irons, the delicious fragrance of tarred oakum and boiling pitch. I particularly remember the epochal day when the sternpost was raised, 'horned'[9] and secured in its exact place; I was almost at the side of 'Skipper' Allen as he directed the operations.

The *Harry* was launched at about ten o'clock at night on the highest spring tide of the full moon — I think it was in the summer of 1892 but am not sure as all my life's records went in the fire that destroyed my home in Port Maitland in 1951. I attended the launching with my father and well I remember my expectant excitement as the wedges, one after another, knocked out, the thrill and the cheers of the onlookers as she started to move down the ways, and then was quickly afloat in the small harbour.

A Yarmouth tug (one of the Cann's I think) that was in waiting alongside the south wharf, took her in tow and towed her around to Yarmouth where she was rigged and soon after she started her voyaging to the sunny islands of the West Indies.

I saw much of the little vessel in the years that followed; I had near relatives in town whom I visited very frequently, particularly when any square-rigged ship was in port that I could board and climb aloft in, or 'talk shop' to the mates and occasionally the captain himself. A day after the *Harry's* arrival in port there would be, amongst the other cargo, long tiers of molasses casks on the Lewis wharf beside her. In the summer time with a hot sun overhead, the slight leakage around the bungs would be reduced to a crust of sugar which boys (myself among them) were wont to scrape off with a chip or pocket knife as a real delicacy. I also on occasions received some of Captain Larkin's 'hand-out' of sugar-cane.

I had the proud pleasure of talking to the jaunty and dapper Captain Larkin on several occasions and told him a lot of what I have written here about the birth of his ship. He was almost a hero to my boyish mind; at any rate I knew he was an extra smart captain from the unusually immaculate appearance of the vessel. With her always clean white paintwork, spotless holy-stoned decks, scraped and oiled masts and spars, polished brass-work fore and aft, neatly folded sails, etc. the *Harry* was maintained more like a millionaire's yacht than a cargo-carrying merchant vessel. I have a distinct recollection of so small an item as the canvas buntgaskets on the harbour-furled square sails. They were painted red, white and blue with a five-pointed star in the middle.

THE GULLISON FAMILY

As previously stated, the ships managed by H. & N.B. Lewis were built in a shipyard at Salmon River, commencing with the *Otago* in 1874. It appears that at some time during the years previous to this, Captain Henry Lewis had become friendly with Captain Benjamin Gullison, who lived in the little community of Brookville, about three miles south of Salmon River. They were men of the same type and had learned their trade in the same school of 'hard knocks'. Hard working, completely dependable and strong in religious convic-

9 Set at the proper angle to the keel.

tions, they would be drawn together as they met in Yarmouth or the various ports where Yarmouth captains got together for a social evening on board one of their ships.

A glance at the map of southwestern Nova Scotia on page 24 will provide geographical details of the home environment of the Gullison family and clarify many of the references in the personal letters included in this narrative.

As you follow the Bay of Fundy coast north from Yarmouth, you come first to the village of Hebron, and a few miles farther is Port Maitland – about eleven miles from Yarmouth. Still farther north, in a stretch of eight miles between Port Maitland and Salmon River, are the communities of Beaver River and Brookville (or Woodvale). Most of the residents of this area between Yarmouth and Salmon River were at that time descendants of the early New England settlers.

Captain Benjamin Gullison was born in 1836.[10] He is first recorded as captain and part owner of the bark *Sarah*, 735 tons, built at Beaver River in 1870. He still owned a share in this vessel when it was wrecked on the English coast in 1877. In the meantime, he had taken shares in the ship *Otago*, 1,095 tons, built in Salmon River in 1874, and was her master when she sailed from Yarmouth on her maiden voyage in October of that year.

Again in 1878 when the ship *Equator* was launched from the Salmon River shipyard, Captain Ben Gullison was the registered owner of four shares. He probably supervised the rigging of the vessel and was also her first master.

Thus began an association of the Gullison family and the firm of H. & N.B. Lewis which continued until the end of their ocean freighting business.

Captain 'Ben' Gullison had three sons, Benjamin Franklin (Frank), Eugene and Ralph. The two older boys went to sea in their teens and became captains in their twenties. Ralph went to sea for one voyage and then came home, finished high school and went on to Acadia University, Wolfville, Nova Scotia. After graduation he went to India as a missionary.[11] Frank became captain of the ship *Republic*, 843 tons, in November, 1883 at the age of 25. Two years later, during the summer of 1885, he assumed command of the ship *N.B. Lewis* which he retained until the vessel was sold in Holland 1893.

As stated in the foreword, it was because of the carefulness of Frank Gullison in saving his papers and correspondence that we are able to re-create a large part of the history of the ship *N.B. Lewis*. Frank's early career was similar to that of hundreds of other Yarmouth County boys. He went to sea as a sailor in his late 'teens'. After a few voyages he stayed home, went to navigation school and passed his examinations for mate. After experience as a mate for a few voyages, he again took time off from the sea to study for his Captain's papers. Following

10 In the *Record of Yarmouth Shipping* a Stephen Gullison is listed as a part owner with Seth Barnes of the vessel *Ranger* in the year 1775. In the plan of division of Yarmouth Township he is listed as one of the grantees (1787).

11 See Appendix B.

FIG. 9. Capt. Benjamin Gullison (seated, foreground) with his sons, left to right, Frank, Ralph and Eugene.

FIG. 10. Beaver River Church and former home of Capt. Frank Gullison.

FIG. 11. Former home of Capt. Frank Gullison.

FIG. 12. Temperance Hall, Beaver River. The first Temperance Society in Canada was established in Beaver River N.S., 1828. The illustration of the Temperance Hall is included because of its historical significance.

FIG. 13. Former home of Capt. Ben. Gullison.

this pattern and with good recommendations from their captains and owners, many a Yarmouth boy was commanding a vessel by the time he was in his middle twenties.

Frank Gullison's logs show that at sea, whenever possible, Sunday was a day of rest. When in port he attended religious services and there is evidence that in some ports prayer meetings were held on board the ship to which would be invited other captains and their wives. At this time there were few ports throughout the world where there would not be a few Yarmouth captains who could get together to have a social evening.

A small portable organ which he bought in Cardiff, Wales, and used on board ship is now in the Yarmouth County Museum, Yarmouth,[12] Nova Scotia. After Captain Gullison retired from the sea, he was for many years superintendent of the Sunday School in the Beaver River Baptist Church.

Captain Ben Gullison's second son, Eugene, was born in 1861, three years after Frank. Like his father and older brother he went to sea at any early age and we find him sailing at nineteen on the maiden voyage of the *N.B. Lewis*, as the second mate. He was discharged from this ship at Philadelphia a year later, and within three years he is recorded as Captain of the *Otago*. Later, for many years, he was master of the *Euphemia*, a sister ship of the *N.B. Lewis*.

Among the reasons given for the success Yarmouth achieved in the world shipping trade, certainly not the least would be the supply of competent captains. While there were, of course, exceptions, most of them were upright in character, sober in habit and had a high sense of duty to their ship and owners. The Gullison family provided fine examples of these traits.

While there was only one Gullison family in the Beaver River area, there were several Corning families. When the *N.B. Lewis* sailed from Yarmouth on its maiden voyage in 1880 the first mate was Thomas H. Corning, a son of Captain Thomas Corning. In March, 1883, Frank Gullison, aged twenty-five, married twenty year old Idella Corning, a sister of Thomas H., and later his brother Eugene married Josie Corning, a cousin of Idella.

As will be seen throughout this narrative, Frank and Eugene Gullison followed the custom of taking their wives to sea with them whenever possible. Della first visited her husband on board ship in Saint John, N.B., in the spring of 1884. Her letters from there to her cousin Josie, who was teaching in a one-room rural school at Hectanooga, Digby County, N.S., provide a picture of her as a young woman not too long married. Other letters seem to show that she was not a robust person. Her cousin Josie appears to have been stronger and better able to stand the rough life of a captain's wife. Two notes written by these wives in ships' logbooks give us an insight into their personalities and demonstrate their deep affection for their husbands.

The note written by Della was found on one of the first pages of the log of the

12 On loan from Mr. and Mrs. Willard Hewey, Lake Annis, N.S.

N.B. Lewis, at Port Eads, Mississippi, October 15, 1887 (page 154) '... How very lonely I am.... May God watch over us and keep us and if separated spare us to embrace one another again'.

A very different type of note was the rather playful one found on the page of a rough log book of calculations used by Captain Eugene Gullison when master of the ship *Euphemia*, written by Josie August 13, 1893. 'The love of my youth by my side and oh he does admire and worship his dear little wife. So nice so nice'.

When Captain Eugene Gullison retired from business he moved from Beaver River to Yarmouth and there are many people who still remember Josie Gullison as being pretty, plump and jolly.

Thus, with some background of the shipping industry in Yarmouth and the personalities of those involved in the following correspondence, we proceed to the actual letters themselves – possibly one of the most complete records of the period for one shipping firm and one captain.

FIG. 14. Yarmouth waterfront, c. 1900.

The career of Frank Gullison as master of a ship commenced when in November, 1883, at the age of 25, he was given command of the ship *Republic*, 843 tons, built at Shelburne in 1871.

Captain Gullison did not keep copies of his letters until 1886, after he had become master of the *N.B. Lewis*, therefore the information about his career as captain of the *Republic* is based on the letters of Captain Henry Lewis, personal letters from his family and other sources.

The original owners of the *Republic* were: William Rogers (32 shares), Benjamin Hilton (16 shares), William H. Cook (4 shares), William T. Kelly (8 shares), and Joseph A. Corning (4 shares). Joseph Corning was the first captain of the ship. William Rogers was married to Chloe, a sister of Henry and Nathan Lewis. In March, 1875, he died intestate and Chloe, Henry and Nathan were named administrators of his estate. From this time until the ship was wrecked near Dunkirk, France, in December, 1886, the ship was managed by H. & N.B. Lewis.

The *Republic* was lying at dock in Baltimore under command of Captain Rose when young Frank Gullison became her new master. The following letter from Captain Henry Lewis describes the arrangement.

Capt. B.F. Gullison   Ship *Republic*   Yarmouth, N.S.
                                                November 3, 1883

Dear Sir:

On Capt. Rose wiring us to send Captain for Republic, Nathan showed me a letter received from you asking for a masters berth. We talked over the matter and decided to offer you masters berth *Republic* and so I accordingly wired you offer of ship and have answer: 'I accept send instructions'. I then wired you, 'Proceed take charge, and wire us on your arrival Baltimore'. No doubt you have seen the *Republic* before and know something about her. She is getting on for an old ship and you will have to use her as such. As you are young man she may do for a beginning. Capt. Rose will give you all information no doubt about her and I have nothing much to say. Do the best you can and get what you reasonably want for safe naviga-tion of the ship. Write often and give us all the information relating to ship.

Yours truly,
Hy. Lewis

P.S. I wrote Capt. Rose a few days ago you were coming to take the ship.

Capt. B.F. Gullison   Ship *Republic*   Yarmouth, N.S.
November 30, 1883

Dear Sir:

Your favor came safe to hand from Baltimore, and also your letters down the Bay.[1] Hope that you are on your way by this time. Hope that you will arrive out in good time. Messers Wambessie and Son have always done our business at Amsterdam and I think that they are as good parties as any that you will find. Therefore, you will take them on as brokers (agents). As the *Republic* has *run off her class*[2] I don't know whether they would be able to procure any back freight to the United States or not.

If so, you could get freight to Baltimore or Philadelphia give Philadel-phia the preference. I have no doubt that if a fair price could be got for the *Republic* it would be better to sell her, and if any price was offered for her you could cable. You speak of your expenses up to Baltimore. I think that if I paid you about what it would cost to send a master from here it would be about right – say 25 to 30 dollars above wages. You would get Capt. Rose's wages $65.00 sixty-five dollars per month.

Yours truly,
Hy. Lewis

---

1 'Down the Bay': The ship had sailed down the Chesapeake Bay from Baltimore and probably the Captain followed a common custom of giving the last mail to the pilot as he was leaving the ship after piloting the vessel 'down the Bay'.

2 Classification: When a vessel was ready for sea, it was given a classification for insurance purposes. Lloyd's of London were the originators of this practice. When Lloyd's began to insure vessels, they early learned they needed to know the condition of the vessel. They therefore began to appoint agents to inspect vessels for them, and on the basis of the inspection report the vessel was given classification number. The term A1 at Lloyd's meant the vessel had the highest possible rating and a number in front of A1, such as 5, meant the rating was for five years. When this time expired, the vessel had to again be inspected. The report of such an inspection would probably state what would have to be done – if anything – for the vessel to continue to have that rating.

Besides Lloyd's, other organizations which classified vessels built in Nova Scotia were the French Veritas and the American Shipmasters Association.

The expression 'has run off her class' meant that the ship was not classified for insurance purposes, although Captain Henry Lewis in his letter of January 9, 1884, stated that the *Republic* was about three-quarters insured.

FIG. 15. Ship *Republic*.

Capt. B.F. Gullison Ship *Republic*   Yarmouth, N.S.
                                                       December 11/83

Dear Sir:

I wrote you last week in care Messers. Wambesse & Son. I wrote you about
all the particulars in answer to your inquiry from Baltimore. Namely that
we would allow you for passage what it would cost to send a man from
here. $25 about and wages the same as Capt. Rose had $65 per month. I
note you sailed from the Capes on 28th. Hope you are well on your way
by this time. You will cable your arrival at Rotterdam (Just say Lewis,
Yarmouth, Nova Scotia arrived). I don't know whether you can get business from Rotterdam or not as she has run off her class. If you have any
offer for New York, Baltimore, Phila you can cable − Phila always preferred. This vessel has been to Messers. Wambessie & Son before. You can
remit as before. Stg. bills on London Bankers − short sight as practical −
trusting you may have a safe passage over.

> Yours truly,
> *Hy. Lewis*

Unfortunately, on this, his first trip in command of a ship, young Captain
Frank got in trouble in the English Channel near Dover. A news item in the
Yarmouth Herald, January 10, 1884, reported the *Republic* bound for Rotterdam had grounded January 4 at Dungeness. She was towed off and proceeded
on her way, arriving at her destination January 17.

A possible explanation is that with strong head winds in the narrow channel
he decided to anchor and await better weather. The wind may have shifted
around to the east with a gale force, and so the ship dragged her anchor and
went aground. He was able to get a tug to tow him off and a later examination
showed that no great damage was done. It is not clear whether or not he had to
jettison any of his cargo.

As we have said, he was only 25 years old and on his first voyage as a captain.
One can imagine his embarrassment at having to notify his agents and owners
that his ship had gone aground. The experience must have taught him a
lesson, however, as he never again left himself open to criticism for the way he
handled his ship.

Capt. B.F. Gullison   Ship *Republic*   Yarmouth, N.S.
                                                       January 9th/84

Dear Sir:

On Friday 4th cablegram from John Black & Co., London reported
Republic on shore at Dungeness. On Saturday morning I had your cable
from Dover − *Republic* stranded at Dungeness, towed off, proceeding Rotterdam. As I don't know under what circumstances you was towed off, I

can't say anything about it. I mean whether towed off under salvage or a stated sum. So we wait until arrival Rotterdam. I hardly know what to say in this matter and anyhow you will make no repairs until you hear from us. The owners think if a fair price could be obtained for the *Republic* it would be better to sell − she is a good old ship with oak bottom and ceiling. If she wants extensive repairs, as far as I am concerned, I am not going to save the money to do it for I own very little in the *Republic*. So on arrival at Rotterdam you will discharge cargo and then wait for orders from here − as far as any expense has been incurred already I hope you have used the ship only for security. In the event of your wanting advice with owners here, see if Messers Wambessie and Son have got one of the T.C. Jones & Co., Liverpool code books.[3] It would save a good deal of expense in cabling and if you had much to say it would pay to ask T.C. Jones Antwerp by telegraph to transmit their cable code to us. The *Republic* is about 3/4 insured and trusting we shall hear of your arrival soon.

> Yours truly,
> *Hy. Lewis*

Capt. B. Gullison   Ship *Republic*   Yarmouth, N.S.
                                              January 16/84

Dear Sir:

On receipt of your cable from Dover I wrote you to Rotterdam in care of Messers Wambessie & Son. I see by the paper reports the vessel is reported at Rotterdam on the 8th. I also had a telegram from Hagar & Co., Phil. He stated you had sent telegram vessel damage slight and that if *Republic* is reclassed you could take a return cargo for Philadelphia. I cabled you last evening asking what it would cost to repair to class Records and also what price ship would bring. Some of the owners would like to '*wind her up*' if they could get about £2600. As the case is, I can't say much for I do not know under what circumstances vessel was got off at Dungeness; whether it was a fixed sum or under salvage. If she has to dock and undergo repairs, in consequence of getting on shore, it would be an underwriters job. This vessel is valued in policy $14,000.00. To make particular average after 1/3 off, is 5% of the bal.[4] The sheathing the underwriters are not liable for as it has been on over four years, so the cost of the shea-

---

3   Cable code books in the hands of sender and receiver enabled messages to be shortened, thus saving costs, which were on a 'per word' basis. T.C. Jones & Co. were ship agents well known to Captain Lewis.
4   The claims will need to exceed the 5% franchise after deductions of 1/3 to be acceptable as a particular average. General Average (insurance) is a partial loss falling generally on all the interests involved in a maritime adventure. Particular Average is a partial loss, not due to a general average sacrifice, falling on one particular interest.

thing does not help to make particular average but bills must amount to 5% outside of sheathing after 1/3 off.[5] You know the *Republic* had no class when this accident took place. She had been in Taylors book.[6] I don't know whether this class is recognized now or not but if it is, and record not being too expensive, she could be put to it again, but it don't amount to much. Should the ship be repaired.

Suppose you could get a freight for U.S. ports; Phila. preferred. You could draw the outward freight to pay up her bills. It is not likely you will have any money to send home, but in case you do, let Messers Wambessie have the bills sent on to London and accepted as we have had a protested Bill lately from Antwerp. Whatever you have done to this vessel or at any time you get in trouble use the ship for security, not me, as I don't own much in the *Republic*. You will understand this matter. If you can get an offer for the *Republic* from £2400 to £2600, you can cable and in case of repair don't get vessel under average so that we do not get anything out of underwriters without of course the damage is too small to bother with. Sometimes a ship's bills almost come to an average and, if not, will by a few pounds being struck out.[7] Will write you again next mail, probably will hear from you before that time.

Hy. Lewis

Capt. B.F. Gullison   Ship *Republic*   Yarmouth
                                                Jany. 23/84

Dear Sir:

I have received your letter from Dover also your two cables from Rotterdam. I note by your letter it cost you $150 to tow off and show, as you say, other expenses, pilot and this would all come in to General Average no doubt.[8]

I have your cablegram namely 'cable instructions whether repair in dock or proceed without reclassing, poor chance of selling'. I am at a loss to know what to say. I am afraid if she is put in dock there will be no end to the matter. Capt. Hilton and Capt. Cook owners are here today and we

5 These bills must amount to 5% (franchise) after deduction of 1/3 for cost of repairs, not counting the sheathing (copper), before the costs of repairs are recoverable under insurance.
6 Taylor may have been an agent for Lloyd's, Bureau Veritas, or possibly the American Shipmaster's Society, which later became the American Bureau of Shipping. B.G. Taylor, whose office was in St. John, N.B., was a subscriber to the Bureau Veritas in 1886. In 1876, a John Taylor of Halifax was a subscriber to American Lloyd's.
7 'Sometimes ... struck out': this appears to mean that if the cost of repairs does not reach the 5% franchise, even if by only a few pounds, the claim will not be accepted under the insurance.
8 Towage and other expenses such as piloting will be recoverable under General Average if incurred either as charges in the nature of salvage or as General Average expenses, i.e. incurred in addition to normal piloting and towage to ensure the safety of the vessel following the stranding.

FIG. 16. N.B. Lewis Esq.

will have to fix up a Cablegram. We have just decided to send on all your documents such as Protest, all Surveys, and Average papers. Of course all ropes and hawsers incident to getting vessel off and labour, goes into General Average.[9] If this vessel has to dock and repair we have decided not to class, but simply caulk and resheath and she may want perhaps some little extra fastening and get certificate for work done from your surveyors but I hope you will be able to proceed back to St. John without docking. If you should have to, sheath. John Black & Co. of London write that part of cargo was jettisoned — is it so?

Yours truly,

H. Lewis

[P.S.] *Republic* particular average bills would come to about £1500. Outside of sheathing, and also the cost of CLASS. Opening up, taking off planks and costs of certificate would not come in.[10] Your agent no doubt, is concerned with all this. Your General Average will be settled on their own merits, and such as getting afloat at Dungeness and extra help getting over, regulated no doubt by Dutch average. We had no invoice on the freight disbursements Baltimore about £600 the inward freight and what you drew on me about 1200 francs would about make that amount.

Capt. B.F. Gullison[11]   Ship *Republic*   Yarmouth, N.S.
                                                    April 9/84

I have received all your favours from Rotterdam and also a letter off Dover. I have also received from Messers. Wambessie & Son all remittances. Bal freight 585,0.0 and also 185 (insurance) secured from General average from cargo. Note the ship was tight when you wrote last. Trusting you may soon arrive. At present, I can not write anything further. At present I do not know what to say about future but after hearing from you by wire will then decide what will be done with the *Republic*.

Yours,

H. Lewis

---

9   Damage to ropes and hawsers and labour charges incurred to safeguard the adventure following the stranding will be recoverable under General Average (as this is normal practice to minimize the loss).

10 'Opening up ... come in'. It would appear here that there is some misunderstanding of the case; it is felt that the opening up and taking off planks was required by the Classification surveyor to issue his certificate (although this appears to be contrary to H. Lewis' letter dated January 23, 1884) and as the vessel was apparently not classed at the time of the stranding these costs in common with the costs of the certificate of class would not be recoverable under the insurance on the hull of the ship. Basically the position is that if the vessel is classed before an accident, reclassing costs are recoverable, but if not classed, then they are not recoverable.

11 This letter was probably sent to St. John to be received by Capt. Gullison on arrival.

Capt. B.F. Gullison   Ship *Republic*   Yarmouth, N.S.
                                              April 22/84

Dear Sir:

On reaching home I got your letter. Note what you say about your decks. If you think they require caulking, and perhaps they do, as you will be taking a deck load, I think you had better commence say, four seams from your water ways and caulk to the side so your water way seam will not be too large and then if you should come back again in summertime I think your carpenter could caulk the balance. We have got to figure so that the ship will not have to draw on the owners to pay running expenses. I hope you have got weather so you can work and will get your mizzen fixed up all right. As regards you taking your wife, I have only spoken to one owner, Capt. Cook. He thinks as times are so very dull you will have to make an allowance for her in your wages. Capt. Phillips makes $5.00 per month difference − of course if the ship was mine I might make no difference in the matter. I shall not say anything to Capt. Hilton about you taking your wife without he expressly asks me, and if he does and makes any up and down objection I will let you know in time.

                                              Yours *Hy. Lewis*

If you see Mr. Magee tell him my folks give me a blowing up because I did not inquire about Miss Ruby & Clara. I told them I forgot all about it.

Just tell Magee this is an oblidge   H.L.

See that the goods I bot from Mr. Finlay came by Packet. I will send you over by packet your bbl. molasses and fish. Give the enclosed to Messers McLaughlin [ship's agents].

Capt. B.F. Gullison   Bark *Republic*   Yarmouth, N.S.
                                              April 29, 1884

Dear Sir:

Yours to hand note contents. Think it quite a saving buying the Grace Cann sails, & I suppose you will get a new lower mizzen staysail. Hope you will soon get to work at loading. Don't think we have had a vessel in St. John spring of the year for some time that there has not been a strike. I had put on board of Schooner *Mystic*[12] yesterday 1 bbl. molasses, 1 quintal cod fish, 1 q. pollock, 1/2 bbl. herring.

They should be in St. John on receipt of this letter. Hope they will load the vessel in *her days*.[13]

                                              Yours *H. Lewis*

---

12 Schooner *Mystic* would be a packet running between Yarmouth and Saint John.
13 'Her days': lay days. See note p. 79.

The following two letters are from Frank Gullison's wife Della to her cousin Josie Corning of Beaver River, who was engaged to marry Frank's brother Eugene, then captain of the *Otago*. Josie was apparently teaching school in Hectanooga, a small village located on the railroad about twelve miles inland from her home.

Ship Republic

St. John, New Brunswick
May 1st, 1884

Dear Jose

I know by this time you are looking for letters – but don't say a word, I'm having what your love says 'tell times' and certainly you will pardon me for not letting you know how I got over [to St. John], but it's likely you have spent a week at Mrs. G's[14] by this time and perused the letter I wrote her. I wonder if she has got through reading it by this time – it was so long and I wrote so nicely. Never mind I've got something more better to tell you. It's the same old story I told Mother and Ma. I left home early Saturday morning, aroused two ladies when I got to B.R. [Beaver River] sorry to say. Told them where I was going and all about it – got to Hebron alright – sent a pair of mits by express I borrowed – was much obliged of course. Took the train car for [Digby] safely landed. Took a cab – went down on the wharf waited three quarters of an hour for the 'Streamer Secret' – jumped in went to Annapolis to see the place and enjoyed it – back to Digby and from there to St. John, where I found my love the minute I landed on the Str. deck before I had scarcely had my eyes opened. It was going to be so late before the boat got in the stewardess made me turn in for a nap. – she said it would be all I would get that night. I was not sick a bit – stood it like a brick – they were all real sick – only one woman besides myself and every once in a while I would peep out and look around at the rest of them – that is how I slept all the way across. But I did not tell you who flirted with me coming over, Doctor Forest. Got my checks and went down aboard of the Str. with me and so long says he.

Frank has gone ashore on business and for a wonder I did not go and while he is gone I thought I would tell you all about it – Oh here he comes – no more writing for today goodby my dear.

Friday morning got a little pain and Frank has stepped out for a few minutes.

Now I'm going to tell you where I've been since I came. I have got acquainted with Mrs. Ring, Mr. and Mrs. Magee, Mr. Lewis the great blacksmith and family – Capt. Jud Durkee's wife – you know her, don't you?

---

14 Mrs. 'G': Mrs. Ben Gullison, the mother-in-law of Della.

Was up there last evening — Capt. Charles Crosby and wife — he married an England lady. I have had some lovely times — went for walks two and three times a day — and they would come over here for tea and we would go there. They went to Yarmouth on Wednesday boat.

The ship is going to be here two months and over and she has gone to Mrs. Annie Durkee's to be confined. They were spliced the same month I was — see what I ought to have had to rock. — but never mind — wait till this voyage is over and I will go home to have something. I have been up to see Aunt Annie and Uncle and she says that she was looking for a letter from you. What a cunning child that is — I could love it myself.

I suppose that you will be greatly surprised to hear that I'm going to voyage. I'm myself too — Jose my old darling I shall long to see you often no doubt. — but I am with my dear Frank whom I love so dearly that what will come during the voyage, I'll not murmur, trusting in Jesus I know I am blest. I know we will miss each other much or at least I will, but I trust God will spare us to meet again, and the good ship *Otago*.

Hope we will meet with Capt. Eugene G. and wife Josie aboard. Oh Jose, I am not going to ask Frank what you wanted me to, unless you tell who told you, and then I will ask him, and he will tell whether true or not. Now there's a square bargain. Let me know soon if you want to find out before the ship sails or barque as she is now.

Now I must tell you what some of my presents were, which I don't care anything about, if I can have Frank with me. A nice rubber cloak — slippers, scrap-book and other things too numerous to mention. I got me a nice sateen wrapper here already made — and twines. You would laugh to see it piled up around me. I have pale blue — old gold, green and white. I have made two bracket lambriquins and on my second tidy. Mrs. Magee lent me one of each to make them by. Now I would teach you if you would run in. Why didn't you come. Fred was here and he said he thought sure you would come and it would not cost you anything — and you and I could be running around. We are going aboard each others ships. Capt. Crosby and wife, Frank and I were aboard of the Mary L. Burell to tea Sunday night. We went to church in the morning and heard Rev. Mr. Cross — Text Collosians 3rd. and I went through the convent last week with Mrs. Ring. Oh, I also saw a Jew baby — Mrs. Magee says she has done her best for me. Now if I don't come home with a nice looking babe she will never try again. Almost every captain has their wives aboard, and the most of them is going the voyage. There are lots of Yarmouth ships here now. Yesterday one was towed in right close us — ain't I having a nice time. We have a splendid mate — Mr. Davidson of Cornwallis and a good steward. He has made me a loaf of cake and plate of doughnuts already and it's misses here and misses there — don't say one word to me now. Frank will soon be here and oh ain't I hurrying before he comes. He has gone to get me some maple sugar. Take a run up to Mother Gullison's and see my clock. Frank says its a beauty. It was all done up so nice I would not let him take the wrappings off. We had a letter from Papa Gullison saying it arrived alright and never got broke. Gave me Eugene's address. I see he is going to Aberdeen. Capt. Frank Corning has gone to Lynn. I heard to get married, and then home for a few days. Well, I must stop writing for it's cleaning house time and you will not be able to spend time to read this unless you get it on Sunday. Frank is going to write you soon. We expect to get away next week if all goes well, and I want you to pray for us, and we will for you. How are the meetings progressing, and has any more joined the church. Have you been to B.[15] to prayer meeting since I came away. I shall never let Tuesday nights go by without praying for the meetings. I sent for my things and looked for them on the last boat, but they did not come or any letters either. I hope they will come tomorrow night. I have heard only a few words from home since I left. You need not wait for me to write first. I will give you liberty to write any time you want to. Tell May I sent for my shawl. That is there, with the rest of my things. I want to finish them so as to have them to put on my bed while in port.

> Yours forever
> *Della*

Ship *Republic*
St. John   May 8, 1884

My very dear friend —
I got your epistle alright — contents noted. I am very sorry you are so lonely, — I might sooth you a little if I was home. Keep up good heart until the *Otago* arrives.[16] You wanted to know what the news was. Les sent me his photo and just wrote a short note, saying give my love to Jose — good-by.

My dear one has gone ashore, and I was not very well. I thought I would begin a letter to you. Got a letter from Bess and was quite surprised to find her at Hartford. She said that she wished that I was there with a plate of hot biscuits. Don't you take the hint — there was a little turnip hash getting warmed up.

Well Jose I wish that you had come over with me — just think what a long visit you would have had, and you could have slept right off our stateroom. Frank and I were up to Aunt Annie's yesterday and we had just an immense time. I was sorry when we had to leave. Oh here is Frank,

---

15 Probably Beaver River.
16 This is a reference to Josie's fiancé, Captain Eugene Gullison.

and he has brought me a lovely basket to put my work in and he says I must have it lined with silk or satin. Oh − he's a gem, Jose, and I don't hardly know how I got along, all those dreary months without him. It's because I had to − says you. I had a letter from Kate since I have been here. She seemed quite surprised to hear I was here, but she says that she prays that I will go home. I will telegraph to you, my dear, to meet me at Hectanooga soon. I see that you still live there. No wonder that you are so lonely, so far away from your Mother. How many children have you now. I hope you have taught them better than to throw the dish-water in the front-door yard.

Della

May 9th

Dear old Jo:

I am going to finish your letter, as it is a very rainy day and I cannot get ashore. Frank has gone to see if there is any letters. Oh − I got lots to tell you. Jake C. was married Wednesday morning and went on the boat to Yarmouth. No doubt you have called on them by this time. They are going to stop at Maitland Hotel until his people call on them. Quite tony. She is going to stop with Aunt Annie and he is going to sea. Bye the bye Jose did you get any wedding cake from the Vandome. I did, and when I came on board I found a white box tied up − with frosted cake inside to Mrs. Gullison with Mrs. Corning's compliments on it. I was greatly surprised. We were over to call the other evening. The captain seems to have a bad cold. I presume it's caused by night sweats. His wife thinks he got it on the sleeping car. I have taken quite a liking to her. − and we are going out walking if the Republic does not sail before Monday. You will have a lovely time to get your quilts and under-wear made this summer.

The brother of Susie's beau, has gone to New York to be spliced. He is the mate of the Mary L. Burril. I see that Ben has arrived in New York and Jess is home. I would like to see him very much.

Jose, I made up my mind to ask Frank that question, before I got your letter, and he says when anybody finds out anything about him, he will always own up. But this is false, Jose, and he says he can say this much, that he was never drunk in his life. He also says that if it had been the last time they went away he would have it cleared up right away, for anything like that going around is false, is something awful, on such dear ones as Frank and Gene.

I knew it was false when you told me, for I can trust mine, and he tells me all that he does. This is true Jose. We have a dear old talk together this time. You may think the reverse but I have this confidence in him Jose, and Oh, how we love one another, God only knows. We are made for one another Frank says, if there is such a thing. But never mind Jose, you and

47

Gene will be made happy soon, and two happier couples were never spliced. Remember me to your dear Mother and tell her I will never forget the happy days I have spent there in the seaside cottage.

> Remember me in your prayers dear,
> *Della May Gullison*

Capt. B.F. Gullison[17] Barque *Republic*   Yarmouth, N.S.
                                              June 3rd/84

Dear Sir:

All your favours came safe to hand also expenses from McLaughlan & Son. Think you must have got away about the 16th. Hope you are well on your way by this time. Hope you may get into Fleetwood all right. I don't know as yet what the *Republic* will do after her cargo is out of Fleetwood and if ballast is dear and no freights, otherwise perhaps it might be as well to buy coals sufficient for ballast only and come to Quebec; that is if coals are reasonable, say for 6 to 7 s. per ton or perhaps you might get a charter for coals from Fleetwood say at 6 s. [shillings]. The *E.H. Duval*[18] now at Hartlepool is chartered for Quebec 6 s. Anyhow, after your arrival I will decide and if you can get charter coals Quebec you can cable, and in having to buy coals to make up ballast you would cable price. If anything should happen when you would have to cable much, you could transmit to T.C. Jones Co., Liverpool and they would use their code. I don't know as I have anything further to say. As soon as you can collect freight remit Bankers draft on London so I may pay disbursements St. John and stop paying interest.

> Yours truly,
> *Hy. Lewis*

P.S. I think the parties that the ship *N.B. Lewis* was with, were good parties. What they are now I don't know. You will have to decide.

Capt. B.F. Gullison   Ship *Republic*   Yarmouth N.S.
                                          June 11th/84

Dear Sir:

I wrote you last week in care of the Post Office. As I have had several letters from Brokers at Fleetwood and don't know any of them I leave the matters with yourself. You will have to look after your Freight and see it remitted yourself, whatever you send me.

---

17 Letter from Capt. Henry Lewis to Capt. Gullison at Fleetwood, England.
18 *E.H. Duval* was a bark managed by H. & N.B. Lewis. She was apparently named after an agent in Quebec.

FIG. 17. Capt. Henry Lewis.

As for future business I will only repeat what I said in my last letter. If you could charter for a ballasting of coals for Quebec at say 6/ perhaps it would be the best thing the ship could do, and that failing, rather than pay a big price for ballast perhaps you had better buy enough coal to make up ballast and proceed to Quebec and as I have written you before if anything should turn up where you would want to do much cabling you had better communicate to T.C. Jones Co. L'pool and let them use their code book and cable me. Trusting we may hear soon of your arrival.

Yrs truly,
Hy. Lewis

Capt. B.F. Gullison   Barque *Republic*   Yarmouth N.S.
June 18/84

Dear Sir:

I have written you several letter in care of the Post Office. No doubt you will receive them all right. I there stated we would look to Quebec for business. You know we shall have to go to Quebec or St. John as they are the only ports that has facilities for docking and caulking. As I have said before, if you can get 5/ or 6/ freight for ballasting coals Quebec you had better close and if you cannot, get charter. Perhaps coal being reasonable you better buy a ballasting of coals. I suppose you would want at least 300 tons.

If Messers T.C. Jones Co, L'pool should send you an account for goods for our firm I want you to pay it. It will probably be about £50 or £55.

Trusting I shall hear of your arrival soon,

I remain yours truly,
Hy. Lewis

Capt. B.F. Gullison   Ship *Republic*   Yarmouth N.S.
July 2/84

Dear Sir:

I have written you before today. After mailing, I had a cablegram from T.C. Jones Co. forwarded for you. Offered New York coal 6/ charter – could buy steam coal for about 8/. No freights for the ports I wrote about. That was Quebec & St. John. I think tomorrow I will cable you through Jones & Co. code to charter coals New York, 800 tons – I have sent a message tonight to see what can be got to fix her oil for back. Where ever she goes she has to be striped & caulked and New York will not be much dearer than Quebec or St. John. I expect you thought the *Republic* did not after being striped of after yards. I heard she was crank – You will find when she is clear of deck load and on her bottom she will be a different vessel. I don't think some extra packing on her rudder would hurt.

> Yrs
> *H. Lewis*

Capt. B.F. Gullison   Ship *Republic*   Yarmouth N.S.
                                                  July 2/84

Dear Sir:

I see by the papers the *Republic* is reported at Fleetwood on 26th ult .... I have written you several letters; no doubt you have got them all right. I gave T.C. Jones Co an order on you for from £25 or upwards to £55. I don't know exactly what their bill is but I want you to pay it as presented.

   Lovitt & Kelly has a bill against the *Republic* for a draft that Capt. Vickery gave pilot some time ago. I don't know the amount but think it is about £5-0-0. You can pay this bill as it is some time due and honestly due them. I don't know whether you can get coals for Quebec or not on charter. I heard they were paying 6/ per ton. I am expecting to hear soon from you by cable stating how things were at Fleetwood so that I may direct you which way to proceed.

   Oil freights are about 3/ French ports, 3/3 has been given for Dunkirk. If you cannot charter for Quebec, as I have written before, it might be as well to buy enough coals to complete ballast and proceed to Quebec. Meantime if oil comes up something better we may bring her to Phila. but no charter will be made before consulting you by cable and finding out position of ship.

> Yours truly,
> *H. Lewis*

Capt. B.F. Gullison   Ship *Republic*   Yarmouth, N.S.
                                                  Sept. 4/84

Dear Sir:

I have telegram from E.H. Duval this morning stating that the *Republic* had arrived and the coal was sold at $5.50 per Chal^n.[19] I had all your letters from Fleetwood and all accounts. You have got to Quebec quite as soon as I expected. The *Republic* will have to dock and caulk; don't know whether we shall sheath yet or not. Will decide later after I talk with owners. Capt. Trefry[20] may take a run on if we conclude to do much repairs, will write to you again soon. Your father has been gone away about a week to take the *Otago*. She is in Phila. and will go to Antwerp with oil 3/3.

19   Chal^n—a chaldron was 32−36 bushels, varying in different localities.
20   Capt. George Trefry was part owner of several vessels with H. & N.B. Lewis including *E.H. Duval*.

Eugene comes home. Hope. Hope you will get along all right and that your coals will hold out. Expect you should make 5 per ton freight on coals. I had some offers freights for *Republic* on passage but thought perhaps you might do as well after arrival. Tell Capt. Crosby Bk *E.H. Duval* that I am looking to hear of an offer for the *Duval* – hope they will be able to sell her. Capt. Cook[21] wants to sell bad.

> Yrs truly
> *Hy. Lewis*

Capt. B.F. Gullison   Quebec   Yarmouth N.S.
                                             Sept. 6/84

Dear Sir:

Capt. G. Trefry will leave here for Quebec next Thursday. The coals then should be nearly out. When out will have the *Republic* docked and if not too expensive will try and get some CLASS[22] for the ship. Trusting you are getting along all right.

> Yours truly,
> *Hy. Lewis*

Capt. B.F. Gullison   Bk *Republic*   Yarmouth N.S.
                                             Sept. 11th/84

Dear Sir:

I have just received your letter and note contents. Capt. George Trefry left here this morning for Quebec. I have talked over with him about *Republic* and he will decide about repairs and also future business for the ship. I received all your accounts from Fleetwood and all is satisfactory. Trusting you may have good dispatch with coal and find some paying employment outwards. I received a letter from Mr. Duval.[23] Capt. Trefry will answer it in person.

> Yours truly
> *Hy. Lewis*

Tell Capt. Crosby I am glad he got such a good price for Duval. Capt. Cook seems pleased.

---

21 Capt. Cook was part owner of *E.H. Duval*.
22 Classification: see p. 36.
23 E.H. Duval was a ship's agent in Quebec for whom the ship was named.

Capt. B.F. Gullison   Montreal   Yarmouth N.S.
                                            Oct. 7/84

Dear Sir:

I had a telegram from Capt. Trefry on Monday stating that the *Republic* left Quebec on Saturday morning. Yesterday I had another dispatch stating that she was at Montreal and commenced loading. I had wired to Capt. Trefry $3000.00 and beside that she has the proceeds of the sale of the coal at Quebec. I suppose Capt. Trefry will pay all the bills at Quebec and the balance of the money, if Capt. Trefry does not send it to you, you had better draw it and pay up your bills at Montreal & I hope you will get good disptach for if you don't get away from Montreal before Oct. 31st all our insurance both on ship and freight will be up and then we are at the mercy of the underwriters whether they will extend the time or not. You must do all in your power to get the work along. If you can get them to work nights, that is if you could get the cargo, you had better do it. The fact is, she must get down from Montreal this month or we will be in a bad box. No doubt you understand all this as well as I do and will do all you can. Write me how you are getting along and what your prospects are for getting loaded and whether any of your crew has standed by you. Hope the old ship is in good order and now if you should get loaded and getting crew at Montreal would detain you, better start and get the balance of crew at Quebec − any how to clear the law. You would have some men so you could call it fully manned.

                                    Yours truly in haste
                                    Hy. Lewis

Capt. B.F. Gullison   Bk *Republic*   Yarmouth N.S.
                                            Oct. 10th/84

Dear Sir:

I wrote you some few days ago at Montreal and last night I had your letter from Montreal stating you was on Monday commencing to load and that you expected good dispatch. I hope you will have good weather and get away quick. I wrote you in my last letter that the limits in all policies on *Republic* both hull and freights, was Oct. 31st from Montreal. Note what you say about ballast & under the circumstances think better take less deck load.

    As I said before when you was home, about provisions, any thing you can buy at the River reasonable − you had better make calculation getting there. You will see that the more bills she has at Montreal the more I have to cover by insurance and the rate is very high. I have had the greatest trouble to get disb.[24] insured and now I can only get insurance on

24 'Disb.' − this word is not clear. It appears to be disbursements. Perhaps added cost of repairs
     to vessel.

$4000.00. I shall write you at the River[25] – Buenos Ayres. If you give me no consignee shall address to British consul. If you should not get my letters at River and you did not find any freight in Brazil you would come back to Florida or Georgia U.S. where we would look for pitch pine freight. Any how on such a voyage a good deal has to be left to the master and you would have to figure carefully in the event of anything offering in way of freight. Of course, a small freight from the discharging port to an oil loading port would no doubt be the best for *Republic*.

> yrs truly
> *Hy. Lewis*

Capt. B.F. Gullison   Barque *Republic*   Yarmouth
                                                   Oct 14/84

Dear Sir:

I had a telegram from E.H. Duval today said you thought to be loaded Thursday or Friday. Hope you will get down all right. I have written E.H. Duval to give you any assistance possible so you may get away as soon as possible. Should you arrive safe at the River as soon as you can collect freight remit on to me Bankers Bills on London. Get sets first, second, third of Exchange in order I may pay disbursements home as soon as I can and stop interest. I will write to you in care of British Consul if you do not name your consignee. I expect you will have to be careful of that timber and protect yourself by Protests if you get bad weather. I have written you before that if you don't get my letters at the River you will, if no suitable business offers from Brazil, come back to Brunswick, Georgia for orders or if you can not get there Tybee but no doubt you will get letters at the River [La Plata] and we may think different then and order her some other port. I wish it could be you could get some freight from the River to an oil loading port.

Any how you will be on the spot and you will have to make your own figuring and do the best you can.

> Yours
> *H. Lewis*

If you should be fortunate to get down to Bic write back by Pilot.

Capt. Gullison   Ship *Republic*   Yarmouth N.S.
                                            April 17—85

Dear Sir:

I had your disptach from Tybee last week and as Nathan was in Phila. I handed the matter over to him and today I have received a dispatch from

25 River La Plata.

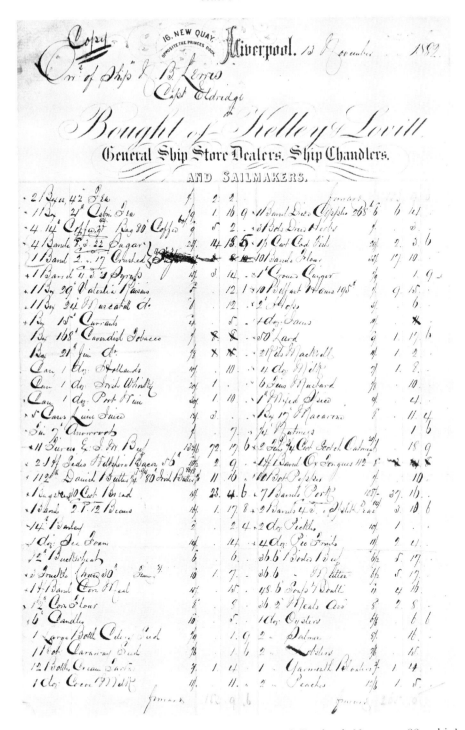

FIG. 18. Invoice of Kelley, ship chandlers, Liverpool, England, Nov. 13, 1882, ship's stores.

him that he has fixed her to load at Sapelo, Georgia, £4/5 U.K. No doubt this was better than coming North for oil at 1/9 per bbl. Hope you may get to you loading port all right. I expect you may tow right down from Tybee [near Savannah]. I have written for Nathan to arrange for funds to be sent from Phila. I expect the *Republic* will be troublesome about getting stiffening in and ballast cut but you will be where you can strap alongside logs of Pitch Pine and hold her up − except she would have some ballast in under timbers but not much & you will know about the *Republic* by this time. Suppose you will be able to take deck load.

I received all your letters and accounts from Buenos Ayres with all the exchange, and everything is satisfactory. Think you done well to fit out as cheap as you did. You must figure as cheap as you can on these voyages. Try to get enough out of it to pay her bills. Your wages a/c you can send home to me and have it paid here. − in haste

Yours truly,
Hy. Lewis

Will write again when I get your charter, of the terms of the charter − then I will know about arranging for funds. They may advance on freight as their charter calls for it some times.

Capt. B.F. Gullison   Ship *Republic*   Yarmouth
April 24/85

Dear Sir:

I wrote you a few days ago in care of J.K. Clarke Co., Darien. No doubt you will get it all right. Yesterday I had a letter from W.F. Hagar Co. with charter party enclosed. It is about all those Timber Charter Parties are like, they claim the priviledge of advancing cash for disbursements and make the ship pay for it well, and we can't help ourselves. There is not much in this business but still I think it better than shifting up for oil at 1/9 per bbl., Hope you may get along all right. Note you have drawn on Hagar & Co. for expenses at Savannah. Think it is well that you provisioned there. I will remit on to Hagar the amount from here. The balance of [indecipherable] and loading they will advance as per charter party. You can send on to me your wages a/c and it can be paid here. As I wrote you in my last letter last week I received all your letters from Buenos Ayres and all your accounts and remittances all in order and everything satisfactory. I am expecting N.B. [Lewis] home tommorow evening. Business is very dull here and freights are dull in all directions. Suppose you can stiffen the *Republic* with logs alongside chained up. You will know about what she will want ballast for stiffening if any. If you find at Sapelo scant water and you can't take much deck load would it not be better to take less small stowage 2/3-freight and put some on deck. Of course this would not do if ship was likely to be tender. But you know doubt will take all this in consideration and I will leave the matter with yourself.

Yours truly,
Hy. Lewis

Capt. B.F. Gullison   Barque *Republic*   Yarmouth N.S.
May 2/85

Dear Sir:
Yesterday I received your letter and note contents respecting mate. I at once sent for Coward which person has been home since you was here. He told me he would go on in case you wanted him, so I at once telegraphed you in care J.K. Clark Darien that if you could not get mate there would I send Coward and now I await your answer. From what you say suppose your articles takes the ship to England. I have sent Hagar & Co. $800.00 for a/c expenses Tybee. The commission I suppose will be paid in Philadelphia so you will only require funds for Sapelo expenses; such as pilotage, ballast out, loading, feeding men loading wages — for this I think you may as well get from shippers. I know their charges are high but at the same time if you have to pay them 2 1/2% for money that we have to supply we might as well let them advance it. Just at this time it costs us high to place money in the States. You speak about Insurance being high, it would be high anyhow as we now have to insure in outside office & so you will use your charter for disbursements Sapelo Yesterday your brother presented an order for $100.00 which was pd. Should you wire me to send Coward he will go first chance. It is expensive but note your mate pays some of the expense. Hope you will get along all right. Could you not arrange down there a note for insurance — or disbursements — I don't suppose you can. Your charter I presume is similar to the Barque *E.H. Duval* which vessel loaded at Darien last spring.

Yours truly,
Hy. Lewis

Messers W.F. Hagar & Co.   Philadelphia   Yarmouth N.S.
May 2/85

Gentlemen:
I sent you through exchange Bank by telegraph $800. on a/c Capt. Gullison wrote me about disbursements at Sapelo. Thought we could do it cheaper by sending the money. I have written that he had better get the balance from the shippers. It will cost more but at same time it will relieve me from responsibility in finding the money. The commission will no doubt be paid in Phila which I can lend. The worst feature on these timber charters in getting advances, is the Insurance which is only decided

at port of discharge. If rate could be named for Insurance at loading port it would be better. Anyhow I suppose we will have to take our chances on it. The barque *E.H. Duval* had a similar charter last spring.

> Yours
> *H. Lewis*

Capt. B.F. Gullison   Barque *Republic*

Yarmouth N.S.
May 8th '85

Dear Sir:

Your letter at hand, note you will get a mate at Phila., if so, it will save expense. Note what you say about cash for disbursements. That, of course, will be only for disbursements at Sapilo. Anyhow if it should include commissions & I don't know as we can help it. I have written you before and that I thought you had better get your funds from shippers. I don't like the idea of having to pay 2 1/2% Coms. for disbursements and then find it ourselves. As regards deck load, I don't think you had better put on deck only a snug deck load for pitch pine is a heavy cargo and folks very often get in trouble being too greedy. Anyhow I leave the matter with yourself. You know about what the old ship can stand both for strength (?) and keeping on her bottom.

  If you find they are going to charge unreasonable you can wire me and I will wire Hagar & Co. to place you in funds. The diff. in exchange will be from $50. to $60.00. That is about the usual thing for these Pitch Pine folk. As there is so many outside owners to the *Republic* I think the ship might as well work her own disbursements. Anyhow, as I have mentioned, if there is any great imposition you can wire me. I think they will do about as they done with the *E.H. Duval* last winter.

> Yours truly,
> *Hy. Lewis*

Note what you say about finding timber crews & I was aware of that fact. You will have to have patience and if necessary replenish your provisions & the more difficulties the more Glory in Surmounting them.

Capt. B.F. Gullison

Yarmouth, N.S.
June 2nd/85

Dear Sir:

I have received all your letters from Sapelo [Georgia, U.S.A.] and also received from Mr. Patton all your accounts and I think you have done the very best you could, but at the same time I think Sapelo a dear place. A little more than some other pitch pine ports. I note you have quite a bill of wages. Been saving for some time; you had better pay yourself in Bristol,

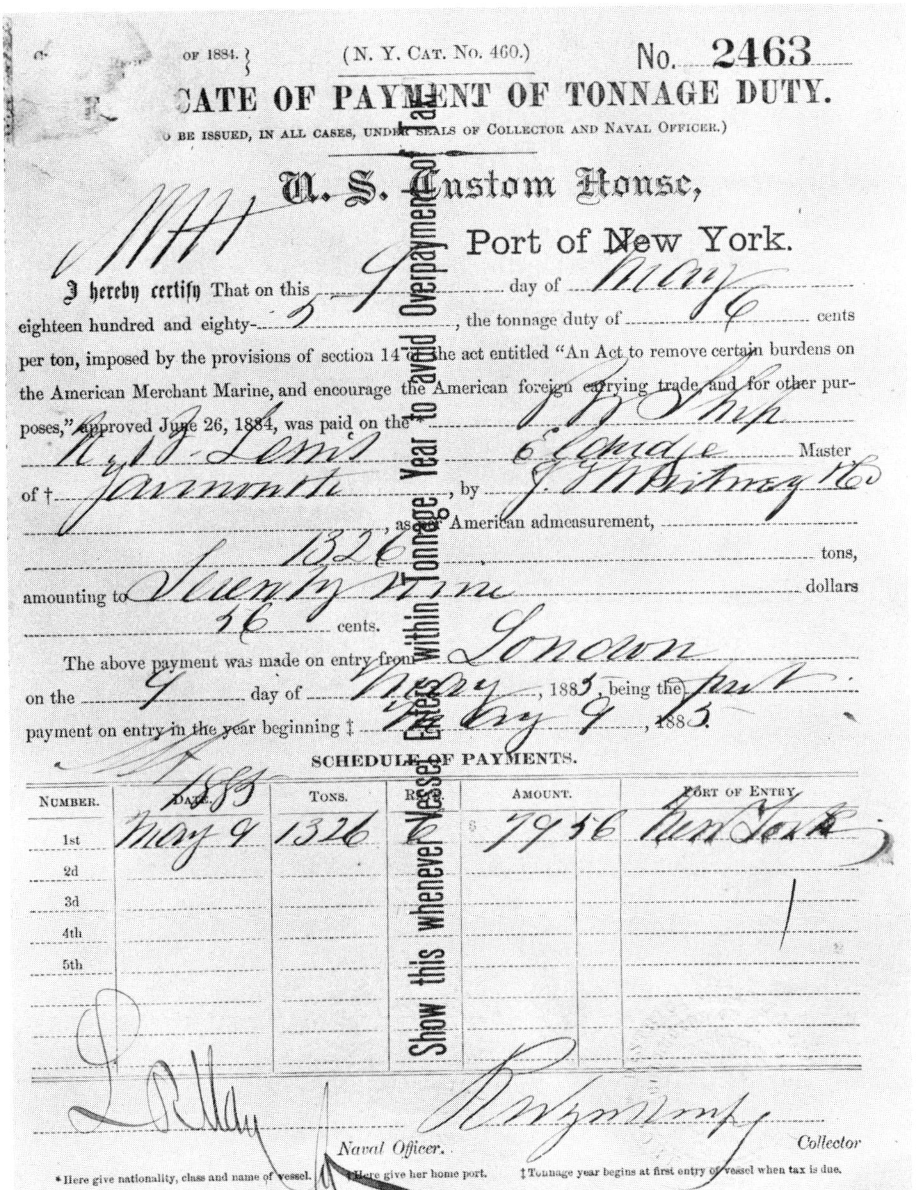

FIG. 19. Certificate of Payment of Tonnage Duty, New York, May 6, 1885.

that is if you have enough freight left to do it after paying off the rest of the crew. In that case you would have to be paid here any balance. Of course, I never have any money on hand on vessels account.

I do not know at present which way the *Republic* will go from Bristol. If you have to cable in reference to business, use T.C. Jones & Co., cable code. No doubt you will find it at the brokers at Bristol. I shall send this letter in care of James & Co. The *Equator* was in to that Firm. Expect he is as good as any one else. Anyhow you can look after your freight. I don't know anything about him since *Equator* was there. I shall write you again in reference to business.

No doubt before this reaches you, you will of heard of the death of Capt. C. Eldridge. He left London on April 3rd and on the 13th small pox broke out. They seemed to get along all right. Arrived at New York on the 8th, took one man out and quaranteaned ship for four days, fumigated and let ship go up.

After about 10 days Capt. Eldridge came home. Arrived on Wednesday, was well up to Sunday evening then went up to Richmond to his mother's and broke out Tuesday and the disease took a wrong turn and he died on Saturday morning. The ship will go across and then probably your father will take the ship again. Will write again.

Yours truly
Hy. Lewis

We all feel Capt. Eldridge's death very *much*.

Capt. B.F. Gullison   Barque *Republic*   Yarmouth
                                                 June 10th/85

Dear Sir:

I wrote you last week in care of H.Y. James, ship Broker in that letter I stated I had received all your letters and a/c from Sapelo. Should you arrive safe at Bristol then we will have to decide future business for *Republic*. Do they load coal at Bristol? If it would pay, we might buy 500 or 600 tons and come to Quebec looking for River [Plate] business again same as last year from Fleetwood. In case of cabling I should think among the brokers you could find T.C. Jones & Co. code book. Anyhow you can communicate after you arrive.

This last few weeks I have been all mudled up. We have had quite a bad time in the shipping line. The *N.B. Lewis* arrived at New York May 9th with small pox on board. They kept her in quarantine until 13th. On the following Monday Capt. Eldridge left for home, arrived Wednesday. Was to N.B.L. up to Saturday; went home to Richmond, took sick Monday, died Saturday. Capt. S. Crosby took the ship. Capt. Phillips was to take the *Equator* over but on Friday last he was taken [sick] and now is in hospital

60

with same disease. I trust he may recover all right. It is a sad business, and I feel very bad. It will be a heavy blow for his poor wife in Liverpool. We understand by cable today that she has an infant within a few days.

> Yours truly,
> *Hy. Lewis*

The following letter, which appeared in the *Yarmouth Herald* of Wednesday, June 3, 1885, pertains to the death of Captain George Eldridge of the *N.B. Lewis*, referred to in the June 2nd letter from Henry Lewis to Captain Gullison. It is followed by an editorial comment from the *Herald* on Captain Eldridge's death.

From Dr. Harris to the Editor of the *Herald*

Dear Sir:

Captain Eldridge, who died of small pox, was doing remarkably well up to Friday noon when he persisted in taking a bath contrary to my orders. He complained of feeling cold immediately after, violent congestion of the lungs followed and he died in a few hours. During the passage to New York there were but two cases (not 5 or 6 as reported) on board Capt. Eldridge's ship — Mr. Murray Lewis, second mate, and a man who was sent to a hospital on arrival. Had the ship been quarantined according to law, small pox would not have been introduced into our community.

I am taking every possible precaution to prevent the spread of the disease and keep it confined to one house. Many absurd rumours in circulation — such as infected bedding being put out the sickroom window to air, etc. have no foundation whatever. The bedding was all burned as soon as the body was removed for burial. The coffin being tarred outside, snugly covered with canvas and again tarred.

Captain Eldridge died Saturday A.M. and was buried the same evening and the next morning thorough fumigation and cleansing was commenced. Outside of his family (six in number) no one has been exposed except myself, so far as I know.

The deceased was highly respected by all who knew him and deep sympathy is felt by the whole community for the bereaved family.

Death of Captain Eldridge

The letter of Dr. Harris fully disposes of the sensational rumours regarding the circumstances attending the death at Richmond of Capt. Eldridge of small pox. Capt. Eldridge was master of the ship *N.B. Lewis* which he left in New York and came on a visit to Yarmouth. As it has now been over ten days since he was in town and no ill effects of his presence has appeared, there is little cause for further anxiety.

Capt. B.F. Gullison   Barque *Republic*   Yarmouth N.S.
                                                  Aug. 4/85

Dear Sir:

I have received all your favours from Bristol and also disbursement account from D. Jarvis & Co. brokers and note the *Republic* was down to
Lundy Island on the 10th. I hope you may have a fair passage to Sydney.
Shall charter her for coals for Quebec and then let her go seeking open
for business from there. I hope we get something for her so we get her
out of debt for I don't like to have anything to do with a vessel that will
not pay her bills & I wish they could sell her. Anyhow, I am in hopes if
nothing happens we may get enough out of her with coal freights and
lumber freights from Quebec to square her up.

   Of course, her heavy repair bills last year has given her quite a drag.
Things are very dull for vessels just now.

   The *Otago* sailed from Genoa 16th ult for Breakwater in ballast.

                                                  Yours truly,
                                                  Hy. Lewis

Capt. B.F. Gullison   Bk *Republic*   Yarmouth N.S.
                                                  August 17/85

Dear Sir:

I have received your telegram this date and in answer I wired you that if
you could for $225 make contract dock, clean bottom, copper paint, shift-
ing included for that amount you could do it. If could not get dispatch
thought probably vessel would go to Europe from Quebec and that fresh
water would clean her bottom at Quebec. For your expenses at Sydney, if
practical, you might draw on Duval which party the vessel would go into at
Quebec, but if not practical, to draw on Duval draw on me at any bank in
Yarmouth at sight. The *Otago* left Genoa on the 16th for Breakwater.

   Saw Capt. Corning today. He will inform your wife of your arrival. Get
along as cheap as you can I want to get her out of debt. Same time you
must have the requirements for safe navigation.

                                                  Yours truly,
                                                  Hy. Lewis

Captain F. Gullison   Barque *Republic*   Yarmouth N.S.
                                                  Sept. 3rd/85

Dear Sir:

I have received your letter of the 28th ult. stating that you had commenced loading and yesterday I saw by the papers the *Republic* passed
LOW POINT for QUEBEC on 31st. I am expecting a letter from you

soon stating particulars of disbursements and how you arranged draft. Up to the present time no business has been blocked out for the ship. Duval thinks better let her arrive.

I note in your letter you say you have a good mate. That being the case you will come home on arrival after you get matters arranged. I have had a letter from Stephen Dousaux the stevedore that loaded the *Equator* & Capt. Phillips was satisfied and the ship had a good cargo. He no doubt is as good a man as you could get, and in the event of your coming home would look out for the ship — with the mate. Trusting you may have a good passage up and expect she will go better now that her bottom is clean.

Freighting is dull at Quebec, hope by the time she arrives we will get something.

> Yours truly,
> *Hy. Lewis*

After the death of Captain Eldridge, Captain S.A. Crosby took command of the ship *N.B. Lewis* for a voyage from New York to Amsterdam and return to Philadelphia.

H. & N.B. Lewis then decided to shift Captain Frank Gullison from the *Republic* to the *N.B. Lewis* and he was so notified while he was at Quebec. He came to Yarmouth for a short visit and then proceeded to Philadelphia, where he took over command of the *N.B. Lewis* from Captain Crosby.

The ship *N.B. Lewis* was a full-rigged ship, that is, she had three masts, each carrying at least five sails, square rigged. Her measurements were: length from the forepart of the stem, under the bowsprit to the aft side of the head of the sternpost: 202 feet; main breadth to outside of plank: 39 feet, 6 inches; depth in hold from tonnage deck to ceiling amidships: 23 feet, 2 inches.

The registered[1] tonnage of 1,327.71 was a measurement of cubic capacity, one hundred cubic feet equalling one ton. The *N.B. Lewis* had a cargo space of 132,771 cubic feet. She was able to carry a little over two thousand tons of coal and on her first freighting voyage from Philadelphia to Ireland she carried 80,117 bushels of grain.

Like the 'Down-Easters' being built in New England, she was designed for medium speed and had larger cargo space than the earlier clippers. She did not carry as great a spread of sail and her crew of eighteen was substantially less than that of the fast California clippers. (The ship *Agenor*, built in the Curtis yards of East Boston in 1870, was considered a typical 'Down-Easter'. She was 202 feet long with a beam of 39.2 feet. The measurements of the two vessels are almost identical.)

Again as a comparison, in a history of the Greenman Shipyard of Mystic, Connecticut, issued by the Marine Historical Association Inc., March 1, 1938, it is stated that the keel of the last large ship to be built by the company was laid down in 1868, and that in September, 1869, when she was completed, she was launched as the *Frolic* of 1365 tons register, length 194 feet, breadth 39 feet and depth 24 feet. It was built at a cost of $70,000.

The *N.B. Lewis* was a softwood ship, so-called because she was planked in spruce. Her keel (and perhaps some other parts of her frame)[2] was of yellow

---

1 See Appendix D, Note 9.
2 Parts of the frame and finish were also of pitch pine and oak.

birch which might very well have come from Lake Annis, where there was a particularly fine stand of this wood which was cut by the owner and hauled to the Salmon River shipyards. According to tradition the logs were cut during the winter and hauled to the farmyard where they were squared off; when a load was ready the driver would get out of bed around two in the morning, yoke the oxen to the sled and start off in the darkness for the shipyard. The distance of twelve miles might take six or seven hours each way. It would be dark again when the driver reached home in the evening.

The financing of the ship *N.B. Lewis* followed the general custom.[3] H. & N.B. Lewis subscribed for 28 of the 64 shares and the master of the new ship Captain Ben. Gullison took 4 shares. In studying the ownership of many of the Yarmouth ships, one notes that much the same group were often the owners of many different vessels. As in the case of the *N.B. Lewis* most of the owners were related by blood or marriage.

The original ownership of the *N.B. Lewis* was as follows:

Nathan B. Lewis	12 shares
Henry Lewis	16 shares
Hugh E. Cann	12 shares
Hugh D. Cann	12 shares
Elizabeth Cann	4 shares
Benjamin Gullison	4 shares
Hugh Kenealy	4 shares

The total cost of the ship fully rigged for sea was approximately $40,000 or $625 per share. This cost estimate is based on the statement of Captain Ben Gullison in his letter of September 23, 1886, to his son Frank, that his one-sixteenth interest in the ship *N.B. Lewis* cost almost $2,500 when she was new.[4]

The ship *N.B. Lewis* was launched from the shipyard in Salmon River, Digby County, Nova Scotia, on July 19, 1880. The *Yarmouth Herald*, in the issue of July 22, stated 'The *N.B. Lewis* was towed from Salmon River to the port of Yarmouth on Tuesday last by tug *Alida* where she is to be rigged and fitted for sea'. This final preparation of the ship took less than a month, for on the morning of August 11, 1880, Capt. Gullison sailed his ship out of Yarmouth Harbour. His first mate was Thomas H. Corning and there was on board a crew of 12 which was evidently considered sufficient to take the ship to Philadelphia in ballast. An agreement and account of crew executed at London in October, 1881, stated 'The vessel shall be considered fully manned with nineteen hands all told'.

It is of some interest to note the family relationships of the captain and mates. The second mate, Eugene Gullison, was Captain Ben's second son.

3 See 'Capital was available' p. 12.
4 Stanley T. Spicer, in *Masters of Sail*, p. 151, states that the 1,268 ton ship *E.J. Spicer*, built at Spencer's Island, Nova Scotia, in 1880 (the same year as the *N.B. Lewis*) cost complete $47,242.

FIG. 20. Site of Ship Yard where Ship *N.B. Lewis* was built, 1880.

FIG. 21. View South from Site of Ship Yard.

The first mate, Thomas H. Corning, was a brother of Idella Corning, who later married Frank Gullison, Captain Ben's oldest son. Thus first and second mates were future brothers-in-law.

Within five years Eugene would become captain of the *Otago*, also managed by the firm of H. & N.B. Lewis.

At the end of two years only one member of the original crew remained with the ship. Murray Lewis,[5] starting as a boy, became first an A.B. (able seaman), then bo'sun (boatswain) and finally second mate before he left the ship.

The crew list as filed at Waterford, Ireland, on completion of the first voyage from Philadelphia shows the number of Yarmouth men on board:

Name	Age	Capacity Engaged	Wages per Month
Samuel Trask	19	Cook	$16.00
Alfred Trask	27	Steward	$30.00
Almon Moses	19	Ordinary seaman	$13.00
Jacob H. Ellis	22	Ordinary seaman	$13.00
Judson Wyman	20	Able seaman	$16.00
Murray Lewis	17	Boy	$10.00
Joshua Lims	24	Able seaman	$16.00
T.H. Corning	28	First mate	$40.00
Eugene Gullison	20	Second mate	$30.00
Charles Trask	25	Boatswain	$18.00
Voris Chute	22	Carpenter	$24.00
Russell Harris	17	Boy	$10.00

The captain and first mate of the *N.B. Lewis* continued to be Yarmouth men, but after the first few voyages the sailors picked up in the various ports were of many nationalities. For instance, on a voyage from Capetown to New Orleans in 1887 the birth places of the crew were listed as follows:

Riga 1	Sweden 4	Germany 3
Denmark 2	Scotland 3	U.S.A. 2
Holland 1	England 3	Belgium 1

The ages of these twenty men ranged from nineteen to forty-seven with an average of thirty-four.

As the ship sailed out of Yarmouth Harbour on her first voyage the first mate, Thomas H. Corning, wrote up the log.

5 Murray Lewis was the son of a cousin of the Lewis brothers Henry and Nathan.

Log of Ship N.B. Lewis 1st Voyage

Yarmouth to Philadelphia

Date	Distance Run	Remarks
Aug. 6, 1880	38	Weather first part light fog. Wind moderate. At one o'clock Cape Forchu bore N.E. dis. 8 miles. Long. 66 9 Lat. 43 41 from which I take my departure.
Aug. 9, 1880	48	Weather fair & moderate.
Aug. 10, 1880	50	Weather fair light winds tacked.
Aug. 11, 1880	55	" " then rainy, wind light, 6 days 3 hours at sea.
Aug. 12, 1880	87	Weather looking stormy and squally with wind increasing.
Aug. 13, 1880	100	Weather fair throughout.
Aug. 14, 1880	82	" " sighted Five Fathom Light Ship bearing s.s. 12 miles. Pilot came on board. At two, ship was taken in tow by tug Cynthia to tow us to Philadelphia. Nine days & three hours at sea.
Aug. 15, 1880		Weather fair wind strong. At 10 a.m. let go anchor off Narrow Gauge wharf with 30 fathom chain.[6]
Aug. 16, 1880		Weather fair commenced discharging ballast.[7] Discharged Bill _____, Roberts & Stewart, seamen.
Aug. 17, 1880		Weather fair Men employed at ballast and ceiling ship for grain. Bedder & Goldfinch seamen discharged.
Aug. 18, 1880		Weather fair. Weighed anchor. Hauled into dry dock to find leak. Men variously employed.

6 Port Arrangements: On arrival in a port the captain usually anchored in the harbour and then went ashore in a small boat to meet his local agents. He was given any information he needed regarding port regulations and loading arrangements.

7 Ballast: The full-rigged sailing ship was designed to be operated most efficiently when loaded. If no cargo was available, the hold of the ship was partially filled with *ballast*. Rocks and beach stones were preferred because they were clean and most easily man-handled. Most ports had an area where ballast could be dumped on arrival and the same ballast might be picked up later by another ship needing it. Sometimes when sailing from an English port for North America without a cargo, the ship might purchase a few hundred tons of coal in the hope it might be sold on arrival. In a French port a cargo of clay would be taken at a freight rate which might just cover expenses when nothing better was available.

Log of Ship N.B. Lewis 1st Voyage (cont.)

Yarmouth to Philadelphia

Date	Remarks
Aug. 19, 1880	Weather fair. In dry dock. Found leak & stopped it.
Aug. 21, 1880	Weather fair. Finished discharging ballast. Men at work ceiling.
Aug. 22, 1880	Sunday weather fair throughout.
Aug. 23, 1880	Weather fair & sultry. Men to work at At 5 p.m. finished.
Aug. 24, 1880	Weather squally. At 5 p.m. unmoored & towed to Girard Point by tug Cynthia and commenced loading corn. Two seamen deserted.
Aug. 25, 1880	Weather fair then squally. Men employed at cargo.
Aug. 26, 1880	Weather fair & cool. Finished loading. 80117 bushels of corn on board.
Aug. 27, 1880	Weather fair. At 5 a.m. cast loose. Six men came on board.[8] Was taken on in tow by tug Newcastle. Anchored & changed boats.
Aug. 28, 1880	Weather fair. Weighed anchor. Dropped anchor again.
Aug. 29, 1880	Weather fair. Weighed anchor & set sail down the river. Discharged the pilot. Secured anchors. Pumps & lookout attended to.
Aug. 30, 1880	Weather fair. Five Fathom light ship bore N.S. by N. distance 8 miles from which I take my departure.

8 Crews: The usual custom to secure any crew needed was for the captain to make arrangements with a 'crimp' for delivery of sailors to the ship just previous to sailing. (See Appendix D.)

First Voyage N.B. Lewis with Cargo

Left	Date	Arrived	Date
Yarmouth	August 6, 1880	Philadelphia 9 days 3 hours at sea 7 days in port	August 14
Philadelphia	August 29	Waterford, Ireland 24 days at sea 22 days in port	September 22
Waterford Loaded 538 tons ballast Drawing 13 ft.	October 16	Philadelphia	November 6

In the agreement and account of crew, filed at Waterford under regulations of the Board of Trade, there is a list of the scale of provision to be allowed and served out to the crew during the voyage. In addition to the daily issue of lime and lemon juice and sugar or other antiscorbutics in any case required by law,[9] the following was to be supplied:

Bread: 1 lb. daily
Beef and/or Pork: 1 1/3 or 1 1/4 lb. daily per person
Flour: 1/2 lb. twice a week
Peas: 1 1/4 pt. twice a week
Tea: 1 1/4 lb. monthly
Coffee: 1 lb. monthly
Water: 1 gal. daily per man

Rice, potatoes or other vegetables at the discretion of the master; also the allowance of suet and raisins.

There was also the notation 'No Spirits Allowed'.

The chart of the first voyage from Yarmouth to Philadelphia and then to Waterford and return shows the courses taken. On the return voyage from Waterford to Philadelphia, on October 26, ten days from port in Latitude 44.31 N longitude 49.07 W, Captain Gullison sounded with his lead and found he was in 30 fathoms of water. As he was at the time about 100 miles East of Sable Island, he was probably making sure he was not getting too close to the shoals of this island so aptly named 'Graveyard of the Atlantic'. Again on the

9 The law enacted in England in 1869 requiring the daily serving of lime juice was to prevent the attacks of scurvy which had killed or incapacitated sailors during long voyages on a diet of salt meat. This led to the English ships being known as 'Limejuicers' and English sailors as 'Limeys'. It was, however, a very far-sighted and humane regulation.

JOHN DOUGHERTY,

STEVEDORE,

No. 30 Christian St.,

Reference,
PETER WRIGHT & SONS.   **PHILADELPHIA.**

FIG. 22. Business card of J. Dougherty, Stevedore, Philadelphia.

J. FINNESEY, Jr.   L. FINNESEY.

FINNESEY & BRO.

MANUFACTURERS OF

Ship Cabooses and Ranges,

Sidelights and Lanterns Ventilators, Deck Pipes, &c.

No. 11 Walnut Street, Philadelphia,

(COR. OF WATER.)

REPAIRS FOR ATLANTIC, PACIFIC, SHIPMATE AND SPARTAN RANGES.

SHIP PLUMBING A SPECIALTY.

TIN AND CORRUGATED ROOFING, HEATER AND RANGE WORK, DECK IRONS
AND VENTILATORS.

FLOORS LAID WITH TILE BRICK, IRON AND ZINC.

FIG. 23. Business card of Finnesey & Bro., Philadelphia.

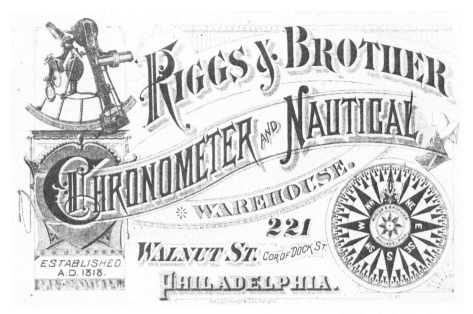

FIG. 24. Business card of Riggs & Brother, Chronometer & Nautical Warehouse, Philadelphia.

FIG. 25. Girard Point grain elevator, Philadelphia (taken from back of J. Dougherty's business card).

31st of October, when he reckoned he was near Georges Bank, he sounded and found 35 fathoms of water. It was a common practice to put tallow underneath the lead, sink it to the sea bottom, raise it, and after examining the sand and gravel adhering to the tallow, fix a position off the coast. In these cases, with favorable weather conditions, Capt. Gullison was perhaps merely sounding for the record, but caution in these waters was always necessary. Under adverse conditions involving low tides and hurricane gales many a vessel has been lost on Sable Island and the Georges Bank.

For the first year under Captain Ben Gullison, the *N.B. Lewis* continued freighting between Philadelphia and ports in Europe. While the records are not complete, it is likely that most of the cargoes were grain. The return trips to Philadelphia were in ballast, except for a voyage from Hamburg in June, 1881, when there was a partial mixed cargo.

On August 12 the *N.B. Lewis* sailed for London. It would appear that on this voyage Captain Ben either took sick or had an accident. On October 10 Captain George Eldridge, another captain from Yarmouth county, took command of the ship. After Captain Gullison recovered his health he returned to Beaver River and worked with H. & N.B. Lewis on a part-time basis. He made occasional voyages as a substitute captain; and when the ships were in port in Boston, New York or Philadelphia he often took charge of the unloading, loading, ship repairs and other port business, while the regular captain, generally one of his own sons, went back to Yarmouth county for a rest and visit.

The amount of time the sailing ships had to spend in port – for loading, unloading, ship repairs in dry dock, and just waiting for cargoes – must have been very frustrating to the owners in Yarmouth. The *N.B. Lewis* arrived in London about September 9, 1881, and it was not until November 1, seven weeks later, that she sailed for San Francisco, probably loaded with a general cargo.

Not much detail is known of the voyages of Captain Eldridge except the bare records. A news item in the *Yarmouth Herald* of February 28, 1884, states: 'Ship *N.B. Lewis*, Capt. Eldridge, which sailed from London December 20th for Cardiff and Valparaiso, while anchored at Gravesend [mouth of the Thames] took fire among her ballast, was obliged to return to London where she was docked and repaired and again sailed for Cardiff, January 25th'.

Captain Ernest Kinney, who for many years commanded the *S.S. Prince Arthur* between Yarmouth and Boston, in his reminiscences in the magazine *Canada East* for Spring, 1931, states that as a boy first going to sea, he was in Cardiff during January and February, 1884, on the ship *Cyprus*, Captain Alfred Parker, owned by Troop & Son, Saint John. They were docked alongside the *N.B. Lewis* and he remembered talking with the second mate Murray Lewis. Other Yarmouth ships in Cardiff docks at the time were *Fanny Cann*, Captain Morrell; *Morning Light*, Captain Ladd; *Fred Taylor*, Captain Tilley.

While Captain Henry Lewis carried on the correspondence with Captain Gullison when he commanded the *Republic*, it was his brother Nathan who managed the *N.B. Lewis* and it was the latter's correspondence with Frank Gullison which makes possible the story of this ship. It is interesting to note that four ships owned and managed by the Lewis brothers arrived in Philadelphia during September of 1885, as the following records show:

Arrived Philadelphia: Sept. 10 ship *N.B. Lewis*, Captain Crosby from Amsterdam

Arrived Philadelphia: Sept. 13 ship *Otago*, Captain Gullison from Genoa

Arrived Philadelphia: Sept. 14 ship *Equator*, Captain Grant from Antwerp

Arrived Philadelphia: Sept. 30 bark *Mizpah*, Captain Cann from Genoa

Captain Frank Gullison joined the *N.B. Lewis* on September 26, 1885. His brother Eugene, who commanded the *Otago*, was in port at the time. We can assume that the Gullison brothers and the two other Yarmouth captains got together in one or other of the ships and that Frank received congratulations on his new command.

On October 1, Eugene in the *Otago* cleared for London and on October 5 the *N.B. Lewis* cleared for the same port. There would no doubt be rivalry between the two brothers as to which would arrive at London first. The records show that the *N.B. Lewis* arrived November 4 and the *Otago* on the fifth. The *N.B. Lewis* was the newer and faster ship, but she must have been made to do her best on this trip. We can imagine Frank meeting Eugene at the London docks and asking him, 'What took you so long?' The *N.B. Lewis* cleared from London on the 16th, but the *Otago* did not get away until the 30th. The former ship arrived at New York January 2, 1886, and the latter at Philadelphia January 21.

The following are two letters sent by N.B. Lewis from Yarmouth to Captain Frank Gullison in London.

Capt. Gullison   Yarmouth
                                                 Oct. 15/85

Dear Sir:
Hope you are well on your way by this writing. Have not done anything with '*LEWIS*' yet for *back business*.[10] No doubt we could get *chalk*[11] for about same as '*OTAGO*' but that seems to be small business to come back with in the winter time. You will *remit* what you have as fast as you can collect.

---

10 Back business: Cargo for return voyage from Europe to America.
11 Chalk: This took the place of ballast and provided some income.

Hope we may find something to pay the back trip. Hope to hear your father is improving soon and able to come home.

> Yours,
> *N.B. Lewis*

Capt. Gullison   Yarmouth
                                                Oct. 29/85

Dear Sir:

Hope you are well on your way by this writing. See *Adolphus* is over. Don't know what to say about future business; don't seem to be anything paying on the other side. Except will have to come back and chance it but if there is anything offering you can let me know if there is any money in it. I wrote you in reference to remitting in my last. Suppose we could get chalk but suppose will be some detention[12] with it. Hoping to soon hear of your safe arrival at New York.

> Yours,
> *N.B. Lewis*

Capt. Gullison   [New York]   Yarmouth
                                                Dec. 16th/85

Dear Sir:

Suppose we might soon look for your arrival. Have closed the ship from New York to Shanghai 31 cents case oil. Think this better than running across the Atlantic at present rates. London accounts and remittances came to hand satisfactory. Shall have to dock and recopper[13]; have engaged Taunton metal 11 1/2 cents. In reference to stevedore, Cummings has applied for the stevedoring; offers one cent per case returns 5%. I believe they are good stevedores. I am going to write Dick & Churchill,[14] they

---

12   Detention: Ship would have to wait to load the chalk and thus could not make as fast a return trip.

13   Recopper: Wooden ships, particularly before they went into southern waters, were carefully covered below the water line with thin copper sheets to prevent the wooden hull from being eaten by worms. The *N.B. Lewis* was then five years old; Mr. Lewis feels it is time to put her in dry-dock and have the copper carefully examined and replaced where necessary.

14   Churchill: This might be the celebrated 'Rudder' Churchill whose story is told in detail by Archibald McMechan in his book *Old Province Tales*. At sixteen years of age he was second mate on the Yarmouth-owned ship *Research*, 1,459 tons. On a trip from Quebec to Glasgow in the winter of 1866, during a very severe storm, the ship lost the use of her rudder. Despite the high seas running, Churchill went over the side, and after repeated attempts, fixed the rudder so they could continue on to Glasgow. His feat was so admired among his contemporaries that he was given the nick-name 'Rudder'. He became a captain in his twenties and retired in 1874 to start a stevedoring business in Savannah, Georgia. He expanded into the steamship business and operated a steamship line between New York and southern ports in the United States. He accumulated a fortune and built a palatial summer residence in Yarmouth County which still stands as a memorial to a great Nova Scotia sailor.

wrote down to Capt. Augustus Cann[15] that they could give us extra inducements. I believe them to be good stevedores and shall give the ship to whoever can give us the best work and best value for our money. I think I will write to Dick & Churchill and see what they can do for us. Cummings has been writing my brokers at Philadelphia; he has been there looking after the *Euphemia*. I think I will, if I can, run on[16] for a while to see the *N.B. Lewis* out of dock. You need not make any announcement about the stevedore until you hear from me. I hear there is a dock that is doing cheaper work; the one that the *Stalwart*[17] was on. Ten cents hauling out, eight cents after first day. J.F. Whitney will do the ships business. Your orders will meet you at New York. I rather favor Dick & Churchill as stevedores, if they will do as well, as Churchill is a Yarmouth man. I have met him several times when he was master [captain of a ship]. Telegraph your arrival and I will come on I think. Should think you would want about not over 50 tons ballast to trim her. *Euphemia*[18] with 70 tons ballast drew 12.10 aft. and 9.10 forward. Hoping to hear of your safe arrival and in the matter of stores and other fittings, better wait till you hear from me before engaging.

Yours,

N.B. Lewis

The *N.B. Lewis* arrived in New York Dec. 31, 1885, from London, completing the first voyage under Captain Frank Gullison. He remained in that port until February 13 while the ship was prepared and cargo loaded for a voyage to Shanghai with case oil.

The first part of the following letter is not available. It was probably written from New York in January, 1886, by Captain Frank Gullison to his younger brother Ralph, at home in Nova Scotia. From other letters it is apparent that Ralph was on board the *N.B. Lewis* when she cleared New York for Shanghai in February, 1886.

... be throwing your time away. Take my advice and try and learn some good trade. I think you will like it better in the long run, but if you insist on coming or going to sea, and your pa and ma are willing that you

15 Captain Augustus Cann was a cousin of Mrs. Nathan Lewis (née Adeline Cann) and one of the successful captains in Yarmouth. By coincidence, the author of these notes owned and lived in the Captain 'Gus' Cann house for many years.

16 The expression 'run on' means he hopes to make the trip from Yarmouth to New York.

17 The ship *Stalwart*, 1,545 tons, was a Yarmouth ship launched in 1883 and owned by Jacob Bingay and others.

18 The records also show that the newest ship in the fleet managed by H. & N.B. Lewis, the *Euphemia*, arrived in Philadelphia on Nov. 12, 1885. The *Euphemia*, 1,367 tons, launched at Salmon River in 1882, while a few tons larger, was practically a sister ship of the *N.B. Lewis*. Under the command of Captain Elijah Phillips, a cousin of Captain Henry Lewis, she loaded a cargo of oil in cases and sailed for Hiogo, Japan, December 21, 1885.

77

should, why pack up your traps and come along as soon as you like. We are working ballast all night and I expect to be up most of the time getting ready for dry dock tomorrow. Expect to make a January shipment so we have to put things up in double quick time. The weather here is very cold at present but has been very fine until lately. I had a very boisterous passage coming out this time; 42 days from London but thankful to survive all safe. I suppose Della is making plans to come on but tell Mother Corning that I do not think I will take her the voyage as the weather out there will be very warm and unhealthy, but suppose she will enjoy the visit on here.

Well, brother be good to yourself and don't stay up too late Sunday nights. Give my love to mother and father Corning, Ed. & Winnie and kiss Lile for me and tell — to strip the cows dry. From your loving brother,

Frank Gullison

Both Captain Gullison's brother Ralph and his wife came to New York — his brother to sign on as a sailor for the voyage, and his wife to visit while the ship was in port, later going on to Philadelphia.

Philadelphia   Jan. 20th 1886

My own true Love[19]:

I have got a bottle of Florida water. Frank I sincerely thank you for all your kindness. Uncle Jim got to the station as I did, so all is well.

Deani is still at B.W. — expect he will be up next July, and trust all will be well. I am happy and content here. The girls are so kind and pleasant. I am right to home. Drop a line to cheer me on. God bless you.

Della

Capt. F. Gullison [at New York]   Yarmouth
                                        Jan. 21/86

Dear Sir:

I[20] arrived at home late on Wednesday; had a rough passage across the bay.[21] Yours of 10th came safe to hand; suppose you are still at 19th street

---

19 Letter from his wife Della to Captain Gullison while he is in New York loading for Shanghai.
20 Letter probably written after return home from a trip to see ship in dry-dock at New York.
21 This would be across the Bay of Fundy from Boston to Yarmouth.

[dock]. Likely they will keep you all your days.[22] Probable will have time to write you again before you get away. In case you want to cable after you get out to Shanghai you can use Jones cable book. Hope you will soon get loaded up and that stevedore will get in good cargo. See the *Otago* has got up all right, I expect, as they report no damage. Letter from Eugene says last hard passage. Suppose shall soon have letters from you.

Yours
N.B. Lewis

J.P. ELDRIDGE AND COMPANY

Painters, Grainers and Glaziers

Dealers in: Paints, Oils, Varnish, Glass and Putty etc.

Corner of Cabot and Dane Sts.

Beverly, Massachusetts

January 26th 1886

Dear Friend Frank:

Your welcome lines of the 24th, came to hand today. I was somewhat surprised but very much pleased to hear from you. I wish it was so that you and Della could take a run up to see us — hoping it will be so one of these days. I have been very much interested in your and Eugene's well fair since ever you took charge. I take the *Yarmouth Times*, and have watched it right up sharp for your clearance and arrivals. It seems almost too hard to have Della unable to get around any better but you must keep up good heart. I hope it will turn out all right by and by. We all have our troubles sooner or later. Well Frank, we are having a very good winter. It is fine sleighing now, and I have been enjoying it today. I have had plenty of work since I came here and a good prospect for the future, if having plenty of work is any prospect. I received a letter from your Father today. They are well as usual. G.A. Raymond is here — he sends his best wishes to you all. Three of my children go to school and Harold will go this summer. Old Aunt Jane McCormach is here and I don't know but what we will have a wedding before long. There is an old widower visiting her quite often. Best wishes to all who inquire and to Eugene and wife. It is

---

22 If the owners had arranged for a cargo through their agent, a charter party (C.P.) would have been signed. The charter party was an agreement whereby a certain shipper would agree to deliver to the ship on a certain date a certain amount of freight to be carried to a certain port for a stated amount and sometimes within a fixed time limit.

    Lay days: When a ship was chartered a *waiting period* or the *number of lay days* was stated during which the ship would wait without charge for cargo to be ready. At the end of the lay day period the ship could charge shippers and demurrage fee for each day held.

bed-time, wishing you every success of life and I hope if we never meet on earth, that we will meet in that better land, from your ever-loving friend.

J.P. Eldridge

The following letter is from the pastor of the church in Beaver River.

Beaver River (Yarmouth Co.)
January 29th 1886

Dear brother Gullison

I have intended to write to you for a long time but I fear now that I have put it off too long, and that you will be plowing the deep before this reaches New York. Both of the times that you have been home I have happened to be absent. We are all glad to hear that your wife stood the journey so well. It must have been a great pleasure to you both to meet again though I suppose that you will both be disappointed that she was not permitted to accompany you on the voyage. I am sorry that you are going on such a long voyage though I expect in some respects it is pleasanter than the Atlantic trips. We were glad that you got the command of a good ship and trust that you may be very successful in the responsible voyage you are about to undertake.

Mrs. DeWolf had a letter from Mrs. Eugene giving an account of the trip. We were glad that your wife fell in with such pleasant companions and enjoyed the journey so well. I trust that she will be returned to us much improved. We do not forget to pray for you both and constantly think of the absent ones. I never had so much interest in ships before but I am getting so that I glance first at the shipping news to see who has arrived or sailed. Such as yourself and brother and Brother Corning (Theo) J. Crosby and other that we feel especially interested in. They expect to commence operations on the Meeting House in March. I know that we can count on you for some help in finishing. I suppose that you are cut off from enjoying meetings very often but then no one can deprive you of meeting with your Saviour by yourself. I think that a Captain has good opportunities of working for the master. You have Ralph with you. He can sing and has a good gift for taking part in meeting. Cannot you hold meetings among the sailors on the voyage? Especially on Sunday.

There seems to be a good feeling in the Church now. I am expecting J.T. Easton from Ohio[23] Church to assist me in a few meetings. Next week pray that they may be blessed. Now remember Mrs. DeWolf and myself to Ralph. Shall miss him but trust that he will be faithful and after the voy-

---

23 Ohio is a village in Yarmouth County. There is a tradition that at the time when the state of Ohio was being opened to settlement, and many New Englanders were emigrating there, some of the Yarmouth people, who were unable to make a trip as far away as Ohio, U.S.A., decided to settle in this area of Yarmouth County and called it Ohio.

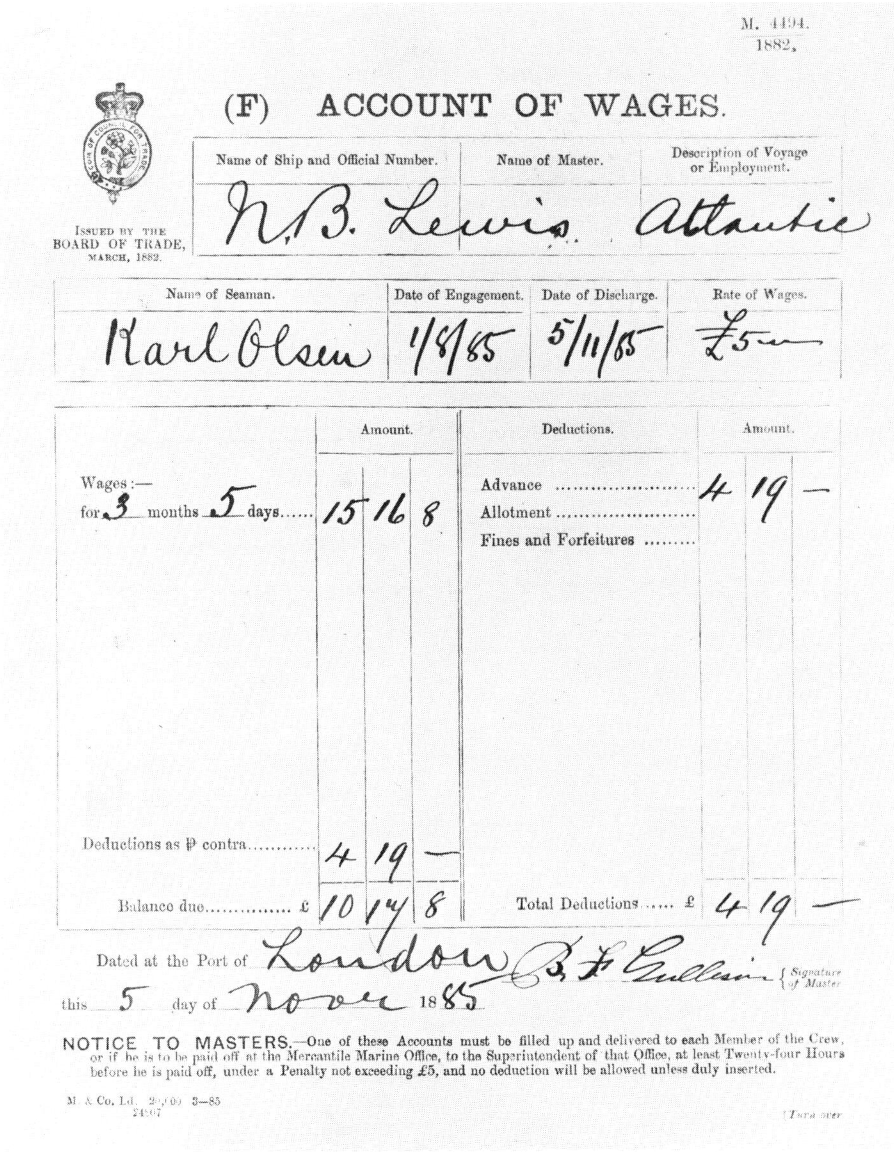

M. 4494.
1882,

(F) ACCOUNT OF WAGES.

ISSUED BY THE
BOARD OF TRADE,
MARCH, 1882.

Name of Ship and Official Number.	Name of Master.	Description of Voyage or Employment.
N.B. Lewis	Lewis	Atlantic

Name of Seaman.	Date of Engagement.	Date of Discharge.	Rate of Wages.
Karl Olsen	1/8/85	5/11/85	£5

	Amount.	Deductions.	Amount.
Wages :— for 3 months 5 days......	15 16 8	Advance	4 19 —
		Allotment	
		Fines and Forfeitures	
Deductions as ℣ contra............	4 19 —		
Balance due.............. £	10 17 8	Total Deductions ...... £	4 19 —

Dated at the Port of London B. F. Gillin { Signature of Master

this 5 day of Novr 1885

NOTICE TO MASTERS.—One of these Accounts must be filled up and delivered to each Member of the Crew, or if he is to be paid off at the Mercantile Marine Office, to the Superintendent of that Office, at least Twenty-four Hours before he is paid off, under a Penalty not exceeding £5, and no deduction will be allowed unless duly inserted.

M. & Co. Ld. 2/500) 3—85
2407

[Turn over

Fig. 26. Account of Wages for seaman Karl Olsen, discharged Nov. 5, 1885, from *N.B. Lewis* after a voyage of three months & five days.

Record of American and Foreign Shipping.

ESTABLISHED 1867.

American Shipmasters' Association, 37 William St., New York.

TARIFF OF FEES.

After January 1, 1881, charges will be as follows:

For Vessels not exceeding 200 tons,					$25
" " 200 and under 300 tons					30
" " 300 " 400 "					35
" " 400 " 500 "					40
" " 500 " 600 "					45
" " 600 " 700 "					50
" " 700 " 800 "					55
" " 800 " 900 "					65
" " 900 " 1000 "					70
" " 1000 " 1100 "					75
" " 1100 " 1200 "					80
" " 1200 " 1400 "					90
" " 1400 " 1600 "					100
" " 1600 " 1800 "					110
" " 1800 " 2000 "					120
" " 2000 " 2500 "					130
" " 2500 " 3000 "					140

When vessels are built under inspection of this Association, or classed under SPECIAL SURVEY No. 5, the above prices will be *increased fifty per cent.*

For *iron vessels, built under inspection*, the charge will be *ten* cents per ton for the first 1,000 tons, and *five* cents for the tonnage above 1,000, in addition to the charges stated in the above table ; but no charge for such inspection of iron vessels will be less than **$25.** The above includes cost of Certificates.

Vessels repaired under Inspection will be charged the following rates :

For Vessels 500 Tons and under				$10
" " over 500 " " 800 tons				15
" " " 800 " " 1200 "				20
" " " 1200 " and over				25

Indorsement of caulking and metalling:

For Vessels 500 Tons and under,				$5
" " 500 " " " 1000 tons				10
" " 1000 " " over,				15

Half Time Surveys:

For Vessels 500 Tons and under,				$15
" " over 500 " " 1000 tons				20
" " 1000 " and over,				25

The above charges will all be in addition to traveling expenses that may be incurred ; and in cases involving extra care and trouble, a special charge will be made.

JAMES PARKER, Secretary.

FIG. 27. Tariff of Fees, American Shipmasters' Association, New York.

FIG. 28. Certificate of Clearance Outward from London, Nov. 18, 1885.

age be restored to us again in safety. Also to Mrs. Gullison if she has not left you before this reaches you and accept kind regards and best wishes for yourself.

Yours in haste
Jas. DeWolf

Capt. F. Gullison   Ship *N.B. Lewis*   Yarmouth
Feb. 1/86

Dear Sir:

Yours of the 27th at hand, contents noted. See they have given you orders. They have about 14 days to load the ship, they will probable take them. See the towage folks jumped the bill a little; that is like them. I think you had better use the Hook [Sandy Hook] going to sea as there may be trouble with ice in the Sound [Long Island] and I notice there is a good deal trouble with crews. You sailing in February should have a fair monsoon[24] up the straits[25] and will probable have no occasion to use the outlaying Passage.

I think you should have the best time of year for going safely. I hope to be able to fix[26] the ship before your arrival at something paying. If you don't hear from me again before you sail, if you have any chance to report yourself on passage, do so as we shall always be glad to hear from you.

Now Captain, as regards taking your wife, I know it would be pleasant to you both, but I feel about just as I did at New York. I can't give consent and think it would be very unwise at present. Another trip she may be able to go. Hope you will see this from my standpoint and not think I want to be hard with you. Eugene has asked the same privilege. I shall write him to the same effect, for this voyage. Hoping you will get a good cargo and make a quick and successful voyage,

Yours truly
Nathan B. Lewis

P.S. the chart bill is charged in ship a/c 2.15.11 pounds.[27]

[The following is a note on the bottom of this letter]:

Mr. Lewis seems to have made a mistake. This is your letter I believe and I suppose you must have got mine.

---

24 Monsoons were prevailing winds in the China Seas which changed direction twice a year. Among the islands and narrow channels it was very important to have favourable winds. Ships' logs show this very clearly.

25 Straits: This refers to Sundra Strait between Java and Sumatra and then up the China coast.

26 'Fix' – to obtain a charter for return freight.

27 2.15.11 pounds (also 2/15/11) – i.e., two pounds fifteen shillings and eleven pence sterling. For English currency or currency of 'sterling area' countries during the period of these voyages, reckon the pound (£) at $4.86, the shilling (s) at $0.24/4, and the penny (d) at $0.02 in terms of Canadian dollars of the same period. (Hence £2.5.11 was the equivalent of approximately $11.15 Canadian.)

He put them in wrong envelopes. You see what he says about taking our wives. Is this not to haw. Write to me and tell me all the news before you sail. Your brother,

E.G. (Eugene)

Capt. Gullison [at New York]   Yarmouth, N.S.
                                 Feb. 6th/86

Dear Sir:

Suppose you must be near loaded. I wrote you last week in reference to going out Long Island Sound. I don't think the small saving equal to the risk so you will take the Hook going to sea.

We have it very cold here now. If the ice is bad, better not go till chances safe even if you have to wait a few days. Hoping to soon hear of your being loaded.

I am yours
Nathan B. Lewis

W.F. HAGAR & CO.
Ship Brokers
No. 111 Walnut Street

Cable address *Hagar*
Use Watkins Code
Philadelphia, Feb. 8th 1886.

My Dear brother Frank

I will drop you a few lines to let you know how we are getting along discharging – expect to finish about Wednesday. Things are going slow. Suppose you have heard about the *Equator*? getting cut down – also Capt. Crangle into St. Thomas – vessel condemned – what a world this is. I thought Mr. Lewis would consent to us taking our wives, but he does not seem disposed so will have to be reconciled. When Della leaves, wire me and I will meet her at the station and look out for her and then if they conclude to go home why they can go together. Hope you will have a pleasant voyage. Trust in God and all will be right.

Your brother
A. Eugene Gullison

Tell me if you credit to the ship with 2/6 per man[28] in London. You know what I mean. Love to Della.   A.E.G.

---

28   2/6 – 'two-and-sixpence' (two shillings and sixpence or approximately 60 cents).

N.B. Lewis Esq.,   New York
                                             Feb. 10th 1886

Dear Sir:

I have settled up business this afternoon. Ships expense here is six
thousand seven hundred & eight dollars and sixty cents $6708.60 & have
given J.F. Whitney a draft on W.F. Hagar[29] for the sum of $4208.60 as
ordered. Will be ready for sea in the morning and shall go weather and
ice permitting. I have had ice to contend with in all my harbour towage
and that is what has run it up so and also stevedores bill I consider quite
high but I believe he did his best. You know about how we were humbugged with that ballast. The 400 tons discharged has averaged about 40¢ per
ton. The *N.B. Lewis* has made more water since we came off the dock; 4
inches in twelve hours but that is not much. I do not think it did her much
good pulling her off drydock; think probable she will take up again.[30] I
received a letter from you this morning stating or advising about not going
Long Island way. It will meet your wishes as I have engaged to go out
Sandy Hook way for the sum of seventy dollars. Mr. Whitney has just telegraphed you amount of the disbursements and number of cases shipped.[31]
I cannot think of anything more to inform you at present but will try and
write again hoping to make a quick and prosperous passage. I shall do my
best to do so Sir and I remain

                                             Your Obedient Servant
                                             B.F. Gullison

---

29 W.F. Hagar & Co., 111 Walnut Street, Philadelphia, were ship agents closely associated with
    H. & N.B. Lewis and the amount of $4208.60 would be an advance against freight. As general
    agents for H. & N.B. Lewis in the United States, W.F. Hagar & Co. might provide cargoes and
    pay port expenses on four or five of the vessels operated by H. & N.B. Lewis in any given
    month. At the end of stated periods – probably each month – Hagars would make up
    statements of their account with Lewis and remit any credit balance. Debits would usually be
    carried over until there was a credit.
       The Captain, in a U.S. port, when needing money to pay expenses, would make a draft on
    Hagar through the banks. In England there was the same arrangement with John Black & Co.
    of London. (See Appendix for information on drafts.)
30 'Take up again' means stop leaking.
31 There is no statement re the number of cases loaded but on a later trip to Java the *N.B. Lewis*
    took a full cargo totalling 48,791 cases of oil @ 31¢; this would amount to $15,125.21 or
    approximately fifteen thousand dollars. It will be noted later that the actual amount for this
    voyage was $15,319.28.

Capt. Gullison

Yarmouth
May 3/86

Dear Sir:

Hope you are half passage by this time. Have not been able yet to fill in back business[1] but shall now go to work and try to have something blocked out by time you are discharged or, if we can, we shall fix now anytime to arrive if possible except it will be hard to get any money to pay much on your arrival. Cable using Jones Code if all right. You will only want to use address 'Lewis Yarmouth Nova Scotia Gullison'. Hope you have a good passage and good dispatch at Shanghai and find it a reasonable port. Remit freight as fast as you can collect in good and approved Bills on London as short sight[2] as possible. Capt. Goudey would be a good man to advise with in all these matters as he has been longer in the business. If on arrival, there is paying business offering you might submit it by cable. We shall try and have something blocked out for the ship if possible. I suppose most of the chartering is done in London. I have written John Black & Co. to let me know what they can get Frisco, Phillipines or Calcutta. Hoping to hear of your safe arrival in good time.

I am yours
N.B. Lewis

[The above letter was written to go by steamer and meet Captain Gullison in Shanghai.]

---

1 By 'back business' he refers to cargo for return voyage.
2 'As short sight as possible': A bill of exchange *at sight* is payable on demand or when presented (within c3 days). In this case the meaning is *as short term as possible*. See Glossary under Freight Payments.

Capt. B.F. Gullison

Ship *N.B. Lewis*   Shanghai[3]

Brookville

May 18th, 1886

Dear Son:

About three months have passed since you left New York. I would drop you a few lines to let you know how we are doing at home. My health has improved beyond my expectations.[4] Your Mother is quite poorly of late troubled with the old complaints – cramps and distress in the stomach. Was in to Aunt – a short time ago to see your boy. He was well. George said he would feel bad to give him up, as the little fellow calls him pa. He is as fat as a little pig, and I think that is the reason he is backward in walking. Della is still in Lynn, Mass. She said she was gaining all the time and that she would surprise us when she came home. We have had a beautiful spring – quite dry and fine but of late considerable rain, starting the grass nicely.

Norman Raymond's daughter Nellie is dead. She was over to the States to get doctored and died suddenly. Her remains will be brought home for interment at Beaver River. I have finished the Meeting House except to paint the inside. Will be ready for dedication on June the 1st. Hope your wife will be home in time to choose a pew. It [the church] will cost from 10 to 12 hundred dollars. I fear it will be some time before we get our money back. Capt. Theoff[5] and I shoulder the bills and hope that all who can purchase a pew will come forward, and do so.

Eugene[6] is on his way from Antwerp to Philadelphia. Makes about £270, Stg. on emptys. Owners have allowed him to take his wife this summer voyage only. I talked with Mr. Lewis and he said that if your wife willed he intended to let you take her next voyage.

I offered them $1300 for one sixteenth 1/16 of the *N.B.*[7] after leaving New York clear of all debts – dues and demands – you to have the benefit of outward freight if any left on Shanghai. I might make it 1400 but $1300 is all she is worth in the market now at the present rates of freights. They would like to sell Eugene 1/16 of *Hugh Cann*.[8]

3 This and the previous letter would be mailed in the expectation it would go via Boston and San Francisco and arrive in Shanghai while the *N.B. Lewis* was there.
4 Captain Ben, who was the first captain of the *N.B. Lewis* and had to give up because of poor health, is now at home and very interested in building the Church at Beaver River. He is hoping his sons will contribute by 'buying pews'. It was the custom at this time when a new church was built to ask members and adherents to 'purchase' a pew which would then become the exclusive pew for the family subscribing. To arrive at a price for a pew the total amount owing was divided by the number of pews.
5 Captain Theoff. Corning lived across the road from Captain Ben Gullison in Beaver River.
6 Captain Eugene is freighting oil in drums across to Europe from Philadelphia and bringing empty drums back. This was not a very profitable business as his return freight only amounted to £270 or about $1100.
7 Captain Ben is trying to buy a share in the *N.B. Lewis* for Frank. The share cost about $2500 when she was built. See note p. 93.
8 The *Hugh Cann* was another Yarmouth ship in which H. & N.B. Lewis held an interest.

Two Voyages of the Ship N.B.Lewis

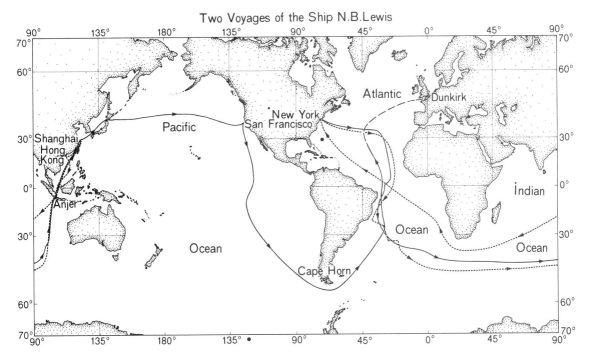

Voyage Around the World

————— Course of Voyage

Sailed from New York February 13 1886
112 days to Anjer 27 days to Shanghai.
Arrived July 2,1886 144 days Sailed from
Shanghai July 24,1886 Arrived San Francisco
September 8,1886 56 days. Sailed
October 29,1886 27 days to the Equator
30 days Equator to Cape Horn 29 days
Cape Horn to Equator 47 days Equator to
Dunkirk Arrived March 11,1887 133 days.

**Voyage- New York to Shanghai and
Hong Kong and Return**

------------------- Course of Voyage

Sailed from New York January 30,1890;
arrived Anjer May 16,1890 116 days;
arrived Shanghai June 18, 1890 139 days;
sailed from Shanghai August 1,1890;
arrived Hong Kong September 5,1890
35 days; sailed from Hong Kong October 4,
1890 arrived New York January 28,
1891 116 days.

Fig. 29.

These interests belonged to George Eldridge and the estate wishes to dispose of them. If I do not buy there will be no danger of them turning you out as they think too much of you to do anything like that. I hope that you may have a safe and prosperous passage and that you may hit on some paying business back. I hope my dear boy Ralph is well and doing well. I miss him very much as I am now all alone. May God watch over him and you and spare you — ere long to meet us all again. Your Mother and little sisters join me in sending love to you and Ralph and may God my heavenly Father keep you in the hollow of his hand and under the shadow of his mighty wing and return you to us again. From your loving father.

Benj. Gullison

Capt. Gullison

Yarmouth
May 22/86

Dear Sir:

I wrote you last mail via San Francisco. Shall look for you along in about a month.[9] See ship *North American*[10] passed Anjer[11] in 86 days from New York for Japan. I have not yet been able to make charter. Hope to do so; if I don't succeed, shall have to do best we can after arrival. Perhaps go to Frisco seeking [a cargo]. Things are dull. Have not heard from *Euphemia* yet[12] at Japan. Soon be out 150 days. I wrote you in my last to remit in good Bankers Bills on London, short sight as possible. Hoping to soon hear of your safe arrival and that paying freight will turn up.

Yours
N.B. Lewis

Capt. F. Gullison

Yarmouth
June 12/86

Dear Sir:

Suppose we may soon begin to look for you along. Sorry have not been able to charter yet. When you get ready, you will have to cable for orders, if we don't succeed in fixing before. If we get you closed,[13] will cable at once. Have been trying to fix for Frisco. Thought we could get 35s[14] Grain

9 The *N.B. Lewis* was 112 days to Anjer.
10 Ship *North American* was launched Boston Mass. Jan. 3, 1873. For her first few years she was considered by many authorities the finest American ship afloat. See: *American Merchant Ships 1850-1900*, by Frederick C. Matthews, published 1930 by Marine Research Library, Salem, Mass., page 212.
11 Anjer, on the Sundra Strait between the Islands of Sumatra and Java, was very familiar to all captains of ships sailing from Atlantic ports to China.
12 *Euphemia* sailed from New York December 21, 1885.
13 'If we get you closed': i.e., if we get a firm charter.
14 35s is thirty-five shillings or $8.40 a ton for grain from San Francisco to Europe.

but the fellow was not reliable. Hope yet to do something from there. We are working with John Black Co., London.

I wrote you in my last about remitting. Can say nothing further. You will see to getting good Bankers Bills. Hope you will soon put in appearance and that we may get something back paying.

Yours
N.B. Lewis

P.S. Capt. Eldrige's 1/16 of the <i>N.B. Lewis</i> will be sold today at auction. Your father will buy, I suppose, if price suites.   N.B.L.

N.B. Lewis Esq.   Shanghai July 14th 1886

Dear Sir:

I write you these few lines to inform you that I expect to [be] discharged tomorrow night. Cargo is turning out fair. Business is dull here most of the shipping is going to Victoria, VI.[15] I have drawn two thousand pounds £2000. In one thousand pound drafts £1000; first has gone to London by this mail to be excepted, will remit to you today by American mail 2nd bill of Exchange for each amount or for each £1000 −, and trust you will receive them in order will forward the other by English mail.

Yours most Respectfully
B.F. Gullison

N.B. Lewis Esq.   Shanghai July 22nd 1886

Dear Sir:

I write these few lines to inform you that I have just made a settlement; have had two days detention on account of trouble with my sailors.[16] Received your telegraph 'proceed for orders to San Francisco'. I shall sail tommorow morning if favourable. My expense here is £561-19-6 or $2569.02 tael[17] @ 4/6 1/2. Have forwarded you 2nd and 3rd bill of exchange[18] to the amount of £2000. Will remit to you balance of freight £586-9-3 and hope you will receive them all in order. I will also send vou-

---

15   Probably Vancouver Island.
16   For further details, see Appendix E.
17   Tael: a far-eastern unit of exchange equivalent to the value of Chinese <i>liang</i> or ounce (approx. 1 1/3 oz. avoirdupois) of silver, and fluctuating in value with the price of that metal. The exchange value of the tael ranged between six and seven shillings sterling from 1745 to 1860, was six shillings eight pence ($1.62) in 1864, three shillings (73 cents) in 1900, and two shillings ten pence (69 cents) in 1904. The exchange rate for Captain Gullison's transactions in Shanghai in July, 1886, was four shillings, six and one-half pence (about $1.10).
18   It was the custom to send one or two duplicate bills of exchange by separate ships in case one should be lost.

chers if not from here will forward from Frisco, and hope Sir you will find everything satisfactory. I have tried to do all for the best and if you find any little mistake please let me know as I am always willing to learn.

From yours most respectfully
Frank Gullison

[Costs approx.	$ 2852.
Drafts Home approx.	12570.
Total freight	$15422.]

The first part of the following letter could not be deciphered. It is evidently a letter to N.B. Lewis from Captain Gullison after arrival at San Francisco in September 1886 from Shanghai. He does not like the arrangement for towage to Benicia where he is to get his cargo of grain.

... today. I think I shall telegraph tomorrow and inquire about this towage agreement. I have not received any word from you about it but see your name signed to a contract at Griffiths tugboat office. This is all I know about it; so perhaps it will be safer to inform you before taking any long tow to *Benicia*[?] as I am not satisfied with a number of persons connected with our business here. I do not wish to find fault Sir, but I must say things seem to turn around very queer. Probably I will take *stiffenings*[19] in the morning. Hope to receive a letter from you soon.

Yours in obedience
B.F. Gullison

Capt. Gullison   Yarmouth Aug. 24/86

Dear Sir:

Suppose you are out now about a month.[20] Think you had good passage to Shanghai and was getting a good dispatch. Suppose I will soon have letters and amount wind up Shanghai. Sorry could not fix[21] the ship before arrival [at San Francisco]. Tried and offered to accept but they would not go through. See things are dull in Frisco. Think it will be as well to take the best offering and get away. See they think about 27/6[22] is the best they can do at present. I.N. Knowles is our agent at Frisco and I have written him in reference to business. Hoping to soon hear of your safe arrival and that there may be paying freight for you on arrival. Get the best offer you can

19 Stiffening: Sufficient ballast for the safe movement of a vessel in harbour or river after unloading, but not sufficient for a sea-going voyage.
20 This letter was written to await Captain Gullison at San Francisco.
21 Fix − obtain a firm charter contract.
22 27/6 − twenty-seven shillings and six pence per ton (about $6.70 U.S. dollars).

or if you can get 27/6 offered with good conditions it looks like the best thing by Mr. Knowles and you can fix her at once. Expect we could of got 4 1/2 for sugar but it did not look like being as good as grain. Things are awfully dull, hope they may improve soon.

Yours

N.B. Lewis

Capt. Gullison   Yarmouth Sept. 23/86

Dear Sir:

Was glad to hear of your arrival over. Sorry could not have you chartered. Hope you may get fixed up. Have been looking for telegram but suppose things must be bad. Had better take the best offering and get away; don't see no use waiting. Hope soon to hear of your charter. Think 27/6 better than anything offering in Manila. Think you got out of Shanghai cheaper than I expected. Shall be glad if we ever get an improvement in freight. Have to live in hopes. I have tried ever since ship sailed to fix her but have not been able. Hope Mr. Knowles[23] will soon be able to get you charter.

Yours

N.B. Lewis

Capt. B.F. Gullison   Ship *N.B. Lewis*   Brookville,[24] Nova Scotia

Sept. 19th 1886

Dear Son:

Your kind favour of the 23 inst. to hand. Pleased to hear from you and that you was well. Sorry to learn that you nor Ralph did not receive any letters at Shanghai. We wrote you both. I addressed them in care of the British Consulate at the above port. Since writing that letter I bought 1/16 [one sixteenth] of the ship *N.B. Lewis* from the estate of Capt. George Eldridge for you for the sum of $1500.00.[25] I thought to get it for about

23 Mr. Knowles was agent for the owners in San Francisco. He had recently made a visit to the owners in Yarmouth, Nova Scotia.
24 Brookville is an area in Digby County between Salmon River and Beaver River.
25 See explanation of ships' financing, Introduction. Captain Gullison (Sr.) says he paid about $2500.00 for this 1/16 interest when the ship was built; this would put the original cost at around $40,000. This is less than building costs in New England at the same period. The price paid for Captain Eldridge's 1/16 interest of $1500 shows the ship valued at $24,000 at this time, when she was six years old. This estimate is based on this particular sale of 1/16 at $1500. However, based on the original cost of the ship and the selling price (in a realistic European market through responsible agents) twelve years later, it would appear that average annual depreciation was about $2000 and that the 'book' value of the ship in 1886 was approximately $28,000 rather than $24,000, and the value of Frank's share $1750 instead of $1500, if the transaction had taken place on a wide-open market. It was expected the ship would make a clear profit of $3200 for shareholders on the voyage New York to Shanghai.

$1300.00 but as she had $7000.00 clear freight after leaving New York for Shanghai, they bid her up high so she was knocked down to me. As you was not here, the bill of sale had to be made out in my name and can remain so until you get home. I can give you credit for your part when it comes to hand. If the assessors find it out they will tax me for it but I shall try to keep them blind. I think after paying disbursements at New York she should leave over two hundred to a 1/16. [$200. in dividends for the four shares of the ship.] They asked over $1800.00 at a private sale but I would not give it. My 1/16 [when the ship was new] cost me nearly $2500.00 and when she left New York on this voyage, after her repairs and new metal she was as good as new.

I hope that you may be able to get some paying business in Frisco. Eugene is making good time in the *Otago* but freights are so low there is little or nothing left. He has got his wife with him this summer voyage but she is coming home this time. I mean the ship is due in Philadelphia about the 25inst. unchartered freights on oil about 2/1 [two shillings one penny].

Note what you say about raising your barn and painting the house and would advise you to wait until next spring. The flues or chimney will have to come down as they leak. I told Della that I thought it would be best to take the top off of the North side and shingle it over as the brick is all coming down. I think your porch ought to be raised up even with the house so I will do what you want in that respect, Dell is home – quite smart. Think if she continues will be able to go with you next voyage or you can come home and fix up your place – and I will take the ship. That is one reason I bought in the *Lewis* – so we could keep her in the family.

The church is all finished and looks well, your wife had picked out a pew and I hope that you will be spared to come home and sit in it. Mr. Goldfinch is dead. George O'Brien has a girl baby. Three days old. She had a hard time and is very sick yet. Your mother has been very sick, but to-night a little better. We all join in love to you and Ralph – trusting this will meet you well at San Francisco. I am dear son, Your loving father – *Benj. Gullison*

N.B. Lewis

San Francisco
Sept. 23rd/1886

Dear Sir:

Closed today at 27/6[26] having obtained about the highest in the market; that is for soft wood[27] ships/but the prospect is poor enough. I calculate

26 See *N.B. Lewis letters* dated August 24 and September 23.
27 'Soft wood ships' were planked with spruce or other 'soft' wood instead of oak or a 'hard' wood. Although only six years old, the vessel is already having difficulty in obtaining a cargo. The era of softwood ships was coming to an end.

they will send us to a third port, they having the priviledge of United Kingdom or Havre, Dunkerque & Antwerp in the Continental Ports @ 2/6 less the above sale; would sooner go for orders.

Will forward you copy of charter party[28] soon as possible. Shall go to the wharf tomorrow and commence loading ballast. Expect they will keep us there all our days[29] which is twenty. Capt. Knowles telegraphed you today concerning closed[30] business. Things in general look blue enough around here. Ships are laying by every day will not accept market rates. There is an iron steamer about our tonnage chartered today for 30/s which is not as good as us comparatively speaking. Well, I am trying to do the best I can and you may be sure will get out of this as soon as possible.

> Yours obediently
> *Frank Gullison*

N.B. Lewis Esq.

Ship *N.B. Lewis*
San Francisco
Sept. 30/1886

Dear Sir:

Moved ship down to sea wall this morning to receive stiffening[31] and have nearly finished lining.[32] Surveyor has been on board and gives the ship an extra good name. J.F. Knowles forwarded you charter party today. I shall telegraph today and inquire about this towage contract as I have not heard any word from you concerning it, only see your name signed to an agreement at Griffiths tug boat office so I shall inquire from you personally before taking any tow to Benicia.

Hope to hear from you soon.

> From your obedient servant
> *Frank Gullison*

Capt. F. Gullison

Yarmouth Sept. 25/86

Dear Sir:

Telegram announcing charter ship *N.B. Lewis* came to hand. Were glad to get her fixed even at this low rate. Never found any money in waiting. Any advances is lost in time and expence with the best of softwood ships. Now we are at a disadvantage from iron and what they call hardwood. The *Lewis*, now being 6 years old, I suppose would make a difference even

28 See note p. 79.
29 See note p. 79.
30 Closed business is the final charter agreement.
31 See note p. 92.
32 Lining – To prepare ship's hold with dunnage, old canvas and/or burlap to protect cargo – especially grain and similar cargoes.

with her as a new ship in way of insurance. This charter I think much better than any money offering in sugar or other cargo India, China or Phillipines. I would think expense should be quite reasonable now in France. The *Euphemia*[33] bills were not big when she was there. She landed last time from Frisco 2060 tons only 1/2 ton short. I will place Funds in either Boston or New York, as Mr. Knowles prefers, for your disbursements and we place the funds subject to his or your draft at sight. Shall soon have letters and charter party I suppose.

Yours
N.B. Lewis

Brookside, Nova Scotia
Sept. 26/1886

Dear Brother Frank:

I thought I would write you a line. Mama and I are all alone. Frank if you could only see your baby, what would you think. He is cunning as he can be – when people goes home from Della's he says by-by dear and shakes hands – awful cunning. This is Sunday – and Mama is reading the bible while I write to you. I go to school[34] now all the fine days and I love it. We are talking about having another teacher this winter – a man in the big school and a woman in the little school. Sometimes there are thirty-four scholars. Oh how I wish that you was home. It has been a long dreary lonesome day. I haven't much more to tell you. Please answer my letter. I would be real pleased to get a letter. Sometime give my love to brother Ralph. I would like to get a letter from him. Please come home, I get so lonesome, I don't know what to do. How does Ralph like to going to sea? Bowmie[35] runs out-doors all the time playing with the kitten. I am going in the big school this winter if I hurry along with the others but I am nearly up to them. Mama sends her kind love from your loving sister. . . . ?

Brookside, Sept. 27th 1886
Capt. B.F. Gullison
Ship *N.B. Lewis*

Dear Son:

Was pleased to note your safe arrival at Frisco. Was down to Yarmouth yesterday and saw Mr. Lewis. Seemed to be pleased to know that you got around so far all safe. Thought your bills was not out of the way. Showed

---

33 *Euphemia* was a sister ship to the *N.B. Lewis.* She left the U.S. for Japan before the *N.B. Lewis* and possibly loaded grain in San Francisco on her way home.
34 There is a two-room school. 'Big school' means the room with older pupils.
35 Bowmie – Frank's baby son Bowman.

me your last letter before leaving Shanghai. Your favors came to hand all right and note what you say as to repairs on your house. Wrote you in my last letter and repeat I thought it would be the best to let the work be until next spring. Will take down north floor and shingle over the hole, and if you wish can get the sills this winter and stock required — before the carpenters go away in the spring — or as I stated before, you can come home when you get out to the States, for a voyage and I will take the ship and you can fix things up to suit yourself.[36] Think I would raise the porch up with the house — then raise all the other buidlings in a line with it and fill up with dirt — cut down your old thorns and put up a nice fence, in front of the house. This would make a great improvement in your place. Eugene is about due in Philadelphia. Now has been out thirty days. He thinks to run home for a few days. His wife is not going this voyage, as the owners are not willing. Times are so hard and ships are making so little. Very few Yarmouth owners will allow their masters this privilege but if your wife improves until you come back they will be willing for you to take her on a voyage or so. But there are some of the owners who object to it in the strongest terms.

Aunt Lydia Raymond died last night. She was a great sufferer, but at last freed from it — we trust.

This is the Sabbath — dark and gloomy enough so I have a good excuse for stopping home. Your Mother is laying on the couch — is not well but much improved. Your wife Della is pretty well — also your little boy. He amuses me and calls me Pa — and will soon follow me everywhere I go. Della told me that she sent a photo of him to you. He is a smart little fellow.

See you have chartered for grain 27/o this is a *good way*[37] to carry grain for the above. Still it is better than lay there long with a full crew on. Must come to a close. Your mother and all your little sisters send love to you and please remember us all to our dear Ralph. Oh may God in this kind mercy watch over you and direct you in all your paths on ocean and land and spare you all to meet us and long will be the prayers of your loving Father Benj. Gullison

---

36 Captain Ben Gullison is offering to take over the ship *N.B. Lewis* for a voyage while Frank comes home to Nova Scotia for rest and change.

37 'Good way': long distance. But the actual rate was 27/6.

Capt. Gullison   Yarmouth Oct. 2/86

Dear Sir:

Your telegram inquiring about towage contract to which I replied 'Have contract with Griffiths schedule rates less 10% off'.[38] I talked with Mr. Knowles about it when here but omitted to write you about it, which slipped my mind. Supposed the towage folks would advise you. I did not know how to interpret your telegraph and asked you to reply if there was any trouble with towage folks; I will enclose the contract.

Hope they will give you good dispatch and bills won't be more than you expect. See your crew have gone; should think there would be nothing lost by them. Capt. Henry goes to Philadelphia tonight. Steamer ran into *Republic*[39] laying at loading berth and cut her to waters edge: badly damaged. Hope steamer will give us enough so we can wind her up. She was run into in Dunkirk and steamer paid the bill. Don't see how they can get clear of paying it, expecting to hear from you soon.

I am yours
N.B. Lewis

Please return contract with ships papers.

N.B. Lewis   San Francisco
                                                   Oct. 5/1886

Dear Sir:

Yours of the 25ult to home yesterday. Contents noted with care as to funds for ship's disbursements. I asked Mr. Knowles; he said either Boston or New York. I inquired of you last week by telegraph about our towage here. I thought it was best to do so Sir as I have not heard any word from you about it. It was worded thus '*Did you contract ship towage here?*' I have received in answer '*Have contract Griffiths schedule rates ten off. Talked with Knowles about it here any question how progressing answer*' I replied, 'Understand contract. Ballast out. Two hundred tons stiffening. Wheat in all satisfactory.'

We are laying at the sea wall yet paying wharfage but doing no work, our lay days commenced on the 4th inst. and no doubt they will keep us here all of them.

I have seen the *Euphemia's* expenses and think I can do a little better, if

---

38   It would appear that Griffiths were the owners or managers of the tug *Monarch*. Perhaps the original price given was $475; 10% off would be $47.50, making bill $427.50. When the bill was presented for $437.50 Capt. Gullison perhaps protested and had $10.00 deducted as an overcharge.

39   *Republic* - See Chapter 1. This ship seems to have had one misfortune after another. The Lewis brothers were hoping to get enough insurance to 'wind her up', i.e., dispose of her. See also letter dated October 9th, 1886.

sailors advances do not raise any higher. Grain market remains dull no improvement, one of the last charters 26/ direct: poor business.

Most respectfully
Frank Gullison
Ship *N.B. Lewis*

Philadelphia,
Oct. 9th, 1886

My dear Brother:
I will try to drop you a few lines tonight and tell you how Josie and I are doing and all about things in general. Well, Frank, I received your letter from Frisco – also one from Ralph and I was much pleased to hear from my dear brothers so far away. Frank, we have just chartered the *Otago* today for Marseille 2/9 up the Mediterranean so I am in hopes to get clear of some of the cold weather and get back here sometime in the spring.

We are now laying at Reed St. getting a new piece of waterways in. The *Republic* lays here also. There was a steamboat run into her at Chester while she was loading and cut her most in two. Capt. Henry Lewis is on here. He is a great old fellow. He expects that Frank felt pretty tall when he got the *N.B. Lewis*. They think that you are doing good work on that round. I heard him tell how cheap you got out of Shanghai. See you are chartered for English Channel. If you come to Havre, get Durkee for stevedore. Josie had not made up her mind whether she will go the voyage yet, but I think that Mr. Lewis will let her go if we like. I doubt if Ralph will come out with you by what he says. I suppose that you have all the news of Della, as Josie wants to say a word.

Your loving brother
Gene

Precious old brother – How in the world are you all this time. How I long to embrace your *tiny* form and gaze into those sky-blue eyes. My heart beats with the memory of thought. My old man, the pilgrim, sits here rubbing mosquito bites with Harts horn. He is a perfect gem. He bought me a nice little organ and a parrot but won't give me an heir. I see that Dell is getting better all the time. I am so glad for you both. God grant that in a few months you will be spared to meet with health and happiness yours, and a bonny time voyage together. I enjoy going to sea – not sick at all. Kiss dear old Ralph for me and take care of yourself. We can't afford sixty dollars for a pew. We are trying hard to get a home laid down by and by – when the surges cease to roll.

Good-by,
Tis Josie

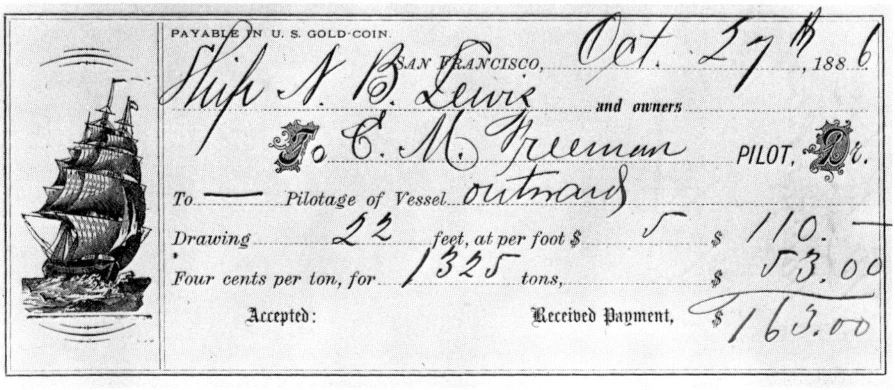

FIG. 30. Receipt for pilotage of vessel out of San Francisco, Oct. 27, 1886.

FIG. 31. Invoice of Thos. Chandler, ship master, San Francisco, 1886.

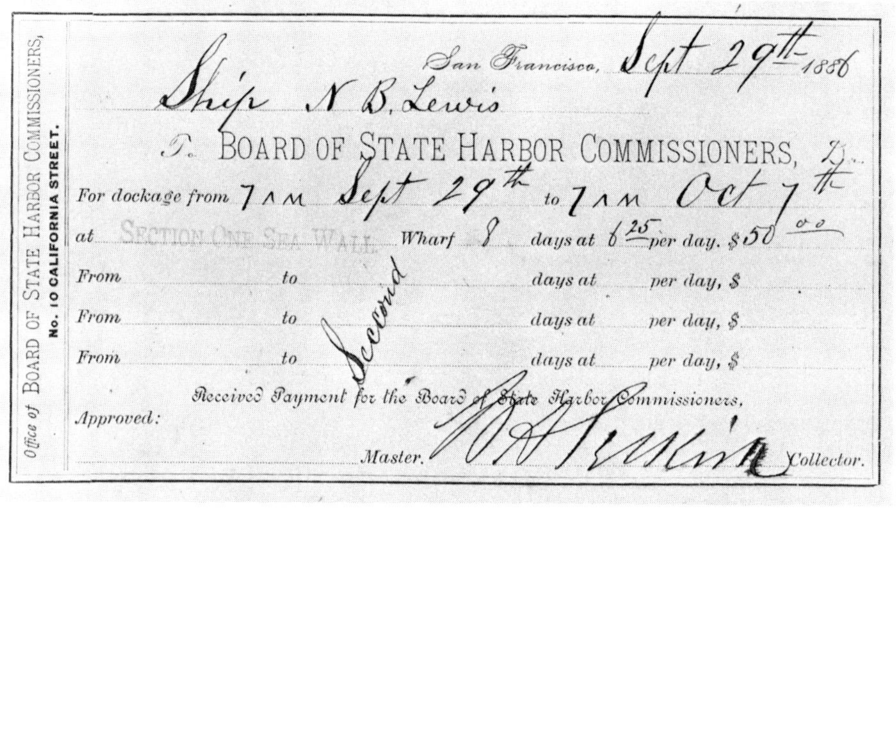

FIG. 32. Receipt for dockage fees from Board of State Harbor Commissioners,
San Francisco (8 days at the sea wall), 1886.

N.B. Lewis, Esq.   Oct. 9th/86

Dear Sir:

I towed to Benicia last Thursday but have not taken in any more cargo, Expect to do a good days work Monday but think they will not load us inside of our days, by the appearance of things now. All the satisfaction I can get from them is to keep cool, twenty days to load the ship in. I could not sell my cordwood here; had to give everything away as it stood in the ship, thought it best to take it all out and be on the safe side as some of it smelled pretty strong, have nothing new to inform you Sir, things in general going on as well as possible.

> Yours respectfully
> *Frank Gullison*

N.B. Lewis Esq.   Oct. 17th 1886

Dear Sir:

I write you these few lines to inform you that things in general are going on as well as can be expected according to our charter; have about 1100 ton wheat in lower hold near finished, will put her down same draught as last time if surveyors do not interfere. Received from you last week contract of ships towage here. Will forward to you with ship vouchers, as ordered, when ready for sea. Will have to get ten barrels of flour here as part of my flour received at New York has spoiled. Have nothing more of any importance to inform you Sir. Hope this will find you well as it leaves me this lonesome Sabbath afternoon.

> Yours most respectfully
> *Frank Gullison*

N.B. Lewis Esq.   San Francisco
                                                    Oct. 28 1886

Dear Sir:

I have got things about squared up today. My expenses here is $4123.27 and I signed a draft less 149.69 commission returned which would be $3975.58 payable at sight. It was not properly made out as I had not received an answer to my letter or to my telegraph to you today asking who to draw on it had to remain so or else I would be detained with ship another day but I think all will be well. J.K. Knowles will telegraph you amount of disbursements and also forward vouchers tomorrow Contract of towage included — I saved twelve dollars by having it with me today. Think you will judge my expenses about medium; you will know Sir what

Frisco is. I have tried to do as well as possible and trust it will meet your wishes hoping to make a quick and successful passage I remain Dear Sir

Yours most respectfully
Frank Gullison

N.B. Lewis Esq.

San Francisco
Oct. 19th/86

Dear Sir:

I write you these few lines to inform you that I finished loading yesterday noon and towed down to Frisco, have on board 1971 ton wheat[40] drawing F 22-02 in aft F21-10 in frd and have F 5 9 in freeboard. My inspector would not allow me anything less than 3 in to every foot depth of hold and as ship was chartered under his inspection did have to comply by those orders.[41] I have signed bill of lading today for Dunkirk direct. I believe it is a hard place to get to especially in winter. Shall be careful and try to get there safe. Shall try and clear tomorrow and sail Friday if possible will write you again tomorrow night and inform you of disbursements and Sectra[42] and trust everything will be according to your wishes.

Yours in obedience
B.F. Gullison

Capt. Watson

Benicia Oct. 22, 1886

Sir:

I received from J.F. Knowles last evening a telegraph stating the freeboard[43] you required the ship *N.B. Lewis* to load at. I have been looking for instructions from you to that effect ever since I came up here but have not received any until last evening through my agent and I wish you to give me them in writing *if you please*. I note you are allowing about 3 in. to every foot depth of hold and 3 inches for difference of water. If I load ship according to these instructions I think I shall be from sixty to seventy

---

40 Cargo of 1971 tons @ 27/6 would amount to £2710 or $13,186.
41 Marine surveyors or inspectors: one of the functions of a marine surveyor is to supervise the loading conditions in regard to cargo. The vessel is to be properly prepared for the type of cargo to be carried and the amount of cargo loaded must not jeopardize the safety of the vessel.
    In this case Capt. Watson, the inspector, is a marine surveyor for the 'Record of American and Foreign Shipping'. He was acting for the shippers and insurers under the ship's charter and the captain had to load his ship to the satisfaction of the surveyor.
42 Et cetera.
43 Freeboard: The distance between the upper level of the water and the upper surface of the uppermost watertight deck amidships, at the side of the hull.

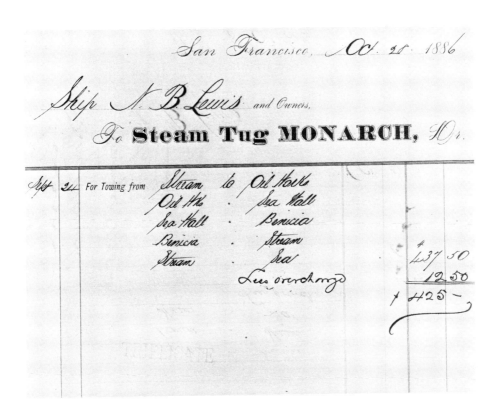

FIG. 33. Invoice for use of steam tug *Monarch*, San Francisco, 1886.

ton short of my last cargo and all of 6 inches less draft which will be too much difference. I think 2 3/4 in. would allow her sufficient clear side and be just as seaworthy. Her last cargo of grain from here was 2060 ton drawing 22 & 22-6[44] and it was delivered in good order and I want to have the same amount this time. Trust you will consider on this and reply.

Yours

B.F. Gullison

mtr

San Francisco Bills

1886				$ ¢
Sept. 18	Pilotage of vessel			120.50
20	Custom house broker			89.98
24	Lumber			360.09
29	Dockage fee at Sea Wall 8 days			50.00
Oct. 4	Oak & iron pieces			7.50
9	Shifting ship in port, docking ship lining ship and lining lumber			91.75
21	Chain repairs			5.75
24	Letter heads 100 sheets 100 envelopes			2.50
26	1 spar 21-19 74 ft. long			67.50
26	Discharging 580 tons ballast 217.50; loading 1971 tons wheat 739.50			956.62
27	Surveys & reports			25.00
27	Doctor's fee			40.00
28	Raling Chronometers			5.00
28	100 grain sacks 3.50 lightering stores 3.00			6.50
28	Cash paid for 12 A.B. (sailors) @ 40.00			
	Fees " " "		@ 5.00	
	Boat hire		12.00	552.00
28	Steam tug *Monarch*			437.50
28	Ship clearage & brokerage			7.50
27	Meat and potatoes			38.25

2826.94

---

44 The ship was drawing 22 feet of water at the bow and 22 feet 6 inches at stern.

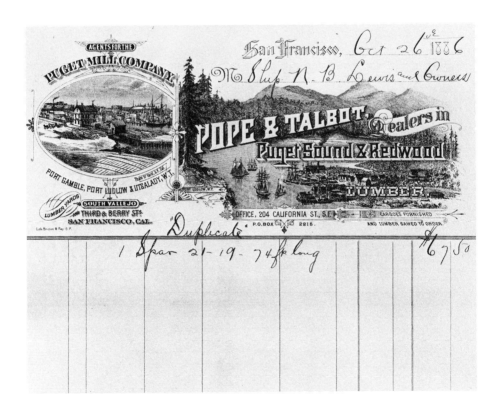

Fɪɢ. 34. Invoice of Pope & Talbot, dealers in lumber, San Francisco, 1886.

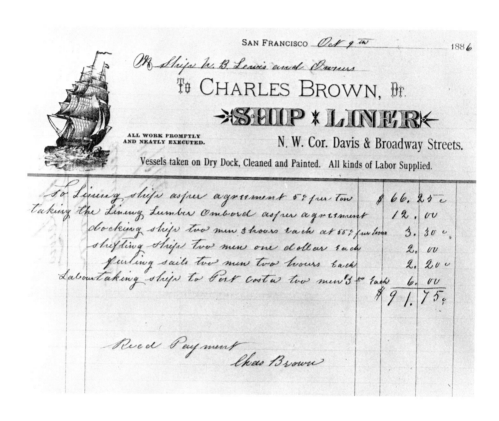

FIG. 35. Invoice of Charles Brown, Ship Liner, San Francisco, 1886.

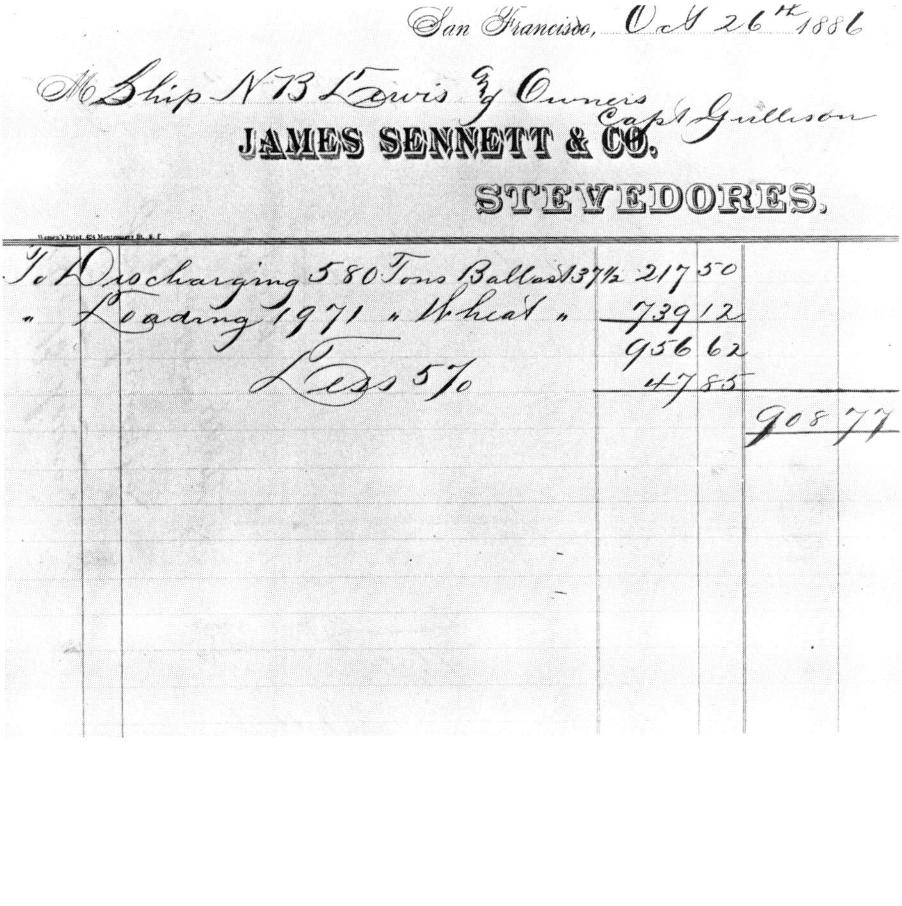

FIG. 36. Invoice of James Sennett & Co., stevedores, San Francisco, 1886.

The *N.B. Lewis* cleared from San Francisco October 20, 1886, for Dunkirk. The following letter was written by N.B. Lewis on the letterhead of Black Bros. & Co., ships' agents in Halifax, Nova Scotia. It would be sent to a ships' agent in London or Dunkirk to be given to Captain Gullison on arrival.

BLACK BROS. & CO.

Halifax, Nova Scotia
Feb. 4th, 1887

Dear Sir:

Suppose it will be time to look for you along. Your San Francisco disbursement a/c came to hand satisfactory. Consignee of cargo some time ago wanted option of u.k. one Port orders Dunkirk Roads. We offered them to shift for 5 per ton, as they wanted all the way from Dublin around to Hull, we thought it low enough. They did not entertain it so you will probable discharge Dunkirk. Hope you will get in safely without any accident as the port is not one of the best. If any cargo offers for the States you can cable. I am here looking after the *Hugh Cann* who put in here in distress. Hope to have her away last of next week and get away home. We have done quite a job on her and she should now be a first class vessel. See freights are still low in Frisco hoping to soon hear of your safe arrival

Yours
N.B. Lewis

Capt. F. Gullison   Yarmouth March 3/87

Dear Sir:

I suppose it will be soon time for you along. Hope to soon hear of your safe arrival. See freights are getting down again Bristol Channel.[45] Hope you will be able to find some paying freights on arrival. Things are awfully dull this side and I would hardly know where to order you. Hoping that things will improve and that we shall soon hear of your safe arrival.

Yours
N.B. Lewis

[This letter was written to meet Capt. Gullison in Dunkirk.]

N.B. Lewis Esq.   March 12 '87

Dear Sir:

I arrived here at Dunkirk roads yesterday afternoon making a passage of 133 days. Have been beating around the channel thirteen days; Had I

---

45   Bristol Channel freights would probably be coal from Cardiff.

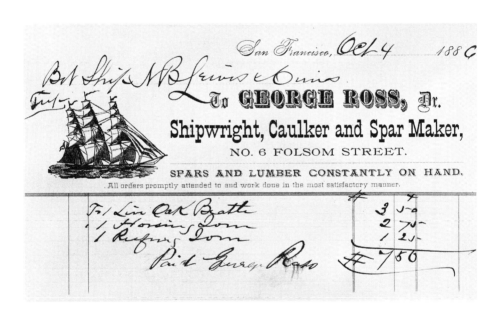

FIG. 37. Invoice of George Ross, Shipwright, San Francisco, 1886.

been bound to Queenstown for orders would made the passage in 119 days. Got most discouraged beating and banging around.[46] There always seems something to spoil my passages but I am thankful to be here today blowing a gale from NE too hard to dock ship. Towed from Beachy Head for 55 pounds: will try and dock tomorrow, well have good dispatch here; hope you will order me out to New York or Philadelphia; telegraphed you last evening '*Arrived possibly empties Petroleum Phil. six pence; hogsheads New York halfcrown; chance stiffening rails four shillings for either.*' Wire received your letter from Halifax contents noted received a letter from Knowles here about the paying of a watchman $5.00. Have you settled it? If not, I will. I believe it was my fault. Trusting to hear from your good self soon, I remain yours most respectfully

B.F. Gullison

P.S. Can I take my wife next, on this voyage?
If so, will you let her know by post card?   B.F.G.

N.B. Lewis Esq.

Dunkirk
March 15th '87

Dear Sir:

I write you these few lines to inform you that our good ship *N.B. Lewis* is in dock and commenced discharging. I received a cable from you yesterday in answer to one sent on arrival here wording thus 'Gullison working with Black[47] on coal cargo, bringing us back states Fall business; nothing here now'. I wrote to Messers Black Co., London last evening to see if they had fixed or expected too and the rates to Rio. The ship is leaking a little more than when we left Frisco: makes about thirteen inches in 12 hours. I think it is under her sheathing and wood ends. Should we load coal for Rio from Cardiff or Swansea, would it not be advisable to sight her bottom, repair the copper, cork the sheathing and wood ends.[48]

Please inform me amount of cash Mrs. Allen[49] had drawn from you on

---

46   He made the passage from San Francisco to the English Channel in 120 days. As a comparison the fast clipper ships of the middle 1800's generally made the run from San Francisco to New York in under 110 days. He must have been so discouraged beating up the Channel against the NE gales that he engaged a tug off Beachy Head on the South Coast of England for tow to Dunkirk.

47   Black & Co. were the English agents for H. & N.B. Lewis in London and Mr. Lewis is working through them to obtain a cargo for the *N.B. Lewis.*

48   'Wood ends' are where the hull planks of a vessel join the stem and the transom. 'Stem' is the upright at the bow of a vessel into which the side timbers or planks are joined. 'Transom' of a vessel is the flat termination of the stern above the water line. 'Sheathing' probably consisted of wooden strips along or above the waterline to protect the hull against ice, etc.

49   Mrs. Allen is the wife of the first mate who was customarily referred to as 'Mister'. By an arrangement with the owners, she had drawn sums on her husband's salary account while he was at sea.

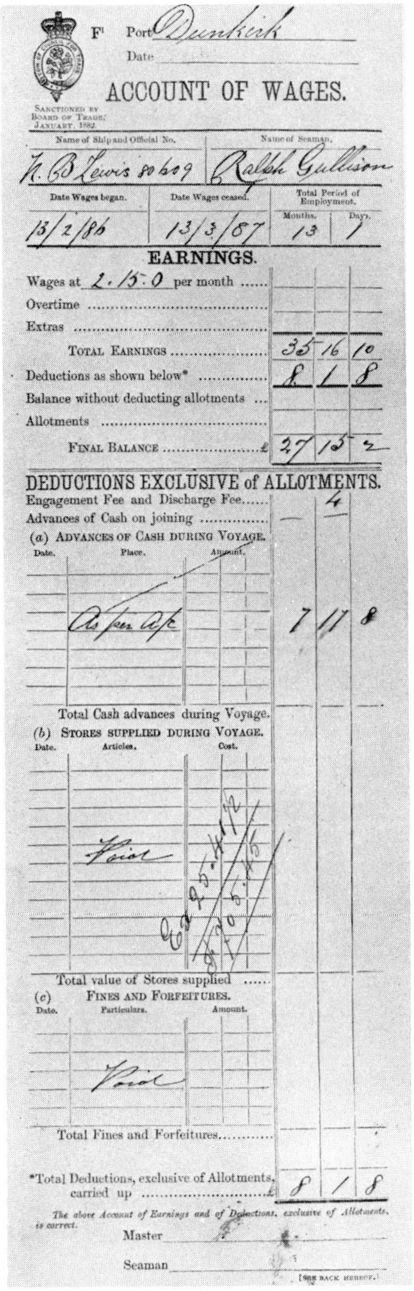

F[1] Port Dunkirk
Date

ACCOUNT OF WAGES.

SANCTIONED BY BOARD OF TRADE, JANUARY, 1882.

Name of Ship and Official No.	Name of Seaman.
N. B. Lewis 80609	Ralph Gullison

Date Wages began.	Date Wages ceased.	Total Period of Employment. Months.	Days.
13/2/86	13/3/87	13	7

EARNINGS.

	£	s.	d.
Wages at 2.15.0 per month			
Overtime			
Extras			
TOTAL EARNINGS	35	16	10
Deductions as shown below*	8	1	8
Balance without deducting allotments			
Allotments			
FINAL BALANCE £	27	15	2

DEDUCTIONS EXCLUSIVE of ALLOTMENTS.

	£	s.	d.
Engagement Fee and Discharge Fee		4	
Advances of Cash on joining	—	—	
(a) ADVANCES OF CASH DURING VOYAGE. Date. Place. Amount. — As per A/c			
Total Cash advances during Voyage.	7	11	8
(b) STORES SUPPLIED DURING VOYAGE. Date. Articles. Cost. — Void			
Total value of Stores supplied			
(c) FINES AND FORFEITURES. Date. Particulars. Amount. — Void			
Total Fines and Forfeitures			
*Total Deductions, exclusive of Allotments, carried up £	8	1	8

The above Account of Earnings and of Deductions, exclusive of Allotments, is correct.

Master

Seaman

[SEE BACK HEREOF.]

FIG. 38. Account of wages of Ralph Gullison Feb. 13, 1886, to March 13, 1887, Dunkirk.

Mister's a/c. Have considerable work to do here but will try to do with as little as possible.... We took a lot of shine off the ship beating in Channel; had more wear and tear there than we had in the whole of the round voyage. I run out some very heavy gales in the South Pacific.

I hove to[50] twice on the passage, once off the Horn for eight hours, once to the eastward of the Western Island; running my NE trades down in the North Atlantic making Northern[51] had to go to long. 50.00 w. Was then at Lat. 40°00 North.

I was 27 days from Frisco to Equator
      30 days from Equator to Horn
      29 days from Horn to Equator
      47 days from Equator to Dunkirk
      ———
    133 Days Passage
     13 off Channel
    —————
    120

50 Hove to: When a sailing ship was meeting gale force winds and heavy seas and unable to make headway it was a practice to reduce sail to a minimum and head the vessel just off the main wind direction, thus easing the main force of the wind and sea against the bow of the vessel.

51 Making northern: In this case the northeast trade winds continued so strong that Captain Gullison continued to head northwest until when he turned eastward he was closer to North America than to Europe.

Financial Statement

Voyage New York – Shanghai – San Francisco – Dunkirk

July 1886	Freight received 49418 cases oil New York to Shanghai		$15319.58
Mar. 1887	Freight received 1971 tons wheat San Francisco Dunkirk		13186.
		Total	28505.58
	Expenses		
Feb. 1886	” New York	$6708.60	
July ”	” Shanghai	2852.70	
Oct. ”	” San Francisco	4123.27	
Mar. 1887	” Dunkirk	5109.30	
		18783.87	
	Sent to Yarmouth from Shanghai	$12570.00	
	” ” ” ” Dunkirk	6889.00	
		19459.00	

New York bills were partly paid from Yarmouth and San Francisco bills
were paid by draft on H. & N.B. Lewis, Yarmouth.
It would appear that the profit on this voyage was about ten
thousand dollars.

John Black & Co.
London & Glasgow

19 Change Alley, Cornhill
London E.C.
15th March 1887

Capt. Gullison   British Ship *N.B. Lewis*
c/D. Spiers Esq.   Dunkirk

Dear Capt. Gullison,
We are in receipt of your esteemed favor of yesterday's date, and note carefully the contents.

We had a cable yesterday from Mr. Lewis asking for quotations to Rio, Monte Video, and Cape Town to which we at once replied and this morning we received cable to close for Cape Town at 18/6 and to advise you when we had done so. We have now pleasure in advising that we have closed the vessel in accordance with said cable authority to load at Cardiff for Cape Town at 18/6.[1] We tried very hard to get a little more, but could not do so, indeed charterers hestiated to give even 18/6 for a vessel the size of the *N.B. Lewis*. As to conditions, we have done the best we could, and we enclose a copy of the charter party. We may also add that we endeavoured to get Penarth Dock for loading but this the merchants were unable to arrange.

We have reserved the right to appoint agents at Cardiff which charterers usually insist upon. Please let us know if you have any choice, so we may arrange with them as to charge for doing business, as we may pay the Custom House fees.

---

1   18/6 – eighteen shillings and sixpence per ton or $4.50 Canadian funds; coal was loaded either at Penarth or Cardiff.

Kindly let us know when you expect to be discharged: if you think of towing to Cardiff, a boat might be obtained for eighty or ninety pounds – always at your service.

Yours very truly
John Black & Co.

Capt. Gullison   Yarmouth
March 17/87

Dear Sir:

Was glad to hear of your arrival at Dunkirk. I was sorry that there was no inducement coming this way. The strikes in the States coupled with usual dull spring business has completely paralized business. In closing the business to Cape Town it will bring us back to the States in the early fall in good time for cotton or oil. I saw a letter from Capt. Bent of the *Charles Baker* from Cape Town. He liked the port, he said. 17s to Cape Town was as good as 16/6 to Rio. This was the rate he said he had. She [the ship] drew 22 feet, but he lightened to 21 before going to the dock [at Cape Town]. Dues and discharging are the principal expenses. Her bills were 346 pounds. Would not take only provisions to bring back to the States if you can get reasonable bill in Bristol Channel.[2] I think there will be more in this than anything else in view. I wrote you in my last in reference to remitting and suppose Charter will provide for advance on coal charter. Shall look for Eugene in Phil.; dull market; also Capt. Dowley[3] had a $1600 bill at Falmouth; more than she is worth. Your father should soon be out.[4]

Yours
N.B. Lewis

Capt. B.F. Gullison   Ship *N.B. Lewis*   BLACK
c/ D. Spiers Esq.   Dunkirk   London 18 March 1887

Dear Capt. Gullison

We are this morning in receipt of your esteemed favor of the 16th inst. and regret to note you do not favor the Cape Town business. The charter is the best we could procure and similar to one we accepted sometime ago for one of our own ships. The commissions are lighter than on Rio char-

2 Nathan Lewis is advising Captain Gullison to purchase provisions from Cardiff to Cape Town and back to a port in the U.S.A.
3 Captain Dowley was commander of barque *Mizpah* which was wrecked on the Cape Breton Coast in May 1887. Note letter of N.B. Lewis dated June 13,1887.
4 His father, Capt. Ben Gullison, had been sick for several years.

ters there being only 2% address besides the brokerage of 5%, at least half of which will be returned.

We are making enquiry about towage and will let you know tomorrow or Monday best we can do. We note you expect to be discharged twenty seventh instant —

> Always at your service
> Yours very truly
> *John Black & Co.*

HENRY LOVITT[5]

Ship Chandler

Ship Store Dealer and Sail Maker

16 New Quay

Liverpool, 18 March

Dear Friend:

I am pleased to hear of your safe arrival and hope you are A1. I hear from Capt. O'Brien you are tip top. Now friend I want your business. No doubt on your arrival at Cardiff you will be met with many plausible people and they will endeavour to explain to you that they can do better than the man that manufacturers the goods and such is not the case. If you will give me your order and leave it in my hands I will guarantee you all kinds of satisfaction and please you. Should you want any sails I have a full draft of the ship and can make you Yarmouth Duck which would be beneficial to your owners as they are shareholders in the cotton mill. Do give me your patronage. I want it badly as business here is awfully dull and poor prospects. Hope to hear from you on receipt and if you wish, on your arrival at Cardiff, send me a wire and I will come and see you.

> Yours truly
> *H. Lovitt*

Tell O'Brien I will place the two pounds ten shillings to his credit if he has not sailed. H.L.

Capt. Gullison   Yarmouth March 19th/87

Dear Sir:

I wrote you by last night's mail but I hear the mail did not connect. Have not much to say. Suppose you will provision only for round voyage back to States. I thought it better to make coal voyage than to come out to the States now as there is nothing doing. Will be in good time for cotton or oil

---

5   Henry Lovitt was a Yarmouth man who had gone into business in Liverpool, England.

next fall. Hope you will get a good dispatch and reasonable bills at Cardiff. I wrote you in reference to remitting Dunkirk. I don't just remember how much coal she took from Cardiff last time she loaded there. Expect about 2050 tons to 2100. You will be best judge of that. Suppose Mrs. Gullison[6] will leave by this mail from Halifax, if she made the connection all right. Hope she will meet you all right.

> Yours
> *N.B. Lewis*

> BLACK
> London 19th March 1887

Dear Captain Gullison

Referring to ours of last evening, we have received two proposals for towage of your good ship from Dunkirk &c and one naming £110 the other £100. We are continuing enquiries and will write you again respecting the matter on Monday.

> We are
> Yours very truly
> *John Black & Co.*

Capt. Gullison
Ship *N.B. Lewis*   Dunkirk
N.B. Lewis Esq.

Dunkirk
March 20th 1887

Dear Sir:

Yours of the 3rd inst. to hand contents noted. Messiers John Black Co. has informed me that he has chartered ship *N.B. Lewis* for Capetown at 18/6 by cable authority from you. Have received copy of charter party also. It reads very one sided and so much commission I told Mr. Black I thought the freight would stand very low after all commissions were paid. He said one half of the 5% would be returned; paying this 5% commission on disbursement at port of discharge where the freight is actually due seems strange but I suppose it is the customary way with coal charters. I expect to tow to Cardiff and the lowest offer is £80-0-0 as yet. Think it is reasonable do you not sir? It will cost me near half that amount from this port[7]; if we sail, to say nothing of the time and expense & towing from Lundy Island.[8] Towing the whole distance will take less crew and less ballast. Ex-

6   Capt. Gullison's wife Della is leaving from Halifax for Liverpool via Cunard steamer to join her husband at Cardiff.
7   Captain Gullison estimates it would cost almost as much to be towed out of Dunkirk and then be towed again into Cardiff from Lundy Island as to be towed all the way.
8   Lundy Island is in the Bristol Channel. As will be seen in later letters it was customary for ships to be piloted and towed between Cardiff and Lundy Island.

pect to be discharged by the 26th inst. Cargo turning out good so far, have drawn 1000 pounds Mr. Spiers sent first bill of exchange Saturday and I will forward you 2nd by next mail. I sent my wife a cable since arrival to ask your permission about going the voyage and have received an answer this morning that she has left Halifax for Liverpool *I Thank You Sir, very much* for consenting to my request. Today I feel very happy and I don't suppose you can blame me. Ralph is going home from Cardiff to go to school. The sea does not suit him. See Father has got well and gone to sea again; will write you again soon.

Yours respectfully

B.F. Gullison

BLACK

London March 21st 1887

Dear Capt. Gullison:

We have your note stating that White Rose offered to do towage to Cardiff for £80 – this is reasonable providing it includes second boat if needed for docking and also the docking at Cardiff – these will amount to £10 to £15. Today we have got estimate of £100 to tow ship from Dunkirk to Cardiff or Penarth Docks – thence to the Westward of Lundy Island with use of the Tug's hawser and second boat to dock the ship at Cardiff if required – The towage from Cardiff to Lundy is a fixed tariff and ships have to pay £20 to £25 for it. We think this offer of one hundred pounds a good one and as the boats named for the work are new and well recommended, we think if you intend to tow that it might be prudent to accept – if so, wire us and write fully when tug will be needed.

The medicine account will be sent receipted.

Yours very truly

John Black & Co.

Capt. Gullison   Dunkirk

HENRY LOVITT

16 New Quay

Liverpool

22nd March, 1887

Dear Friend:

I am in receipt of yours this p.m. Thanks for your offer for sails and I trust your order will arrive soon as my sail maker is idle and do promise me your stores as I want it badly owing to recent failures lately. I shall have much pleasure in meeting your wife and putting her in comfortable quarters and advise you after arrival.[9] You can rest assured I will attend

---

9   Captain Gullison must have written Mr. Lovitt asking him to meet his wife on arrival at Liverpool from Nova Scotia.

to this properly. Should you sail from Dunkirk before the wife's arrival, I will keep her in Liverpool and you can wire me your arrival at Cardiff and say if you are coming. Don't leave your order until you arrive at Cardiff. If you sent it to me I can have it ready and if you do not arrive at Cardiff I shall never charge you for the stores & sails. If you send the order along, I can have ready by time you arrive. Hoping to hear from you soon.

> Yours truly
> *H. Lovitt*

BLACK
London
March 22,1887

Dear Capt. Gullison:
Referring to ours of yesterday — we beg to say we have now arranged with Messers Harrison Bros. and Moore to attend to your vessel's business at Cardiff and we shall be glad if you call on them upon arrival there.

> Yours very truly
> *John Black & Co.*

Messers John Black & Co., London   Dunkirk March 24 '87

Gentlemen:
Your letters of 21 & 22 to hand. Contents noted; as to towage from Dunkirk to Cardiff; I have received about the same estimate as you £100-0-0 from the White Rose Co. at Cardiff so the only thing that remains now is which Co. has the best boats. Perhaps it would be advisable to close with a written agreement and the usual clause, 'Act of God' etc. If not, I can arrange it here with White Rose Co. Let me know what boats you are working with before you close business. I cannot give you a decided answer now when I will require them but will give two to three days notice. Expect to be discharged by Monday; hoping to hear from you soon, I remain Yours Respectfully

> *B.F. Gullison*

JOHN BLACK & CO.
London March 25th 1887

Dear Capt. Gullison:
We have your favour of yesterday's date about towage and we think it may be best for you to make your own arrangements — this will save any confusion or misunderstanding — The boats we had in view were the Earl line these boats are new and we believe a little more powerful than some

of the *Roses*. We have had ships towed by the *Roses* and always with good satisfaction.

We suppose you will be out on Monday and suppose you will leave toward end of next week for Wales.

Yours very truly
John Black & Co.

N.B. Lewis Esq.   Dunkirk March 25th '87

Dear Sir:

I write you these few lines to inform you that we have discharged 1410 ton wheat. It is coming out in fair order and expect to commence taking in ballast on the 28th inst. We will probably get away about the 2nd April. I will send you my account of wages also deserters a/c at Frisco,[10] hope you will find it satisfactory. I have drawn my balance of wages amounting to £175-16-04 stg. and will remit to you Sir First Bill of Exchange to said amount. Will you please place it in the Saving Bank and oblige. I would like to turn it over to Father as part payment for my interest in the *N.B. Lewis* but as he is away and I expect Mother also, will let it stand or place it in the bank until I hear from him. Trusting you will receive both bills in order.

I remain
Yours faithfully
B.F. Gullison

N.B. Lewis Esq.   Dunkirk March '87

Dear Sir:

I wrote you on arrival here about the ship's leaking and received an answer yesterday by cable stating 'think no need sighting ship's bottom.[11] Get windmill pump[12] Cardiff'. Ship has not made any water since copper has rose out of the water. I have examined the topsides and find them quite soft in places and along under the Bluff of the bows, very open, also wood ends. *Now the copper*. On our passage from Shanghai to Frisco I sighted two places on the side abreast the Main rigging when ship was laying over; I tried hard to list her enough in Frisco to replace it but could not do it. Since I arrived here I find there is more off abaft the former

10 Deserters at Frisco. See Appendix H.
11 Sighting the ship's bottom – the hull of a wooden ship sailing into southern waters was covered below the water line with thin copper sheets to prevent its being eaten by worms. Sighting the ship's bottom meant putting the ship in drydock for a careful examination of the hull.
12 Windmill pump was a pump in the bottom of the hold operated by a windmill on the deck. It came to be considered by sailors the sign of a leaky ship.

place I would judge about three sheets [of copper] and I am afraid if it is not repaired ship will get wormed. Think it got scraped off coming down Woosung [river at Shanghai] and sailing through fisherman's fishing stakes. If I was sure of this being the only place it could be easily repaired by a diver. So I cabled you today 'Leak is in the topsides and they require caulking.[13] Metal requires patching; will sail tomorrow'. It is going to cost considerable more to caulk topsides and patch copper than Windmill pump would cost but the danger of getting wormed and the name of a Windmill pump on board sounds like neglectfulness on my part and a leaky ship but I do not wish to dictate to you Sir but only want to explain matters to clear myself. My expenses here will be about £1050 stg. Mr. Spiers will forward you Vouchers and balances of freight which amounts to about £600 stg. In your last letter of the 19 inst. you say you informed me about remitting freight? I have not received the letter. I have sent first and second exchange in the amount of £1000 stg. and Spiers will forward you balance. I am towing to Cardiff; docked and towed down to Lundy for £100. I expect you will think I am growing extravagant but I have done it for the best. I corresponded with Black & Bros. about it.

Yours respectfully
Frank Gullison

Captain Gullison   Dunkirk

HENRY LOVITT
16 New Quay
Liverpool 28th March '87

Dear Friend:

I am in receipt of yours this morning including order for sails which shall have my best attention. The *Sarnia*[14] is expected at Morille today and if she arrives will be in Liverpool tomorrow. Up until the time of writing there is not word of her. I am thankful to you for your kind promise of your order for stores and I assure you they will be A1. And no reflections to be cast either in price or quality. I will wire you immediately on the arrival of Mrs. Gullison and if able to proceed will say so in my wire. Hoping to hear from you again soon.

Yours truly
H. Lovitt

---

13 To caulk the topsides is to fill the seams with oakum above the metal sheets. Oakum is a loose fibre made by untwisting and picking apart old ropes. It is driven into the seams with a caulking iron.

14 *Sarnia* – the Cunard steamer from Halifax on which Mrs. Gullison is a passenger.

Capt. Gullison   Dunkirk

HENRY LOVITT
16 New Quay
Liverpool 30th March '87

Dear Friend:

I wired you this morning that the wife arrived all right and rather fatigued and considers it would be advisable to see you in Cardiff as Dunkirk is an awful journey. I gave her the address and no doubt you will have a letter tomorrow. I have a good mate and 2nd mate, wages as you say; £8 and £5.[15] Shall I send them on? I expect to have to go to London tomorrow, if so, will not return until Friday. In any case, your orders shall be attended to as I have left a good man in charge. Awaiting your reply in reference to the mates.

Yours truly
H. Lovitt

Capt. Gullison

Yarmouth
April 2/1887

Dear Sir:

Your cable at hand. Notice what you say about topsides and caulking; suppose boot topping[16] better come off. She will be more likely to be slack under it. The question is whether to put it on. If we should go East from Java would want it on. While you are at it, better caulk from metal up. I should think metal would be good for another deep water voyage. I cabled you to buy windmill pump. I think we shall put them on all our vessels as they are a good standby, not because we want to sail leaking vessels, but to use in case of emergency. I cabled you mate's wife had received $280 on this voyage. I will cable you about caulking topsides and under boot topping. Think this will be worst part of them; hope metal will turn out good. I thought we would come North this fall but if freights should be good in Java or West coast we might want to go there so I expect it would be as well to put on boot topping again but we will let you know by cable. Capt. Cann leaves today to take *Euphemia*; have not heard from *Otago* yet. It has been a hard March to get on the coast. Business in the States is about at low water.

Yours
N.B. Lewis

P.S. Suppose Mrs. Gullison is with you by this time.

---

15 i.e., – wages per month.

16 Boot-topping – the area of hull between the waterlines of a ship when fully loaded and unloaded. The term also is used to refer to a distinctive brand of paint covering this area, and to the procedure of cleansing the hull near the surface of the water by scraping off grass, slime, barnacles and other shells, and treating it with a preservative mixture of tallow, sulphur and resin (before special paint was developed for the purpose).

BLACK & CO.
London
29th March 1887

Dear Capt. Gullison:
We are in receipt of your favor and are much pleased to hear your cargo is turning out so well and that you expect to leave on Friday – we hope you will get across to Cardiff quickly and safely.

Yours very truly
John Black & Co.

BLACK & CO.
London
April 5, 1887

Dear Capt. Gullison:
Today we have the following cable from Mr. Lewis 'Advise Gullison sight metal – caulk topsides, renew boot topping' – which instructions will no doubt have your very best attention.

We enclose check for £ one hundred toward payment of your disbursements and further sums will be sent from time to time as you request.

We notice the tug is reported off St. Catherines [Isle of Wight] early this morning and we look for your arrival Thursday.

With kind regards
Yours very truly
John Black & Co.

BLACK & CO.
London
12th April 1887

Dear Captain Gullison:
We were pleased to hear of your vessel reaching Cardiff safely and docking. We enclose order to enable us to collect freight from charterers, please sign and return to us. We understand it may interest you to hear that we have just introduced Capt. Fred H. Corning[17] who came here mate of the *Vandalia* to the command of the ship *Don Enrique*; this ship leaves here in tow on Thursday for Cardiff to load for Japan. We shall be pleased to hear how your loading progresses and will send you further funds when required.

We are
Yours very truly
John Black & Co.

17 Another Yarmouth County man.

HENRY LOVITT
16 New Quay
Liverpool
6 April 1887

Dear Friend Gullison

I received your valuable order from Dunkirk and also telegram 'Spices' notifying your sailing Monday morning 4th. I hop this will find you safe arrived. I am sorry to say I have been very unwell for the past few days and I understand Mrs. Gullison has been the same. You had better come to Liverpool as soon as you get things in working order as I do not think Mrs. Gullison able to travel alone. I have everything ready for shipment as soon as required. There is a young man at Cardiff by name of John Davis. He will attend to your bonded stores and see everything in order for you and if you wish you can take your stores on board while taking out ballast by telegraphing me to send them on and should you miss the Rail Co. will hold them until you are ready to take them. I hope to see you soon in Liverpool. Mrs. Gullison is in care of Mrs. Robinson, 39 Wesley Street, Toxteth Park. Let me know if you are coming up and I will meet you. Have mate and 2nd ready at any time.

Yours truly
H. Lovitt

N.B. Lewis Esq.   Cardiff
April 10, 1887

Dear Sir:

Does the two hundred and eighty dollars as you cabled me include the order that I sent you from New York if so I have charged Mr. Allen $20.00 too much. If it does not include it, it remains O.K. as I have charged him the above amount when paid off. I will give him an order on you for twenty dollars on these conditions.

Yours most respectfully
B.F. Gullison

N.B. Lewis Esq.   Cardiff
April 10, 1887

Please pay bearer John C. Allen the sum of twenty dollars (If) the allotment cabled me at Dunkirk amounting to two hundred and eighty dollars includes the order I sent from New York.

B.F. Gullison

HENRY LOVITT
16 New Quay
Liverpool
11 April '87

Dear Friend Gullison

I hope you and Mrs. Gullison arrived all safe and none worse for her journey. Mrs. Robinson says the Dr. has ordered Mrs. Gullison Claret and Beer. You have none ordered. Shall I send you say two bbls. beer and one case of claret? I will make it all right. Please wire on receipt of this.

Yours truly
H. Lovitt

6 doz. in bbl. beer
1 doz. bottles in case of claret

Capt. Gullison   Ship *N.B. Lewis*

HENRY LOVITT
16 New Quay
Liverpool

Dear Sir:

This will be handed to you by Mr. Eaton the party engaged as mate for your vessel — wages £8 — no advance. He pays his own way which you will refund him.

Yours truly
H. Lovitt

HENRY LOVITT
16 New Quay
Liverpool

Dear Friend Capt. Gullison:

I have sent your mate away today and no doubt will be with you ere this reaches you. Wages £8, no advance here, he pays his own passage which you will refund him. I have also sent the greater portion of your stores off and will send the remainder tomorrow with Bonded stores. Will attend to the beer and claret, pleased I thought of it. I will forward a/c as soon as in order and hope to see you before you sail and will arrange settlement. I will write Davis to give you any assistance you may require in getting stores in order and bond passed. The rail Co. will call for your empties when ready and cause you no troubles.

Your father arrived at New York on the 6th with decks swept and loss

of main yard; not so very serious. I shall send list of stores tomorrow including everything. Hope Mrs. Gullison is none the worse of her journey.

> Yours truly
> *H. Lovitt*

N.B. Lewis Esq.

Cardiff
April 13, 1887

Dear Sir:

I arrived here on the 9th inst; ten days towing around. Will take ship off
Gridiron[18] tonight. Copper is in a very bad state, thin as paper some parts,
like a honey comb. I thought to have about four or five sheets to put on
but instead of that amount it took 123 sheets and two cwt. nails and the
fact of the case is, Sir, the copper is not fit for the voyage. The old that we
took off at New York was 100% better than this is at present. It seems to
be all eaten off around the nail heads and butts of the sheets more especially along under the bows. I shall send you a sample from here and I
know you will be astonished. Will do all my caulking and sheathing by the
day.

> Yours most respectfully
> *Frank Gullison*

Capt. Gullison   Cardiff

HENRY LOVITT
16 New Quay
Liverpool
13 April '87

Dear Friend:

I have shipped the remainder of your stores today and now enclose your
list of all and how packed and I hope you will find all correct when you
cheque them off. I suppose your mate is with you ere this and I hope he
will suit you. I received your telegram and sent you the two bbls. of beer
and case of Claret. Will send you invoice tomorrow. Excuse me saying
more today; very busy. Please give me sufficient time of your 2nd mate in
case the one I have in view will not go. Kind regards to self and wife.

> Yours very truly
> *H. Lovitt*

---

18 Gridiron — a framework of fixed parallel beams to support a vessel at low tide. Not a drydock,
since work on the hull could only be carried out between high tides.

The following are all letters from John Black & Co. to Capt. Gullison at Cardiff:

London April 13, 1887

Kindly let us hear if you received ours with check and Mr. Lewis' instructions. Trusting your business may proceed to your entire satisfaction.

Yours etc.

London April 14th, 1887

We have your favour yesterday's date and we regret to learn that the metal is not up to your expectations. We see it was put on in New York.

We suppose you will get your carpenter to give you a letter showing its conditions and with this you should send a sample to show what it is like. These would enable Mr. Lewis to make a claim upon the makers.

Your advance freight will be paid here, after sailing, and we will have to supply what funds you need. When we have your advice of needs will send funds. We look to you to advise us in this case.

Yours etc.

London 19th April 1887

We enclose letter received for you this morning. The Canadian mail has not arrived yet, but we expect it this afternoon or in the morning, trusting you are getting on well.

Yours etc.

London April 21st, 1887

We have yours and regret ship requires so very much oakum. It is very disappointing no doubt as charterers are anxious to get ship away. It will be quite in order for you to give Mr. Lovitt order upon us for stores.

Yours etc.

London 26 April 1887

We are in receipt of your favor and will give due protection to your order on us for £299-14-4 in favor of Mr. Henry Lovitt and we also enclose as requested cheque your favor £200 the receipt of which kindly own. We regret delay and trouble you have had over caulking and repairs – but hope you will get through in time to commence loading Thursday.

Yours etc.

London April 28th, 1887

We have your favor of yesterday's date and we can only regret the very serious detention you are having. It is very annoying no doubt but you cannot help yourself under the circumstances. We have asked Messers Harrison to assist you all they can towards getting her loaded promptly and we hope you can manage to sail next week. Mr. Lewis will be looking anxiously for ships sailing and we trust he may be advised of this next week. You have no doubt written to him referring to cause of detention.

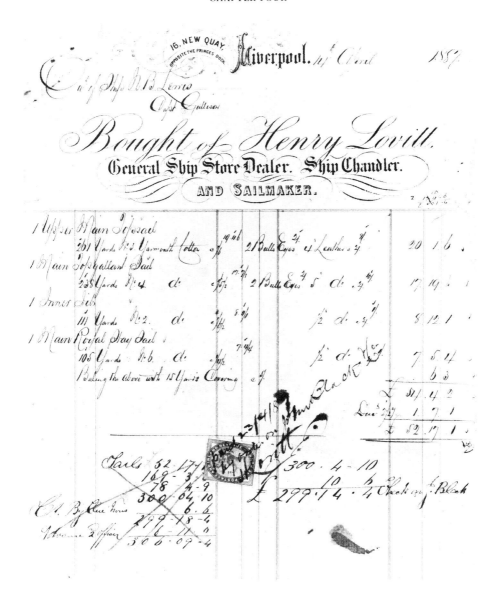

FIG. 39. Invoice of Henry Lovitt, ship chandler, Liverpool, Jan. 14, 1887 England, for sails, etc.

N.B. Lewis Esq.   Cardiff April 18th, 1887

Dear Sir:

I write you these few lines to inform you we are getting along very well with our caulking and boot topping[19] expect to be finished about Thursday. Will probably get away about 25th instant. I am buying all my own stock and having my work done by the day. Caulking is very soft especially under sheathing. Enclosed please find 2nd bill of exchange balance amount freight £415-15-1. Spiers forwarded first bill to said amount hope you will receive them all in order. Have 400 ton coal on board.

> From yours obediently
> *Frank Gullison*

Capt. Gullison   Cardiff   HENRY LOVITT
                                      16 New Quay
                                      Liverpool 18 April 1887

Dear Friend:

I received a telegram from Cardiff this morning with no signature and presumed it was from you and replied and up to the time of writing have no answer. I don't know of any person else that would wire me under the circumstances. Enclosed please find your a/c's and trust you have received all the stores in order ere this. I pin a list of emptys charged, to be deducted if you return them. The rail Co. will call for same and you should have no trouble. I am in hopes to see you before you sail. I may possibly be in Cardiff this week but cannot mention the date. I hope Mrs. Gullison has recovered her health and that all will be satisfactory.

> Yours truly
> *H. Lovitt*

P.S. The 2nd mate I had in view has escaped but will endeavour to find a suitable man tomorrow and will send him off if you require him. H.L.

Capt. Gullison   Cardiff   HENRY LOVITT
                                      16 New Quay
                                      Liverpool 19 April 1887

Dear Friend:

I am in receipt of your two telegrams this afternoon. The 2nd mate will leave tonight to join you – wages £5-10. I have given him an advance note for this amount payable 3 days after he leaves Cardiff providing he sails in the ship. Also advanced one pound to pay expenses in all including tele-

19 See note p. 125.

grams 6 pounds 11 shillings for which I enclose you bill. I also enclose you credit for clews. I received them yesterday and give you credit for what I did not use which you can deduct from the sail account before remitting. You will see I have not charged you for head lining irons in the a/c. Hope to see you before you sail. Kind regards to self and wife.

Yours truly
H. Lovitt

Capt. Gullison   Cardiff

HENRY LOVITT
16 New Quay
Liverpool

Dear Sir:
This will be handed to you by Mr. Henty the party engaged as 2nd mate for your vessel, wages £5-10 advance here payable 3 days after he leaves Cardiff providing he sails in the ship. I gave him £1 to pay expenses. Hope he will make you a good officer.

Yours truly
H. Lovitt

Capt. Gullison   Cardiff

HENRY LOVITT
16 New Quay
Liverpool 21st April '87

Dear Sir:
I am in receipt of your two favours this morning, note contents. At present there is no vessel bound for West. If you send your brother on here I will see he gets a ship soon for the States or St. John. Note you have returned the empties and the cheque on John Black & Co. will be very acceptable. I will send you perhaps before you sail.

Yours very truly
H. Lovitt

N.B. Lewis Esq.   Cardiff April 26th, 1887

Dear Sir:
We are getting along with our work very slowly, in fact, I am disgusted with this dock and the carpenters in it. I have had the surveyor down here to inspect our repairs. He examined us within and without and found one iron knee in lower hole cracked in the points and he said he thought it was an old break and that it was a defective knee situated on the port side two beams forward of main hatch the mizzen

mast. I bought a second hand on for 18/o, just as good as new. The caulking under boot topping is very poor, in fact, the whole of it. It is taking four or five double threads [of oakum] under boot topping; six in some places in wood ends and bow, three double above using a lot of oakum and time. We are moving around this confounded dock in all directions and it eats up so much time from carpenters work. I think if I had went into dry dock when I arrived here and finished repairs, I would have saved time and expense. My towage around about this dock pulling and hauling is going to amount to £32-0-0. It worries me very much Sir, but I cannot help myself, I am trying to get along as cheap as possible but the best I can do will be very dear, and I know you will think my bills very high when you receive them but if you could see how I have been situated since I arrived here you would not wonder at the expense. I may be loaded by the 30th but it is doubtful. Charters are in a hurry to load me this week but I do not expect to be ready as we are having a rainy day. Carpenters have had to knock off work and we have got to move again so I will close my writing. Remaining yours obediently

B.F. Gullison

P.S. I have sent you a sample of the copper.

The following letters are all from John Black & Co. to Capt. Gullison at Cardiff:

London 2nd May 1887

We have your favor of Saturday's date and are pleased to hear of vessel being out of the carpenters hands. We hope shippers will load her up quick and shall be glad to hear of any services in our power.

Yours etc.

London 3rd May 1887

We are in receipt of your favor and note contents. We thought we had sent you copy of colliery guarantee as to the loading of your vessel and regret our omission to do so. We now enclose copy and hope to hear that hereafter the loading is progressing to your satisfaction.

Yours etc.

London May 10th, 1887

We trust your loading is proceeding and that we shall very soon hear of your being ready. We are sure you will be glad to clear of Wales, your stay having been so long. We know this was no fault of yours. Will you require any more money? Is there anything we can do for you to hasten your getting clear?

Without further to advise

Yours etc.

London 12th May 1887

We are in receipt of your esteemed favour of yesterday's date and are pleased to note that you are likely now to get under the Tip.[20] We trust you will have no further delay. Enclosed we hand you cheque for £100 on account of ship's disbursements, receipts of which please own.

Yours etc.

N.B. Lewis Esq.   Cardiff May 6th, 1887

Dear Sir:

I finished repairs last Friday 29 ult and sent in notice I was ready for receiving cargo but up to the present have no more than stiffening in; will have to lay our lay days out now which will take until the 10 inst. Charters wanted me badly when I was not ready but now they have changed their minds and tell me to wait my lay days. This is very aggravating after being detained here as long as I have. Repairing expences whole amount will cost £215-10-0. This is high, I know, but rainy weather and shifting so much has increased it Sir; the work done cannot be beat that is one satisfaction. I have not got Windmill pump this time as I thought other bills would be so high. Trust it may meet your wishes.

Yours obediently
B.F. Gullison

N.B. Lewis Esq.   Yarmouth   Cardiff May 13th 1887
Nova Scotia

Dear Sir:

No doubt you are getting tired of receiving letters from me here, I, for my part, am sick and tired of the *name* and *sound* of Cardiff but under the circumstances I have been placed since I arrived here I could not do better. I commenced loading on the evening of the 11 inst. Hope to have my cargo in by 8 a.m. tomorrow morning if so will sail 11:30 a.m. Have been trying to push business very hard throughout the day so as not to lose this tide as it is my only one for the next week to come on F 22.2 in. draft.[21] I sincerly hope I shall be fortunate enough to do this for I am getting nearly discouraged, everything seems to be against me since I arrived here.

   I have shipped my people today and have made an approximate a/c with my brokers here Harrison Bros. and Moore who are very fine people I think. They will forward you all vouchers after my clearance. Disburse-

20 Tip — the coal loader.
21 Cardiff harbour was too shallow for a full load.

FIG. 40. Penarth dock, Nov. 17, 1896, showing all tips engaged, & eleven steamers waiting (Courtesy National Museum of Wales).

FIG. 41. Barry pilot cutter "Kindly Light" (Courtesy National Museum of Wales).

ments amount to £999-17-11 approx. a/c. These are large figures I know Sir, but *I have done my best.*

I tried to work saving on my repairing here by keeping out of dry dock and it would have been such had I not been humbugged so with shifting and rainy weather. I cannot think of anything further to inform you Sir, I hope to get out safely and make a quick and prosperous voyage. Will write you again and send letter by pilot boat. Trusting these comments will find you in good health and that you will not think this detention here Sir, is any fault of mine. I am yours obediently

B.F. Gullison

N.B. Lewis Esq.

Ship *N.B. Lewis*
May 14th 1887

Dear Sir:

I write you these few lines to inform you that I am now passing Lundy Island where I will discharge tug boat. Wind northerly moderate breeze. Things in general working good as can be expected after such hurrying out of dock. Thank goodness I am clear of this place and very glad of it.

I have on board 2027 ton of coal and drawing 6 inches more water than the cargo of 1882.[22] Draft 22.5 and 22.9[23]; 53 ton short of her proper cargo. I would have put her down 4 inches more had I plenty of water. Please excuse writing and mistakes as I am in a great hurry.

Yours obediently
Frank Gullison

Capt. Gullison

Yarmouth June 13/87

Dear Sir:

Suppose you are getting well on your way. Accounts came to hand; bills were about what I expected although it makes a big hole in a small freight. You did not send me the chandlery account from Lovitt, Liverpool. See by general account it was 299 pounds. Hope you will get a quick dispatch at Cape Town; remit your freight to Messers Black, they will send returns to me. Suppose you will be able to get enough stone ballast for cotton or oil. My mind now is to order you to Barbadoes for orders[24] or to S.W. Pass[25] for cotton. I will decide in my next. You need not cable arrival but cable

22 Cardiff to Rio de Janeiro under Captain Eldridge.
23 Ship was drawing 22 feet 5 inches forward and 22 feet 9 inches at stern.
24 "Orders": When no cargo had been arranged for a vessel, owners would *order* her to a convenient port, where, on arrival, the captain would receive instructions through local agents as to his next course. Ports commonly used for this purpose were Brest, France; Falmouth, England; The Breakwater, at the mouth of Delaware Bay; and Barbados.
25 i.e., Port Eads at the mouth of the Mississippi River.

when you sail using the Port you are bound to – if Barbadoes you can use address and Barbadoes without any signature; if to the Pass the same way using the word 'Pass'. Hope you will find things better this side. It would suit cotton business. Suppose if all goes well, you should be up by November first which would be a good time for cotton or perhaps oil. In the event coming to Barbadoes, could order North or South. Dowley has wound the 'Mizpah' up – on Cape Breton about a total loss. No insurance of any account. Think he will do better hauling kelp and raising potatoes from this out.

Yours
N.B. Lewis

P.S. If anything in way of business offering where you are, you could cable. Don't expect it would be safe on the metal to charter for any eastern port or West Coast S. America so I think better to make tracks North.

J. ELLIOTT & SONS[26]

(John H. Robinson)

Bute Docks

Capt. F.B. Gullison   Cardiff
Ship *N.B. Lewis*   Cape Town C.G.H.   June 30th 1887

Dear Capt. Gullison:

I suppose it is about time to write you a few lines just to let you know how things are going on this side of the line. For the most part their has been nothing unusual to report. All things remain as they were. *Abbie S. Hart*[27] got away nicely then came the *Fred B. Taylor* and bound for Manilla. I fitted her out and in fact was Broker for her. He had 20/s. John Bunyan also has sailed hence for ... 18/s. I have present ship *Rossignol Monte Video* 17/9. *Lennie, Rio*, at 18/6. *Annie Goudey* sailed yesterday for Monte Video 19/6. *Lizzie C. Troop* is at Sharpness yet; been reclassing. Goes to Montreal in ballast to load lumber for South. *Monrovia* is at present at Antwerp. Times are generally dull and freights low. I suppose you will come North this voyage. I trust you and Mrs. Gullison are in the enjoyment of good health. My family are all well and Mrs. Robinson wishes to be kindly remembered to you both. We are having extreme warm weather in England and very dry and the prospect for good crops is poor if the dry weather continues. I got your rope the morning you sailed and have it in the store for you. I hope to see you back in Cardiff soon again. Also trust you may get some good inducement to come. Our mutual friends the ... seem to enjoy life pretty well. We have had a general Jubilee[28] in England and

---

26 A ship's broker in Cardiff.
27 See Appendix F for further information regarding vessels mentioned.
28 Queen Victoria's Jubilee of 1887.

there is not half the colliers working, consequently ships have to wait long days and many have been on demurrage. I trust you will make a good passage out and also secure some good homeward business. Wishing you all prosperity in life. Kind regards to Mrs. Gullison and don't forget to kiss the baby for me a lot of times.

from yours faithfully,
John H. Robinson

Write me a few lines.

Capt. Gullison   Yarmouth July 4th, '87

Dear Sir:

I wrote you by last mail. I can say not much in addition; remit your freight to John Black & Co., London. Hearing nothing to the contrary, come to Barbardoes for orders calling on De Costa commission merchants. We can then go to the Gulf or come North hoping there may be some improvement in rates by that time. In case there may be anything offering where you are, you can always get us by cable. If possible, get enough stone ballast for cotton or oil; hoping you will make a safe and speedy passage. Cable when you leave, not on arrival.

Yours
N.B. Lewis

Cabling if Barbadoes destination – cable thus – 'Lewis Yarmouth Nova Scotia Barbadoes.'

N.B. Lewis Esq.   Cape Town July 19th '87

Dear Sir:

I arrived here on the morning of the 15 inst. after a fair passage of sixty days. I did not cable you as Lloyd agents did so on my arrival and you will probably hear very near as soon. I think I shall cable you when I commence taking in ballast. Hope this will meet your approval. I have been laying in the bay since my arrival waiting my turn to Lighter[29] which I trust will take place about last of this week. We go to a wharf outside the docks built on to the breakwater to lighten to about 20 feet 7 inches or 21 feet. We will then go into dock. Merchants take it out on Bill of Lading quantity after deducting about £32.0.0 thereabouts which is a fraud but it will be cheaper than having it weighed which cost 9 pence per ton beside.

Frank Gullison

---

29 The ship is drawing too much water to go into docks so some coal is being unloaded onto a lighter (or barge) to lighten her.

MESSRS. JOHN BLACK & CO.
No. 19 Change Alley   London

Gentlemen:

I arrived here on the 15 inst making my passage in sixty days all well and right side up with care. Received your letter and also disbursement and freight a/c and I also had a letter from Messers Harrison Bros. & Moore and I must here say that I found them to be perfect Gentlemen in all my business with them at Cardiff; I have been laying in the bay since my arrival. Will go in discharging berth about 22nd.

I will not have much of a remittance on this voyage and it seems discouraging. Did you receive £4.0.0 from Harrison Bros. & Moore on a/c of advance note?

Yours truly
Frank Gullison

Messers Harrison Bros. & Moore   Cape Town
Cardiff   July 20th '87

Gentlemen:

I arrived here on the 15th inst after a very pleasant passage of sixty days. I will not get a discharging berth before the 22nd. Your letter to hand on arrival contents noted all a/c seems to be in perfect order. The only trouble is they are very large; this we cannot help. I cashed the carpenter's & O.S. note myself and forgot to mention to you about it.

Wishing you the compliments of the season.

I remain yours
most respectfully
B.F. Gullison

Messers Donald Currie & Co.   Cape Town July 21st '87

Gentlemen:

I hereby give you notice that ship N.B. Lewis is now ready for discharging cargo and that my lay days will commence from the present date.

Trusting you will favor me with a quick dispatch.

I remain, yours respectfully
B.F. Gullison

N.B. Lewis Esq.   Cape Town July 26th 1887

Dear Sir:

We are discharging slowly outside of dock yet. Have lightened to F20 00 in [vessel's draft] and expect to go into dock on Thursday if they will give me a quay berth; then we shall probably work much faster. I received your letter and note contents; I will send you my Chandlery a/c or ask Mr. Lovitt to forward you one. Shall remit John Black & Co. balance of freight as directed; will also cable you when ready for sea. My bills will be near £400,0,0 stg. here. Have to pay 1/8 [1 shilling and eight pence] for discharging and 8/o per ton of 2000 lbs. for ballast, dirt and stone mixed. Cannot get any other. I tried hard to get my coal discharged by allowing 1% discount on amt. of freight. This would be reasonable for a quick dispatch but when they come to make us pay out price 12/6 for this 1% is unreasonable.[30] They should by rights take it by bill of laden [lading] quantity; other ships *have paid* the 1 3/4% thereabouts and are now doing it so there is no help for me this time but I shall write to Mr. Black about it so if we should come down here again he would perhaps be able to arrange it a little different. There is a number of ships here and they must all have a letter of credit for their (owner) and save on disbursements. Charles Baker's expenses here next to me was £386-13-9, *Queen of the Fleet* £418-14-11, Ship *Ryerson* £452-8-2. Ship *Caledonia* of Pictou is trying hard to get fixed for Manilla by J.F. Whitney.

Bark bound to Bay of Bengal for Jute $500 New York $550 Boston. As our copper is poor, I think, as you, Sir, we should make tracks North.

I hope I shall hear from you by coming mail.

Yours obediently
B.F. Gullison

---

30 It appears from other references in this correspondence that cargoes sometimes turned out on delivery to be somewhat less than bill of lading quantity (whether because of carelessness, loss, water damage, breakage, desiccation, theft, or just human nature). Messrs Donald Currie & Co., to protect themselves, have adopted the custom of deducting one per cent of the bill of lading value of the cargo from the amount of their remittance when paying freight charges on cargoes received. In this case they would have deducted the value of 20.27 tons of coal at 12 shillings and sixpence per ton or approximately $51.75. Captain Gullison resents this and feels that if his cargo were weighed out it would be shown that there was no such shortage. However, Curries are unwilling to bear the cost of weighing out the coal, and the cost, if borne by the ship, would probably amount to more than $51.75. Gullison prefers to take this loss rather than to incur even greater expense by having his cargo weighed out. Donald Currie & Co. have been able to take advantage of the ship because the terms of the charter party drawn up by the ship's agents (Black) had not been specific enough on this matter.

Messers John Black & Co.   Cape Town Aug. 2nd 1887

Gentlemen:

I write you these few lines to inform you that I am about 1/2 discharged and expect to leave here about 14 inst to Barbadoes. My coal merchants, Donald Currie & Co. would not take my cargo on Bill of Laden quantity but as a customary rate with them deduct 1% on amount of freight and also charging me cost price 12/6 per ton which is actually on board ship is what I call a piece of imposition. They say it is the custom of the port to pay the 1 3/4% thereabouts; *but it is not*. Some are taking it by bill of laden and some by allowing 1% discount, this is outside DC. & Co.'s office. I partly arranged to have my coal weighed but was given to understand that I could not have it weighed out the ship as it was not the custom of the dock. Also that I would have to pay for weighing of the said coal which they say would be [?] per ton but find it is [??].[31] I would here ask, am I compelled to pay for the weighing, and also to deliver coal to [indecipherable] before being weighed, will you please inform me this and oblidge. My expenses here will be about £400-0-0 stg. Will remit you balance of freight as ordered by my owner N.B. Lewis.

> Remaining yours most respectfully
> *B.F. Gullison*

The following is a letter from Frank Gullison to his father at home in Nova Scotia.

I am much oblidged for your information concerning my 1/16 of the good ship *N.B. Lewis*. I am very anxious to get my debt paid and I assure you it will be a long while before I am in debt again without I am compelled to and I think Father you are making a great mistake when you say neither Eugene nor I have ever thanked you for what you have done for us. It is not Eugene's principle neither is it mine to do anything like this and I think myself if you remember right you will recall the time that I thanked you for offering me assistance and beside offering my thanks I paid you like any other stranger would; not only money affairs but for every trifling thing you have done around my place and I do not want to say too much concerning this but I want you to know Father that your sons have feelings to be overbalanced and I think when you reconsider what you have wrote me in your first letter relating to offering thanks for favours done you will say that *you have been* a little too *hasty*. I am getting a very poor dispatch here. Was waiting a week before I could get a discharging berth. Expect to get away from here about the 16 inst. My expences here will be

31 Unable to decipher the figures in the original letter.

upwards of £400 stg. Everything is very dear. 8/ per ton for ballast; stevedoring 7/6; dockage 6^d; six pence for 21 days and 3 [three pence] per ton after.

from Frank

N.B. Lewis Esq.   Cape Town August 10th 1887

Dear Sir:

We expect to take in ballast in the morning. Will probably be discharged about Saturday. We have had great detentions here on a/c of drawing so much water and having so many ships here together in so small a dock and have to wait our turn. Another fault is our fore and after hatches are very small but you may be sure sir I am trying to do my best. We leaked considerable coming out. Made about 1 inch per hour. I find now it is between the lower part of the boot topping and copper. I expected her to leak a little there but not so much as she did. It will have to be looked after before loading again. I think Barbadoes will be a good port to call. Will cable as directed.

Yours most respectfully
B.F. Gullison

P.S. Enclosed you will find a small painting of your ship upon a silver leaf. Please accept. Yours B.F. Gullison

---

N.B. Lewis Esq.   Cape Town August 17, '87

I write you these few lines to inform you that I come out of dock this morning and anchored in the bay. Will probably be ready for sea Saturday if all goes well. I have had a *very poor* dispatch here on a/c of merchants having so much coal on hand on my arrival here and I wrote you in my last letter about other detentions and I have had trouble with my crew. My bills will be more than you expected no doubt but I assure you Sir, it is no fault of mine. I shall remit balance of freight to John Black & Co. and forward you all vouchers. I wrote and asked Mr. Lovitt, Ship Chandler to send you store bill as I have only one.

From yours faithfully
B.F. Gullison

N.B. Lewis Esq.   Cape Town August 19th 1887

Dear Sir:

I write you these few lines to inform you I will tow out from here in the morning. My bills here are heavy over and above amount stipulated in charter party. You will see by account which will be sent you enclosed with

FIG. 42. Painting of Ship *N.B. Lewis* & view of Capetown.

145

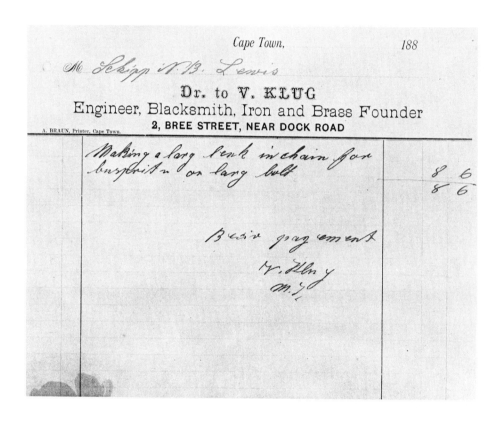

FIG. 43. Invoice of V. Klug, brass founder, Capetown, 1887.

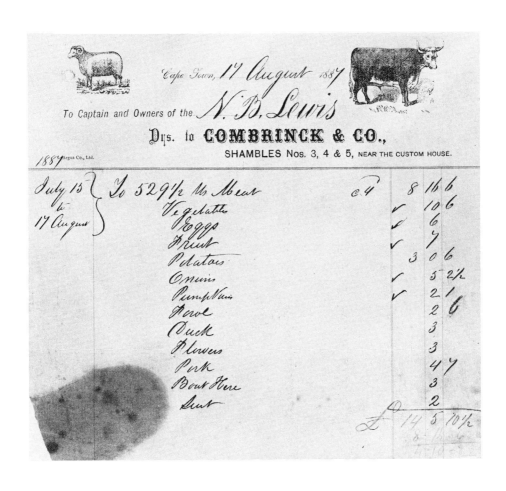

FIG. 44. Invoice for ships' stores from Combrinck & Co., Capetown, 1887.

FIG. 45. View of Capetown Harbour, 1898. (Reproduced with the permission of the
Trustees of the National Maritime Museum, Greenwich).

vouchers that my expenses amount to £533-2-1. I gave Donald Currie & Co. a draft on John Black & Co. to the amount of £186-2-1. Had to pay 5% on this and also 1/2% for exchange bills. I forwarded to B. & E. Stamford copy bill of lading duly receipted and reg. the same. Will send you enclosed in this letter press copy advising J.B. & Co. of my draft on him.

Sir, I regret my detention and expenses here. You will be somewhat surprised at the time and expense and *'time means expense'*. I have *worked faithful* and might come here a dozen times again and never be in the position that I have been placed in since my arrival.

Frank Gullison

The following was likely meant for delivery at Barbados c/o Da Costa & Co.

Capt. Gullison   Yarmouth August 24/'87

Dear Sir:
Your cable announcing sailing for Barbadoes came safe to hand. See you arrived down July 15th at Cape Town. No letters yet on arrival. Hearing nothing to the contrary proceed to Port Eads for orders. I think New Orleans for cotton will be our best place; should be in good time for cotton. On arrival at Port Eads you will find letters and if any arrangements for towage will advise you there. If no letters it would be safe to wire before making any arrangements as sometimes they miscarry. I am in hopes we may strike something fair in cotton here. Don't seem to be anything North to pay at present; might do 23¢ to Japan for case oil, nothing in that; we might remetal on the other side.

If I make any different arrangements will cable Messers Da Costa, Barbadoes. When you arrive, if you don't find any different orders, cable me the word 'Eads'[32] which will let me know you understand my orders and have sailed. Hoping you will have a good run down to Barbadoes.

I am yours
N.B. Lewis

Your Father arrived at New York yesterday.

---

32 The cost of a cablegram was figured on each word. 'Eads' (Port Eads) was the port at the mouth of the Mississippi river to which the *N.B. Lewis* was bound and Mr. Lewis in his instructions was simply trying to save money. The expression 'The Pass' or 'The Passes' refers to the seaways leading to various channels at the mouth of the Mississippi river. Port Eads is situated on one of these channels.

CODES USED.

SCOTT'S 1880.
SCOTT'S Reprint 1883. Vide pages 127 and 129, and "Advertisement."
WATKIN'S, Boston, 1881.
TELEGRAPHIC CODEX PORT CHARGES OF THE WORLD, by
Theo. Hunter & Jarvis Patten, New York.

N.B.—OBLIGE BY ALWAYS SIGNING CABLE MESSAGES.

CABLE ADDRESS—
DAÇOSTA,
BARBADOS.

Memoranda

CABLE ADDRESS—
DACOSTA,
LONDON.

FROM

DA COSTA & CO.,

SHIP BROKERS AND GENERAL AGENTS,

BARBADOS,

AND

117, LEADENHALL STREET, LONDON.

To Owners and Shipmasters,

The importance of the Island of Barbados, as a port of call for Vessels seeking employment, has of late years been considerably enhanced by the introduction of a sub-marine cable, which places the Island in connection with all the neighbouring ones, as well as with Europe and the United States of America.

Its geographical position, Lat. N., 13° 5′ 42.″ 50, Long. W., 59° 37′ 18.″ 45, is of great advantage, being to windward of all the other Islands.

There are three **LIGHTS** on the Island, the particulars of which are as follows, viz. :—

REVOLVING LIGHT ON RAGGED POINT.—This Light is exhibited from a Lighthouse erected on Ragged Point, a little North of the extreme Eastern end of the Island, position in Lat. N., 13° 9′, Long. W., 59° 26′. It is a revolving holophotal one, elevated 213 feet above the level of High Water, giving flashes at intervals of two minutes, and in clear weather should be seen from a distance of 20 to 25 miles. The Lighthouse is situate 300 yards from the extremity of the cliff, at a distance of two miles and-a-half North-west from the Eastern end of a group of dangerous reefs, called "The Cobblers' Rocks," running parallel with the South-Eastern Coast of the Island. It is thirteen miles in a direct line North-east of the South Point Light. Mariners are advised to keep **WELL OFF** to the North-east of the Lighthouse, to avoid the prevailing strong current running Westward on the "Cobblers."

[P.T.O.

Fig. 46. Memorandum from Da Costa & Co., ship brokers, Barbados.

To Capt. Gullison:

Dear Sir:

We have your valued favour of the 27th ulto and note contents. We duly received the Certificate of Delivery of coal at Cape Town and have collected balance of freight, sending accounts to Mr. Lewis.

We put forward a strong representation to the Castle Co.[33] respecting charge made for coal allowed in lieu of weigh − but failed to secure anything in the shape of a return. We sent the correspondence to Mr. Lewis.

> With kind regards
> Yours very truly
> John Black & Co.
> *Irving Chester*

Capt. Gullison   Yarmouth September 28/87

Dear Sir:

Your cable at hand from Barbadoes. I am writing A.K. Miller & Co., ship brokers, New Orleans in reference to business at that port. On arrival at Port Eads you will communicate with them. I have written him to advise you in reference to tonnage and other matters in event of ship going to Orleans you will probable find a letter there on arrival. If we have not then decided where to go for business you will await instructions at Port Eads. I expect you have dirt ballast I think you wired me it was mixed dirt and stone. Would it be practical to work out the stone as it is early for cotton. You may have to wait a while. On arrival telegraph Miller and Co. and they will telegraph us.

> Yours
> *N.B. Lewis*

---

33   The Castle Co. was operating a line of steamers, and while Currie & Co. were local agents, the coal no doubt was destined for the steamship company.

Capt. Gullison   Yarmouth Oct. 15, 1887

Dear Sir:

Telegram at hand yesterday announcing arrival *Lewis* at, I suppose, New Orleans. Don't see anything to do now but to wait for cotton to move. Hope you will be able to work something out. If you don't ballast. The Cape Town business is very small of its size, as the Irishmen would say. It seems to me the lower the freight the more the charges and impositions. They are a regular set of sharks, however, must live in hopes of doing better. I think for these voyages vessels, as a rule, lay in too much salt provisions.[1] I suppose in the event of going East it is well to have a good stock but going to Cape Town or Rio and River Platte is not much more than Atlantic voyage. Expect we will have to wait some time for cargo. Hold things up as cheaply as possible and make all you can out of it. Expect your crew will clear out. Suppose Liverpool would be the best port to take cotton, all other things being equal. You may be able to get some stiffening cargo. I got the little leaflet picture of the ship which is very pretty. Hope this will find you and your family all well.

I am yours
N.B. Lewis

P.S. Think Drysdale will give good satisfaction as stevedore.

1 Salt provisions – Usually pork and beef are stored in barrels containing a salt pickle.

[The following is a note found in the front of one of the log books evidently written by Capt. Frank Gullison's wife Della:]

Saturday evening
October 15th 1887 Ship *N.B. Lewis* at Port Eads
Della all alone in the cabin. Bowman confortably in bed. Frank has gone to N. Orleans on business.
How very lonely I am. This is a foretaste of what is coming. Oh, if it was not for these bitter partings. I trust I shall see my darling tomorrow, in time to wind the chronometer. It is blowing hard but the 'good ship' is lying in here beside a bank with the willows and rushes waving on both sides. We do not know where we shall go to load — but perhaps to New Orleans, if so, I expect Della will say (good bye) for a little while. I have been reading xc Psalms and so lonely. Now I will retire and try to forget my little troubles.

May God watch over us and keep us and if separated spare us to embrace one another again.

This day has been a week to me.

(Della Frank)[2]

Capt. Gullison   Yarmouth Oct. 19th '87

Telegraphed you Monday to proceed to New Orleans. I thought by Messers Miller telegram you was there all the time. Expect things are going to be slow. Think it will be as well not to discharge ballast until we see what is to be done. If your crew stay by, which they probable will not, and if there is stone mixed with your ballast, could you not keep them working it out of the dirt and save buying that much stone. You, of course, know all about this. You wrote me from Cape Town ballast was stone and dirt mixed.

Yours
N.B. Lewis

N.B. Lewis Esq.   Port Eads Oct. 28, 1887
Dear Sir:
Your favour to hand yesterday of the 15th and 19th ult.

Note what you say about ballast, also cable proceed to New Orleans. I am still at Port Eads and will now explain my reason for doing so. I got

---

2 Expressions such as Della Frank (the name of wife and husband combined) are still occasionally heard in Western Nova Scotia. The practice may have originated when two men with the same last name married women with same first name.
    See also letter from Capt. Gullison to Dr. Harris dated Dec. 6/87 and letter from Mrs. Corning (Della's mother) to Capt. Gullison dated June 30/88.

favoured by the tug boat company discharging ballast. I had it hoisted out by steam Derrick which cost me 30¢ per ton by filling with my crew. I had about 150 tons stone picked out on arrival here. I have now about 250 ton and that *trimmed* and *ready*. We were very *fortunate finding so much stone.* Have put ship down two feet by the stern. I think she ought to load about right with that. The quarantine and fumigating expenses closes on the 1st November which amounts to $100.00. This saved will be quite an item which can be if we remain unchartered. There is a lot of copper off; it is like decayed brown paper and seems about useless to try and repair it. I shall use what I have aboard and let the rest go trusting what I have done will meet your wishes.

> Yours truly
> *Frank Gullison*

Capt. Gullison   Yarmouth Oct. 22nd 1887

Dear Sir:

Yours of the 15th at hand contents noted. Glad you have been able to get so much stone out of your ballast. Hope you will be able to work out some more. We shall have some patience waiting for business. Am in hopes next month will show some business worth taking. Our Cape Town business did not seem to turn out much but suppose it is no use to cry, as we all, I think, done the best we could under the circumstances. The confounded metal[3] seems to be at the bottom of the whole thing.

    As you will have stone ballast for stiffening, you will use your own judgement about discharging the dirt.

> Yours
> *N.B. Lewis*

Capt. F. Gullison   Yarmouth October 29th 1887

Dear Sir:

I telegraphed Messers Miller & Co. today in reference to telegram to consult with you and as you know the situation and being on the spot you are in a position to judge whether to take business as it is or wait longer. The business is small but it costs money to wait and if there is no immediate prospect of improvement it will be better to take present rates and move off. Anyway you will, with Mr. Miller, be in position to decide and do for the best in your judgement. Write me what you are paying for stevedore, compress and other principal charges. Hoping you may be able to get her

---

3 Confounded metal – Mr. Lewis is complaining about the quality of copper or alloy sheets which were put on the *N.B. Lewis* in New York.

fixed up at a paying rate. I see by Mr. Miller's letter we would save 20 cents per bale compress and stevedore and 5 cents per ton on tonnage.[4] This on last year rates could make on a ship like *N.B. Lewis* about $1400 saving which is quite an item.

Yours

N.B. Lewis

N.B. Lewis Esq.

New Orleans
November 3rd 1887

Dear Sir:

On my arrival at the city today with the good ship *N.B. Lewis* I received a letter from you of the 29th ult. I talked with Mr. Miller concerning present rates of freight and also prospects of the future which are not at present looking upwards as demands have decreased during the last few days. The many sailing ships which are waiting here at present are getting little or no cotton and present freight rates are low. In all probability, in a week's time they may be higher, so perhaps it will be wise to hang on for a while as cabled you by Miller and Co. In my last letter, I informed you about ballast, discharging, trimming & sutra [et cetera] fumigating expense is saved. Drysdale and Husites have become partners. Their charge is 60¢ per bale, compressing 50¢. Have not agreed to dis. [disbursements] yet. Will let you know farther on.

From yours obediently

B.F. Gullison

---

4   After cotton is picked, it is put through a gin to separate the fibres from the seed. The cotton is then baled in a gin box at the gin, making a large and cumbersome package, which goes next to a warehouse for storage.

Before 1887 very few interior warehouses were equipped with a compress so the cotton was shipped to the port in 'flat' bales which had a volume of about 40 cubic feet. At the port this flat bale was compressed to a volume probably between 15 and 20 cubic feet. The smaller the volume the greater number of bales that could be loaded; the freight cost per bale would decrease with the volume.

It would appear that Captain Gullison received the 'flat' bales which were then compressed and loaded by stevedores under contract.

The question of weight – It has always been the custom to 'plug' lading weights, by adding 5.10 or more pounds per bale to the actual weight for bill of lading purposes. Freight is paid basis B/L (bill of lading) weights which are always furnished by the shipper. The reason for this is the fact that cotton normally absorbs some moisture in transit and additionally should the ship suffer some type of marine disaster the insurance companies settle on the basis of the B/L weight. Hence, even if the actual weight of the bales was 490 pounds, the chances are that the B/L weight was at least 500 or more. The practice of 'plugging' weights is known as 'franchising'.

N.B. Lewis Esq.   New Orleans Nov. 8th '87

Dear Sir:

We cabled you yesterday, 'Chartered ship with two thousand bales free of consignment for Liverpool market; business very quiet, improvement doubtful'. Which is the case, there is sail tonnage arriving every day and taking the rates offered; that is the most of them. There is not enough cotton sold to make them any higher although they had a sale yesterday of 12000 bales for Havre. We thought it better to make a commencement on his sale as we have been waiting now about long enough.

> Yours most respectfully
> *Frank Gullison*

N.B. Lewis Esq.   New Orleans Nov. 12, 1887

Dear Sir:

I telegraphed you yesterday. Afraid too many vessels took Liverpool berths: can change to Havre Three thousand bales nineteen thirty seconds $(19/32)$[5]; consignment, better prospects for Havre than Liverpool, recieved your answer this morning 'You on the spot knowing situation thinking best take Havre offer'. I wrote you on the 8 inst in reference to Liverpool business; it looked encouraging enough, but since then there has been little or no cotton shipped outside of engagement and as the prospects looked higher for a quicker dispatch at Havre we thought it advisable to turn her over for that port. Much same figures but gaining consignment as telegraphed you. We will commence loading Monday.

> Yours respectfully
> *B.F. Gullison*

Capt. Gullison   Yarmouth Nov. 19, 1887

Dear Sir:

Yours at hand. I think the change to Havre will probable be better. The rate is small but in hopes will save something of it. Oil rates are better, think can get 3/6 rate Dunkirk. Wish they would keep as good as that. Would be better than deep water business. When you want some money for disbursements, let me know. How is your crew? Do they hang on or have they skipped? Hoping you will get a good cargo and dispatch – write often and let me know how you are getting along.

> Yours
> *N.B. Lewis*

---

5   i.e., 19/32 cents per pound or 59.376 cents per hundred pounds.

N.B. Lewis Esq.   November 21st 1887

Dear Sir:

I write you these few lines to inform you that loading is going along slowly, have on board three hundred bales averaging 490 lbs.[6] Will try and get her squeezed up tight as possible. Freights are on a stand still, no improvement whatever.

I wrote you about stevedore's rates for loading. It is Nett figures and as I have nothing more of importance, to inform you, sir, will close. The weather here since Sat. evening has been quite cold; found ice on deck this morning.

> Yours obediently
> *B.F. Gullison*

N.B. Lewis Esq.   New Orleans Nov. 23, 1887

Dear Sir:

I telegraphed you on Saturday asking you to send me mate. I received yours today. 'Can't find mate will have to do best you can'. I am very sorry as I am in want of one very much, the fact is I cannot get along with the one I have and there is none here at present that I would take and no likelihood of there being any very soon. I know the cost is considerable from home here but sometimes the dearest article is the least expense in the end especially if we have to pay for cotton and staves in Havre and I hope if you find a good man you will send him on. Freights have taken a fall today. 18/64[7] is now offered. We have on board 1400 bales. I hardly know what we are going to do for the balance of our cargo. To take the rates now offered will be sinking money. I have four sailors, carpenter, mate and second mate, cook and boy.

> Yours respectfully
> *B.F. Gullison*

N.B. Lewis Esq.   New Orleans Dec. 5th '87

Dear Sir:

I write you these few lines to inform you that we have on board today 3000 bales. I hope to have her pretty well filled up by the 15th. I have raised main hatch combings to the heights of 3″ 7′ and also put short stringers of oak in between deck's beams under main hatch. I have bought two spars one fore top gallant mast and mizzen upper topsail yd. I picked

---

6   See note p. 156.
7   18/64¢ would be a very decided drop to around 28 cents per hundred pounds.

up a beautiful stick at the passes 40 ft. by 12″ square which was very near enough for main (hatch)? but the iron work has cost considerable. The weather here remains very warm. My wife left here for home Saturday evening.

Your letter of the 22nd ult came to hand yesterday. Has been in the Post Office at the 'Passes'.

From yours most respectfully
Frank Gullison

Dr. H. Harris[8]   New Orleans
Beaver River   Yarmouth Co., N.S.   Dec. 6th '87

Dear Sir:

My wife left here for home on first. She is quite miserable and has been under Dr. Lewis treatment for about one month. One of the best Physicians in New Orleans. He pronounced her case alhumanuria, a disease accompanying pregnancy and informed me that she would have to be *watched* very closely as this complaint was often followed by *convulsions* at child birth and in many cases *premature labour* was needful. This I have not told my wife but thought it advisable to inform you. She will call your attention on arrival home and now Doctor, I will say do best possible and please drop me a few lines on receipt of this. Wishing you the compliments of the season, I remain

Yours respectfully
Frank Gullison

N.B. Lewis Esq.   Yarmouth, N.S.   December 9th '87

Dear Sir:

I write a few lines to inform you that we have 3369 bales on board; have engaged 3650 @ 19/32 and 250 @ 9/16.[9] I hope we will have her all taken up by the last of the week. There seems to be plenty of cotton in the market but the merchants on the other side will not pay a price for it, 17/32 has been taken by a number of ships to fill up on.

I have not got a mate yet and do not know what I shall do.

From yours obediently
Frank Gullison

---

8   This is the same doctor who treated Captain Eldridge when he had smallpox. Dr. Harris later sold his house in Beaver River to Captain Ben Gullison and moved to Yarmouth.

9   9/16 − i.e. 56 1/4 cents per hundred pounds.

Capt. Gullison   Yarmouth Dec. 10 '87

Dear Sir:

Your telegram at hand this morning. I had been looking around for mate. They are not plentiful. Those that are worth having. I have shipped Mr. Robert Patten who seems like a fine young man. He has passed the Board for Master lately. Has been some time mate. He don't want to leave here till next Saturday boat. Going through by rail suppose he would get along about Christmas. I have telegraphed you to this effect asking for reply also how progressing with cargo. You will have to be guided by your judgement about filling up at going rate. Was in hopes rates might stiffen for balance of cargo instead of weakening but we shall have to take things as they are if no prospect better. There is several ships wanting mates now. Eugene wants one for the *Otago*. What there is home seem to want to stay for a while — before you get ready let me know time enough to get funds along for disbursements.

> Yours
> *N.B. Lewis*

New Orleans Dec. 10th 1887

My Dear Mother [10]:

This is a Sabbath morning and I am sitting in my 'now' lonely cabin. I have to improve my time, if I allow my mind to wander, I am shedding tears before I know it and how hard it is to be parted from those who are so near and Dear. These partings make my poor heart ache but it is one consolation to know that time will help these feelings. Oh May God in his kind mercy spare us all to meet again is all I can say and this will be my prayers to him that ruleth all things. I have been greatly worried about Della since she left me. I know she has had good care but the journey was so long and tiresome. I expect little Bowman required a great amount of watching he is so mischivious I should have liked to went home with her and spent the winter with you all. *I do want a change* but my means will not allow me. My interest in this ship stands unpaid for and at this present of voyage I have not made enough to cover insurance let alone principal. *Times are so bad.* Well, Mother, I suppose you are all together this morning and enjoying yourselves immense. I trust my Darling one will improve rapidly and hope God is blessing you all with good health and now Dear Mother, I will say let us forget the past difficulties that have arose from time to time and if *I* and *mine* have caused your heart to be anxious I pray

---

10 Letter written to his mother-in-law, Mrs. Frank Corning. See her letter in reply dated June 31st 1888, in which she describes Della's condition on arrival in Yarmouth after she had a miscarriage on the steamer, p. 188.

you at this moment to forgive us and as the old year goes out, let us bury them so deep that they will not spring forth again and may this coming year of '88 renew our love double fold but Mother I do not mean to preach a sermon. I have wrote as my heart feels trusting you will write me a few lines in the same way I wish to *love* and be *loved* if I am allowed to do so. Give my love to my darling wife and babe and if the words I have wrote meet your wishes *Seal* them with a *kiss* to *them both.* Remember me to Capt. Corning and tell him I shall write, also Annie and Ed with fond love to yourself and Lila I wish to remain,

Your loving Son
Frank Gullison

N.B. Lewis   Yarmouth, N.S.   December 10, 1887

Cargo engaged thirty six hundred fifty bales nineteen thirty seconds, balance nine sixteenth will be ready next week. Am afraid mate will be late unless he leaves immediately.

B.F. Gullison

N.B. Lewis Esq.   Yarmouth, N.S.   New Orleans
                                                              Dec. 20th/87

Dear Sir:

I cleared from the Customs today. Will have onboard '*today noon*' 4460 bales cotton and will sail this evening. I took my last 33 bales @ 1/2c lost about $10.00 but it is better than having to wait for another week. My expenses here is $8246.47. I gave A.K. Miller & Co. sight draft on National Citizen Bank to this amount and advised them of the same. Brokers will forward you all vouchers and I trust you will find everything in order Sir. My mate arrived here Sunday morning 10 a.m. His passage was $55.00 he gave me $15.00 which I will credit the ship with. No improvements in freights. Lizzie Burrill gave consignment to Havre for 2500 @ 19/64 enclosed please accept Aprox. A/C of wages from your Obedient Servant

Frank Gullison

To aid in the understanding of the transaction concerning the bales of cotton, the following is included.

Estimate of freight received on cargo of cotton via ship *N.B. Lewis* from New Orleans to Havre, Dec. 21st, 1887.

Total cargo 4460 bales (bales were considered to weigh 500 lbs.)

Rate on 3650 bales was 19/32 or 59.375¢ per 100 lbs.	$10835.94
Rate on 777 bales was 9/16 or 56 1/4¢ per 100 lbs.	2185.31
Rate on 33 bales was 1/2¢ or 50¢ per 100 lbs.	82.50
	$13103.75

The above is figured on bales weighing 500 lbs. The captain stated in one letter the average weight of a bale was 490 lbs. If this was the accepted weight, the above amount would be less 2%

	262.00
	$12841.75

Estimated financial statement for voyage New Orleans to Havre

Approximate freight received		$13103.00
Expense New Orleans		8246.47
Havre	£1190 (approx.)	5790.00
Total expenses		$14036.47

The expenses at New Orleans were paid by a draft on the National Citizens Bank[11] before leaving New Orleans, which would be charged to the account of H. & N.B. Lewis. Capt. Gullison sent £1700 (approximately $8262) from Havre to N.B. Lewis, February, 1888, to cover the New Orleans expense. Repairs to ship at Havre amounted to more than the balance of freight, so Soley & Co., the agents at Liverpool, advanced funds which they later collected from advance coal freight.

Capt. Gullison   Yarmouth Jan. 12/'88

Dear Sir:

Suppose you are getting pretty well along towards Havre. Think we done as well as it was possible to do under the circumstances. New Orleans this year had not done much in way of freights. One good thing expenses was not high. You will find the ship closed for Rio at 21s[12] to load at Cardiff.

---

11 The New York City Directory of 1885-86 shows a National Citizens Bank at 401 Broadway, which is now part of Chemical Bank.
12 This would be a cargo of coal at twenty-one shillings a ton.

This is an extra rate for the times. The charter was made through George Durkee and Soley of Liverpool who will duly advise you and send Charter Party. The worst feature is the metal.[13] I booked at 7 3/4 [seven and three quarters] pense subject to any decline and usual discounts. I thought it best to do this as we can't tell where they will carry the price. Now as to the best place to do it, you will have best idea. If there is dock accommodation in Havre, which I understand there is, and you can get in at once, I believe it would be best to do it there as you are liable to detention in Cardiff.[14] You had better caulk the vessel, I think by the day. You will be best able to judge as to the best place to do work, also of the advisability to doing it by the day. I will write you next mail and send memorandum of last suit of metal; see she had 2557[15] sheets. Hoping to soon hear of your safe arrival which you will cable.

> Yours
> *N.B. Lewis*

Following are copies of letters confirming booking of ship *N.B. Lewis* for metal.

> G.T. SOLEY & CO.
> Liverpool 11th Jan. 1888

Dear Sirs:
With reference to the '*N.B. Lewis*'. We can supply her at Havre at the same terms and price as at Cardiff.

> Yours faithfully
> for Vivian & Sons
> (signed) *Rich. J. Phillips*

> G.T. SOLEY & CO.
> Liverpool 9th January 1888

Dear Sirs:
We confirm the booking of the *N.B. Lewis* for a suit of metal with the necessary nails for supply at Cardiff at the following prices: Metal 7 3/4 d [pence], nails 9 3/4 d less 2 1/2 and 1%. The old metal to be returned to us and credits to the ship at 5 3/4 d per lb. less 5 lbs. per cwt. draft and 2 1/2% discount settlement by cash.

13 He is referring to the problem of re-coppering the hull of the ship.
14 Previous experience had shown that repair work was not done as quickly in Cardiff as in Havre.
15 It took 2557 sheets of copper for re-coppering.

The ship to have the benefit of any fall in the official price up to the date she leaves the graving dock.[16]

> Yours faithfully
> for Vivian & Sons
> (signed) *Rich. J. Phillips*

Capt. Gullison   Yarmouth Jan. 19/88

Dear Sir:

I enclose metal bill. You will find it handy to refer to. If you think it to your advantage, you can do your work in Havre or, if you think best, go to Cardiff and do it there. I don't think coal freights are quite so good now. You may remit me say the amount of your New Orleans draft say 1800 pounds. The balance keep for metalling. One half of the coal freight is advanced. After paying your bills in Cardiff, whatever is left can come home. Think it best to use balance of cotton freight and that will give you ready cash to work with.

> Yours
> *N.B. Lewis*

N.B. Lewis Esq.   Havre Feb. 2nd 1888

Dear Sir:

I sent you a cable on the 31st ult reading thus, do you accept Jones price, or days work, as we expected you had received his estimate by this time forwarded by Franque before my arrival. Answer received yesterday. 'Do work according your judgement'. I was anxious to know this as I wanted to get booked for dry dock. We have two more estimates, one from Masion and one from Cooper, ship carpenters here, but they are far above Jones prices and I think it advisable, Sir, to give him the preference as he bears a very good name and have it done by the 2Fs [two francs][17] per sheet as specified in contract, he finding all materials except copper and nails and pay particular attention to his work; − I thought at first sir that it would be better to do by days work but I find now in the hauling to and from dock he can beat me 50Fr and there is always so many frivolus things to charge for too, in days work. Taking all things into consideration, I think it better to do it by the job and trust it will meet your wishes.

We expect to be discharged in eight days. Do you want ship fitted out for one year's stores or do you intend ordering her North from Rio, Sir? I have wrote to Soley at Liverpool about copper and I have with me Sir ev-

---

16 Graving dock − a drydock used for cleaning and repairing the underwater section of vessel.
17 The exchange value of the franc would have been approximately 19 1/2 cents.

erything pertaining to our last fit of copper including all carpenters time and all dry dock expenses: will order about same quantity of Vivian's and same No. but will have to have about 100 sheets of 24 oz. for keel. You remember last time, sir, we kept the old on which will be played out now. I am afraid our old metal is going to turn out *low* in *weight* but you may depend Sir that everything will have *close attention*. The English nails too will be heavier. We expect to be in dock about four days. I am inquiring into towage, from here to Cardiff. Weather here is quite cold, wind light and easterly. Ship *Prince Lucine* that towed down Mississippi River with us has not arrived yet. Have 1122 bales out tonight in good order. Will write you again as soon as discharged.

> Yours
> Most Respectfully
> *Frank Gullison*

Please excuse blots.

G.T. SOLEY & CO.
Ship & Insurance Brokers

Captain B.F. Gullison   Liverpool
Ship *N.B. Lewis*   Havre   2nd Feb. 1888

Dear Sir:

Your favor of 31st ulto to hand and contents noted. We are pleased to learn of your safe arrival. We have been watching the report to send you charter, but you have not been reported in the 'Gazette' before today.

We now beg to enclose copy of charter, which we trust you will find in order. We had stipulated for Penarth loading, as we know by experience, it is the cheapest and most convenient for vessels and masters. The agents at Cardiff are Messers Barnes Guthrie and Co. We also enclose copy of metal contract, in which we got option of using at Havre or Cardiff. The terms are the usual ones, less 2 1/2% discount and 1% commission. Old metal returned at 2d per lb. less than the new and to be taken delivery of and weighed at the dock. The nails you are free to sell, lump sum, or return to the metal company. At the same price as old metal − at 5 3/4 d per lb. they will come to a big sum. The agent for Vivian's metal at Havre is A. Christiansen to whom please apply. We suppose you will get your work done cheaper at Havre than at Cardiff as it costs about 15 to 16 pence per sheet at latter place, which you no doubt know. We shall be pleased to be of any assistance to you here, and remain

> Yours truly
> *G.T. Soley & Co.*

Capt. F. Gullison   Yarmouth Feb. 2/'88

Dear Sir:

Was glad to hear of your safe arrival at Havre after a good passage. In reply to your cable yesterday I answered to do as you thought best as you, knowing the circumstances, would be best able to judge. I always would rather do the caulking by the day but some times you can do as well, with reliable folks, by the job. I did not understand the reference to Jones offer but suppose it was an offer made by him that had not come to hand. In provisioning for the voyage do so with a view of coming North as probable I shall order you to Breakwater[18] or to the Hook unless there should be extra inducements to go the other way and, if so, we can always buy fit-out provisions.

I presume you are metalling in Havre. I believe I wrote you we bought Vivians metal through Soley, Liverpool, they being the parties that made the Charter. I wrote you in my last to remit me, say $9000. and use the balance towards your metal or if it suits better, to pay for metal work and ships account in Havre and send balance home. Then you can have more to remit of the 1/2 coal freight. The metal is to be cash less discount. It will have to be paid either out of the cotton freight or the 1/2 coal advance. I think you will understand this as it does not make any difference which way you do it. Hope you will get a good suit of metal and a good job caulking. Suppose you will tow over to Cardiff. In towing, should think you could save some ballast. See Eugene has got over to Dunkirk all right. Business looks better now for ships. Hope it will hold as we are having a very hard winter here. Hoping this will find you all well.

> I am yours
> *N.B. Lewis*

                                     G.T. SOLEY & CO.
                                     28 Brunswick Street
Capt. Frank Gullison   Liverpool 6th Feb. 1888
Ship *N.B. Lewis*   Havre

Dear Sir:

Your favor of 3rd inst. received today and contents have our attention.

A Liverpool tug has gone to Havre to take the Cashmere to Cardiff, about 80 pounds is the price asked, and 20 pounds Cardiff Docks to Lundy, but we think we could secure a good boat here for about 70 to 75 pounds. Have you tried Cardiff? They might do it cheaper.

---

18 'Breakwater' would be for Philadelphia and 'Hook' would be Sandy Hook for New York.

When you get through your dock work, will you kindly let us know what it costs you per sheet to strip, caulk and remetal? We would like the information for reference.

> We are, Dear Sir,
> Yours truly
> *G.T. Soley & Co.*

N.B. Lewis Esq.   Havre Feb. 8th 1888

Yours of the 19th ult to hand this morning with enclosed copy of metal bill. Will I return it again as I have one similar. We finished discharging tonight. Cotton came out all right, expect to get in dry dock tomorrow night. I shall send you £1800-0-0 and keep the balance for expenses here. I have an offer of £75-0-0 stg. to tow ship to Cardiff one of W. & T. Jolliff powerful tug-boats, including Havre. All the ships are towing from here as it is quite reasonable.

> From yours most respectfully
> *Frank Gullison*

N.B. Lewis Esq.   Havre Feb. 9th 1888

Dear Sir:
Enclosed please accept 2nd bill of exchange to the amount of £1500.0.0.

   Fifteen hundred pounds

Franque has forwarded 1st bill today's mail. Your last letter ordered £1800.0.

   I asked for exchange draft for this amount but Mr. Franque thought it would be advisable to send £1500 by this mail and the balance to make up New Orleans disbursements by next or following mail. I trust it will meet your wishes.

> Yours obediently
> *Frank Gullison*

N.B. Lewis Esq.   Havre Feb. 13th 1888

Dear Sir:
Enclosed please accept 2nd exchange to the amount of £200.0.0 (Two hundred pounds Stg.). I wanted to send three hundred but Mr. Franque thought it would be advisable to send balance after settling bills; we hauled into dry dock yesterday and commenced work. The metal is in very bad state. I counted about three hundred sheets entirely gone; the remainder, with the exception of the runs aft, is *very very* thin. I am keeping a sample;

find ship quite slack especially buts and wood ends, also six bolts broke on rudder brace and one dumb brace which will have to be renewed *'Having splendid caulking done'*.

> Yours most respectfully,
> *Frank Gullison*

G.T. SOLEY & CO.

Capt. B.F. Gullison   Liverpool 13th February 1888
Ship *N.B. Lewis*   Havre

Dear Sir:

Your favor of the 11th received this morning, and as requested we engaged the tug *Thomas Joliff* now at Havre about to tow the *Tuskar* to Cardiff, to tow your ship, to be ready about end of this week or first of next, or as soon as she can get back, a couple of days grace on either side, the ship to wait a day or two for the tug, or tug for ship, use of tugs hawser, price agreed £70. Messers Joliffe would like the preference of towing ship to Lundy for £20,[19] should one of their boats be available at Cardiff when the ship is ready. We wired you as requested 'Engaged Thomas Joliffe' and trust everything may turn out satisfactory. We are pleased to hear your cargo turned out well, and hope your metalling will be equally satisfactory.

> We are, Dear Sir,
> Yours truly
> *G.T. Soley & Co.*

G.T. SOLEY & CO.

Capt. B.F. Gullison   Liverpool 18th February 1888
Ship *N.B. Lewis*   Havre

Dear Sir:

Your telegram received yesterday stating 'ready Monday night Joliffe will be too late reply' to which we replied 'No other screw available Paddle tug wants 90 pounds'. We saw the owners of *Thos. Joliffe* and found she had put back to Havre with the *Tuskar*.

Your message just in 'Cannot wait Joliffe must try elsewhere if contrary wire', to this we do not reply as you are of course free so far as she is concerned and we hope you may secure suitable tow − if not when the *Joliffe* reaches Cardiff, we can get her to go back for you. It is unfortunate

---

19 The proposition was that the firm of Joliffe would tow the ship from Havre to Cardiff for £70 but would like to have the business of later towing ship out of Cardiff harbour (to Lundy Island). It is interesting to note that at this time the tug boats with screw propellers were beginning to replace the type using side paddle wheels.

that the weather should so upset your arrangements. We hope you will get around without any other vexatious delay.

> We are yours truly
> *G.T. Soley & Co.*

N.B. Lewis Esq.   Havre Feb. 19th 1888

Dear Sir:

Yours of 2nd inst to hand on 16th contents noted which shall have attention. I came out of dry dock on Friday, was detained there one day after work was finished on account of bad weather which has lasted here about one week. Two ships left here Thursday under sail and have become total wrecks, all hands saved. The ship *Tuskar* left here same day in tow; had to put back after coming very near going ashore. She still remains here. As the weather looks finer today, think they will make a start as she has the boat I engaged. I shall have to look elsewhere. Will have my ballast in about Thursday night; will take from 250 to 300 tons beside what I have in, making in all about 500, better to be *sure* than *sorry*. Shall settle a/c tomorrow; think they will be near £600 stg. Copper and dry dock and carpenters expenses.

> Yours obediently
> *Frank Gullison*

The following letter to Frank Gullison is from his brother Ralph. From previous letters we know that Ralph wrote Frank at New York in the fall of 1885 asking if he could join the ship for the next voyage. He was then 16 years old and apparently was thinking of following in the footsteps of his two elder brothers and becoming another sea captain. Frank advised Ralph against this plan but added that if his 'ma' and 'pa' agreed he would take him.

Ralph joined the ship in New York and, as mentioned elsewhere, made the voyage to Shanghai, San Francisco and Dunkirk. He decided the life of a sailor was not for him and returned to his home in Nova Scotia to resume his education.

At this time he was almost 19 years old. He later graduated from Acadia University and went to India as a missionary.

Brookville Feb. 19th/'88

Dear Brother Frank:

This is a beautiful Sabbath afternoon. We were all down to Beaver River this morning, and listened to a sermon on benevolence by the Rev. Cahoon Porter of the Hebron baptist church with whom Mr. DeWolf made a change to-day.

Father and Mother have gone over to see Della. She is quite smart and doing nicely. I steal a few minutes every night to play with little Bowmie. I think he is as cunning and smart as they make them. Father goes over there and gets down on the floor and lets Bowmie roll him and fist him, as he calls it.

Mrs. John Tedford who has been a great sufferer for sometime died last night, leaving two children and a husband to mourn her death, which was caused by a cancer in her stomach. There was an old Mr. Cann at Port Maitland taken sick a week ago – was seized with three strokes of paralysis leaving him speechless. These two diseases are getting more common every day. Poor old Aunt Susy Kelly is ailing. She is not expected to re-cover. Grand-ma is better again. I guess under the head of sick, that will do for now.

I don't suppose you like the news of going to Cardiff again, on account of it being such a dirty place. I had a letter from little Billy, our cabin boy and he would like to get with you again. I told him where you was going and advised him to write you.

Capt. Theop. Corning or at least the Ship *Munro* is chartered for Shanghai with cases of case oil at thirty cents. Thank you very much for the pencil you sent and Leila says to thank Frank for her present. I will put on my coat and see Aunt Susy and Clara will finish.

From *Brother Ralph*

Dear Brother Frank:

This is a beautiful Sabbath day and I am keeping house. Pa and Ma and the baby is over to Della's place and I don't know much news for Ralph has told you all. I was over to your dear wife's place last night. She had put Bowmie to bed and he heard my voice and wanted a kiss. When I came out he wanted me to kiss again and Della told him to lay still or she would shut the door, and Bowmie said, why Mama I am astonished at you. He is smart and hearty. Frank, my pen you sent me is just lovely. Well, I don't know anything to write but I have great fun with Bowmie. Don't be disgusted with this letter. I will put a little more etiquette next time.

[Continuation of Ralph's letter:]

I suppose you would like to know how I am progressing in school, and judging from my letter you have the opinion that I am not making much head-way. But you must make an allowance for I have not taken up writing or spelling this winter. My time is more important for other studies. I have taken the full Academy's course and it gives me all I can jump to. I am not naturally very quick to learn and my memory is poor, in fact, it has been so long since I went to school, to the others it is mostly review, but my teachers encourage me greatly (taffy on the broom-stick). I want to try to stay here until next fall then enter the college, after a year in the academy. By so doing will save about $100.00.

I don't know whether I will be able to keep on the right side of father, till that time. It is pretty hard, Frank, to see poor old Dad get up and go to the shore or woods etc. and not able to assist him except on Saturdays. And of course it is hard for Dad to see the way things are going. He gets out of sorts and acts cross at times but such is life. He says if I don't get away next summer that I will have to go to work. However, I think that I can come to an agreement with him sometime. I study from 8 until nine o'clock at night and from four to seven in the morning. Uncle William Raymond expired on January with paralysis. He and his wife were here last summer. She is one of the best little women that lives I think. Poor Mother can't think of taking up a pen because of her hand.

I was over to Della's last night.[20] We had frosted cake and barbadoes tamarinds and brown bread etc. Our lodge has a pie social on Thursday. The old cow hasn't had a calf yet and corn-meal is 4.00 per bbl. That's all the news.

Ralph

N.B. Lewis Esq.   Havre Feb. 22nd 1888

Dear Sir:

I finished ballast today and settled all accounts and now ready; tug boat has not arrived owing to *'bad weather'*. The docks are crowded with wind-bound ships, some having been detained for two weeks and tonight it is piping from N.N.E. and prospects for tomorrow start not very encouraging. Mr. Franque will forward all vouchers which may arrive as soon as this; gave him a check on Soley and Co. for the amt. of £59-9-3 stg. to square accounts; I will now *sir* give a note of expenses. Jones carpentering and dry dock expenses including extra work in dry dock; new dumb brace and copper bolts for rudder and one extra day's dock dues on account bad weather F5711.90 or £228 stg; copper bill 370-15-10 pounds. Total expenses F27438.65 or 1090-0-0 pounds Stg. I have not paid my wages here thought best to do so at Cardiff; also towage there which will be 70 pounds. Having such a poor return on old copper made the new come high and now sir I will say we have a *'good job done'* everything in *first class order* the expense of which I will leave for your good self to judge. Waiting your reply, I hope you will receive your 1500 pounds and 200 pound drafts in order.

From your obedient servant,
Frank Gullison

---

20 At this time Captain Ben Gullison and Captain Frank Gullison were next door neighbors so it
    was easy for the family to visit back and forth.

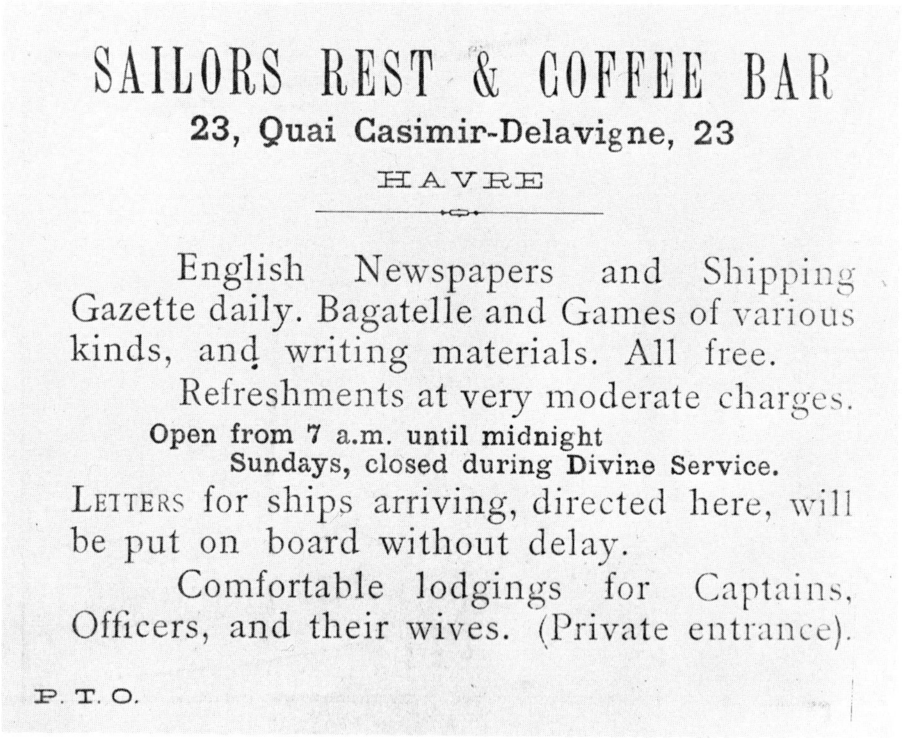

SAILORS REST & COFFEE BAR

23, Quai Casimir-Delavigne, 23

HAVRE

English Newspapers and Shipping Gazette daily. Bagatelle and Games of various kinds, and writing materials. All free.

Refreshments at very moderate charges.

Open from 7 a.m. until midnight

Sundays, closed during Divine Service.

LETTERS for ships arriving, directed here, will be put on board without delay.

Comfortable lodgings for Captains, Officers, and their wives. (Private entrance).

P. T. O.

FIG. 47. Business card for Sailors' Rest & Coffee Bar, Havre.

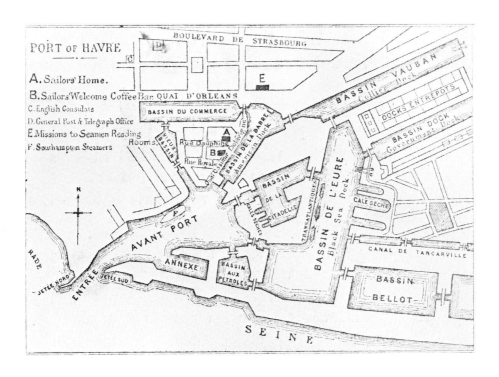

FIG. 48. Reverse of business card for Sailors' Rest & Coffee Bar, Havre, with map of dock area.

APPROVISIONNEMENT GÉNÉRAL DE NAVIRES

JARNET

SHIP CHANDLER AND PROVISION MERCHANT

14, Quai des Casernes

HAVRE

Imp. Maudet-Godefroy. — Havre

FIG. 49. Business card of Jarnet, Ship Chandler, Havre.

CHAPTER SIX

Loading the ship with coal at Cardiff was much simpler than unloading. Small railway carriages from the Welsh mines were brought to the docks loaded with coal which was transferred to *tips*. These latter had chutes which could be placed directly over the holds of the ships thus loading the ship by gravity. In the holds were sailors or stevedores who acted as trimmers to see that the coal was evenly distributed in the hold to keep the ship on an even keel.[1] This loading was under the general supervision of the first mate although the responsibility for a satisfactory job also rested on the contracting stevedore.

Unloading the coal at its destination was more difficult. Several methods were used depending upon the facilities of the port.

Sometimes the coal would be put in baskets or canvas bags and hauled up by means of block and tackle by men on the deck who then swung the tackle to unload the coal on the wharf or possibly a lighter.

Another method was to use larger wooden buckets which would be pulled up by a team of horses or oxen working on the deck. Horses would be harnessed to swivel trees to which a long rope was attached. The rope ran through a block attached to the dock and thence went up through other blocks and down into the hold of the ship. The dump bucket was lowered into the hold, loaded and when the horses received the command *Giddap* they started off along the wharf, thus pulling up the bucket. This was then swung out over the wharf and dumped.

The most up-to-date method was to use a donkey engine which served the same purpose as the horses or oxen but was quicker and more convenient.

---

1   Trimming a ship properly is a skillful job requiring much experience. Note that Captain Gullison often mentions the draft of the *N.B. Lewis* forward and aft. Trimming also covers the stowage of bulk cargo, especially under the side decks. Any empty spaces in the hold might allow the cargo to shift during the voyage.

G.T. SOLEY & CO.

Capt. B.F. Gullison   Liverpool 28th February 1888
Ship *N.B. Lewis*   Cardiff

Dear Sir:

We have your favors of 21st and 22nd from Havre, also your telegram about tug, to which we replied and today we have yours of yesterday from Cardiff, and are pleased to hear you got around in good time and have a prospect of quick dispatch.

Your bill of £59.9.3 from Havre was duly honoured and we will pay Watkins bill for towage when presented and send you an account of both, which you can remit us from Advance Freight. We are much obliged for particulars of cost of metalling and note you paid Vivians bill at Havre. We presume they allowed the 1% and 2 1/2% discount all right.

We are advising Charterers to credit ship with one fourth brokerage at Cardiff, as agreed with Mr. Lewis.[2]

You have a good freight to start on and hope you may strike good business abroad.

> Yours truly
> *G.T. Soley & Co.*

N.B. Lewis Esq.   Cardiff
Yarmouth   Nova Scotia   February 28th 1888

Dear Sir:

I arrived here at Penarth Dock Saturday night, had very windy weather towing around. I see Eugene[3] cleared on 22nd inst. Same day as I, he has had and is having a beautiful chance as we have had a continental N.E. gale blowing since his departure and I hope he will make a good passage. We hauled under ballast crane this afternoon. Will probably have it out in three days and have written notice given for cargo. I am well pleased with *Penarth* and everything looks favourable for a good dispatch. I hope to receive a few lines from you in the coming mail.

> Yours Respectfully,
> *Frank Gullison*

---

2   Soley & Co. had evidently agreed to give Nathan Lewis a discount on their regular brokerage fee.
3   His brother Eugene had been at Dunkirk in the ship *Otago.*

Capt. B.F. Gullison
Ship *N.B. Lewis*   Cardiff

G.T. SOLEY & CO.
Liverpool 29th Feby. 1888

Dear Sir:

Your favor of yesterday received and in regard to necessary disbursements, these are provided for in advance freight as per charter, and it is
better for you to draw against same, as is the usual custom, than for us to
make further advances.

We have today paid your order on demand £70 in favour of Watkins
for towage at Havre to Cardiff and now enclose an a/c for it and draft at
Havre, showing amount £129.16.9 due us which kindly remit to us out of
advance freight.

We note you would commence putting out ballast yesterday afternoon
and trust you will secure quick dispatch in loading.

We shall be glad to hear from you as to your progress

> and remain Dear Sir
> Yours truly
> *G.T. Soley & Co.*

N.B. Lewis Esq.   Yarmouth, N.S.

Cardiff
March 12th 1888

Dear Sir:

We commenced taking in cargo Saturday, have on board 600 ton. They
must have us finished by Thursday or else we will be on demurrage.[4] The
docks are so crowded with ships several steamers are on demurrage now.
The Ocean Co. *promised* me cargo *two days* after my ballast was out but
kept putting me off day by day, the consequence was I kept booms alongside nine days with the expectation of saving time and having a good dispatch but I got greatly disappointed *as I generally do*. We had a very heavy
blow yesterday, Barometer fell to 28.50 but this morning is looking fine.
Hope to get away about 17th.

> Yours Obediently
> *Frank Gullison*

N.B. Lewis Esq.

Cardiff March 16th 1888

Dear Sir:

We finished loading on the 15th inst. Have on board 2082 ton of coal beside 10 ton for ship use. I think it is about the largest cargo our ship *N.B.*

---

4 Demurrage is charged by the ship to the shippers if vessel is not loaded within the time set in the
   charter.

Lewis has ever taken. Draft of water F22-4 in. fore F22-8 in. aft and *tight* as a *bottle*. I squared up my business today. Expenses £837-12-8. Will enclose you receipt for money left in agents hands to the amount of £255-8-4 being balance of 1/2 freight collected they will send you Bank Draft to said amount also vouchers and supplement a/c should there be any small difference in disbursements sheet, which I will also forward you and trust you will receive all in order. Expect to sail in the morning. Wind has been easterly today and has the appearance of remaining for a while. I cannot think of anything more to inform you good sir, so will close my epistle hoping to make a *quick* and *successful* voyage I remain

Yours Most Respectfully
Frank Gullison

P.S. I had to draw £10.0.0 after squaring my personal account.   B.F.G.

Messers G.T. Soley & Co.   Liverpool   16th March 1888

Dear Sirs:

I beg to advise you that I have finished loading and will sail tomorrow.
  The quantity of cargo is 2,082 tons.
  I enclose cheque for £129.16.9 which I trust will be found in order.

Yours respectfully
B.F. Gullison

Towing down Bristol Channel March 17th '88

N.B. Lewis Esq.

Dear Sir:

These few lines will inform you that I left Penarth Dock this morning at 8 a.m. expect to discharge tug off Lundy at 4 p.m. Weather fine, wind northerly; looking Easterly; Sent you by yesterday's letter disbursement a/c and receipt for balance of freight. *Please* let me know what you think of *expenses* at our *last two ports*. One thing we have not been '*cheated*' out of our cargo this time. I like Penarth Dock much better than Cardiff and you will see by a/c it is the least expensive. I have everything arranged for discharging[5] with my crew. If I can *only keep them*, they came on board this morning quite sober but my cook has layed by on the shelf.[6] I think we are going to have a beautiful chance out and hope Sir to make a quick and prosperous voyage.

From Yours Respectfully
Frank Gullison

---

5   He is planning to have his crew discharge cargo.
6   His cook is drunk.

Cardiff, *March 2ᵈ 1888*

CAPTAIN OF *R. B. Lewis*

𝕸𝖊 𝖆𝖌𝖗𝖊𝖊 to Tow your Vessel ~~from Dock to Roads for Tariff and from Roads to Lundy, per stages, at £~~ · · ~~per stage, or~~ from Dock to Lundy Island for the sum of £ *19 : 0 : 0*

MARTIN & MARQUAND,

Per *J. A. Hawker*

AGENT.

Agent—J. A. HAWKER,
4, ELEANOR STREET, DOCKS.

FIG. 50. Statement of towage fee from Cardiff to Lundy Island, March 2, 1888.

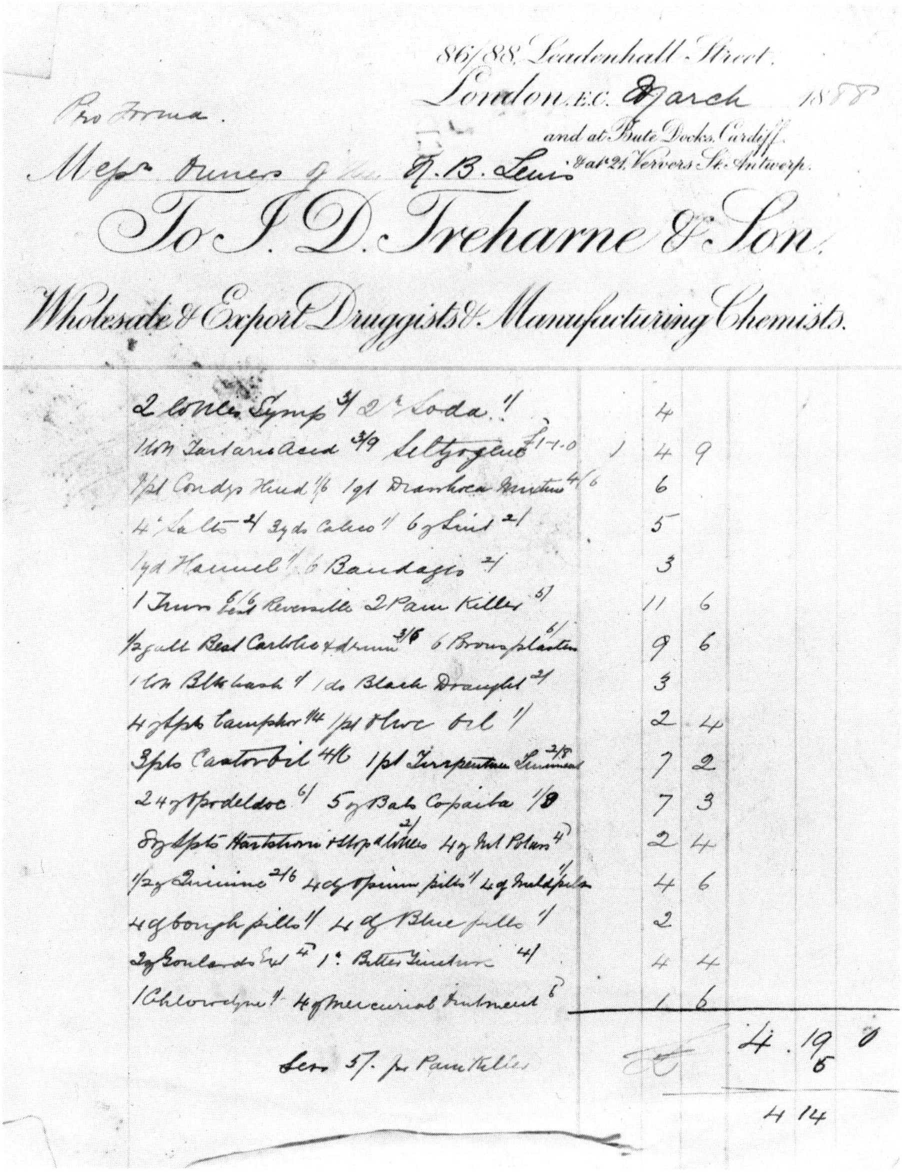
86/88, Leadenhall Street,
London, E.C. March 1888
Pro Forma.
and at Bute Docks, Cardiff,
& at 21, Ververs St. Antwerp.
Messrs Owners of the R. B. Lewis
To I. D. Treharne & Son,
Wholesale & Export Druggists & Manufacturing Chemists.

2 bottles Syrup 3/ 2 lb Soda 1/		4	
1 lb Tartaric Acid 3/9 Seltzogene £1-1-0	1	4	9
1 pt Condy's Fluid 1/6 1 qt Diarrhoea Mixture 4/6		6	
4 lb Salts 2/ 3 yds Calico 1/ 6 oz Lint 2/		5	
1 yd Flannel 1/ 6 Bandages 2/		3	
1 Truss 5/6 Pain Reliever 2 Pain Killer 5/		11	6
½ gall Best Carbolic & drum 3/6 6 Brown plaster 6/		9	6
1 lb Blk Wash 1/ 1 do Black Draught 2/		3	
4 oz Spts Camphor 1/4 1 pt Olive Oil 1/		2	4
3 pts Castor Oil 4/6 1 pt Turpentine Liniment 2/8		7	2
24 oz Opodeldoc 6/ 5 oz Bals Copaiba 1/3		7	3
8 oz Spts Hartshorn & Sp. Nitre 2/ 4 oz Nit Potass 4		2	4
½ oz Quinine 2/6 4 doz Opium pills 1/ 4 doz Mild pills 1/		4	6
4 doz Cough pills 1/ 4 doz Blue pills 1/		2	
2 oz Goulard's Ext 4 1 oz Bitter Tincture 4/		4	4
1 Chlorodyne 1/ 4 oz Mercurial Ointment 6		1	6
Less 5/- pr Pain Killer	£4	19 / 5	0
	4	14	

FIG. 51. Invoice of I.D. Treharne & Son, Druggists, London, March, 1888.

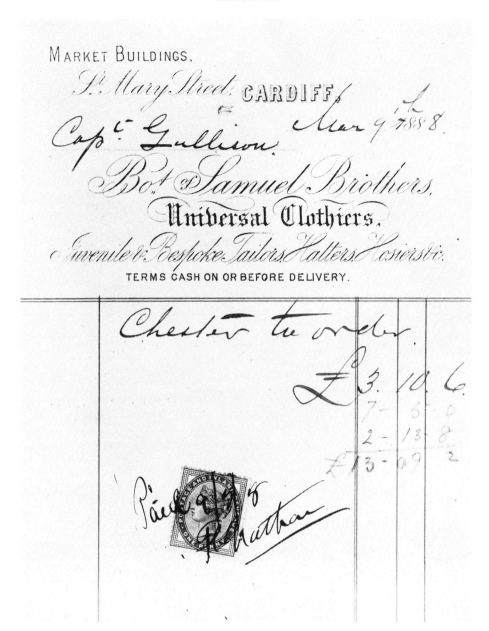

FIG. 52. Invoice of Samuel Brothers, Clothiers, Cardiff, March 9, 1888.

FIG. 53. Invoice of Arkell Bros., Drapers, Cardiff, March 10, 1888.

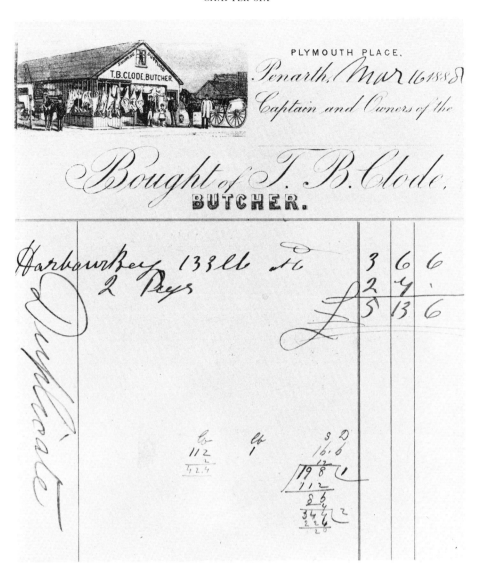

FIG. 54. Invoice of T.B. Clode, Butcher, Penarth, March 16, 1888.

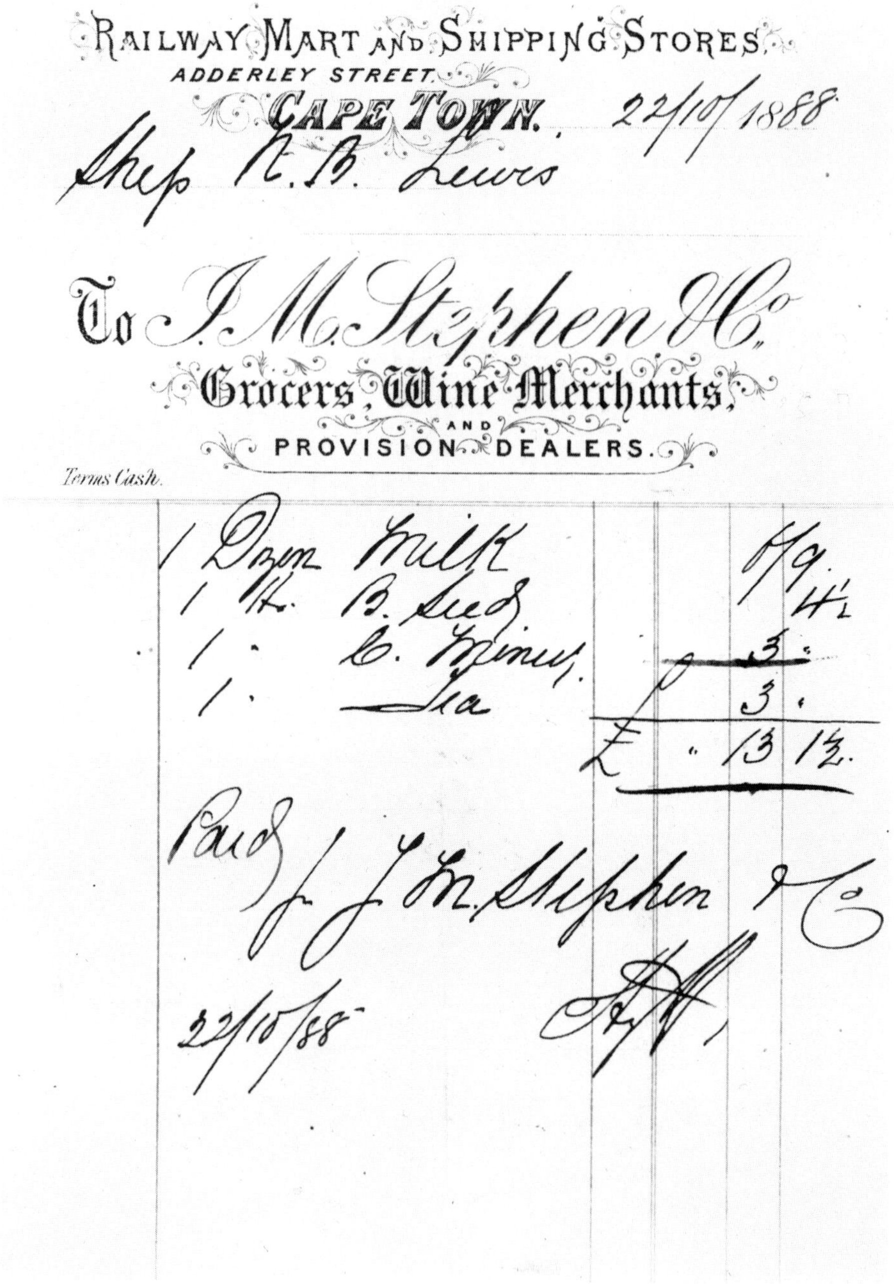

RAILWAY MART AND SHIPPING STORES
ADDERLEY STREET.
CAPE TOWN. 22/10/1888

Ship R.B. Lewis

To I.M. Stephen & Co.
Grocers, Wine Merchants,
AND
PROVISION DEALERS.

Terms Cash.

1 Dozn	Milk			1/9
1 tt.	B. Seed			4½
1	C. Wines		3	
1	Tea		3	
		£	. 13	1½

Paid f/ I.M. Stephen & Co

22/10/88

FIG. 55. Invoice of I.M. Stephen & Co., Grocers & Wine Merchants, Capetown,
Oct. 22, 1888.

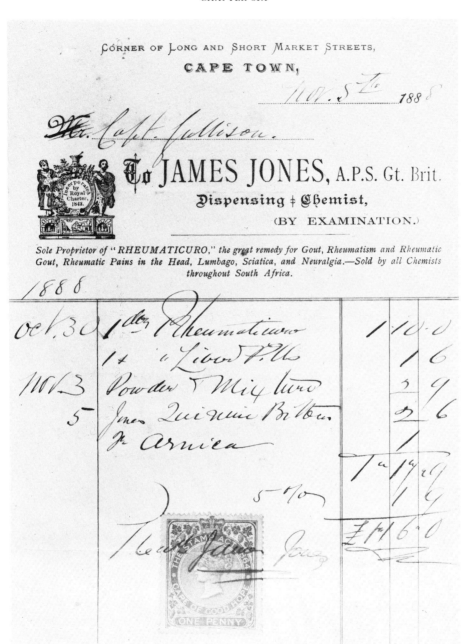

FIG. 56. Invoice of James Jones, Dispensary Chemist, Capetown, Nov. 5, 1888.

Capt. B.F. Gullison   Ship *N.B. Lewis*   G.T. SOLEY & COMPANY
c/o Messers Wilson & Sons   Rio   Liverpool 4th April 1888

Dear Sir:

Your letter of 16th March, from Cardiff was duly received with enclosed cheque for £129.16.9 and we are obliged for your attention. We note your sailing with a fine fair wind, and trust this may mean you safely arrived all well.

We got a copy of your metal a/c from Vivians, and found that they had not allowed you full discount at Havre, so collected the difference £2.7.6 and remitted it to Mr. Lewis.

> We remain
> Yours truly
> *G.T. Soley & Co.*

Capt. Gullison   Yarmouth April 7, 1888

Dear Sir:

Suppose you are getting along towards Rio pretty well by this time. Cardiff a/c came to hand all satisfactory. Think you done all could be done to save money. Metalling means a good bill now with $7 \ 3/4^d$ per pound [of weight] but it must be done. If you don't hear anything to the contrary about ten days before you are ready to leave Rio, cable me and I will cable you orders. Freights now are very low in Atlantic North. Coal freights seem to be the best thing going now. Freights North may improve before you are ready. I don't see anything at present in the East or West Coast to go for. Remit me as soon as you collect freight what you have left in good bankers bills on London in as short sight as practical. Hoping to soon hear of your safe arrival and that will get a good dispatch.

> Yours truly
> *N.B. Lewis*

Capt. Gullison   Yarmouth Apr. 21/'88

Dear Sir:

I wrote you a few days since and will now drop a line. Hope you will have a good passage and soon report at Rio. I was asked a few days since to allow charterers to send vessel to Montevideo at 24s,[7] they giving orders at Rio on arrival. I told them it was worth at least 6s extra to shift — expect it would take two months longer. Coal freights seem to keep up pretty well.

---

7   This would be an increase of three shillings over rate of 21. Mr. Lewis says it would be worth six shillings more to shift from Rio de Janeiro to Montevideo.

I wrote you to let me know about ten days before you are discharged and I will give you orders if you have not received them previous to that time. Remit as usual. Hoping you will get a good dispatch and we may be able to find some paying business. Things are very flat in the States at present but hope they will improve later on. Coal freights have been 24s to Montevideo. Hope they keep up as it will help other business. Mr. Baker[8] chartered 3 ships to Cape Town at 23 shillings. Would make quite a difference in cargo such as N.B.L. Hoping to soon hear of your safe arrival.

> Yours
> *N.B. Lewis*

P.S. I will use Jones cable code when I cable.

N.B. Lewis Esq.   Rio de Janerio May 4th 1888

Dear Sir:

I arrived here today noon making passage in forty-seven days. Had a very poor chance down. Crossed the line on the 13th approximately Long. 29 10. We could not fetch down past Pernambuco. Was delayed beating around there in a strong Westerly current for three days, had three days dead calms off Abwhilse Rocks with heavy squalls or wind and rain from S.W. quarter the remainder of my passage, but thank the 'Giver of all Good' I am here at my destination and I think probably I shall feel a degree of Happiness when I leave again. One thing, there is no sickness to speak of.[9] I have not received any letters from you yet sir. Did not think it worth while to cable until ready to sail. I see by a circular April 11th that freight is still looking up. If I thought you had our good ship *N.B.L.* fixed again I think I would give it out to a stevedore as I would get a better dispatch as he and the merchants I presume are linked together.[10] I know I shall be bothered greatly as the lighters have poor attention and long days, but I think I shall try my luck.

I should like to go down to the Cape [Cape Town] again outside of *Curries people* or to *Simons Bay*. I think I could do a great lot better than last time. I hear that *Simons Bay* is a very *cheap port* indeed would like to try it.

Well, sir, the Good Ship *N.B.L.* was tight as a bottle this passage and

---

8 Mr. Baker: Hon. L.E. Baker was a prominent Yarmouth ship-owner. He was one of the organizers of the Yarmouth Steamship Company and was a leading promoter of the tourist trade.

9 He is probably referring to yellow fever.

10 He now thinks he will not save money by using crew to unload instead of hiring a stevedore.

behaved splendid with her cargo of 2100 ton and she looks tip top too. Will write to you often and hope to hear from *your good self* soon.

> Yours Obediently
> *Frank Gullison*

Agents at Havre for Vivian & Son
A. Christiansen   11 Quai de L'ile   Havre

Dear Sir:

I write you these few lines to inform you that on re-examining my copper bill I find you have made a mistake on discounting. The 2 1/2 and 1% should have been taken off before deducting the old metal which makes a difference of eight pounds and five pence stg. in ship's favour. Trusting you will rectify this error and remit the said sum of 9.0.0 pounds to our Agents at Liverpool, G.T. Soley & Co.

Please give this your immediate attention.

> Yours
> *B.F. Gullison*

G.T. Soley & Co.   Liverpool   Rio de Janerio May 5th 1888

Gentlemen:

I arrived here all well after a passage of Forty-seven days was pleased to receive a note from you. I do not understand the difference of £2.7.6.

On re-examining my bills on my passage here, I find a *blind mistake on my part.*

The discount should have been taken off before deducting the old metal which makes a difference of £8.0.5. Eight pounds and five pence in ship's favor. I have wrote to Christiansen about it and will enclose a copy of the same to you.

I am now waiting for the Customs movements. Will probably commence discharging about the 8th inst. See coal freights have rose since my departure.

> Yours Respectfully
> *B.F. Gullison*

Messers Wilsons Sons & Co.   Rio de Janerio May 7th 1888

Gentlemen:

I hereby give you notice that the Br. Ship *N.B. Lewis* under your charter has this day entered at the 'Customs' and is now ready for discharging cargo that the lay days will commence from the above named date trusting you will favor me with a quick dispatch.

I remain
Yours Respectfully
B.F. Gullison 'Master'

[notation in pencil:]
24 hours notice   commence 9th inst.

N.B. Lewis Esq.
Yarmouth   Nova Scotia

Rio de Janerio
May 14th 1888

Dear Sir:

I write you a few lines to inform you that I have out about 500 ton cargo. I had to give the discharging out[11] as first *one* and *two* and sometimes three men would be layed out to a time and I could not depend on them so I thought it advisable to do this @ 1.200 per ton. He pays me at the rate of 5/0 per day for my men all that I can give him.

I am trying to get a good dispatch and leave here soon as possible. Please let me know if I cannot buy a small donkey engine for discharging purposes as one would more than pay for itself in one cargo of coal here.

Yours Respectfully
B.F. Gullison

N.B. Lewis Esq.
Yarmouth   Nova Scotia

Rio de Janerio
May 22nd 1888

Dear Sir:

Your letter of the 9th ult. came to hand yesterday. Contents noted which shall have attention. I have about 1250 ton out tonight and expect to finish by Saturday or Monday next. We had three holidays last week; Liberation of the slaves in Brazil. I hope to sail about 3rd June. Will cable you tomorrow for orders thus; Lewis Yarmouth Nova Scotia same as Cape Town.

Wishing you Sir, compliments of the season.

Yours obediently
Frank Gullison

---

11 He has now decided to employ a stevedore.

N.B. Lewis Esq.   Rio de Janerio June 4th 1888

Dear Sir:

I squared up accounts today. My expenses here is about £532-0-0 including provisons which is near £64.0.0. I consider the expenses high, Sir, but I have *'saved time'*. I am going to do better *next time* by 150.0.0 if you will allow me to invest in a Donkey Engine about 45 to 50 pounds. I could sell it again after discharging. I will forward you vouchers and disbursements accounts, also first bill of Exchange to the amount of £559.2.3 registered; will send the 2nd by American mail. I could not obtain them under 90 days sight on Wilsons & Co. which they say is good as the Bank. I had to use four words in my cable to you as they would not accept the address alone. Received your 'Proceed to Cardiff'. I expect to sail tomorrow: Your letter of the 31st May to hand today. I do hope we will be able to get a good freight for the *Cape* or Montevideo. Rio is quite sickly. American ship *Theresa* went to sea yesterday in charge of the Mate. Well, Sir, I will close my letter hoping to make a quick and successful passage.

> Yours Respectfully
> *Frank Gullison*

Enclosed please find first bill of exchange.

The following letter is from Mr. Thomas Corning, the mother of Frank's wife Della. It refers to Della's trip home to Yarmouth from New Orleans in December 1887. (See letters dated Dec. 6th and 10th, 1887, from Frank Gullison at New Orleans).

> Brookville June 31st 1888
> Yarmouth County
> Nova Scotia

My Dear Son:

I received your kind letter. I was much pleased to get it. It has been a long time – something like four years – not so long as that. I will try to answer in my poor simple way. You wanted me to write you all about Della's travel after she left the ship for home. Della has written herself and others so I will be behind all the friends as I am with everything. Well, dear, I had my nerves all shaken up as you can imagine when I heard that my poor Della was in Yarmouth aboard the boat in her berth laying there – could not move – uncertain whether she would ever be any better. I arose from my bed in haste – dressed and went to her as fast as the horse could take me, when we got there everything seemed still as death. We stepped softly when we went into the cabin to find my child in her state-room all alone. Quite a number aboard the boat asleep. We would not have known where to find her if her state-room door had not been open. All we could see was her eyes. Her face was white as the sheet — still she was quite chipper, but it was only excitement. The sight of her lashed onto her bed and carried on a hand-barrow up to her boarding house was a sad sight and almost killed me. She is now in her snug little home as well as can be expected. I thank the Lord for his kindness for it is in and through him that we live and without him we are nothing. I feel very lonely at the present time for your little boy has been with us for seven weeks and Della a fortnight. It seems that half the house has gone. Oh Frank, I think that if you had come to Boston with Della she would not have been sick on the boat. She was too sick to come alone with the care of little Bowman. If she ever gets over this she will do well. For all concerned do not take her from home again until she gets strong again or you will not have her long. Well, dear Son, we shall all go sooner or later. We know not when. You asked very kindly to forget the past. Do you think there is anything to ask forgiveness for? I did not know as you did. Do you think that anyone could forget being accused of making and talking what they never thought of. No God knows I am not guilty. You think I did and so do others. It is wearing me to death. Your father and mother have not been inside in three years. I have been in there four times this last summer. I shall not go again of course, for they do not want me. Well, God bless you all whatever comes of me. Since I commenced to write we have heard of your arrival. I am so glad for Della was getting anxious and Gene had arrived. I would like to see you very much indeed. Hope to before many months if God spares our lives. Della will write the news. This is my second attempt to write, and it is not fit to send. Excuse the poor writing and spelling. Write to me again if you think me worth writing to. I think of you often in your lonely cabin without your loved ones.

Mother C. (Corning)

Capt. F. Gullison   Yarmouth July 5, 1888

Suppose you are out now about a month for Cardiff. Shall look for you along in about a fortnight. You will find the ship closed through Soley, Liverpool for 21s Cape Town. Perhaps we might have done better by 6d but did not like to keep it open. It seems to be the best business going now, carying coal. Your a/c came to hand yesterday from Rio. Letters may be along today. Notice what you said about Donkey Engine in your last. As you are going to the Cape, perhaps it would be as well to leave it another voyage. I expect they would soon pay for the cost. I suppose Mrs. Gullison by this time is on way to meet you. Hope you will get a good dispatch in

Cardiff. If I want you to provision for longer than the voyage to Cape Town and back again this way, will let you know. I don't know what will be offering for the East from Cape Town. The rates lately have not been worth shifting for. Shall look for Eugene out in about ten days — hoping soon to hear of your safe arrival.

> Yours truly
> *N.B. Lewis*

P.S. Letter at hand with exchange notice. What you say about Donkey Engine, if you can get it for the price you name, better get one; that is if practical to use in Cape Town. Soley said something about arranging your advances in Cardiff. If there is any advantage in it had better do so. I will write you fuller about this in my next. N.B.L.

Capt. B.F. Gullison   G.T. SOLEY & CO.
Ship *N.B. Lewis*   Cardiff   Liverpool 13th July 1888

Dear Sir:

We were glad to get your favor of 5th May, from Rio de Janerio advising your arrival at that port, and we note by papers you are reported as having sailed again on 5th June; you had good dispatch. In reference to the discount on metal bill, it is the custom to take 2 1/2% off the amount remaining, after old metal has been deducted, and an additional 1% on gross amount for the new metal. In your case the 2 1/2% was taken off rightly, but instead of allowing further 1% on new metal, they took it off net amount. This we had rectified and remitted the difference £2.7.6 to owners as advised you.

Acting on instructions from Yarmouth, we have fixed your vessel to load at Cardiff for Cape Town @ 21/6, under the enclosed copy of charter, which we hope will be found in order. It is the usual form Cape [of Good Hope] Charter, Curry's, but we got the allowance for weighing reduced from 2% to 1 1/2%.

Ship is free of consignment at Cardiff as we thought you would prefer your own agents for doing ship's business. We are sending this c/o Capt. Robinson of Messers Elliott & Sons, and trust to hear of your safe arrival all well.

We shall be glad to be of service to you in any way we can.

> and remain, Dear Sir
> Yours truly
> *G.T. Soley & Co.*

Capt. F. Gullison   Yarmouth July 19/'88

Dear Sir:

I am looking for you along, hope to soon hear of your arrival. I wrote you last month Mr. Kelly of the firm of Soley & Co. was here last week. He thought that he could make some arrangements through their friends on Bristol Channel that could make things easier for you. You will be able to judge of the matter. They will most likely write you in reference to the matter. I wrote you in reference to Donkey Engine. If you can get one for about price named better get one that is if you work one to advantage in Cape Town. In provisions, better calculate on coming back in Atlantic. If you should go East, suppose could fit up without making much difference. Hoping to soon hear of your safe arrival,

> I am yours
> *N.B. Lewis*

Capt. Frank Gullison   G.T. SOLEY & CO.
Ship *N.B. Lewis*   Cardiff   Liverpool 20th July 1888

Dear Sir:

We beg to enclose you a letter to our care received today. [See next letter.] The writer has just returned from Nova Scotia and when in Yarmouth was told by Mr. Lewis that you would report at Cardiff to agents of our recommending as the charter for the Cape does not bind ship to any. This is of no other importance to us than making it more convenient to supply you with funds for disbursements, as we have to collect advance freight after you sail. We beg to recommend Messers Tylor and Lewis, collier agents and shipbrokers. Will you please call on them, as we are tendering you our service here, we are

> Yours truly
> *G.T. Soley & Co.*

N.B. Lewis Esq.   Cardiff
Yarmouth   Nova Scotia   July 23rd 1888

Dear Sir:

I arrived here on the 20th inst. making a very good passage of forty-four days all well and everything in order. Docked Saturday afternoon and hauled right under-ballast crane, working tonight will have all discharged tomorrow 10 a.m. and written notice given for cargo; received charter party on arrival and think it much better than last time to the Cape; hope to have a good dispatch here and get away soon; if I can strike a good bargain for Donkey Engine think perhaps it would be advisable to so do as it would come in handy for all purposes. Will pay crew off tomorrow wages a/c about £140.0.0 not including self not much repairs to do this time *'thank fortune'* waiting your orders in reference to stores I remain,

> Yours obediently
> *Frank Gullison*

Capt. B.F. Gullison   Ship *N.B. Lewis*   G.T. SOLEY & CO.
Liverpool 24th July 1888

Dear Sir:

We are pleased to note your safe arrival at Cardiff, and trust this may find you ready for loading and that you may have a good dispatch. Messers Tyler and Lewis write us you have reported to them, for which we thank you, and that they will furnish you with what you may require for disbursements, meantime taking your order against the Advance Freight, which is payable after sailing. They will then remit us the balance, if any, which we will forward to Messers Lewis [H. & N.B. Lewis], Messers Tylor and Lewis will also collect or charge in account, the brokerage which is due us under the charter. We will account for returns to Messers H. & N.B. Lewis, when remitting balance of freight.

We explained the metal a/c in writing to you before which we trust is satisfactory to you.

> We remain
> yours truly
> *G.T. Soley & Co.*

N.B. Lewis Esq.   Cardiff
Yarmouth, Nova Scotia   July 30th 1888

Dear Sir:

I have nothing of any importance to write as I think of. We are laying to the buoys waiting for cargo; think probably they will order ship under tip Thursday. I have ordered six month's stores. Should your orders require more can do so easily. We are having very disagreeable weather here, rainy and blowing near all the time. East Bute dock is so full of shipping that there is hardly room to move.

I was to Liverpool to meet my wife and made the acquaintance of *Capt. Kelly*,[12] and I wish, Sir, to acknowledge *your great kindness* to *cable* allowing me the privilege of taking wife the voyage.

> Yours very respectfully
> *Frank Gullison*

---

12 Captain Kelly, of the firm of Soley & Co. Liverpool, had recently visited Yarmouth.

Captain B.F. Gullison Ship *N.B. Lewis*   G.T. SOLEY & CO.
Cardiff   Liverpool 1st August 1888

Dear Sir:
We trust this will find you at a loading berth. This East wind will make
you feel like getting away.

We have been through the Havre metal account with Vivians and find
that the agent at Havre in making up a/c took 2 1/2% discount *off the old
metal* which is different from the custom here and makes the 2 1/2% disct.
due off the gross of new metal instead of balance so you were right in
demanding a further return from them. They have paid £5.9.11 to us with
apologies for the error and we enclose you cheque for said amount which
with return previously sent Messers Lewis will make everything right.
> We remain
> yours truly
> *G.T. Soley & Co.*

Captain B.F. Gullison   G.T. SOLEY & CO.
Ship *N.B. Lewis* Cardiff   Liverpool 3rd August 1888

Dear Sir:
We have your favor of the 2nd inst. and are glad to learn you are getting
loaded. Hope you may finish before the holidays. In regard to disbursements at Cape, £400 is the sum that should be in the charter — they came
to us from London with only £300 which was not according to agreement,
and we have a letter authorizing £400, and it must be our oversight that
your copy is not altered same as ours. You will find £400 all right and we
think charterers agents at the Cape will have no objection to increasing it
if required, anyway, we will write them to furnish you with more funds, if
required, taking if necessary, a short draft on us. What had you last time?
No doubt your hat[13] has suffered deterioration on the Rio voyage, and we
have much pleasure in enclosing you a fund for its renewal at our expense.

We enclose a letter which came in this morning,
> and remain
> yours truly
> *G.T. Soley & Co.*

---

13 This is a little present the agents are giving the captain — a custom of the time.

N.B. Lewis Esq.   Cardiff
Yarmouth, Nova Scotia   August 7th 1888

Dear Sir:

I settled up my business this afternoon. Have on board 2082 ton coal: expenses here is £959.7.1. Gave Tylor & Lewis and Co. an order on Donald Currie and Co. to the amount of One thousand three hundred and fifty seven pound, sixteen shillings and three pence £1357.16.3 being 2/3 advance freight less deductions as per charter party they will remit balance to G.T. Soley & Co. who will a/c for returns and forward you. Brokers here, will forward all vouchers and I trust Sir, you will find everything in order. I expect to sail in the morning 5 a.m. if nothing prevents and I hope to make a quick and successful voyage. Wishing you compliments of the Season I remain

> Yours Obediently
> *Frank Gullison*

N.B. Lewis Esq.   Lundy Island August 8th 1888

Dear Sir:

These few lines will leave me at Lundy 5 p.m. and will be forwarded by tug boat. Wind West, dead ahead and blowing quite strong. I wrote you last night informing of expenses and hope you will receive all vouchers and that you will find everything satisfactory. *Hoping to make good time* I remain Yours Most Respectfully,

> *B.F. Gullison*

Enclosed please accept a/c of wages.

Captain B.F. Gullison   G.T. SOLEY & CO.
Ship *N.B. Lewis*   Cape Town   Liverpool 29th August 1888

Dear Sir:

We duly received your favors of 7th August from Cardiff and note contents. Messers Tylor & Lewis forwarded from Cardiff to us all a/cs and vouchers, excepting the riggers bills, which they say you took with you. We forwarded everything to Messers Lewis at Yarmouth with bank draft for balance of freight, which we have no doubt they have received before now and hope will be found in order.

   We have arranged with Messers Donald Currie and Co. that their agents at the Cape shall supply you up to £550, if required, under the terms named in the charter and we trust this will fit you out all right.

   We shall be pleased to have the opportunity of getting you a good freight next time and *will not press* Rio on owners. Freights are now booming 23/ Rio 25/ M. Video 22/6 Cape etc. Homeward freights from California and the East are also better. Oil has been up to 4/, 4/6 as you will see by circulars and papers. We will write again to meet you at Cape Town

> and remain
> yours truly
> *G.T. Soley & Co.*

Capt. Gullison   Yarmouth Sept. 6/'88

Dear Sir:

I have accounts and remittance to balance a/c £566-11-5 to hand today from Soley & Co. all satisfactory freights seem to be improving all around. Oil freights are from 4s to 5 according to reports. Cotton seems to be opening fair also coal freights to Rio are quoted 23s Cape Town 22/6. I think if you hear nothing to the contrary, proceed to Barbadoes for orders. If any other business comes up, I will cable you; not hearing from me proceed as above. Try to get as much stone in your ballast as possible so if you should take cotton or oil. There is a coal freight to be in the market this fall from Philadelphia to Honalulu, Sandwich Islands at $10.00 per ton. I think if we could get that, it would be fair business but it is a good way off and nothing may come of it. Hagar has the order but I think business will be fair both in oil or cotton by the time we should get around. Cable me when you arrive and you can find a word in Jones Code that will tell when you will probable be ready to leave. Take the word in Code Book 'Preemptor' would mean you would be ready October 31st. Find the word in the dates that will cover the date probable cable thus: Lewis Yarmouth Nova Scotia (here fill in the word to cover the date which will be all that will be required).[14]

> Yours
> *N.B. Lewis*

Capt. F. Gullison   Yarmouth Sept. 26/'88

Dear Sir:

I wrote you by last mail in reference to cabling on arrival and giving me probable time of getting away from Cape Town. Freights seem to be improving all around. Calcutta is offering $8.00. I believe N.B.L. should take about 2400 tons measurement goods. I think cotton from the gulf should be fair business this fall. I wrote you if you heard nothing to the contrary

---

14 The cable which was sent read as follows: 'Lewis Yarmouth Nova Scotia prefecture'.

to come to Barbadoes for orders. If I should make any charter or change, I will cable you in time. If I do so, to make sure you have got orders you can cable reply. For instance, if I should cable you 'Closed Calcutta' you can cable me the same back thus; Lewis Yarmouth Nova Scotia Calcutta or using the name of any other port I might order you to. If you don't hear from me by cable proceed to Barbadoes. When you leave you can cable me the word Barbadoes. Hoping to hear soon of your safe arrival and that you will get a good dispatch. Coal freights to Rio are 24s now — not bad business to come back to Cardiff for.

Yours
N.B. Lewis

N.B. Lewis Esq.   Cape Town Oct. 24th 1888

Dear Sir:

We arrived here on the evening of the 18th inst. making a passage of seventy one days all well. We had a very poor chance to the Equator Forty four days crossed in 25.00 degrees W. Long. from there to the Cape 27 days, towed to the North Jetty to lighter[15] next morning and will have to pay cartage from there to the coal stores which will amount to 1/0 per ton probably will have to discharge about 200 ton. I cabled you on arrival here this: 'Lewis Yarmouth Nova Scotia Prefecture'. I gave you as near as possible the time we ought to be ready. I think by the appearance of things now we might get a good dispatch, so I gave you the 8th Nov. Will proceed to Barbadoes for orders, according to your instructions, unless I hear anything from you to the contrary. I am very much pleased to see that freights are improving. I hope that the good ship N.B. Lewis will obtain one of them. I think we need a little encouragement after such a long spell of low freights; will write to you again about next mail.

Yours very respectfully
Frank Gullison

N.B. Lewis Esq.   Yarmouth, Nova Scotia   Cape Town Oct. 31st 1888

Dear Sir:

As the mail leaves tomorrow, I thought I would write you a few lines to inform you that we have discharged about 1200 ton coal and the prospects of a fair dispatch here this time say the 9th or 10th Nov.

I received your cable reading thus: chartered New York Cururbit: regardful which being interpreted from your code means oil in cases N.Y. to Java. 40¢ this is good business no mistake. It cheers me up greatly to see

15 Ship had to be lightened before entering harbour.

freights improving and I assure you nothing will remain undone that lays in my power to do, to get away from this port and arrive at N.Y. as quick as wind and weather will permit.

Yours Obediently
Frank Gullison

Captain's statement of his account with ship

Ship *N.B. Lewis* and Owners in a/c with B.F. Gullison Master 1888

DR	Pounds	Shillings	Pence
Stevedore a/c £173.3.6, Harbour towage £14.0.0	187	3	6
Boatman 15/0, Koch & Dinie ironmongers 14/9	1	9	9
Stephen & Co. Provisions £3.15.4 Heyland ironwork, 11/4	4	6	8
Kling, Blacksmith, 5/6 Duffett, tinsmith, 14/0		19	6
Eles, Boatmen £1.0.0, Ross & Co. ironmongers 15/6	2	15	6
Obletta, Green Grocers £1.8.0, £1.9.3, £8.0.6	10	17	9
Cambrinck, Butcher, £14.18.9 Shipping Office £1.0.0	15	8	9
Towage outwards £11.0.0			
Cash to Officers & crew £10.9.0 Personal expenses			
£3.10.6	13	19	0
Cash to B.F. Gullison Master Balance a/c	16	9	7
CR	£265	0	0

By Cash Donald Currie & Co. £265.0.0

E&OE [Errors and omissions excepted]

N.B. Lewis Esq.   Cape Town Nov. 9th 1888

Dear Sir:

I have settled up accounts today. Expenses £457.7.6 forwarded stamped bill of Lading, receipted to G.T. Soley & Co., who will collect balance of freight and remit you. I got the best of Currie gang this time and it makes me feel good. I made them pay for *'Lighterage'* which I thought I would have to pay on arrival here, but after talking with the *Habour Board*, I found that the ship was at *Cape Town dock* outside of Alfect Dock and under jurisdiction of said dock so I made them pay the Lighterage necessary to enter Alfect Dock Cape Town.

I kept very cool until I got my coal discharged and then I let out and gained my point. Will forward you all vouchers and personal a/c and hope you will receive all in order. I cabled you today Lewis Yarmouth Nova Scotia New York as ordered, I hope to make a quick and prosperous passage, Sir, and will close wishing you a *Merry Xmas* and a very *Happy New Year*.

Yours Most Respectfully
B.F. Gullison
(Sail in the morning)

Excerpt from log of voyage of the ship N.B. Lewis, Capetown to New York.

Saturday 10th November 1888

    9 a.m. received two men on board, weighed anchor, set sail and proceded to sea. Wing w.n.w. light breeze, passed between Robin Isl. & mainland.

    7 p.m. passed Dassen Island wind hauling w.s.w.

    Fresh breeze & fine weather, no ship in sight.

Wednesday 14th November 1888

    Fine weather predominated. Passed one brigantine bound north, Seaman exployed picking over ballast for stone and arranging the same.

Thursday 15th November 1888

    Seaman employed washing hold and cleaning ship.

Friday 16th November 1888

    Finished washing hold.

Saturday 17th November 1888

    Commencement s.e. Trades.

Monday 19th November 1888

    Men employed scraping yards.

Thursday 22 November 1888

    Men employed scraping yards.

Friday and Saturday

    Employed painting outside.

Sunday 2nd December 1888

    Fine weather throughout the day. Crossed the equator last night making twenty-two (22) days from Cape Town. All well and everything in order.

Monday 3rd December 1888

    Lost s.e. Trades.

Tuesday

    Weather squally throughout the day with dark passing clouds; doing very good wind N.E. Fresh breeze. I think this must be commencement of N.E. Trades is so we have had no Doldrums passing from a fresh S.E. to a N.E. wind in Lat. 3° 02′ W.

Tuesday 25th December 1888

Fine weather throughout the day. Have spent a very pleasant Xmas. All sail set.

Wednesday 26th December 1888

Arrived New York this day at 3 P.M. and made ship fast at 42 South St. Brooklyn making a fair passage of 46 days.

Paid $65.00 towing in & docking.

Captain B.F. Gullison
Ship *N.B. Lewis*   New York

G.T. SOLEY & CO.
Liverpool 15th Dec. 1888

Dear Sir:

Your two favors of 24th Oct. and 9th Nov. were duly received and contents noted.

We are very much obliged for the information you give us respecting Cape Town and congratulate you on getting on so well with Messers Currie. How did you manage to get B/L endorsed for full quantity without discount for non-weighing? or did you weigh out all right? We have collected balance of freight as per certificate and forwarded same to Messers Lewis – We are pleased to hear that your ship is fixed for a good case oil freight and hope to have the privilege of fixing her for a good homeward freight in due course. Freights are very good all over and better prospects for the next year, than for a long time past.

We have fixed several ships for Cape Town lately at from 28/ to 30/ and hope they will get out as well as you did. *Otago* is about loaded for there.

We enclose freight report, and with best wishes and compliments of the season, We remain

Yours truly
G.T. Soley & Co.

Capt. Gullison

Yarmouth Dec. 22/'88

Dear Sir:

I suppose we may soon begin to look for you along. Got letters and a/c from Mr. Cupe all satisfactory. I expect, as we are going to Java, it would be as well to sight the bottom[1] as they are very particular there and with a ship under charter to come back they take every opportunity and chance

---

1   Sight the bottom – to put the ship in dry dock to examine the hull and in particular the copper sheathing.

to make you dock your ship if they can find any metal rough or off. We may be able to fix back from Java same voyage as *Euphemia*. It only cost her loading and discharging about £400 including 2 1/2% commission. It saves a good deal in time and expense to load there. *Euphemia* was 9 months 8 days on the round trip. With the chances of loading in Java think we had better sight metal. Let me know what you think of it on arrival. Shall probably receive balance of Cape Town freight from Soley & Co. next mail. Expect we could do some better now on ship if not chartered. Hoping to soon hear of your safe arrival. Telegraph arrival also what you think about sighting metal.

Yours

N.B. Lewis

p.s. I am of opinion it would be safer to sight metal and get certificate of being in order. Suppose it would cost about $300 to $400. Many thanks for the pictures; they are very nice; wishing you the compliments of the season.

Yours

N.B.L.

You may work out enough stone out of your dirt from ballast under your oil. Should think 100 tons would not be too much. Hope she will take the high 7% right.[2]

Capt. Gullison   Yarmouth Dec. 26th/'88

Dear Sir:

I omitted to mention when I wrote you about sails we can save about 8 cents per yard by getting them made in Yarmouth. We can ship them through in Bond.

Hoping to soon hear of your safe arrival.

I am yours

N.B. Lewis

N.B. Lewis Esq.   New York Dec. 29th 1888

Dear Sir:

I arrived here on the 26th after a fair passage of forty six days and reported to J.F. Whitney and Co. My expenses at Cape Town will be eleven pounds cheaper as I sailed out [instead of using tug] and will credit ship to said amount. I telegraphed you the amount for docking received reply 'do

2   Additional note to letter dated Dec. 22, 1888.

not want Guineres Creek, prefer Townsend Egett dock'. As I have not made any arrangement for this place, I suppose it will be all right, my figures to you was for the best dock in New York, Sectional Dock above the bridge. I think perhaps it would be advisable to sight her bottom, but *cannot think* there is any metal off. Surveyors fee will be $12.00. I think we will have a good dispatch as the charterers gave me considerable encouragement. I suppose we had better fit for one year's stores. Received your note concerning sails. Will take canvas enough for Main Top Gallant sail. I made onboard this voyage mizzen top gallant sail, main lower topsail, inner jib and outer fore topmast staysail and all our old sails are in good repair. I am paying Mr. Patten off today. Very sorry to lose him, he is a good man, *can recommend him highly*; Have shipped another N.S. man today by the name of Graves, has appearance of a *good* man.

Discharging ballast slowly, will get enough stone for oil. Had about 75 ton picked out on arrival here. I would like you to see the *N.B. Lewis* this time very much, she gets great praise.

Yours respectfully
B.F. Gullison

Capt. F. Gullison   Yarmouth Dec. 28/'88

Dear Sir:

I was glad to hear of your safe arrival in such good time. I telegraphed you in reply to yours to give preference to Townsend and Edgett but not to go to Gunieres Creek. Any how I have no love for that place. Of course, if you have got any other dock it is all right. I believe their dock, Townsends and Edgetts, is very easy access. Notice you expect to have ballast out on Monday. Suppose you will find enough stone for Dunnage Bottom and any ballast required. Hope Mr. Churchill [Stevedore] will get a good cargo in. Tell him he must do his best. Suppose Mr. Hagar [Philadelphia agent] will supply any funds you may want to pay off crew and other purposes. Hoping you will get a good dispatch. I believe Java is a bad place for worms. Capt. Cann[3] said they got in around his rudder pintals[4] where the metal was off. You will please see that every exposed place is covered with metal. If you could not get into such places as around the rudder, might give it a good coat of copper paint. Let me know about sails if you require them as I suppose you will need some. Hoping to hear from you soon by mail.

I am yours truly
N.B. Lewis

---

3 Capt. Herbert Cann had recently been in Java in command of ship *Euphemia*.
4 Pintles – heavy pins on the forward edge of the rudder (to which they are held by heavy straps) by which the rudder is hinged to the gudgeons on the sternpost. A vessel like the *N.B. Lewis* would have had at least 5 sets of gudgeons and pintles.

Capt. Gullison   Yarmouth Jan. 3/'89

Dear Sir:

Your letters at hand yesterday by Mr. Patten. Notice what you said about
sails. Will have upper topmast and main topmast staysails ready to go by
Dominion[5] Saturday. Will send canvas for top gallant sail; Mr. Weddle-
ton, Yarmouth sailmaker, will cut it. We can save quite a little sum on
these sails. Will have Spencer[6] made if I hear from you in time. I telegraphed you this morning asking you to reply when you got out of the
dock. Hope you will find metal all right. I expect the *Lewis* is looking fine.
Should like to run on board and see you but can't this time. Hope they
will load you up quick. Would like it if we could strike a good freight back
from Java. If not, shall have to shift to some of the other ports. With the
S.W. Monsoons will be in good position to go to Manilla, Hong King,
Singapore or any of those ports. I suppose it will be best to take a year
stock of provisions especially the heavy stores. Capt. Cann in Euphemia
sold several bbls. of salt provisions and had quite a lot when he arrived. Of
course he did not know he was going to load in Java. Suppose shifting
from there would make 3 months difference at least in length of voyage.
Tell stevedore to figure her up for a good cargo. Better write Eugene[7] to
the Cape (Capetown) and give him any points you can about the place.
Got ballance of freight account yesterday from Soley, Liverpool. *Euphemia*
is now loading expect you will be getting away about the same time. I will
write you by *Dominion* when I send sails. They will go from Boston by
steamer next Monday or Wednesday in bond.

Yours

N.B. Lewis

P.S. Capt. Herb Cann sold in Java 3 bbls. salt provisions and had when he
arrived 14 but don't you go short. Lay in plenty for a year's voyage. It
seems to me his crowd could not have eaten much — appetites must have
been poor.

N.B. Lewis Esq.   New York Jan. 6th 1889

Dear Sir:

We went on dry dock Thursday and came off Friday; copper in good
order with the exception of a few places on the keel or shoe, which used
up about one half dozen sheets. Metal surveyors have taken our classification and will have it endorsed to that effect. We commence to load in the

5   *Dominion* — a steamer operating between Yarmouth and Boston.
6   Spencer — a gaff sail on the after mast of a square rigger is always the driver or spanker, while
    gaff sails on any other square-rigged mast are known as 'spencers'.
7   Evidently Capt. Eugene Gullison was taking the *Otago* to Capetown with a load of coal.

morning, I telegraphed you on Friday, in loading berth, commence loading seventh; make spencer[8]; send four bolts No. 5; one bolt number one,
two, three, and four (canvas). The No. 5 is for making a mizzen topmast
staysail, the other for any necessary work. I thought it better to wire you
as perhaps you would have the sails off before you received a letter. My
crew have all left but two. All forfeited one month's pay, steward on a
drunk today. I told Capt. Churchill what you said about the loading, he
said he would certainly do his best. Yesterday and today has been stormy,
cold, raw wind N.E. with light rain. Rather poor prospect for doing any
work.

Yours respectfully
B.F. Gullison

Yarmouth Jan. 5/'89

Capt. Gullison:
Your telegram at hand this morning. Glad you are in loading berths. Presume you found metal all right. It is worth something to know that. I am
sending tonight by steamer *Dominion* one bundle of sails marked L. They
will go by the Metropolitan line of steamers to New York from Boston.
Will probable get off Monday next if *Dominion* gets over on time, if not on
the Wednesday boat. I got the spencer [sail] in time for today. The saving
if any is only in the making as I have ascertained today that they are making 37 1/2% on canvas. If so you had better get it in New York for your
top-gallant sail and spare canvas; we have sent the *Euphemia* about 1800
yds. of sails; all the saving is in the making. Hope they will give you a
good dispatch. We have very fine weather here for the last ten days.
Eugene on way to Cape. *Otago* was detained by bad weather but sailed
29th and passed Lundy Island. I will enclose bill of lading by *Dominion* for
the sails. The agent in Boston will ship them by the Metropolitan line.
Hoping they will arrive in due time. They are shipped to Java by the ship
N.B. Lewis in bond; this is the way we do it. After they are on board you
appropriate them to the ship's use.

Yours
N.B. Lewis

---

8   Captain Gullison was asking to have spencer sail made in Yarmouth.

Ship N.B. Lewis & Owners in account with B.F. Gullison Master

DR	$ ¢	CR	
To wages from Aug. 26th		By Cash Rec.	
to Jan. 26th	350.00	Cape Town £27.6.9	
5 months at $70.00		By Cash G.T. Soley	
Cash and supplies made during		Copper a/c £5.9.11	$159.48
voyage £67.3.2 @ $4.86	326.38	By Cash J.F. Whitney	
		& Co.	549.88
Expenses N. York travelling			$709.36
& board	17.20		
Aug. 1st cash paid cooking			
Cardiff			
8th paid water			
” ” Boatman			
” ” Watchman	15.78		
	$709.36		

N.B. Lewis Esq.,   Jan. 15, 1889
Yarmouth, Nova Scotia

Dear Sir:

On the 15 day of each month commencing March 15/'89 Please pay to Mrs. Emerson Graves Twenty Dollars, the same being half pay of her husband for services rendered as Chief Mate of Ship *N.B. Lewis*. These payments to continue until I inform you of the contrary.

> *B.F. Gullison*
> Master

[The above was countersigned by Emerson Graves to validate the notification for the benefit of N.B. Lewis.]

N.B. Lewis,   *Nite Telegram*   a/c N.B. Lewis
Yarmouth, N. Scotia   N.Y. January 16, 1889

Disbursements sixty three hundred sixty eight dollars fifty two cents cargo forty eight thousand seven hundred ninety one cases. Sail Friday.

> *B.F. Gullison*

N.B. Lewis Esq.   January 16th 1889

Dear Sir:

We have settled a/c today and would be ready for sea tomorrow but our sails detens us. We received instructions tonight concerning them and I think probably we will get them onboard tomorrow. I think the time and expense will amount to more than they would have come to here. I had to employ a customs Broker, also cartage, literage[9] and Sutra [etc.] will come to considerable. I towed from my loading berth direct to Staten Island, made ready for sea and tonight crew is all onboard and everything in order. I cabled you this evening disbursements $6368.52 cargo 48,791 cases seven less than I informed you in last letter, draft of water 22.00 and 22.06. I expect you will think expenses high especially store bills but I have tried to work economical but somehow bills will swell in spite of one. I paid myself off up to 25th inst. and hope you will receive a/c of wages and that all business will turn out satisfactory. I hope to make a quick and prosperous voyage. I gave my 1st officer half pay note on you, will you please accept.

> Yours respectfully
> *B.F. Gullison*

Capt'n Corning[10]   New York
January 17th 1889

Dear Father:

We expect to sail in the morning if weather is favourable. I received your cable in answer to my letter and thank you for so doing. If Father goes away he will hand you over my business account. Please get your house painted next *spring* or *fall*. I think Uncle George Goudey will be a good hand as he and wife Della were talking about suitable colours. Have the fence also painted to correspond with the house, also roof painted *brown*, window sashes drawn and sectra. We have on board 48,791 cases, will make a very good freight if everything goes favourable, which I trust will. We are all well, thank the Good Lord and trust ere long to meet you all at home. As I am in a great hurry, I will bid you Good Bye again. Della is writing to Mother Corning. Kiss her for us, also Love to Lila and all the family.

    Please write to Java in care J.F. Van Leeveven, Batavia, Java.

> From your Loving Children
> *Frank & Della*

---

9 Literage – transportation from shore to ship.
10 Captain Thomas Corning was Della's father.

N.B. Lewis Esq.   New York Jan. 18th '89

Dear Sir:

We are towing down the bay, wind Westerly and light, weather looking fine. I informed W.F. Hagar our disbursements and sent him vouchers and he will remit you. Gave J.F. Whitney draft on him for disbursements. Hope you will receive everything in order. Please let me know what you think of all my bills. J.F. Whitney recommended me to a good house in Batavia, J.F. Van Leeveven & Co. I think they would be good people to send letters to. I have a good crew onboard and everything in order. Hoping to make a quick and successful voyage from yours,

Most Respectfully
Frank Gullison

Capt. Gullison   Yarmouth Feb. 27/'89

Dear Sir:

Hope you are well on your way by this time; have not much to say at present; don't know as yet anything about home business; I think it will be as well to leave that until your arrival, unless something turns up that is really good. If we could get same business from Java that *Euphemia* got – only I think should command better rate the way business is now – but time will tell. On your arrival at Batavia, cable your arrival and I will see what I can find in the way of business and cable you. If you don't hear from me in a week and can get an offer of freight to load at Java or any of the other ports, you can submit it to me and we will decide and let you know but do nothing positive until you hear from us as we might be about making a charter or, in other words, if we did not understand each other, get chartered twice. Remit your freight as fast as you can collect Bankers Bills. *Euphemia's* were drawn on Baring Bros., London. I think 60 day date bills would be most profitable if you can get them at as good advantage. We had quite a fall short in our cases in *Euphemia* – cost about 50 pounds – think mate must have been careless.[11] Don't see if oil is

---

11 It would appear that the *Euphemia* delivered about 140 cases short of the consignment recorded on her bill of lading. By the custom of the sea, the first mate was normally responsible for the safe-keeping and delivery of cargo. However, the shortage might well have not been the fault of the mate. Captain Gullison was to have similar difficulties in accounting for his cargo, and it would appear from his letter dated August '89 (page 225) that port customs and procedures in Surabaya provided abundant opportunity for undetected pilfering by stevedores and lightermen.

    It is interesting to note that two days after this letter was written in Yarmouth the *N.B. Lewis* and the *Euphemia* under the command of Capt. Herb. Cann of Yarmouth signaled each other in Lat. 34° 35 N, Long 29° 17 W about 200 miles South of the Azores, one on the way to Java and the other returning. See letter from Capt. Gullison dated June 12, 1889.

piled in a block and counted how there can be any mistake unless they steal it. I thought your bills were all right and reasonable in New York. I think you have large load of salt provisions. If you load at Java should think you could sell some beef and pork if you have a chance. You will be able to judge yourself. In any case always be sure you have got plenty, don't go short. Hoping to hear in good time of your safe arrival and that we will get a paying freight home.

> Yours
> *N.B. Lewis*

P.S. The bottom is out of freight now. [Freight rates are very low.] N.B.L.

The next letter would have been sent by steamer to Java and so arrive before the *N.B. Lewis*.

Capt. Gullison   Yarmouth March 21st 1889

Dear Sir:
Suppose you are getting pretty well along on your way to Java. I have closed the ship to load at Java from two ports. This is a duplicate of *Euphemia's* business last fall. Her rate was 27/6, our rate now is 33/9 this is equal to $8.10 gold. This is good business to load up without shifting ports. I think 30 clear days for loading this clear of Sunday and surf days. If wet, sugar paid on intake weight, if dry in baskets on delivery custom weight. The *Euphemia* took in about 1940 tons and was paid freight on 1900 tons. The charterers are the same parties. Soley in Liverpool made the charter and will probable send you the charter party at once from England. Hoping you will have a good passage and good dispatch. I have not seen charter party yet. I expect they have. Ship is to arrive in Batavia by July 1st and be ready for cargo not later than July 31. You will see this gives lots of time. I expect it optional with them whether they commence to load you before July 1st. I have not seen this charter party but think it is about like *Euphemia's* in these clauses. Hoping this will find you in good health and safe arrival in Batavia. You will cable arrival. *Euphemia* had 26 1/4, 27 3/4, 28 3/4[12] on cases and 27/6[13] back to Boston. She made a good round. Should think Lewis would gross $8000 profit on round trip if all goes well.

> Yours
> *N.B. Lewis*

---

12 These are rates on cases of oil from New York.
13 27/6 is return rate on sugar to Boston.

Capt. B.F. Gullison   G.T. SOLEY & CO.
Ship *N.B. Lewis*   Batavia   Liverpool 22nd March 1889

Dear Sir:

We have fixed your ship by cable authority received from Yarmouth, to
load at one or two ports in Java for New York, Boston or Philadelphia
direct, as ordered on signing B/L at 33/9 on dry sugar net weight delivered, option of wet sugar payable on net intake weight and we have
much pleasure in enclosing copy of Charter, which we trust you may find
in order and at top rates.

   We fixed the *Euphemia* to the same people last year. She carried a cargo
of dry sugar to Boston and everything turned out most satisfactory on
both sides. We believe she did very well at 27/6 so your business ought to
be a good one. With big freight out she will make a fine round. The merchants say if sugar is ready they will give you cargo before 1st July if ship
is ready, but we scarcely think you will be able to get to loading port and
ready for cargo much, if any, before that date.

   Freights are keeping up here and the prospects are for a good year in
Atlantic trade. Barrel Oil is the only sick business at present being 1/9 for
U.K. and Cont. but this will right itself when the season comes on. Deals
60/, 62/6. P. Pine 16.5/, 6.10. Quebec 28/. 29/ and coal to Rio 29/ Montevideo 31/ Cape 28/ B. Ayres 34/ &c are current rates. We trust this will
meet you on arrival all well and that you may have a pleasant voyage altogether.

                                        We remain
                                        yours truly
                                        G.T. Soley & Co.

                                        Yarmouth April 4/'89

Capt. Gullison:

I wrote you some time since in care of J.F. Vanleeveven which you will
receive no doubt on your arrival at Batavia. I got Charter Party yesterday
from England. See by the terms you have to arrive at your final port of
discharge July 1st and they are not bound to take you before that time.
This should give you ample time. You may be able to facilitate matters in
the way of dispatch by a little grease.[14] Some times a few dollars and a
little attention goes a long ways with some of these folks. Hope you are
getting well along and will have a good passage. Freights don't seem to
improve just now. *Otago* is on her way up to Montreal 17 1/2 Lumber
River.[15] I wrote you in my last about all I could think about. Do all you

14 A bribe to facilitate work being done more quickly loading, unloading, etc. (A term used was
    'greasing the palm'.)
15 A load of lumber to the River de la Plata @ $17.50 per thousand.

can to facilitate dispatch and get along as easy as you can with the Dutch-men. I believe they are never in a hurry. Capt. Cann had it quite sickly when he was there. Look out for health and your crew also. You will keep enough money out of Inward Freight to load her out and remit me as soon as you can collect. I see *Euphemia* remitted in Bankers Bills on Bar-ings London 30 days sight. A sixty day Bill at the same rate would be cheaper than 30 days sight by about a gain of 30 days. I merely speak about this. You will be able to judge in these things best, being on the spot. Hoping to soon hear of your safe arrival at Batavia and that you may have a good dispatch. You will cable on arrival.

> Yours
> *N.B. Lewis*

Yarmouth April 25/'89

Capt. Gullison:

I have written you twice before in reference to business and don't know as I can say much that I have not written before. The Charterers say they will be ready with cargo as soon as ship is ready. Hope soon to hear of your safe arrival. If you can facilitate dispatch by using a little grease, do so. Some times it will go a good way in the way of getting dispatch. I wrote you about remitting in my previous letters. Prospects seem good for busi-ness this fall again. Suppose your father is getting his ship loaded. Don't know if he will go or not. Writes me he has bought another small part. Eugene should be nearly half passage to Montreal now. Expect it will be well to keep a sharp look out for the tally[16] of those sugar folks. I believe you can insist on sealed lighters[17] if you choose to. Sugar has taken a great jump on this side. I don't know how this will affect freight. Hoping to soon hear of your safe arrival and this will find you all well.

> Yours
> *N.B. Lewis*

Capt. Gullison   Yarmouth May 9/'89

Dear Sir:

I will drop you a few lines. I have written you three times before this. I am now looking daily to hear of your safe arrival. See the Bottom has gone out of freights East entirely. We have the *Euphemia* at Melbourne and can't get an offer. We are thinking very seriously of ordering her back in

---

16 The count as given by stevedores is not always correct.
17 Sealed lighters would have cargo in an enclosed space to prevent stealing.

ballast. Think it would be better than taking a low freight and spending say five months to get it when we could be in New York in say 95 or 100 days. It would take 50 or 60 days to get up to the East India Ports and probable 50 days there even if we could get any business for her to do. Hope you will soon arrive so as to have no chance of losing our freight which looks good just now.

See you have to be at last Port of Discharge July 1st. In the event of your finding yourself jamming for time perhaps you could get consignees of oil cargo to let you discharge at first or second port by paying them something. In the event of anything turning up to hinder you getting your cargo sooner than say an indefinite time for business I would sooner clear out in ballast for United States. In that case you might pick up something for ballast and that would give enough to pay your inward bills this side. I only heave out[18] these suggestions hoping to soon hear of your safe arrival and that you will get a good dispatch and good cargo of sugar which should make us a good round.

Yours
N.B. Lewis

The following Note of Protest is included here as it gives a description of the weather during the voyage — gale force winds were encountered in the North Atlantic and it was at this time a sailor was killed in a fall from the fore top-gallant yard. The filing of a Note of Protest shows that damage to the ship was not due to any fault of the Captain, and thus an insurance claim can be made if necessary. It is included here primarily because of the description of weather during the voyage.

NOTE OF PROTEST

On this eighth day of June in the year of our Lord One Thousand Eight Hundred and Eighty-nine personally appeared and presented himself before me Samuel Rushton Lankester, British Vice Consul at Samarang, B.F. Gullison, Master of the British ship *N.B. Lewis*, Official Number 80609 and 1325 Tons Register, which sailed from New York U.S.A. on or about the 18th day of January last past, with a cargo of Petroleum bound for Samarang and arrived at Samarang on the eighth day of June instant, and fearing damage owing to boisterous weather during the voyage, he hereby notes his protest against all losses, damages, —c reserving right to extend the same at time and place convenient.

Signed before me British Vice Consul
at Samarang this 8th day of June   *Sd. S.R. Lankester*
One Thousand Eight Hundred and 89   British Vice Consul

18 'Heave out': a sailor's expression.

NOTE OF PROTEST.

On this *eighth* day of *June* in the year of

our Lord One Thousand Eight Hundred and *eighty nine* personally

appeared and presented himself before me *Samuel Rushton Lampester*

British Vice H.B.M. Consul at *Samarang. R. F. Gullison*

Master of the British *ship* the *R. B. Lewis*, Official Number

88609 and *1325* Tons Register, which sailed from *New York U.S.A.*

on or about the *18* day of *January* last past, with a cargo of

Petroleum bound for *Samarang* and arrived

at *Samarang* on the *eighth* day of *June* instant, and fearing

damage, owing to* *boisterous weather*

during the voyage, he hereby notes his protest against all losses, damages, &c., reserving

right to extend the same at time and place convenient.

British

Signed before me, Her Britannic Majesty's

Vice Consul at *Samarang*   *pd S. R. Lampester*

this *8* day of *June*

One Thousand Eight Hundred and *89*   *British Vice Consul*

I certify the foregoing to be a true and correct copy of the original Note

of Protest, entered in the Acts of this Consulate and copied therefrom.

British Consulate, *8 June* 18 *89*

S. R. Lampester *Vice* Consul.

* Here designate shortly the suspected source of damage, e.g., "boisterous weather," "collision," "fire."

M. & Co. Ld. 5000 8-83

FIG. 57. Certification of Captain Gullison's 'Note of Protest' to the British Vice-Consul, Samarang.

I certify the foregoing to be a true and correct copy of the original note of Protest, entered in the Acts of this Consulate and copied there from.

British Consulate   8th June 1889

S.R. Lankester   Vice Consul

PROTEST

BY THIS PUBLIC INSTRUMENT OF PROTEST be it known and made manifest to all people that on this 17th day of June one thousand eight hundred and eighty nine personally came and appeared before me Samuel Rushton Lankester, Her Britannic Majesty's Consul at Samarang.

Frank Gullison Master of the British Ship *N.B. Lewis* of Yarmouth N.S. of registered tonnage 1326 tons or thereabouts, official number 80609, Emerson Graves Mate, and Alexander McQuarrie seaman of the said vessel, who did severally and solemnly declare and state as follows: that is to say,

that on the eighteenth day of January 1889, these appearers and the rest of the crew of the said vessel, set sail in her from New York, bound on a voyage thence to Batavia for orders, laden with a cargo of Petroleum, the said vessel being then tight, staunch and strong, well manned, victualled and found in every respect fit to perform her said intended voyage.

That on the 19th of January a strong breeze from the North West set in, with a heavy sea, causing the vessel to ship some water.

That on the *following day* set in under like circumstances, the wind veering towards North around noon. That on the 21st of January the wind increased with heavy squalls, causing the ship to labour heavily and ship heavy seas for and aft. That towards night the wind increased to a gale from the South West, accompanied by heavy rain, which continued during the night and part of the following day, the vessel lying to and shipping heavy seas. That the wind afterwards moderated and veered to the North West, but that it again increased towards evening, the day ending with a strong gale and heavy sea. That on the *23rd of January* the wind and sea moderated towards the evening and all plain sail being set the vessel proceeded on her way, with fair wind and moderate breezes until the *27th of January* which day began with a fresh breeze and squally weather. That the wind increased during the day, a heavy sea getting up, which caused the vessel to labour heavily and ship much water. That the sea calmed down during the next day, but that the wind increased again on the 29th of *January* with a heavy head sea which however abated on the *next day* after which the vessel sailed on her way with fair wind and weather until the *3rd of February*, on which day heavy squalls and a head sea caused the vessel to labour heavily. That during the *following* day the violence of the wind increased causing the vessel to ship much water and that on the 5th of February and the *following days* heavy weather was experienced the ship labouring heavily and the sea running mountains high. That on the *8th of February* the wind moderated, and the sea began to go down, and that all plain sail having been set the vessel proceeded on her way. That up to the *6th of March* variable winds, rain and squalls of more or less violence were met with and that on that day a heavy squall blew away the mizzen top mast and staysail. That the *next day* with a light variable wind, all sail was set and that the weather continued fair until the *27th of March* which began with heavy squalls from the South East which increased in violence during the day causing the vessel to labor heavily and ship much water. That this weather continued the *following day* the ship laboring heavily through out, but that on the *29th March* the weather began to improve and continued fair until the *12th of April* on which day heavy squalls from the North West set in, causing the ship to roll and ship heavy seas. That the squalls moderated during the following day but set in with renewed violence on the *14th of April.* That similar weather prevailed during the following ten days, the sea only beginning to moderate on the *20th of April* when all sail was set, and the vessel proceeded on her way with steady breezes till the *3rd of May*, which day commenced with a strong breeze from the North which increased towards night, causing the ship to labour heavily. That the wind moderated on the following day but that the sea remained rough the vessel continually shipped heavy seas. That on the 5th of May the weather continued very uncertain, the wind veering continually, but increasing in violence towards midnight, with heavy squalls and rain and a very heavy head sea causing the vessel to ship heavy seas. That the weather improved on the *following day* and that nothing further worthy of mention in these presents took place until the *13th of May* which began with a strong breeze. That the wind increased during the day and was accompanied by heavy squalls causing the vessel to ship heavy seas for and aft. That on the *next day* the wind was less violent, the sea still remaining rough and the vessel labouring heavily. That the same kind of weather prevailed with the same results during the following 2 days. That on the *17th of May* the violence of the wind increased assuming the character of a hurricane towards the morning of the *18th of May*, the ship running under lower topsails and reefed fore sail and shipping very heavy seas throughout the day, and it was not until the morning of the *next day* that the wind began to moderate and the sea calmed down. That during all these days the pumps, lights and look out were properly attended to. That the 19th of May commenced with a fresh breeze and that all sail was set and the vessel proceeded on her way, nothing further worthy of record taking place until the *31st of May* when Java Head was made at 2 p.m. That the ship passed New Anjer on the following day and anchored in Batavia Roads in ten fathoms of water on the *2nd of June.* That orders were received to proceed to Samarang, at which port the vessel arrived on the *8th of June* and anchored in 7 3/4 fathoms of water.

And this appearer Frank Gullison further declares, that on the eighth day of June, he appeared before me, Her Britannic Majesty's Consul, and caused his protest to be duly noted.

And these appearers do protest against the aforesaid Bad Weather, Gales, Storms, Accidents, and all loss and damage occasioned thereby, the same being entirely owing to the facts and circumstances before mentioned.

And the said appearers do solemnly and sincerely declare that the foregoing statement is correct, and contains a true account of the facts and circumstances; and they make this solemn declaration, conscientiously believing the same to be true, and by virtue of the provisions of an Act made and passed in the sixth year of the reign of his late Majesty King William the Fourth, intitled 'An Act of repeal an Act of the present Session of Parliament, intitled, 'An Act for the more effectual abolition of Oaths and Affirmations, taken and made in various Departments of the State, and to substitute Declarations in lieu thereof, and for the more entire suppression of voluntary and extra-judicial Oaths and Affidavits, and to make other provisions for the abolition of unnecessary Oaths.

Signed – *F. Gullison*, Master

Signed – *Emerson Graves*, Mate

Signed – *Alexander McQuarrie*, A.B.

Declared and protested before me the said Samuel Rushton Lankester Her Britannic Majesty's Consul at Samarang this 17th day of June one thousand eight hundred and eighty nine on eight foolscap pages of which this is the eighth.

Signed – *S.R. Lankester*, British Vice Consul

ATTESTATION CLAUSE

This Form of Attestation is only to be filled up for Copies. In the Original which is to be preserved in the Consulate it is to remain blank.

I, Samuel Rushton Lankester Her Britannic Majesty's Vice Consul at Samarang do hereby certify and attest to all whom it doth concern, that the foregoing is a true and faithful copy of the original Protest entered in the Acts of this Consulate, copied there from and compared therewith. In testimony whereof I have hereunto set my name and affixed the Seal of this Office at Samarang this 18th day of June one thousand eight hundred and eighty nine.

S.R. Lankester, British Vice Consul

Ship *N.B. Lewis*   Samarang

N.B. Lewis Esq: Yarmouth, N.S.   June 12th 1889

Dear Sir:

I wrote you a few lines at Batavia but I did not think of cancelling date in charter at the time. I tried very hard to get Merchants here to take all the cargo, when this failed I tried to get them to take the half but it is no use they have no facilities for giving a quick dispatch in fact they only want part of the cargo here and part at Sourabaya. They say they will take it from us as fast as they possibly can, we have up to date discharged about six thousand. I have engaged help from the Stevedore here, I received your cable but could do nothing as stated above. I cabled yesterday, Impossible ship ready sugar charter advise I will not report myself to sugar merchants until last of the month. I do not like to appear too anxious. I have talked to several experienced people in the business here. They think our merchants will hold us; more so if weather continues dry. Custom of port discharging here is 15 to 1600 [cases] per day. I feel greatly worried about this business, my long passage has made bad work all around. I will here give you a few remarks concerning it. Sailed from N.Y. Jan. 18th. Signalized ship *Euphemia* Feb. in Lat 34° 35′N Long 29° 17′ w. Between these two dates I lost twenty days on my passage owing to continual gales or more properly called Hurricanes from South & SE I never saw the wind blow so steady from this quarter before in the N. Atlantic it was something unusual in fact the whole passage has been a *hard one.*

March 5th Edward Anderson A.B. fell from the Fore top Gallant yard to deck and died eight hours after. Crossed the Equator March 11th Long. 27° 58′ w Passed Cape G.H. [Good Hope] Apr. 22nd, Java head May 31st. Came to anchor Batavia June 1st., Samarang 7th.

June 14th up to date 7530 cases discharged. There is small talk of discharging all cargo here. First lot seems somewhat damaged by steam and seawater. I do not know of anything more to inform you Sir, so will close trusting things in general will turn out all for the best.

I remain Dear Sir
Yours Obediently
B.F. Gullison

Capt. Gullison   Ship *N.B. Lewis*   June 7th, 1889

Dear Sir:

We expected to have seen you in passing Anjer[19] but weather etc. has been so bad that we have missed you in passing. We now enclose our cards trusting that in passing this way when homeward bound and if requiring water or fresh supplies we may have the pleasure of doing business with you. Having no funds, shipmasters can always have what they require and we will accept their draft for any amount.

Our place is at 4th Point, now Anjer, where the post and telegraph office is stationed and all letters sent to our care are forwarded on board vessels passing Sunda straits free of charge.

The anchorage here is good and safe at all times as the reef that was formerly off 4th Point entirely disappeared with the eruption of '83[20] leaving deep water close to the rocks. Vessels anchor anywhere off the Point in from 13 to 15 fathoms, mud always giving the cable buoys a good berth. There is a Red light 1000 yards to the Eastward of 4th Point light-house,

---

19 Anjer was on Sunda Strait between the islands of Java and Sumatra. This strait was used by most ships going to the Far East.
20 The eruption of '83: an allusion to the explosion of the volcanic island of Krakatoa in August, 1883, which killed 36,000 people, scattered debris across the Indian Ocean, and caused many changes in the configuration of Sunda Strait.

VAN BRUGGEN & KRUISINGA,
SAMARANG.

Scheepsleveranciers.	Shipschandlers.	Fournisseurs de navires.
Belasten zich met laden en lossen van schepen, leveren koelies en bronwater aan boord.	Take charge of stowage and discharge of the ships, deliver coolies and wellwater on first demand.	S'occupent avec le chargement et déchargement des navires. Fournissent des coolies et de l'eau à bord.
Groote voorraad van alle scheepsbenoodigdheden.	Great stock of all shipsprovisions.	Grand magasin de toutes sortes de provisions.

FIG. 58. Business card of Van Bruggen & Kruisinga, Samarang.

which is a range for the cable. Vessels coming into the roads at night *must not* anchor with this light in sight.

We have late home papers to which captains calling here are welcome. Being the only ones here in our business we have all the vessels that call for water, supplies or for orders and trust we may add the *N.B. Lewis* to our list of American ships, also have the pleasure of making your acquaintance. We have the only *water boat* in *Anjer*.

Trusting to have the support of shipmasters in general,

> We remain
> Yours truly,
> *Scott, Rairden & Co.*
> Anjer Point 7/6/89

P.S. Our Captain Rairden was along side your vessel on the 2nd when off Batavia but did not go on board as he was in a hurry to get on shore to be in time for the English steamer that he had to pilot down.

N.B. Lewis Esq;   Surabaya July 1st 1889

Dear Sir:

Since my last letter to you dated Samarang June 12th ult. I have had many difficulties to contend with but I feel happy to inform you tonight that everything has turned out all for the best respecting our sugar charter. I cabled you today 'ship ready sugar' and hope you will receive it in order: I arrived here on 29th ult. with about 16000 cases on board; received lighters same day and discharged 3000, worked double gangs Sunday and this morning I held survey and sent report of same with written notice that our good ship was ready to receive cargo one hour before the time according to charter would expire. So you see Sir, that I did not have much time to spare. I finished discharging at Samarang on the afternoon of the 26th ult. and as good luck would have it I got a chance to tow to Surabaya for the sum of £40.0.0 Stg. (forty pounds sterling) that same night by the French steamer *Cheribon*. If I could have not got this chance I should have lost my charter, and as it was I had to leave my freight there in the hands of a firm called J. Daendels & Co. to settle my accounts and as they have only squared up today with Petroleum merchants I will not receive it in time to send by this French mail which leaves tomorrow. The draft will be £2454.0.0 Stg. Expenses at Samarang F 1906.58 @ 11.9[21] equals £160.4.4 not including commission. Sugar is very scarce here now owing to heavy rains and a very backward season. I know our sugar merchants did not want ship, but they cannot help themselves now. There is a merchant

21 'F 1906.58 @ 11.9' – i.e. 1906.58 Dutch florins (gulden) at 11.9 to the pound sterling. The florin was thus worth about 41.9 cents. It is currently (December, 1974) worth about 38.6 cents.

firm here which have 36 steamers[22] chartered to load this month and there is no cargo in market yet. I expect our sugar merchants will send me pedaling all around North coast for cargo. They asked me on my arrival here why I did not inform them that I was short of time and they would have tried to help me but I knew even if they did it would all mean money and I suppose now they will try and find fault as my cargo will not be discharged before tomorrow noon. Anyhow, I feel somewhat better in mind than I did a week ago: let what will come. I tried very hard to get a quick dispatch at Samarang. I offered them a store house for their oil for one month but they only laughed at me and said they did not as a rule put their oil in other store houses and that the ship would be discharged according to custom of Port but it came out all right after all. I left three men in prison at Samarang for refusing duty and attempting to stab 2nd officer. The Government have taken the matter in charge. Now they are waiting their trial which may come off soon. Probably they will get from 6 months to 1 year. 1st mate and myself was absent from the ship at the time signing protest at Br. Consulate. I hope they will give me enough sugar here to save expense of ballasting; anyhow I am trying to do best possible.

> From Yours Most Respectfully
> *B.F. Gullison*

Messers G.T. Soley & Co.
Liverpool   England

Surabaya
July 11th 1889

Gentlemen:
Your letter containing copy of charter to hand on my arrival at Batavia 31st May. I was very much pleased to know you had fixed ship at such a good rate.

Owing to a very long and tedious passage I came very near losing my charter, had survey & written notice sent in to my Sugar Merchants July 1st 11 a.m.; you will see I did not have much time to spare. I have had to work very hard for it, as my Petroleum Merchants at Samarang would not assist me in discharging. I received orders here to proceed to Cheribon[23] and finish cargo at Surabaya, or give them one *month* as *extra* time. I chose the latter and I am now waiting with patience for the time to come.

> Yours truly
> *B.F. Gullison*

---

22   This is an indication of the competition sailing ships were now receiving from tramp steamers.
23   The French steamer *Cheribon* was evidently named after this port on the north coast of Java.

Messers J.F. Whitney & Co.   Surabaya July 11th '89
New York

Gentlemen:

Your letter to hand on arrival at Batavia contents noted. Many thanks for papers received from your office; they come very acceptable. I arrived at Batavia May 31st. Was ordered to 'Samarang'; discharged 33000 cases finished balance of cargo here at Surabaya, came very near losing sugar charter, was ordered to 'Cheribon' to take in part cargo and to finish loading here, or, to give them thirty extra days. I preferred the latter and I am now waiting the time. Owing to heavy rains and a very backward season, sugar has not come in as early as usual but we are waiting with patience. Wishing you Compliments of the Season,

    I remain Gentlemen,

                          Yours Respectfully,
                          B.F. Gullison

N.B. Lewis Esq. Yarmouth, Nova Scotia   Surabaya July 11th '89

Dear Sir:

I wrote you last mail 1st inst. concerning business in general since then I have received orders to proceed to 'Cheribon' and load part cargo and return here and finish, or give them until July 31st as extra time, they have to give me Surabaya as a first loading port and Pasourawan last, or I will give it you as drawn out in Charter: 'With reference to Article II of this Charter party it is today agreed, that the laydays are to commence on or before the 31st July 1889 provided that the ship receives a full and complete cargo at Surabaya and for Pasourawan; Surabaya to be the only or first loading port.' I believe myself they haven't any more sugar at Cheribon than they have here and that this is only done to give them more time as sugar is scarce; they knowing full well that I would not take up with said offer, in preference to loading and discharging ballast, pilotage and sectra to go to Cheribon and having the s.e. monsoons to face again coming back. If charter had stipulated loading ports in rotation it would have saved me considerable time and that would mean money, but as it was, they had any two ports North of Java and they have now taken advantage of it and I am now trying to wait with patience but find it tedious. I will remit you by today's mail first bill of exchange to the amount of £2454 Stg. Two thousand four hundred fifty four pounds Sterling and hope you will receive it in order. I could only get 30 days sight bill. Sorry to keep you waiting so long. I will try and send balance which will be about £700 Stg. next mail holding enough for expenses as ordered.

                          Yours respectfully
                          B.F. Gullison

N.B. Lewis Esq. Yarmouth, N.S. Surabaya July 16th '89

Dear Sir:

I forwarded to you by last mail first bill of exchange No. 432 to the amount of £2454 st. I will now remit you by this French mail £700.0.0 stg. Seven hundred pounds being balance of freight outward cargo reserving for expenses here F 5355[24]; approximately £466.0.0 thought it better to keep enough in case of emergency.

   We are now to our sugar berth and moored. Sugar is now coming in quite brisk but the steamers taking it all. Nothing more of any importance to inform you, Sir. Will send 2nd bill of exchange next mail.

Yours Obediently
B.F. Gullison

S.R. Lankester Esq. Surabaya
British Vice Consul   Samarang July 24th '89

Dear Sir:

As my ship will soon be ready for clearing from this port, will you please inform me whether I shall have the liberty of cancelling the names of Robert Panson, Charles Cruger, Thos. Milton from my articles. I do not care about taking these men without I am compelled to, and as suitable people are now on hand I should like to have the privilege of shipping them at once. Waiting your reply.

I remain yours respectfully
B.F. Gullison

Capt. Thos. Corning Surabaya July 25th '89
Brookville N.S.

Dear Father:

Since my last letter to you dated Jan. 17th, we have received one from Mother, March 16th in which she said you were not in very good health, but we trust you have improved before this. We thought, as you, that perhaps it would be better to postpone the painting of our house and write you to that effect. I received a letter from Father Gullison from New York. He said he could not hand you over the receipts for the money he deposited in the Merchants Bank, as he holds these as vouchers for the money intrusted. I was under the impression that he had put my money in the Government bank; but no doubt you understand it all.

24 'F' – florins

Well, Dear Parents, we are all quite well on board. The Bark *Romanoff*,[25] Capt. Doty is here, wife Della and Mrs. Doty are on the go steady, having lots of fun. We all stand this climate much better than we thought. Bowman makes himself sick once in a while by eating too much fruit and getting out in the sun, but taking everything into consideration we are doing remarkable well.

I suppose you know, that I am chartered 33/9 on sugar Boston, N.Y. or Phil. I came very near losing the charter as my passage from N.Y. has been a long and tedious one of 133 days. Had one A.B. fall from fore top-gallant yard to deck. Died eight hours after. But thank the giver of all good we arrived safe at Batavia roadstead, May 31st. Received orders June 3rd and proceeded to Samarang, discharged part cargo, held survey, sent written notice to sugar merchants, only one hour before cancelling date in Charter Party expired. They wanted to do it bad as sugar is very scarce owing to heavy rains and a backward season. Steamers are lying here on demurrage. There is one house Eaton & Co. have thirty six steamers chartered and no sugar as yet. Sailing ships are leaving here for Singapore.

Yours truly
Frank Gullison

N.B. Lewis Esq.   Yarmouth N.S.   Surabaya July 25th '89

Dear Sir:
Enclosed please accept 2nd bill of exchange No. 432 to the amt. of £2454 stg. I forwarded to you on 16th inst. first bill to the amt. of £700 stg. and trust you may receive them in order; We have not done anything yet in shape of cargo. Sugar is coming in slowly; my time will be up on the 31st, then lay days commence as per Charter.

I have sent aloft Main Top-Gallant yard here, new top-gallant Cross trees & trestle trees & fitted iron supporters to same. Scraped & painted ship outside also lower hold inside & dunnage[26] laid & etc.

I will sell some of the salt provisions here. Things in general going along fairly well.

Yours Obediently
Frank Gullison

---

25 Bark *Romanoff*, 1049 tons, built 1876, owned by A.F. Stoneman and others of Yarmouth. Captain George Doty was a Yarmouth Captain. The Stoneman wharf was next to the Lewis wharf and Captain Henry Lewis and A.F. Stoneman were next door neighbours.

26 Dunnage − loose material laid beneath or wedged among objects carried by ship to prevent injury from chafing or moisture or to provide ventilation.

Ship *N.B. Lewis*   Surabaya July 1889

It is this day mutually agreed between B.F. Gullison Master of Br. Ship
N.B. Lewis & Stevedore Joe of Surabaya, the said stevedore engages to load
ship *N.B. Lewis* with sugar at Surabaya and Pasoeroean laying all dunnage,
supplying all labour, and sufficient men to keep lighters going and ship
working, dunnage laid as required by master, stevedores men taken to and
from the ship at his expense, no money to be advanced until the ship is
loaded, and should the said ship *N.B. Lewis* finish at Pasoeroean, the said
stevedore is to go with her and his men to complete the loading under a
penalty of forfeiting the whole money already earned at Surabaya.

    Taking in and stowing cargo at Surabaya &/or Pasoeroean.

    Thirty Dutch cents .30 per ton Nett [about 13¢ Canadian]

    Stowing only   .23   "   "   " [about 10¢ Canadian]

Stevedore guarantees to load said ship with 2000 tons sugar Nett.

Witness   *B.F. Gullison Master*
E. Graves Mate   Stevedore

N.B. Lewis   Yarmouth Nova Scotia   Sourabaya July 30th '89

Dear Sir:

Please accept 2nd of exchange to the amount of £700 (seven hundred
pounds) 2nd of first remittance sent last mail; I will keep the third until
called for; We commenced loading sugar yesterday. Have onboard about
three hundred baskets. Sugar is now coming in quite fast and things in
general looking more encouraging; I hope they will soon load up for I am
getting tired doing nothing. Bark *Romanoff* sailed today for Singapore.
Weather here is quite warm & s.e. Monsoons have now taken a good hold.

                         Yours respectfully
                         B.F. Gullison

N.B. Lewis Esq. Yarmouth Nova Scotia   Surabaya Aug. '89

Dear Sir:

In reference to our discharging here, I have to inform you that we delivered the forty nine cases short of our cargo, was paid on bill of Laden
quantity and charged f4.32 per case short equal to f211.68 or near £18 stg.
This looks bad no mistake and I am very sorry about it, we would naturally
think this was neglect of duty. I was informed on my arrival at Surabaya
that the custom of the Port was for our ship to unload 1500 cases per day
and that I was to deliver them to lighters alongside, they giving no receipts
whatever until the same was landed at the stores. Notwithstanding this they

had a tallyman onboard who agrees with the mate, still he is not allowed to give a receipt. The dispute originates with the lighterman; they have all the chance to get away with whatever amount they like, it is no use sealing their lighters without one does the cabin and the whole business. I know full well they have received our whole cargo and had I not been beholding to them *for time*, I would have made them pay for each & every case as it went over the ship side.

They should be made to give a receipt for each lighter before it leaves the ship which would save all humbugging. They know this full well too, but they say it is not the custom of this port.

Capt. Doty Bk. *Romanoff* finished discharging here and came out all right, *but he is an exception*.

We have onboard about 300 ton cargo.

I have paid 2nd officer off here and will probably sail without one.

J. Daendels & Co. have assisted me here and Samarang and I propose with your consent to pay for it say two or three Guineas.

Today is Java New Year, but we are working one lighter.

From Your Obedient Servant
B.F. Gullison

A.F. Stoneman Esq.   Sourabaya Aug. 8th '89
Yarmouth Nova Scotia

Dear Sir:

As requested by Capt. Doty I now take pleasure in forwarding you two letters, left in my care and trust you will receive them in order.

Bk. *Romanoff* sailed from here on the 29th ulto for Singapore.

Yours respectfully
Frank Gullison

J. Lankester Esq.   Sourabaya Aug. 9th 1889
Br. Consul Samarang

Dear Sir:

Will you please receive personal effects of Robert Pearson, Charles Cruger and Thos. Milton forwarded by S.S. Frans L/D Putte. She sails from here tomorrow. I have omitted to charge the freight to said seamen. You can please yourself about forwarding the same.

Yours most respectfully
B.F. Gullison
Br. Ship *N.B. Lewis*

N.B. Lewis Esq.   Sourabaya Sept. 5th 1889

Dear Sir:

I have about squared up business today having had a great amount of
trouble just as our good ship was ready for sea. I loaded here at
Sourabaya to 19 ft. 6 in. and finished outside the bar. Merchants paying
for lighterage and towing the distance of twenty-three miles, which took us
four days, while doing so my steward was taken sick and died in thirty-six
hours with all the symptoms of cholera. After this the boatswain died in 11
hours from a healthy strong man and four others laid up. I took them
ashore to the hospital and have had to leave two behind, the ship being so
far away and the dangerous sickness required assistance for which you will
see by a/c. I have been greatly worried and it is a wonder that I am not
sick myself but thank the Giver of all Good I am still able to attend to my
business and trust for health and strength to continue. I have had to take
a man out of the forecastle who will be in the place of a steward home. We
are loaded with 1853 tons of sugar Nett or about 1964 gross. We have averaged little over 23 Ric per reg. tonnage which is considered very good
carrying bound for New York. My disbursements here is about 675.0.0 stg.
I will remit balance of money here which amounts to about 131.0.0 and all
vouchers and hope Good Sir you will find everything satisfactory and that
I will make a quick and successful passage and have no more sickness.

From Your Obedient Servant
Frank Gullison

Captain B.F. Gullison   Ship *N.B. Lewis*   G.T. SOLEY & CO.
c/o Messers Boyd & Hincken   Liverpool 15th Nov. 1889
New York

Dear Sir:

We were pleased to receive your letter of 11th July from Sourabaya and
note all you say.

We saw report of your sailing for New York on 23rd August and hope
this may find you safely arrived all well.

We are very glad you saved the sugar charter, as nothing so good has
been done since. Business is very dull in the East at present, but some very
good case oil freights outwards. There are not as high rates being paid on
coal and iron from this side as during last winter but still fair business. We
suppose you will be going out East again.

We will send bill for Commission on Charter to our agents Messers Scammell Bros. and you can pay same at your convenience after cargo is delivered.

> Shall be glad to hear from you
> and remain
> yours truly
> *G.T. Soley & Co.*

Account of freight for Mr. Gullison Master of the Ship N.B. Lewis

15,791 4	Petroleum	$ .39	$6158.49
12 4	do unloaded		
too much at Samarang		.39	4.68
			$6163.17
Commission 2 1/2%			−154.18
			$6008.99
		4.80	
			£1251.17
			−700
			£550.17
			£6594.85

Disbursements

Paid to Captain *Cheribon*		496.	
To Surveyor		60.	
Pilotage		118.	
Captain Gullison		350.	
Clearing in		2.50	
Telegram to Samarang		1.67	
Short delivered 49	(4.32)	211.68	1239.85
	Balance		5355.

Verified, found correct
and balance received

Sourabaya 11th July 1889

B.F. Gullison   *D.G. Septwear*

Capt. Gullison   Yarmouth Dec. 9/89

Dear Sir:

Suppose we may begin to look for you along. See you was spoken 23rd Oct. 300 miles N.W. Cape Good Hope was pleased to find you making so good time. Suppose you got away about Sept. 7 notice you had a lot of sickness and deaths among your crew at Java. It is a hard place where you have a lay so long. Everything in shape of remittances and accounts came to hand all satisfactory. You will find the ship chartered for Shanghai 37 cents this is 6¢ more than last time you went there. I did not like to risk it longer as freights don't look too healthy. I expect to leave home last of this week for the States. Have *Otago* now about due at Boston and *Hugh Cann* in about 3 weeks. I shall close up my house and take my wife and shall probable stay away couple of months. You was lucky in getting your sugar freight. Think they would have got out if they could. *Otago* is fixed to load back B. Ayres 15 1/2 could not get $12. now. *Equator* left Boston last week for B. Ayres 15 1/2[27] made $15,900. I shall come along probable as soon as I hear of your arrival at New York. Telegraph home when you arrive and they will let me know where ever I am. Hoping this will find you and your family well.

                                                        Yours
                                                        N.B. Lewis

27 Probably $15.50 per thousand on a load of lumber. This would mean a cargo of over one million feet. It would appear that the *Otago*, *Hugh Cann* and *Equator* are all in the lumber trade to South America. This business would be obtained through James G. Hall & Co. of Boston who were agents for H. & N.B. Lewis for many years.

The *N.B. Lewis* arrived at New York from Java in January, 1890, and after unloading the cargo of sugar prepared to leave for Shanghai with a load of case oil.[1] The captain's wife, Della, returned to their home in Yarmouth County with their baby son.

When the ship sailed January 25 there were on board 21 souls.[2] They included the captain, first mate, second mate, steward-cook, carpenter, 12 able seamen, two ordinary seamen, a boy and the wife of the first mate. The first mate, Emerson Graves, had made the previous voyage to Java with the ship; he must have proved very satisfactory, because permission for a first mate to have his wife accompany him was very seldom given. Evidently, like the captain, the mate and his wife were of a religious turn of mind, for Captain Spicer in his letter of July 22, 1890, from Hong Kong, mentions that Mr. and Mrs. Graves had been attending the prayer meetings on board the ship in Shanghai.

The *Mary L. Burrill*,[3] another Yarmouth ship, under command of Captain Kinney, was in New York loading case oil for Shanghai at the same time as the *N.B. Lewis* and sailed one day earlier. The two ships arrived at Shanghai the same day, sailing up the Woosung River together.

---

1   The complete log of the voyage from New York to Shanghai to Hong Kong and return to New York has been included in this chapter. A perusal of the daily entries in the log book gives an insight into the daily life on board a sailing ship during a long voyage. Through the islands of South East Asia it will be found that the *N.B. Lewis* used the Sunda strait between Sumatra and Java and that another passage used was the Ombai strait north of Timor.
2   See Appendix E for crew list for this voyage with wages paid.
3   See Appendix F particulars, *Mary L. Burrill*.

Capt. Gullison

United States Hotel
Tilly Haynes Prop.
Boston January 27, 1890

Dear Sir:

I got so interested in loading the ship I did not have time to go down to lower part of city after she got filled up – trim came out all right. Think she was about on even keel suppose if not too stormy today you got her down below. *Otago*[4] had shifted down to deep water wharf but has done nothing loading lately. I believe lumber is alongside to finish her now. *Hugh Cann* arrived at St. John Saturday. I shall leave tomorrow night for St. John. In writing me direct, care Messers McLaughton & Co. give me amount of disbursements and all particulars. The *Equator* arrived B. Ayres last Friday 55 days from Boston; good passage. Suppose *Mary L. Burrill* is ready by this time to get away. You must not let her get away from you. I was pleased with *Lewis* cargo suppose if we had filled up every where she would have taken the 51,000 cases. I think she is just as well with a few out forward. It has been snowing here all day and thawing very hasty. Eugene's mate came this morning. I don't expect to get home for several weeks yet. Hoping you will have a safe and pleasant passage to Shanghai and we shall be able to secure a paying freight back. I think you said you wanted 5 shares in Yarmouth Steamship Co. if they were to be had.[5] Balance of amount due you will deposit in bank.

Yours
N.B. Lewis

N.B. Lewis Esq.,

January 29th 1890

Dear Sir:

We squared up a/c yesterday and would have been ready to sail this morning had the riggers attended to their work. I went on board last night supposing every thing would be ready, but instead, found that the riggers had brought grog on board and part of them got drunk, the foreman of the gang in the bunch. The sober part of them refused to obey his commands so the day ended and work hanging. It will take all the day to get squared up onboard with my crew. So you see Sir, how things goes. Captain Churchill had a bill on his a/c of $4.00 for putting lumber on board. Jones refused to charge ship with this amount said he did not make an agreement with you to load wood on ship. It is the usual custom to do so though no doubt you understood this, he also tried to charge for delivery

4   Mr. Lewis and his wife are staying at the United States Hotel in Boston for the winter. *Otago*, *Hugh Cann*, *Equator* and *Mary L. Burrill* are all Yarmouth ships.
5   It would appear that Captain Gullison must have by now paid for his shares in the *N.B. Lewis*.

of the remaining boards. I settled the bill but told him I would inform you about it.

Our expenses here $12,239.04; whole amount that is including $4250.00 you draw makes it $16,489.04. Draft on W.F. Hagar $1774.91, the a/c was forwarded to Mr. Hagar last evening, the vouchers will probably go today; ship draft of water f22.00 on even keel and starboard list.

Your letter from Boston to hand yesterday. So I will send this to St. John. Suppose you have heard of the *Emilia L. Boyd*[6] being lost, Collision; crew saved.

Ship *Burrill* sailed yesterday.[7] I shall probably sail this afternoon or to-morrow morning. *Do not think he will beat me.* Hoping to make a quick and successful voyage. I remain

Yours respectfully
Frank Gullison

J.F. WHITNEY & CO.

15 State Street   P.O. Box 1793   New York

Capt. B.F. Gullison Ship *N.B. Lewis*	New York
Care China & Japan Trading Co.	Feb. 28, 1890
Shanghai, China	

Dear Sir:

Your favour of 30 ulto was duly received. We insured your effects and slops[8] $300 at 6% and sent the policy to your wife.

Enclosed we hand you letter received since you sailed, also freight circular which will show the state of our market.

---

6   The bark *Emilie L. Boyd*, of Yarmouth N.S., John B. Killam master, from New York December 23, 1889, for Hong Kong with a cargo of 35,000 cases of oil, collided with Norwegian tank ship *Rolff*, Capt. Jorgensen, from Havre December 20 for New York, on the morning of January 15, 1890, and foundered. Captain Killam reported that on the morning of January 15 he was steering S.E. with wind almost on the port bow and blowing half a gale.

   The *Rolff* was running free and could have passed clear of the *Boyd* but she changed her course slightly and attempted to cross the *Boyd's* bow. She struck the *Boyd* on the port bow, crushing it in so that hundreds of cases of oil tumbled through the breach overboard. The *Rolff's* topmast and bowsprit were carried away and her bow was slightly injured but she kept on her course. The *Boyd's* crew had to row nearly four miles before the *Rolff* unwillingly took them on board. They landed at St. Thomas. The day was clear and there was no excuse for the accident. The *Emilie L. Boyd* was valued at $40,000. She was 1240 tons register, was launched in 1881 and was owned by Wm. Law & Co., G.H. Guest, T. & E.S. Perry, George Crosby, John B. Killam and others.

7   See letter dated June 27/90 at Shanghai.

8   See Appendix D.

Vessels are chartering to arrive 30 cents Hong Kong, 37 cents Shanghai, 34 cents Japan — nothing doing in bbl. oil.

Hoping you are well and wishing you success.

Yours
J.F. Whitney & Co.

DIARY OF CAPTAIN FRANK GULLISON SHIP N.B. LEWIS

Voyage from New York to Shanghai
Jan. 30th 1890 to June 18th 1890

Jan. 30th
2:30 p.m. weighed anchor & proceeded to sea in tow by tug Vosbrug Pilot Edward Devlin. 4:30 discharged tug & pilot: Increasing wind from NE: 8 p.m. Highland bore w by s.

Jan. 31st
Lat 39.57 N   Long 72.18 w Acc.
Moderating wind backing NW: noon put anchor on the bow & bent mainsail, getting things in general snugged up.

Feb. 1st
Lat 38.39 N   Long 71.14 w Obs.
First part light air from various quarters: Middle part moderate from wsw: later hauling NW & NNE: moderate breeze & fine weather: nothing in sight: 1 bbl. pork.[9]

Feb. 2nd
Lat 37.29 N   Long 69.46 w Acc.
First part wind NE increasing breeze: shortened down to reefed topsails: middle light rain: Later heavy squalls of wind & rain hauling sw Bar. 30.40 Ther. 75.

Feb. 3rd
Lat 37.20 N   Long 65.18 w
Wind remaining steady from sw attended by fine weather. 5:30 p.m. passed *S.S. Benguella* bound to New York: passengers as well as her captain seemed to be all in good humour waving their caps and handkerchiefs; passed very close so it was very easy to recognize her name: no doubt he will report us in a few days. Bar. 30.32 Ther. 68.

---

9   The captain makes a notation in the log each time a barrel of beef or pork is opened or 'broken out'.

Feb. 4th
Lat 36.57 N   Long 60.48 WC [Course] E 1/2 S. 225[10]
Wind moderate attended by rain at times veering from SW to W
NW & N: sea quite smooth, nothing in sight, day ends fine. Bar. 30.21
Ther. 67°.

Feb. 5th
Lat. 36.39 N   Long 58.37 W
Wind hauling East around by South to SW attended by fine weather. Capt.
quite sick unable to attend to his duty. Bar. 30.20 Ther. 70

Feb. 6th.
Lat 36.24 N   Long 54.58 W Course E 1/2 S Dis. 178
Wind remaining steady from SW; Fine weather continues. Somewhat better
today, have turned out and dressed. Bar. 30.20 Ther. 70.

February 7th
Lat 36.40 N   Long 51.02 W Course E 1/2 N
Dis. 172 log. 200 Chro.
Wind remaining steady from SSW: smooth water and everything going
along lovely: feeling more like myself again: what beautiful weather we are
having to what we experienced one year ago. Flour 450 lbs. taken out since
24th Jan. Bar. steady 30.20 Ther. 70 Rove off new main L. topsail brace
'Port'.

Feb. 8th
Lat 35.37 N   Long 47.43 W Course E by S 3/4 S 182
Wind hauling from WSW to North coming out strong; reduced sail from
royals to reefed topsails in short order; later part blowing gale from NE
making good weather under reefed topsails Bar. 30.51 Ther. 70.

Feb. 9th
Lat 35.08 N   Long 47.07 W Course SE 1/2 S 40
First part wind blowing strong from East under reefed topsails Middle
hauling ESE moderating later; wind & weather moderate all sails set. Bar.
30.40 Ther. 66.

Feb. 10th
Lat 34.37 N   Long 44.16 W Course E by 1/4 S 155
Steady from SW beautiful breeze and fine weather; one skysail yard ship in
sight steering more northerly than we. Bar. 30.16 Ther. 70.

10 This notation means that course was east half south; and distance sailed in 24 hours was 225
    nautical miles.

Feb. 11th

Lat 33.16 N Long 41.22 W Course SE by 1/2 E 165

First part light rain squalls, looking very black (clouds) middle part hauling west, later NE & ENE, hauled around very moderate company keeper in sight. Bar. 30.04 Ther. 70.

Feb. 12th

Lat 32.37 N Long 38.34 WCE by S 1/2 S 148

Wind first part light from S hauling SW later part balling off 10 knots. Signalized steamer. Bar. 30.00 Ther. 69

Feb. 13th.

Lat 30.32 N Long 35.25 WC SE 1/2 E 200

Wind hauling from SW around by W to NW & NE; shortened down to reefed topsails; later part strong breeze, squally at times Bar. 30.26 Ther. 66.

Feb. 14th

Lat 27.55 N Long 33.19 WC SE 3/4 S Dis 192

Wind NE & ENE throughout the day; nothing in sight, day ends finer looking, weather having the appearance of trades Bar. 30.30 Ther. 66.

Feb. 15th

Lat 25.10 N Long 31.40 WC SE By S 1/2 S 190

Wind strong from East & NE but sea very smooth for the wind; very heavy squalls at times, nothing in sight, day ends strong breeze and squally.

    TRADE WINDS HERE bar. 30.30 Ther. 70.

Feb. 16th

Lat 22.06 Long 29.35 W SE by S 1/4 S

Dist. 215

Strong breeze and squally weather throughout the day. Bar. 30.20 Ther. 70

Feb. 17th

Lat 19.09 N Long 28.25 W Course S by E 1/2 E 190

Strong breeze from E attended by very heavy squalls of wind & rain but we are doing good work and must not murmur 'cut out mizzen royal' Bar. 30.10 Ther. 71.

Feb. 18th

Lat 17.57 N Long 27.35 W S by E 1/4 E 195

Strong breeze from East, with squalls of wind & rain; carried away fore T. gallant yard, sent aloft a new one at once. Bar. 30.04 Ther. 72.

Feb. 19th

Lat 13.02 N   Long 26.48 W C S by E 1/2 E 183

Moderate breeze from NE all sail set; Weather looking more settled. Signalized two steamers today, one bound North, the other South the both were large two funneled boats, the last one signalized was bound to Rio and no doubt he will report us; the former I could not vouch for; Day ends fine weather. Bar. 30.00 Ther. 74.

Feb. 20th

Lat 9.56 N   Long 25.51 W Course S by E 1/2 E 197

Steady breeze and fine weather; weather feeling softer, new moon tonight. Bar. 30.00 Temp 77.

Feb. 21st

Lat 7.29 N   Long 24.33 W Course SE by S 1/2 S Dis. 162

Wind NE attended by fine weather throughout the day. One barkentine bound South Bar. 29.90 Ther. 80.

Feb. 22nd

Lat 5.25 N   Long 24.35 W Course South 125

Steady breeze with heavy dark passing clouds, rainy looking weather, feeling quite soft. Thomas Baeren fell from crossjack yard to deck injuring his face and hip but very little; think probably he will be able to resume duty in a few days. Bar. 29.86 Ther 83.

February 23rd

Lat 4.00 N   Long 24.09 W Course S by E 1/4 E 90

Wind veering from SE to North, dark passing clouds with squalls of rain at times; filled about 1000 gals. water: two barks and one brigantine close too. Signalized Swedish Bark from Newport bound to Rio 27 days out and wished him to report us. Bar 29.82 Ther. 85.

Feb. 24th

Lat 3.04 N   Long 24.16 W

Wind variable from North around by east to South & SW; squalls of wind & rain with heavy inky looking clouds. Bar. 29.82 Ther. 82.

Feb. 25th

Lat 3.00 N   Long 24.05 W

Light variable airs throughout the day; three sail in sight trying to get South. Bar. 29.84 Ther. 83.

Feb. 26th

Lat 1.46 N   Long 24.05 W

Wind variable from N to E; some very heavy squalls; several ships in sight steering South. Bar. 30.81 Ther. 80.

Feb. 27th

Lat 00.46 N   Long 24.23 w dis. 60

Wind light from SSE to SE having more the appearance of SE trades. Sick man resumed duty. Bar. 29.82 Ther. 84.

Feb. 28th

Lat 00.30 s   Long 25.37 w Course sw 1/4 w 108

First part fine breeze and beautiful weather; later hauling South & ssw in a heavy squall; day ends fresh breeze from South; signalized ship Piako of Llyttelton N.Z. from Canterbury to London 70 days; he received our signals in like order & will probably report us. Bar. 29.80 Ther. 84.

March 1st

Lat 2.26 s   Long 28.00 w c sw 1/2 w 182

Wind s to sse, Fresh breeze and fine weather; bent new mizzen royal, sets like a top; several sail in sight steering South. Bar. 29.82 Ther. 85.

March 2nd

Lat 4.32 s   Long 29.54 w Course sw dis. 169

Steady breeze from SSE true; this being Sabbath day everything quiet; so ends the day. Bar. 29.82 Ther. 84.

March 3rd

Lat 6.12 s   Long 31.32 w Course sw 1/4 s 133

Wind moderate from SSE. First part squally; later fine beautiful weather.

March 4th

Lat 7.44 s   Long 32.5 w Course sw by s 3/4 s 100

Squally weather throughout the day. One bark in sight sailing South. Rove off new main upper topsail brace; 36 fathom 3 1/4 in. Bar. 29.92 Ther. 85 Fahr.

March 5th

Lat 10.25 s   Long 33.56 w Course sw 3/4 s 198

Signalized Bark *Petitcodiac* of Moncton from Cardiff for Buenos Ayres; 39 days out; he will report us. Boatswain laid up. Bar. 29.94 Ther. 86.

March 6th

Lat 12.12 s   Long 34.54 w Course wsw by s 1/2 s 119

Wind SE true, heavy squalls middle part of the day nothing in sight. Day ends fine weather. Bar. 30.00 Ther 85 Fahr.

March 7th

Lat 13.20 s   Long 35.50 w Course sw 1/2 s dis 87

Wind light from SSE. Fine beautiful weather. Bar. 30.00 Ther. 86 Fahr.

March 8th
Lat 15.05 s   Long 36.04 w c s 1/2 w Dis 100
Wind ESE attended by fine weather. Passed bark bound North. Bar. 30.00
Ther 85 Fahr.

March 9th (Sunday)
Lat 17.03 s   Long 35.38 w Course s by E 123
Squally first part of evening; day ends fine.

March 10th
Lat 18.29   Long 35.29 w Course s 1/2 E Dis. 80 mile
Wind veering from East to North; squally, at times, very hot day. Bar.
29.94 Ther 86 Fahr.

March 11th
Lat 19.49   Long 35.02 w Course s by E 1/2 E 81 miles
Wind veering from SE to NE squally; overhauled salt provisions; in good
order; opened 1 tierce beef. Bar. 29.96 Ther. 86.

March 12th
Lat 21.59   Long 34.05 w Course SSE 140
Wind veering from ESE to NNE; squally towards evening. Bar. 29.96 Ther.
86 Fahr.

March 13th
Lat 24.10 s   Long 32.57 w Course SE by s 1/2 s 143
Wind moderate from East to NNE at times squally strong sw heaving in,
nothing in sight. Bar. 30.02 Ther. 84 Fahr.

March 14th
Lat 26.10 s   Long 31.55 w Course SE by s 1/2 s 138 miles
Wind E moderate breeze, fine weather; repairing No. 2 foresail; carpenter
overhauling yards & masts; repairing heel of main topmast. Bar. 30.20
Ther. 84 F.

March 15th
Lat 28.29   Long 31.18 w s by E 1/4 E dis. 142
Fine weather and a moderate breeze ESE throughout the day; 1 box of lime
juice Bar. 30.30 Ther. 84.

March 16th (Sunday)
Lat 29.56 s   Long 31.12 w Course S 1/4 E
Dist. 85 fine weather. Bar. 30.34 Ther. 81 F.

March 17th

Lat 31.16 s   Long 31.29 w Course s 1/4 w Dist. 78

Wind veering from SE to SSE: passed one bark steering North also sighted one ship to leeward bound East. expect it will be the *Narwhal* or *Minnie Burrill* Bar. 30.36. Ther. 80 F.

March 18th

Lat 32.19s   Long 29.53 w Course SE dis. 93

Wind variable & light from SE around by N to NW; trade winds absconded weather very poor & squally LOST THE S.E. TRADES. Bar. 30.30 Ther. 77 F.

March 19th

Lat 32.55 s   Long 28.24 w Course SE by E 1/2 E Dis. 85

Wind NW light breeze & hazy. Bar. 30.20 Ther. 77 F.

March 20th

Lat 32.24 s   Long 25.12 w Course E 1/2 N Dis. 161

Rove off prt main brace new 39 fathoms. Bar. 30.24 Ther. 74 F.

March 21st

Lat 32.37 s   Long 24.42 w by acc.

Wind light & variable; very heavy sea from sw Bar. 30.16 Ther. 75 F.

March 22nd

Lat 33.40 s   Long 21.52 w by acc

Wind veering to ENE; later part rain & heavy sw swell throughout the day; bar. falling & weather looking threatening Bar. 29.80 Ther. 74.

March 23rd (Sunday)

Lat 34.17 s   Long 19.46 w by Obs

First part wind increasing; furled light sail; 6 p.m. heavy lightening from sw increasing to all parts of the heavens with loud peals of thunder; shortened down to lower topsails; heavy rain continuing until 8 p.m. wind hauling to NW mid-night hauling sw came out very strong; came up on 2 ships under short sail. Bar. 30.00 Ther. 74.

March 24th

Lat 34.11 s   Long 18.34 w Course E 1/2 N Distance 60

Wind moderating from the s; hauling E & NE; fine weather throughout the later part of the day. Bent main spencer bent No. 1 main topsail & fore two bbls. flour opened (1 bbl. 18 days). Boatswain laid up. Bar. 30.00. Ther 72 F.

March 25th

Lat 35.34 s   Long 14.53 w Course s by E 3/4 E dis 192

Increasing wind from the NE with rain; hauling N & NW; shortened down to Reefed upper topsails Bar. 29.90 Ther 75.

March 26th
Lat 36.29 s   Long 11.29 w Course E 1/2 s dis 185
Wind veering to sw & moderating, set sail accordingly; westerly swell making. Bar 30.30 Ther 72 F.

March 27th
Lat 37.03 s   Long 9.08 Course E by s 1/2 s 118
Light breeze from the NW throughout the day; heavy NW swell regular Cape Horners. Things in general going along smooth. Oh what a lonesome life this is. Bar. 30.40 Ther 74 F.

March 28th
Lat 37.42 s   Long 7 w
Wind moderate throughout; heavy westerly swell continues. Bark in sight steering SE; day ends fine weather. Rove off new wheel ropes 12 fathoms 3 3/4 Bar. 30.30 Ther. 70.

March 29th
Lat 39.10   Long 2.32 w Course ESE Dis 225
Wind steady & fresh from the NNW; westerly swell running; nothing in sight. Doing good work. Course SE Var 2 Rt − W. Finished repairing No. 2 mainsail.

March 30th
Lat 40.07 s   Long 2.13 E Course ESE Dis 230
Wind steady from the NW; fresh breeze doing good work. Westerly swell continues; nothing in sight. Bar 29.91. Ther 70.

March 31st
Lat 40.58 s   Long 7.00 E Course E by s dis. 222
Wind increasing from the NNW, hauling NW with rain, later part steady strong breeze under reefed fore & mizzen topsails & whole main doing very good work. Sea quite regular. Course by compass SE by s Bar. 29.70 Ther 68 F.

April 1st
Lat 40.55 s   Long 11.03 E Course E Dis. 188
Blowing strong from w. Our good ship is doing her duty riding the high seas like a young sea gull. Bar 29.90 Ther 69 F.

April 2nd
Lat 41.05 s   Long 15.17 E Course E 1/2 s dis. 191
First part blowing fresh from w, middle moderating & hauling N & NE increasing in force and backing to NNW & w; threatening weather under lower topsails, reefed main, upper & reefed foresail. Blowing strong light rain at times. Lowest Fall [barometer] 29.62 Bar. 29.62 Ther. 67 F.

April 3rd
Lat 40.59 s   Long 19.01 E Course E dist. 175
Blowing a gale from the w; under topsails; high sea but running even.
Our good ship runs before it like a top 63 days from New York all well.
Bar 28.80 Ther 65 F.

April 4th
Lat 41.07 s   Long 23.07 E Course E 1/4 s dis. 185 true
Wind from w & wsw moderate gale and high sea; weather looking South-
erly Bar. rising; day ends heavy squalls. Bar 30.11 Ther 63 F.

April 5th
Lat 40.36 s   Long 26.39 E Course E by N 155
Wind wsw heavy squalls throughout the day. Caught four large albatros.
Bar. 30.40 Ther 68.

April 6th (Sunday)
Lat 40.39 s   Long 28.57 E Course E 1/2 s Dis. 105
Fine weather throughout the day. Bar 30.50.

April 7th
Lat 40.39 s   Long 31.48 E Course E 129
Light breeze ... *cured my albatros skins* Bar. 30.50.

April 8th
Lat 40.27 s   Long 35.18 E Course E 3/4 N
Wind steady with fog squalls Bar. 30.40 Ther. 66.

April 9th
Lat 40.16 s   Long 38.12 E Course E 1/2 N 130
Fine weather moderate swell from West. Finished repairing No. 2 mainsail; 1 bbl. pork 32 days. Main tank sounded 5 ft. 5 in water used (Tank
18 ft. 6").

April 10th
Lat 40.29 s   Long 40.6 E Course E by s 80
Fresh breeze, light squalls, sw swell increasing. Commenced repairing No.
2 crossjack. Day ends dirty looking. 70 days from NY; about 13 ft. water
main tank; 3 bags flour 65 lbs.

April 11th
Lat 41.44 s   Long 44.37 E Course E by s 3/4 s dis. 220 miles
NE wind throughout the day, smooth water & fine weather. Later part
doing good work logging 10 & 11 knots; Bar. falling gradually Bar. 30.10
Ther. 70.

April 12th
Lat 41.48 s   Long 49.48 E Course E dist. 237,
Fine steady breeze throughout the day from NE; water keeping very
smooth; heavy dew at night. Bar 30.10 Ther 66.

April 13th (Sunday)
Lat 42.00 s   Long 54.20 E Course E 205
Rather squally Bar. 30.10 Ther 66.

April 14th
Lat 42.06 s   Long 57.02 E Course E 1/4 s dis. 121
Wind increasing from NE with rain & high sea; shortened down to lower
topsails; later moderating and sea decreasing. Bar. 30.11 Ther 66.

April 15th
Lat 41.52 s   Long 59.56 E Course E 1/2 N dis. 125
Light winds Bar. 30.10 Ther 66.

April 16th
Lat 42.05 s   Long 62.28 E Course E 1/2 s dis. 115
Wind N light rain & fog. 1 tierce of beef 34 days. Bar. 30.10 Ther 66.

April 17th
Lat 41.24 s   Long 64.55 E Course E by N 3/4 N dis. 118
Wind moderate from NW high swell from West; finished repairing No. 2
C.J [Cross jack]. Tank sounded 7 ft. out sucking 1 ft. 7 in. per week. Stew-
ard receives 6 buckets or 12 gals; sailors 1 bucket (2 gals.) Bar. 30.10
Ther 65.

April 18th
. Lat 41.21 s   Long 66.16 E Course E 1/4 N 65 miles.
Light breeze, heavy swell; commenced repairing No. 2 main upper topsail.
Lecture to sailors about grub. Bar. 30.00 Ther. 68.

April 19th
Lat 40.50 s   Long 69.23 E Course E by N dis. 142
Moderate westerly wind; bent[11] No. 2 main upper topsail. Bar. 30.26 Ther.
64.

April 20th (Sunday)
Lat 40.34 s   Long 71.00 E Course E by N 76
Fine weather. Bar. 30.22 Ther. 66.

11 'Bent' – replaced No. 1 main upper topsail with No. 2.

April 21st
Lat 40.16 s   Long 73.31 E Course E by N dis. 116
Wind west fine weather; finished repairing No. 2 fore upper topsail. Bar.
30.20 Ther. 65.

April 22nd
Lat 39.28 s   Long 75.18 E Course NE by E
1/2 E 98 Light breeze; men variously employed, *caught 7 beautiful albatros.*

April 23rd
Lat 39.45 s   Long 76.35 E Course E by S 1/2 S dis. 62
Wind hauling around NE, light breeze & steady Bar. SW swell running. So
ends the day, not making very good time lately. Bar. 30.50 Ther. 67.

April 24th
Lat 39.28 s   Long 80.36 E Course E 1/2 N dis. 185
Wind NNE fresh breeze; men employed at sails; things in general going
along satisfactory; 84 days out.

April 25th
Lat 38.51 s   Long 85.07 E Course E 3/4 N Dis. 216
First part fresh breeze NNE; all sail; middle increasing wind & sea. Later
strong breeze, shortened down to reefed topsails; wind & sea increasing &
threatening weather. Bar. 30.10 Ther. 65; 10 ft. 3 in. water main tank.

April 26th
Lat 38.26 s   Long 88.39 E Course E 3/4 N Dis 168
Wind N blowing strong under reefed topsails & foresail. Bar. keeping very
high for the wind we are having. Bar. 30.10. Ther. 65.

April 27th (Sunday)
Lat 37.58 s   Long 91.50 E Course E by N dis. 158
First part under reefed topsails, middle all sail; bar. 30.20. Ther. 65.

April 28th
Lat 37.21 s   Long 95.10 E Course E by N dis. 165
First part wind increasing with fine looking weather and high Bar. shortened down to reefed topsails midnight, blowing strong from N. *One sailor
gets obstrepulous* [obstreperous], *had to give him a trimming.* Bar. 30.10 Ther.
65 F.

April 29th
Lat 36.21 s   Long 97.31 E Course NE by E dis 128
Day ends fine weather all sail wind SW overcast. Westerly sea running. Bar.
30.30 Ther. 64 F.

April 30th
Lat 35.15 s   Long 100.12 e Course ne by e 1/2 e 142
Squally weather. So the month has past & gone and I am just as homesick
as ever. Bar. 30.20 Ther. 63.

May 1st
Lat 31.50 s   Long 102.55 e Course ne by n 246.
Wind hauling from se in to s & ssw increasing in force; reduced sail to
lower topsails; reefed upper main & foresail; blowing a gale, doing good
work. Bar. 29.90 Ther. 63.

May 2nd
Lat 29.45 s   Long 104.43 Course ne by n 157
Wind south strong breeze throughout the day; under reefed topsails &
foresails. Bar. 29.74 Ther. 68 f.

May 3rd
Lat 26.53 s   Long 104.59 e Course n 1/4 e dis. 170
Wind se first part blowing strong; later more moderate; fine weather. Bar.
29.74 & Ther. 72.

May 4th (Sunday)
Lat 24.48 s   Long 105.07 e Course n 1/4 e 129
Moderate breeze; fine weather Bar. 30.00 Ther. 75.

May 5th
Lat 22.55 s   Long 105.16 e Course n 1/4 e dis. 112
Fine beautiful weather; men employed bending No. 2 sails; things in gen-
eral working satisfactory. Bar. 30 Ther. 75.

May 6th
Lat 21.04 s   Long 105.24 e Course n 1/2 e dis. 111
Wind veering from s to e fine beautiful weather, men employed repairing
No. 1 fore t.g. sail Emptied 4 bbls. flour into bags and put in flour tank.

May 7th
Lat 19.14 s   Long 105.19 e Course n Dis. 110
Wind S. steady throughout the day; carpenter stripping t. gallant bulwark;
men repairing sails side sticking mainsail. Bar. 29.94 Ther. 77.

May 8th
Lat 17.19 s   Long 105.27 Course n 115
First part wind s, later part hauling se & e. commencement of trades. Bar.
30 Ther. 80.

May 9th
Lat 15.27 s   Long 105.27 e Course n dis. 112
Wind veering from ese to sse throughout the day, heavy swell from s mod-
erate breeze & fine weather Bar. 29.96 Ther. 83.

May 10th
Lat 12.31 s   Long 105.22 e Course n 177
Wind ESE moderate breeze; overcast & dark inky looking clouds Bar. 29.90
Ther. 84.

May 11th
Lat 10.26 s   Long 105.19 e Course n
Heavy squalls of wind & much rain throughout the day. 6 p.m. sighted
Christmas Island. Noon bearings put Riggs Chro. °8″ west course bearing;
Adams chro. °45″ west course bearing Bar. 29.80 Temp 83. 101 days from
NY all well.

May 12th
Lat 9.11 s   Long 104.51 e Course NNW 80
Wind variable and light throughout the day; first part rain; later light air,
heavy southern swell; putting wire rope on main lower t'sail. Bar. 29.82
Ther. 86.

May 13th
Lat 8.27 s   Long 104.54 e Course North dis. 44
Wind light & variable; very poor days work; 1 bbl. pork 33 days Bar. 29.90
Ther. 86 F.

May 14th
Lat 7.30 s   Long 105.23 e
8 a.m. sighted land; noon Java Head bearing n by w dis. about 45 miles. Current
set ship SE 24 miles during the day; 1 tierce beef 1 bbl. flour. Bar. 29.89
Ther. 86

May 15th
Lat 6.19 s   Long 105.40
Passed between Java Head & Princess Island; Wind sw unsteady in force
and baffeling through the straits. Noon passing up Sunda strait Bar. 29.80
Ther. 86

May 16th
8 p.m. passed Anjer Light; Scott Rairden & Co.[12] boat came off with papers & letters; he will report our ship. Wind throughout the day from ssw
later hauling ENE [See letter of N.B.L. June 7/89.] Bar. 29.81 Ther. 85

Yarmouth April 9, 1890
Capt. Gullison:
Suppose it is about time to drop you a line. I saw report of you in Lat.
11 – and Long. 34 w. You had made very good time. Expect you will be

---

12 See letter from Scott Rairden dated July 6, 1889.

rather soon for Monsoon to get a good run up. I have done nothing with ship back yet. Things look very dull. If we could get anything that would pay to load in Shanghai, it would be as well as shifting. They have been talking about $9500 to $10,000 to load Shanghai and Hong Kong. Sugar may start up later in the Phillipines. I shall be looking around and if any paying business comes up will advise, if I close.[13] Hope there may be a change for the better before long. You will remit as usual being careful to get good and reliable Bankers bills. Date bills would be preferable if the difference is not too large between them and sight. You will be guided by your own judgement being on the spot. If you load at ports nearby, keep money to disburse you home, but if you have to cross over to North or South America to load (for instance, there may be business from Puget Sound, Frisco or other ports) in this case we would send funds for disbursements from here. I took 4 shares for you Yarmouth Steamship Co. at $100 instead of $105. Baker allowed this on a/c I deposited Exchange Bank at 3% deposit receipt subject your order. Hoping to hear of safe arrival in good time.

> I am yours
> *N.B. Lewis*

P.S. Cable arrival. *Otago* not yet reported. About 62 days gone, should hear from her in week or so.   N.B.L.

Capt. Gullison   Yarmouth April 23/'90

Dear Sir:

I wrote you fully by last mail. Have not much to say. Nothing new in freights which keep very dull. Have been trying to fix but nothing comes out of it so far. If we could get say $10,000 to load at Shanghai and Hong Kong it would be as good as going further for more money. Perhaps, however, I am in hopes something paying will turn up before you are ready. I wrote you to reserve enough money to pay disbursements if you loaded near by where you discharge. If you cross the Pacific to load we can send funds from home or draw on homeward freight. Hoping to soon hear of your safe arrival at Shanghai. I suppose we should look for you in about 140 days. *Otago* got out in about 70 days, expect had light winds. Things look very dull this way in freights and business. Shall use Jones Code. Hoping this will find you all in good health.

> I am yours truly
> *N.B. Lewis*

---

13 'If I close' – if a charter is signed.

N.B. Lewis Esq.   Yarmouth, N.S.   Anjer Java May 15th '90

Dear Sir:

Just a few lines to inform you that everything is in *good order* and condition on board our Good Ship N.B.L.

One hundred and five days passage to Anjer. Have had several days calm on the coast. I do not know if Narwhal or M.L. Burrill have passed here or not.

You will no doubt Sir take notice there is a mistake of $50.00 in my a/c of wages. I gave the ship Cr. for the sugar, for which, I should have charged for the same, I trust I shall have good chance through Gasper Straits.

Yours Obediently
Frank Gullison

The log continues:

May 17th
Noon North Watcher [light] abeam 3 miles; variable weather squalls of rain attended by thunder & lightening Bar. 29.81 Ther. 85.

May 18th (Sunday)
Lat 4.10 s   Long 106.45 E
Ligh variable air Bar. 29.81 Ther. 85.

May 19th
Noon passed through Macclesfield Channel Jilka Island east 1 mile; had a beautiful chance through; carpenter overhauling top gallant bulwark. Bar. 29.81 Ther. 85.

May 20th
Lat. 1°−56 s   Long 107−22E
Had a very heavy squall this morning. Lasted about an hour. Wind NNE. Day ends light variable airs. Bar. 29.8 Ther 85 F.

May 21st
Lat 1.39 s   Long 107.28 E
Light variable airs throughout the day; nothing in sight seamen employed at sails & various jobs. Bar. 29.80 Ther. 86 F.

May 22nd
Lat 0.50 s   Long 106.58 E
Light variable airs & calms; very hot day; bent No. 1 main lower tops forward to replace fore. Bar. 29.80 T. 87.

May 23rd
Lat 0.31 s   Long 106.52
Light variable airs, light rain at times. Bar. 29.82 Ther. 87 F.

May 24th
Lat 0.23 N   Long 106.37 E
Light southerly wind throughout the day; St. Julien Island bearing N by E
1/2 E. Bar. 29.79 Ther. 88 F.

May 25th (Sunday)
Lat 1.45 N   Long 106.40
Calm & light air predominating; passed two steamers to & from Singa-
pore. Bar. 29.80 Ther. 86 F.

May 26th
Lat 3.00 N   Long 106.55 E
Passing between Natuna & Anamba Islands China sea NE current 1/2 Bar.
29.81 Ther 86.

May 27th
Lat 4.12 N   Long 106.51 E
Passing between Natuna & Anamba Islands; variable light air from all
quarters & calms; almost seems impossible to get North; NE current 1 knot.
Bar. 29.80 Ther. 87.

May 28th
Lat 5.15 N   Long 106.55
Wind light & variable from West around by SW to S. Had a very heavy
squall last evening. Bar. 29.81 Ther. 88 F.

May 29th
Lat 5.49 N   Long 107.35 E course NE dis 52' current NE 3/4 mile per
hour.
This has been a very hot day & mostly calm & light variable airs. Signalized *S.S. Jason*, English, who will report us, at any rate he answered our
signals. Bar. 29.80 Temp. 89.

May 30th
Lat 6.13 N   Long 108.16 E
Calms & light airs; signalized another steamer bound North Bar. 29.80 T.
89.

May 31st
Lat 6.54   Long 108.41 E by D.R.[14]
Light air & calms; later heavy squalls from all quarters caught some water in main tank about 300 gals., 100 in deck tank; very bad chance to get North. Bar. 29.72 T. 85.

June 1st (Sunday)
Lat 7.40 N   Long 108.43 by D.R.
Rainy squally weather throughout the day; very light variable airs; Caught some rain water today. Bar. 29.80 T. 88.
6 boxes tobacco of 20
3/4 boxes tobacco opened

June 2nd
Lat 8.36 N   Long 109.14 E
First part light breeze from the South; 1 bbl. flour 19 days. later hauling SE with rain squalls & fresh breeze. Bar 29.83 Ther. 86 F.

June 3rd
Lat 10.28 N   Long 110.28 E
Wind quite steady from s & ssw. By the appearance of things, in general, I think we have the commencement of the sw monsoons; one ship ahead, overhauling her fast. Bar. 29.78 Ther. 87.

June 4th
Lat 11.46 N   Long 11.43 E.
Steady breeze from the ssw throughout the day; nothing in sight. Bar. 29.74 Ther. 88.

June 5th
Lat 13.16 N   Long 112.38 E.
Wind veering from s to sw; cloudy weather, but fair; painting outside. Nothing in sight; current set ship 18' East during the day. Bar. 29.74 Ther. 88.

June 6th
Lat 15.05 N   Long 113.40 E
First part dark inky looking clouds, attended by moderate breeze; Later part heavy rain squalls, overcast sky; strong rippling on water. Bar. 29.76 Ther. 82.

---

14 D.R., dead reckoning -- when the sky is overcast and the captain cannot fix his position from the stars, he uses the log to obtain his average speed, thus finding number of miles sailed during day, and then makes allowance for tacking, wind, currents, etc. and estimates his position.

June 7th
Lat 17.1 N   Long 114.25 E
Moderate breeze from s to sw attended by rain squalls & overcast sky;
Two funnell ss passed steering for Hong-kong Bar. 29.80 Ther. 86.

June 8th
Lat 18.44   Long 115.8 E
Wind quite steady from s & ssw with frequent squalls Bar. 29.80 T. 87.

June 9th
Lat 20.27 N   Long 116.00 E
Wind ssw & steady & light; passed through very heavy tide ripps; Current
set ship East 17 miles during the day. Bar. 29.80 T. 87.

June 10th
Lat 22.00 N   Long 116.25 E
Fine weather throughout the day; wind s by w; tide ripps continue but not
so strong Bar. 29.76 T. 87 F.

June 11th
Lat 23.26 N   Long 117.47 E
9 a.m. sighted Lannock Island & 11 a.m. Brothers Islets; fine weather
rather hazy over the land; nothing in sight but a fleet of junks inshore;
Easterly current 1 knot per hour. Bar. 29.82 T. 85.

June 12th
Lat 24.28 N   Long 119.44
Wind s & sse; fine weather; one bark in sight beating down Formosa
strait; two steamers, one bound up the other down; cut out new main
lower topsail Bar. 29.86 T. 83.

June 13th
Lat 25.49 N   Long 120.54 E
Wind ssw moderate breeze & fine weather; sailor Jacobs fell from aloft to
the deck, nothing serious. Bar. 29.82 Ther. 81.

June 14th
Lat 28.11 N   Long 122.19 E
First part fresh breeze from South & ssw, later hauling west NW North &
NE came in foggy. Bar. 29.82 T. 78 F.

June 15th (Sunday)
Lat 28.35 N   Long 123.4 E
Wind NE fresh first part; light rain & fog; later light breeze & fog. Lost my
deep sea lead & sounder & 60 fathom of line; $35.00 gone to Davy Jones
locker. Bar. 29.80 T. 76.

June 16th
Sighted Bairen Island at 4 p.m.; 8 p.m. North Saddle Island light bore
West distance 20 miles; strong ebb tide making; Wind E & ENE fresh
breeze, hazy, & light rain, very disagreeable weather Bar. 29.80 T. 74.

June 17th
Came to anchor in 10 fathoms of water, mud bottom, North Saddle Island
Light bearing SE by S; Elliott Island SSW.

June 18th
8 a.m. weighed anchor & proceeded on our voyage; received pilot on
board at 11 p.m. Light ship bearing NW by W 1/2 W dis 6 miles. 10 p.m.
came to anchor at Woosung; 139 days from New York. *Mary L. Burrill*
anchored 3 hours before us.

Capt. Gullison   Yarmouth April 30/'90

Dear Sir:
I shall send this via San Francisco. I have written you twice before and
since doing so I have closed the ship to load at Shanghai and Hong Kong. I
expect you will think the rate very low but I figure it as good as $6.00 for
sugar for Manilla. The port of discharge is New York, Rate $9500. Things
are very dull out East with ships laying waiting for business. It seems to
me there must be an accumulation of Tonnage and with the large fleet
gone out I can't see much chance for improvement. I have written W.F.
Hagar & Co. to enclose you particulars to Charter and charter party via
Frisco. The *Euphemia* is loading at Japan at same rate $9500. I wrote you
in my last about remitting. I see *Narwhal* is at Batavia 86 days, fine passage.[15] Expect you will get the NE Monsoon which will make it hard getting
to Shanghai but hope you will be able to make fair passage and report in
good time. Cable on arrival. Trusting this will find you all in good health.

I am yours truly
N.B. Lewis

P.S. In cabling arrival if you have particulars charter use the word Frank
and I will understand it as meaning you have particulars of charter.

If you arrive before this and have cabled arrival you can cable me Frank
on receiving C/P [Charter Party]. N.B.L.
[Note On Letter]
Messers W.F. Hagar & Co.

Gentlemen:
Will you please enclose this letter to Capt. Gullison ship *N.B. Lewis* via San
Francisco and oblige. N.B.L.

---

15 *N.B. Lewis* took 135 days for the same voyage.

Capt. Gullison   Yarmouth June 19th '90

Dear Sir:

I was glad to hear of your safe arrival this morning. I sent you some time since letters in reference to business charter back and so on which I expect you have before this. The rate is low but perhaps as good as anything going at present. Things don't look very favourable in freights at present but hope they may improve before you get moving again. Suppose you will keep money enough to discharge Shanghai and Hongkong, remitting balance of inward freight from Shanghai. Suppose this letter will meet you in Hongkong that is if they don't load you up quick. When you get loaded cable me the word 'sailing' thus

Lewis Yarmouth Nova Scotia sailing

Otago is on way up to Breakwater [Delaware Bay] for orders. Lost her rudder head going down, three days out from Boston but managed to steer her down. Hoping this may find you all in good health. Haven't heard from *M.L. Burrill* yet. See you passed Anjer previous 19th May.

Yours
N.B. Lewis

N.B. Lewis Esq.   Shanghai June 27th '90

Dear Sir:

I arrived at Saddle Islands June 16th, Woosung 18th, Shanghai 19th and commenced discharging on 21st and count my passage 139 days from New York. All well and right side up with care. *Mary L. Burrill* and the *Lewis* towed up the river and docked together although he beat me to Anjer; ship *Narwhal* must have had a better chance than us. We made very good time to the Cape, 63 days, had we got any show at all *running our eastern down*[16] which we did in 42°.00 South Lat. could have made Anjer in 93 days as it was, we were 105 as I informed you in my letter from Anjer. Crossed Equator Feb. 27th Long. 24.23 w 28 days. Cape Good Hope Apl. 3rd Christmas Island 101. Anjer 105. We made a little water in our topsides[17] coming out. When I went to overhaul them here found them very slack in places so concluded to have them caulked, also main deck another piece of rail in poop which I think is decaying underneath, this will cost us about $250.00 (Mex),[18] ship finding material. I am doing it for the best Mr.

16 'Running our easting down'—this is a reference to the strong winds, often of gale force, which continually blow from West to East across the South Atlantic and South Indian Oceans. It will be noted the course was along latitude 42° s.
17 Topsides: outer surface of the hull above the water line.
18 The 'Mexican dollar' was currency formerly minted by the U.S. mint for the far eastern trade. It represented 420 grains of silver. In Shanghai in 1890 Capt. Gullison valued the Mexican dollar at 87 1/2 cents on the gold standard.

Lewis, and trust it will be accepted. Our homeward freight is small compared with our outward but no doubt it is better than Pacific ports, we could at present get about one shilling more per ton. I will send you, Sir, by this mail, £1000 stg. (One thousand pounds) date bills as requested.

We did not have to lighten any this time, towage very high, cargo coming out in excellent order. Things in general working satisfactory.

Your Obedient Servant
Frank Gullison

TUESDAY, OCTOBER 20, 1891

For the *Yarmouth Herald*
A Visit to Shanghai[19]
By a Yarmouth Mate

On the morning of the 18th of March last, a bright and beautiful day, some friends and myself went to visit the ancient town of Shanghai, or 'Chinatown' as the ancient city is called. As our ship lay on the opposite side from Shanghai at Jardine's wharf, our native Sambaugaman[20] offered to put us across the river. The countenance of Mr. Joyce, No. 419, was illuminated with pleasure, as he with great rapidity and wonderful dexterity sculled his sandpan across the beautiful river, and with his broken English entertained us on our journey. We were not long in crossing the Woosung, that beautiful tributary of the Yang-Tse-Kiang that meanders serpent-wise far into the interior and constantly filled with native craft of different descriptions from the sandpans and junks to the huge war-ships that lay at anchor mid-channel. As we reached the opposite bank several 'Rickshaws' were eagerly awaiting our arrival, offering us their assistance with violent gesticulations and forcible language, reminding one of the hackemen or expressmen for the transportation of baggage around some great Metropolitan Central railroad depot.

The Rickshaws are beautiful little vehicles, originally of American construction, provided with a small, narrow seat, capable of seating one person, covered with a cushion of bright green, red or some other loud color, and two light high wheels. They also have a folding top, as our buggies have, to shelter the inmate from the rain in wet weather and protect him from the sun in hot — the turnout reminding one of our two wheeled baby carriages at home, only of larger size. They are also provided with a small pair of shafts, to which the native Chinaman will attach himself by means of a belt or sircingle [wide leather strap] across his shoulders, and for the matter of a little cash will

19 This account of 'A Visit to Shanghai' was published in the *Yarmouth Herald* of October 28th, 1891. Written by a Yarmouth sailor, at that time a mate and later a captain, George Baker, it provides a colorful picture of the city of Shanghai at this time. It should be remembered that at this time the city of Shanghai contained both the International Settlements and the local Chinese city. The 'Settlements' were in turn divided into three divisions, English, German and French, each with a local government.
20 The operator of the sampan or Chinese water taxi.

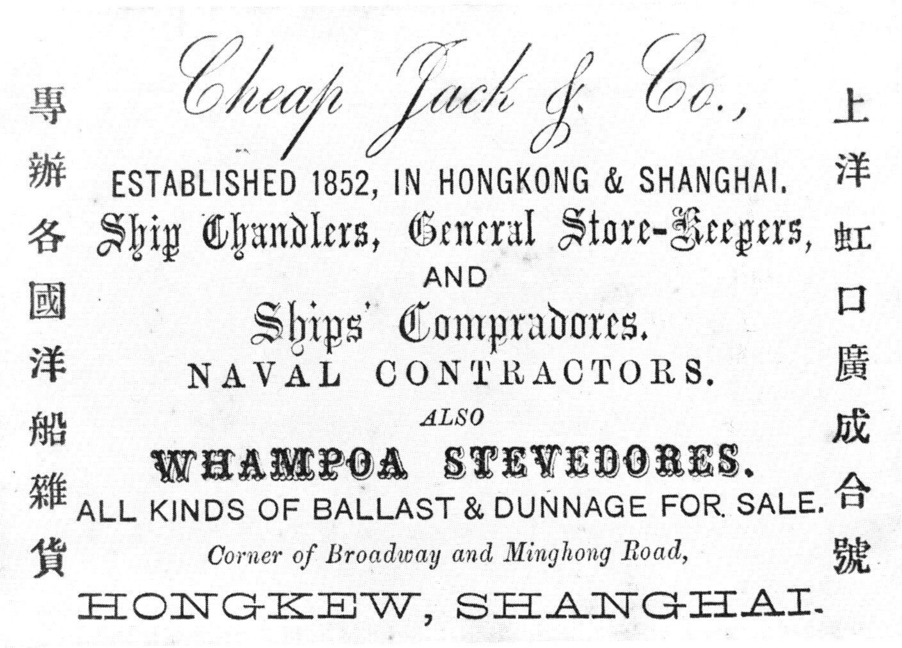

專辦各國洋船雜貨

Cheap Jack & Co.,

ESTABLISHED 1852, IN HONGKONG & SHANGHAI.

𝕾𝖍𝖎𝖕 𝕮𝖍𝖆𝖓𝖉𝖑𝖊𝖗𝖘, 𝕲𝖊𝖓𝖊𝖗𝖆𝖑 𝕾𝖙𝖔𝖗𝖊-𝕶𝖊𝖊𝖕𝖊𝖗𝖘,

AND

𝕾𝖍𝖎𝖕𝖘' 𝕮𝖔𝖒𝖕𝖗𝖆𝖉𝖔𝖗𝖊𝖘.

NAVAL CONTRACTORS.

ALSO

WHAMPOA STEVEDORES.

ALL KINDS OF BALLAST & DUNNAGE FOR SALE.

Corner of Broadway and Minghong Road,

HONGKEW, SHANGHAI.

上洋虹口廣成合號

FIG. 59. Business card of 'Cheap Jack', Shanghai.

run for miles with the un-wavering speed of the fleetest horse. Having selected four of the most comodious, we proceeded down the old Kong Kew to the store of Cheap Jack[21] the ship's compodore[22] and stevedore, where we employed a native to accompany us as guide. As the Chinese gentleman who runs this shop, and goes under the cognomen of Cheap Jack, was indulging in a cup of tea, he asked us to join him in the proceeding. We were pleased to accept this invitation, and took our tea in true oriental custom, sitting around a table with no cover, drank our tea with no sugar in ornamental cups or bowls, with no handles. After a brief stay here we again continued our journey, passed the Astor House, and the monument erected in memory of Sir William Knight, who was murdered in '65 by the natives, passed through American and English Shanghai at great speed, with the untiring efforts of our human horses and continued down the French settlement, then through a short distance of open country, where, as far as the eye could reach, were the graves of the Chinese dead. The Chinese have no cemetery or grave yard (set apart and dedicated as holy ground wherein to bury the bones of their departed) nor are their graves marked with expensive granite monuments of marble tombstones, that future generations may ask, 'What mean ye by these stones?' but the country is thickly interspersed with mounds, arising at frequent intervals, and held in as great religious awe as the most costly memorial in the most fashionable cemetery. After the space of half an hour we arrived at China-Town.

This city is surrounded by two high walls and six huge gates, which open at 6 a.m. and close at 6 p.m. with the regularity of a clock. I learn that this ancient city had existence at the time of the Tsin and Kitan dynasties as far back as 222 BC and was visited by Yhenghis Khan and Kublai Khan, the great conquerors in the thirteenth century. We left our Jimmie Rickshaws outside the gates as they had no licenses to enter, and accompanied by our guide proceeded on foot. A small river or brook runs through the city, which is constantly filled with all refuse, its waters of a greenish cast, and the odors arising therefrom sickening to the aesthetic tastes of the European.

On entering the streets of the city (and when we refer to these, don't let the reader picture a Broadway with its thousands hurrying to and fro! nor a Girard Avenue, with its tall and shadowy pines, but long narrow dirty lanes hardly of sufficient width for two to walk abreast) we could see the signs of the various business places, protruding in every conceivable direction and covered with the Chinese hieroglyphics. Among the most interesting places we visited were the silk makers, shops or factories, several of which we passed and paused to inspect. In a long filthy room with low roofs, they were at work, weaving the most beautiful and costly silks — silks fit for princes, of all shades, colors and textures — silks, with beautiful flowers and other designs worked in and interwoven in them. Other shops were engaged by blacksmiths, carpenters, tailors, shoemakers, and all trades people — places where old leather was taken, picked to pieces, and after the addition of straw, rags and bamboo &c., they pressed it until it resembled and was sold for the finest French Calf — places where all cotton and wool were picked to pieces, washed, represented and sold for new. A busy city indeed,

21 See Cheap Jack's business card, found among Captain Gullison's papers, reproduced on pg. 255.
22 'Compodore' — comprador, or Chinese business agent. See Appendix D.

reminding one of New York on a smaller scale, its inhabitants as eager to obtain cash and as zealous in the worship of mammon as the many thousands who daily walk the busy streets of our great cities, 'jostling each other in their race for gold.' Our attention was taken by the numerous beggars, who, half naked, filthy and in rags, beat their heads against the ground and otherwise inflicted self torture, that the stranger may take notice and give a few cash. One in particular was afflicted with the dropsy and had his leg swollen to a terrible size, kept hammering his head and breast and crying for help. We gave several small donations of a few cash, and when the news circulated that we were distributing alms in such wonderful profusion we were soon surrounded by a young thousand.

Time will not permit me to dwell longer on the abject misery of these poor heathan. We next crossed a winding bridge and entered the native Jugernaut or Chinese Joyce [Joss] house.[23] Several Joyce [Joss] were there, some of wood, bronze, metal, silver and gold, and several decorated and gilded and resembled gold. There were the God of the Sowing, the God of Harvest, the God of Peace, the God of War, &c., &c. Each one we noticed attentively but our guide paid no apparent attention until, arriving at the pedestol of the Cyclone God, he prostrated himself on the ground and did obeisance. It was the anniversary day of the Cyclone God and a great feast was abundantly provided and sacrificed in his honor. A table abundantly filled with poultry, game, fish, meats and fruit, was before him. Sandal wood and incense were burning in huge urns; and there he stood in all his splendor, with two arms uplifted, two hanging down, a satisfied expression on his face, as if he in reality appreciated the attempts made in his honor. Among other places of interest we found opportunity to visit, the most worthy of mention was the Tea Gardens. It is really the Chinese Park, small buildings containing tables for tea drinking, their walls formed exclusively of a clear transparent shell the most beautiful specimen of conchology I have ever seen. They also have beautiful highly colored silk curtains, behind which is the Chinaman's stage, theatre, or Boards of Thespis. These gardens contain many different varieties of plants, trees, &c. Among these our notice was particularly attracted by a singular specimen of a large tree, a species of palm, though smaller in size. Its longevity was so great, that while lifting its bushy head high above the earth, and spreading its leaves to the rains and sunshine from heaven, and in every way enjoying health and still growing, its bark and outside had become petrified. One was in a complete state of petrification and stood there as a memorial, a huge pillar of stone, containing fossiliferous strata more wonderful than the Palaeozoic Rocks of Pekin [Peking] or the cretacious stones of the Yang-Tse Kiang.

Other noticeable plants were the camellias, the orange and lemon trees, different varieties so trained and tortured in youth, that they represented contorted, stunted plants, twisted and bent in every imaginable direction, possessing a grotesque beauty in their extreme ugliness; and the palms seemed to look down upon us with the passion-less calm of some animated articulated superior human beings as we sat down to rest under the canopy of their shadowy branches.

South End   *G.A. Baker*

---

23   Chinese temple for idol worship.

Messers R. Brockelman & Co.   Shanghai June 30th '90

Dear Sirs:

Under reference to the charter party dated New York 26th Apl. 1890, I beg to inform you that I am today ready to receive cargo, and would request you to send the same as quick as possible. Hoping you will favor me with a quick dispatch here.

>   I remain Dear Sirs
>   Yours Faithfully
>   *B.F. Gullison*
>   Commanding Br Ship *N.B. Lewis*

Messers Reuter Brockelman & Co.   Shanghai July 1st '90

Dear Sirs:

Under reference to charter party dated New York 26th April 1890, I beg enclosed to hand you the certificate of seaworthiness from Lloyds surveyor of this port. I further inform you, that I am today ready to receive cargo trusting you will favor me with a quick dispatch.

>   I remain Dear Sirs
>   Yours Faithfully
>   *B.F. Gullison*
>   Commanding Br Ship *N.B. Lewis*

N.B. Lewis Esq.

Dear Sir:

Our lay days commenced July 2nd and we are now waiting cargo. We finished discharging 27th ult, cabled you Frank, discharged, *meaning* have received *Charter Party* ship *discharged*. I sent you by last mail 27th 1st bill of exchange to the amount of £1000 stg.

And will today send you First bill of exchange to another £1000 stg. and also 2nd of Exchange to First amount. Hope, Sir, you will receive all in order. I wrote to you about the work I was having done. Have decks and topsides caulked. Commenced taking up some of the rail[24] aft today, find it very bad underneath, so much so, that instead of 40 feet we shall have to make it 56 feet.

>   Yours Obediently
>   *B.F. Gullison*

---

24 Top of bulwark.

Mrs. Daniel Wardell[25]   Shanghai
85 Selwood Street   London S.E.   July, 1890

Dear Madam:
Your letter was received at New York, contents noted. I could not pay the
money due your husband there or deliver his effects.

   Had to wait until I arrived here at Shanghai.

   His wages which amounted to $206.29 Gold including his effects which
were small was delivered to the British Consulate of this port.

   My ship is bound from here to New York via Hongkong.

>   Yours Respectfully
>   *B.F. Gullison*
>   Commanding Br. Ship
>   *N.B. Lewis*

Messers Reuter Brockelman & Co.   Shanghai July 9th '90
Shanghai

Dear Sirs:
Referring to our conversation of the 8th inst. regarding the stowage of tea
with a mixed cargo, containing untanned hides and undressed wool.

   I have carefully considered this matter with all the precautions you have
suggested and cargo stowed with stevedore of your approval, and have
come to the conclusion that hides and undressed wool throw off such
odours as may be very detrimental to the tea stowed in the same bottom
and in event of your shipping the tea with the same, I must insist upon
the 'Bills of Lading' containing the clause 'Ship not liable for deterioration'.

>   I remain Yours Faithfully
>   *B.F. Gullison*
>   Master Br. Ship *N.B. Lewis*

N.B. Lewis Esq.   Yarmouth N.S.   Shanghai July 11th '90

Dear Sir:
This will inform you that we have not commenced any cargo yet. They
informed me yesterday that they had some tea and wool and I had to explain to them that tea and wool, or undressed wool was not fit articles to be
stowed on same bottom and I sent a letter to this effect and also telling

---

25 Daniel Wardell was engaged in New York January 12, 1889, as cook and steward at twenty-five
    dollars per month for the voyage to Java. He died in Surabaya from cholera and was thus
    recorded as discharged August 28, 1889. It is not clear why the captain could not remit from
    New York the balance of wages and effects to the widow in London.

them in event of them shipping tea with wool or hides I should insist on bills of Lading containing the clause 'Ship not liable for deterioration' to this I have not received an answer. We have 350 ton of shingle[26] ballast on board but if they give all tea I shall take 50 ton more. I have had to condemn my Main Lower Topsail yard; expect bill will be high. Enclosed please accept 2nd bill of Exchange to last amount (£1000).

> Yours faithfully
> *Frank Gullison*

Messers Reuter Brockelman & Co.　　　Shanghai July 12th '90
Shanghai

Gentlemen:

Yours of the 11th inst. to hand contents noted; I accept your offer in which you say, if I sign clean bills of lading you will give me a letter of guarantee, not holding me responsible for deterioration the tea may suffer from smells of other cargo in said ship.

> Yours respectfully
> *B.F. Gullison*
> Commanding Br. Ship *N.B. Lewis*

N.B. Lewis Esq.　　Yarmouth, N.S.　　　Shanghai July 18 '90

Dear Sir:

As the mail leaves today via San Francisco I thought I would write you a few lines, although we have done but very little as regards loading. About 1/4 of our lay days are up and 50 tons of wool and straw onboard. We will not take any tea although they came to my terms and I have it in black and white too. For my part I am very glad the tea question has dropped. I know if we took tea and wool together there would be damaged tea at New York as the smell of this undressed wool is very bad.

Typhoon signals were up yesterday and we are having it in earnest this morning. Ship *Troop*[27] arrived here last night 108 days from New York.

> Yours Obediently,
> *Frank Gullison*

P.S. I have sent you two £1000 bills First and second exchange of the same. Exchange now is very high owing to the silver bill being passed in

---

26　Shingle – water-worn smooth stones from a beach.
27　Ship *Troop* was owned by Troop firm of Saint John, N.B. This passage of 108 days compares favorably with that of *Lewis* and *Burrill* of 140 days. Another comparison is the first voyage of the *Cutty Sark* made in 104 days.

Washington. The bank quoted 4/11 (four shillings and eleven pence) per Tail[28] dollar yesterday and it is expected to rise above 5 shillings.

I will not send any more sterling until I square up here Sir. Will probably get an extra good rate for balance.

Ship N.B. Lewis and Owners in a/c with B.F. Gullison Master

1890 July 31	Dr. $ ¢	Cr. $ ¢
To cash paid deceased steward	246.25	
" " paying off three sailors $29.06		
	67.18	$38.12
" " Blacksmith $8.50 + $1.00	9.50	
" " A. Chay-Wing-Wa Gilder	25.00	
" " Kwang-Hong-Sang, Carpenter	333.73	
" " Tai Mow, Potatoes and veg.	11.67	
" " Ah Ming, Flags	18.00	
" " Mactavish & Lehman, druggist	2.90	
" " Sam Pan[29] & Ric Shas[30] wan	42.00	
" " Supplies and Cash to Officers		
& crew	487.95	
" " Hotel expenses	15.00	
" " Personal B.F. Gullison	140.82	
	$1400.00	$1400.00
Cr.		
By Cash Received C.J.T. Co.		$1400.00
E. and O.E.		

Shanghai July 31st 1890   *B.F. Gullison*, Master

28 'Tail' – tael.
29 Sam Pan – water taxi propelled by one oar over the stern.
30 Ric Shaw – rickshaw – a two wheeled vehicle pulled by a man.

Ship *Charles S. Whitney*
Parsboro Nova Scotia
GEORGE D. SPICER Master[31]

Capt. Gullison   Ship *N.B. Lewis*   Hongkong
Shanghai   July 22, 1890

Dear Sir:

I will try and fullfill my promise to write you a few lines. Well, Demmence, the pilot, left on the morning of 2nd inst. so you see what a tedious time getting out the river and that whole week was nearly calm and hot weather with the exception of a heavy squall about two days after the pilot left. We had some current to the Eastward as soon as we was out to the Barren Islands but when we got to Turnabout Island there was about two kinds of current to the N.E. so you see it was slow work getting to the s.w. Was nearly a week getting around that Island. If there had not of been a Typhoon passing on the 14th got a breeze which runs us to Breaker Point then we had another siege to get along. Light winds and sea from Southward which would roll the ship to near the shore. On the 17th was another typhoon and very bad rainy weather. Changeable weather, got within 15 miles of the light (Hongkong) when had to tack ship and stand off. Was 24 hours getting here. Anchored here 10 a.m. 20th. Sailed in the Tymoon pass. Got a compadors man for pilot just by the light.

Now. Capt. Gullison, my opinion is the *Charles S. Whitney* would of been about 20 weeks in the place of 20 days getting here if we had not of got some good slants. Perhaps the *N.B. Lewis* would do better. And it is very hard work I never got a good nights sleep on the pass and was about used up when we got here. We did not have so much wind at any time. Some very heavy squalls, lost one sail. The weather has been bad ever since we arrived. The *Thiorva* and *Ann Stafford* arrived the evening of the 20th then there are 5 American ships and the *Z. Ring* here. I can't say I like Hongkong as well as Shanghai but I have seen none or very little of the place. Expect to be here all the days. We are quite well. Mrs. Spicer had a few days of indisposition but is quite well now. Gertie is well and they both join with me in sending kind regards to you and all the friends in Shanghai. Heard you was having meeting[32] every week on your ship and I trust they will be a blessing to you and all concerned. Please write me all the news and where all the vessels are going or what they are going to do. Tell Mr. Harris at the C. & J. Trading Co. I have his note and will send the canarys.

With kind regards
I remain Yours Truly
George D. Spicer

31 Captain George D. Spicer was grandfather of Stanley T. Spicer, author of *Masters of Sail*.
32 Prayer meeting.

P.S. I hope Capt. Kinney[33] found his cigars before he left for Puget Sound. Kind regards to Mrs. Graves.[34] *Gertie*

P.S. Please give my kind regards to Mrs. & Mr. Graves. I forgot to tell you what that Vice Consul in Shanghai is trying to do. You know the man I shipped there did not join and I had to get another man in his place and Every the Superintendent of the Home was with me at the time I got the other man. He was to blame that the other man was not on board. After I left they sent the man down here and wrote to the Harbour Master to collect $15.00 for the passage and the advance but of course I declined to pay any such bill so they have wrote back to the Consul. That man beats anything I ever seen in the shape of a Consul. He is not worth to be called a man as there is no part of a man about him and by the correspondence. The sailors Home man has acted like everything but a gentleman. There is a great many very bulky official documents. This might be of some benefit to you. Tell Mr. Every I am extremely obliged to him, as well as the Consul. I fancy they will have some trouble to get the money. I must tell you a little about my finger, it is far from well. There was a piece of loose bone I wanted the doctor to take out before I left which he did not do and it got quite solid and the finger was running quite a lot lately so today I got the doctor to work and they cut the end of my finger up and took out 2 pieces of bone. I hope it will get well now.

G.D.S.

N.B. Lewis   Yarmouth, N.S.   Shanghai July 31st '90

Dear Sir:

This will inform you that the Good Ship *N.B. Lewis* will sail for Hongkong tomorrow. The merchants did not have sufficient cargo for us, so they had to put onboard 'Ballast' and as we have 25 of the lay days used up here. My expenses here is about £50 Stg. I expect you will think them high but money does go somehow. I have sent you two £1000 drafts and will enclose in this; First Bill of exchange 50 days sight to the amount of £800-2-9 Stg. making in all £2800-2-9 have reserved £200 for Hongkong expenses. I trust I may be favoured with a short down?[35] I do dread it so much.

From Your Obedient Servant
Frank Gullison

---

33 Capt. Kinney was master of the *Mary L. Burrill.*
34 The first mate of *N.B. Lewis* was Emerson Graves and it would seem from this letter that Mrs. Graves was with him on this voyage.
35 Voyage from Shanghai to Hong Kong.

J.F. Whitney & Co.   New York   Shanghai July 31st 1890

Gentlemen:

This will inform you that the good ship *N.B. Lewis* sails for Hongkong tomorrow. Your letter of Feb. 28th was duly received and contents noted; please accept thanks for your kindness.

   Will you please hold the enclosed documents until my arrival at New York.

   Wishing you sirs, compliments of the Season.

> I remain Yours Respectfully
> *B.F. Gullison*

Messers Reuter Brockelman & Co.   Hongkong Sept. 6/'90

Gentlemen:

I beg to inform you that the Br. Ship *N.B. Lewis* is this day ready to receive cargo, hoping you will *favor me* with a quick dispatch here.

> I remain Gentlemen
> Yours faithfully
> *B.F. Gullison*
> Commanding Br. Ship
> *N.B. Lewis*

N.B. Lewis Esq.;   Hongkong Sept. 16th '90

Dear Sir:

We arrived here on the 5th inst. after a long and tedious passage of 35 days. I never had such a drubbing before, and never wish to experience the same again. North of Formosa Strait I was hard at it for 14 days steady drill, tacking about every three or four hours whenever I could make a point either one way or the other, and the wind during this time never moved over two points. I did think sometimes the yards and sails would go out of her. I had to carry a press of sail to try and hold on but it was impossible and at the end of these 14 days I was about 10 miles to leeward of where I started from and I always kept well inshore too; but never anchored only once for about an hour during the passage, after this seige we had calms and light variable breezes from North and N.E., at times not sufficient to stem the current which runs at the rate of 1 to 3 knots and the tide rip at times would whirl her around in all shapes and it is a thing impossible, Sir, for any ship to beat down the China sea against the 'Monsoons'. Certainly they do stand a chance at times; I am sure if I hadn't got one I would have been to the North Pole by this time instead of

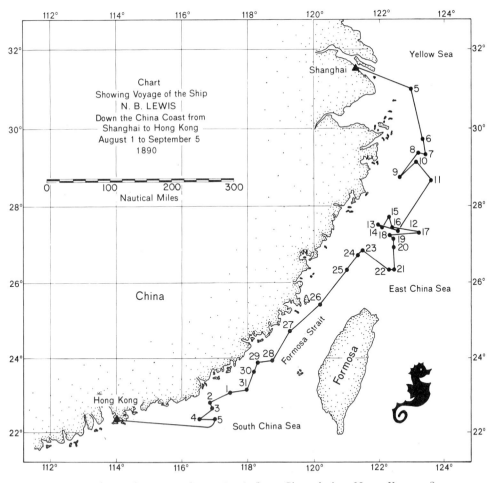

FIG. 60. Chart of voyage of *N.B. Lewis* from Shanghai to Hong Kong, 1890.

Hongkong and I must say I was pretty near used up when we arrived here and according to my idea we have had more wear and tear during this time than our passage from New York to Shanghai. Had considerable sickness too; one sailor fell and broke his arm and he is now in hospital doing well. I hope you have received your bills of exchange and all vouchers from Shanghai.

Your letter of June 19th I received on arrival here. Note what you say about cabling on sailing. We expect now to sail from here about the 30th if things go favourable. I am painting yards and masts here this time. Think it will be better than scraped and cheapest in the end. I have all my crew, except one in the hospital, so I will conclude by saying that I am in good health and trust this lengthy epistle will find you the same. Hoping soon to get clear of this place and make tracks for New York.

> I remain, Dear Sir,
> Yours faithfully
> *B.F. Gullison*

Shanghai 24/9/90

Dear Capt. Gullison:
It was indeed with great pleasure I received your welcome letter from Hongkong: also glad to hear you are quite well, after such a trying passage.

DIARY, VOYAGE FROM SHANGHAI TO HONGKONG 1890

August 1st 1890
2 p.m. tugboat & pilot came along side, weighed anchor & proceeded in tow tug *Fokelin.* 8 p.m. anchored at red buoy; Wind westerly.

Aug. 2nd
Working tides down Yang tese Kiang; wind westerly.

Aug. 3rd Sunday
Light air from East; weighed anchor this morning at 3 a.m. & anchored at 8 a.m. Ship *Troop* in company with us. Weather very hot this morning swell setting in from NE; discharged pilot 8 p.m.; flood making; Day ends fine; beautiful weather; wind veering from SE to ESE Bar steady.

Aug. 4th
Light air and fine beautiful weather throughout the day; wind first part East & ESE later ENE Bar 29.74 T 86.

Aug. 5th
Lat 30.38 N   Long 123.00E
Light variable airs throughout the day attended by fine weather Bar 29.70
T 88.

Aug. 6th
Lat 29.50N   Long 123.10 E
Light variable airs & light rain.

Aug. 7th
Lat 29.31 N   Long 123.22 E
Wind light & southerly; clear blue sky.

Aug. 8th
Lat 29.35 N   Long 123.14 E
Light variable airs & northerly current here about 1 knot per hr.

Aug. 9th
Lat 28.58 N   Long 123.29 E
First part of this day begins with light variable airs; middle continual lightening in the SE quarter, later blowing fresh from SW; royals in, hardly holding our own; current setting NE 1 knot per hr.

Aug. 10th Sunday
Lat 29.28 N   Long 122.56 E
Wind blowing strong from SW; current setting NE 1 knot per hr. almost
impossible to hold our own under these circumstances but will have to
bear with it I suppose. Bar. 29.62 T 88.

Aug. 11th
Lat 28.50 N   Long 123.39 E
First part of this day begins with fresh breeze from SW; midnight heavy
lightening from all points of the horizon; later part wind hauling West NW
& NE with a very heavy squall; reduced sail to lower topsails & fore sail
Bar. 29.50 T 83.

Aug. 12th
Lat 27.40 N   Long 122.18 E
Light variable breezes; later hauling SW fresh: HARD HARD SIGHT.

Aug. 13th
Lat 27.51 N   Long 121.51 E
Wind blowing strong from SW; all light sail furled & fore & mizzen top
gallant sail. Current setting NE 1 knot per hr. during the day, cannot but
hold our own – This is rough on rats.

Aug. 14th

Lat 27.48 N   Long 122.00 E

Blowing a gale from ssw; under reefed topsails & courses Bar. 29.70 T 85.

Aug. 15th

Lat 28.5 N   Long 122.19

Wind nailed fast at sw blowing a gale; under reefed topsails & courses, drifting to NE 30 miles dead to leeward, short chopping sea; Sighted land this morning. Bar. 29.72 T 85.

Aug. 16th

Lat 27.56   Long 122-24 E

Wind steady from sw; current setting NE I knot per hr. This is very discouraging Bar. 28.76 T 85.

Aug. 17th Sunday

Lat 27.41 N   Long 122.51 E

Wind holding sw & ssw; fresh breeze & steady, looking sw monsoons HARD, HARD SIGHT to get sw Bar. 29.78 T 85.

Aug. 18th

Lat 27.38 N   Long 122.7 E

Wind holding ssw & sw Strong breeze & dead on end; sw monsoons in earnest.

Aug. 19th

Lat 27.32 N   Long 122.13 E

Stood in Wan Ghu Bay this morning & made Pan-Shan Island bearing North Taluk Isle NW by N; 14 fathoms water, mud bottom Wind sw to ssw not so steady as usual Bar. 29.84 T 85.

Aug. 20th

Lat 27.7 N   Long 122.17 E

Winds sw & wsw; moderate & fine; current setting NE 1 knot per hr.

Aug. 21st

Lat 26.25 N   Long 122.33 E

Wind West & WSW; moderate breeze & smooth water Bar. 29.80 T 85.

Aug. 22nd

Lat 26.31 N   Long 122.21 E

Wind light from West smooth water (*poor prospects*).

Aug. 23rd

Lat 26.56 N   Long 121.30 E

First part light from sw; later increasing, sighted Namke Island 3.30 p.m. bearing N 3/4 E, Tai Isle sw by w Bar. 29.62 & 84.

Aug. 24th Sunday
Lat 26.42 N Long 121-21 E
Wind veering from sw to w & later light squall off the land; not making much progress as Namke Island bears tonight at 6 p.m. N by w; Tai Isle w 1/2s; current setting NE 1 to 2 knots throughout the day.

Aug. 25th
Lat 26.29 N Long 121 E
Calm & light variable airs, ending with cloudy sky & a heavy squall from NW: Victor Anderson fell & broke his arm, set it and laid him by.

Aug. 26th
Lat 25.37 N Long 120.12 E
Squally from NW to NE, heavy dark passing clouds; later fine weather, wind North, sighted Turnabout Island. Bar. 29.82 T 84.

Aug. 27th
Lat 24.40 N Long 119.30 E
Wind light from N to NE & ENE; fine beautiful weather Bar. 29.80 T 85.

Aug. 28th
Lat 23.55 N Long 118.38 E
Wind light & variable from NW around to N & E Bar. 29.76 T 87.

Aug. 29th
Lat 23.53 N Long 118.13 E
Light variable breezes from ssw to sw Bar. 29.70 T 83.

Aug. 30th
Lat 23.38 N Long 118-5 E
Wind light & variable from ssw to sw, smooth water & Fine weather current setting constantly to NE from 1 to 2 knots Bar. 29.72 T 85.

Aug. 31st Sunday
Lat 23-04 N Long 117-47 E
First part wind light from sw; later light variable airs & calms VERY HEAVY TIDE RIPS Bar. 29.74 T 85.

Sept. 1st
Lat 22.51 N Long 117-13 E
Wind light & variable from NW around by N to E & s; later part quite steady from SE & fair looking. Bar. 29.70 T 85.

Sept. 2nd
Lat 22.41 N Long 116.40 E
Wind hauling s & sw, light airs & calms. Current as usual setting NE; Oh what a hard time we are having Bar. 29.72 T 86.

Sept. 3rd
Lat 22.23 N   Long 116.54 E
Wind veering from ssw to w, later part, heavy dark clouds rising over land
& to the NE quarter but the wind does not seem to come that way.

Sept. 4th
Lat 22.11 E   Long 116.20 E
Light variable airs & calms; getting most discouraging. Current setting SE,
heavy tide rips. Bar. 29.60 T 87.

Sept. 5th
Lat 22.19 N   Long 116.50 E
First part light air from the N; later part hauling NE; light wind; Spoke a
pilot boat off Pedro Blanco & received him on board 4 p.m. Boston Jack
came off in a steam launch; as the wind was light and the weather looked
threatening I engaged this boat to help ship in. 11 p.m. dropped anchor
in Hong Kong Bay after a long & tedious passage (35 days).

NOTE: The following letter was evidently written to Captain Gullison by a
missionary living in Shanghai. No signature.

I do hope this will reach you before you sail, if it does be sure to let us
know where to write to in New York, won't you?, and next time you come,
don't forget Mrs. Gullison.

I am so glad Capt. Park had such a fine run to Hongkong, I said to him
I would give him a week, but he said longer. I wish you had had such a
slant. I expected a letter from Mrs. Graves in answer to mine. Hope they
are both well, and that he is at least trusting in *Him* who alone can save to
the uttermost all that come unto him.

We often think and talk of you at home and the pleasant evenings spent
at Brits wharf.[36] We are so glad to hear Capt. Kinney is coming back soon.
Mary L. Burrill chartered from the Sound (Puget), Timber. The *Mary Pend-
leton* is about half loaded, do not know when she is likely to get away. The
wife was so disappointed she could not get down with the *Luzon*. Please
give our best chin-chin to Capt. Park and Mr. Williams. She did manage to
go down with the *Lilan*, Capt. Allyn, she enjoyed it fine. Sorry to say the
meetings are not so strong now, as they used to be, but two ships have just
arrived, the *Ellen A. Kirk*, Capt. Dennis and his daughter and the *Stamboul*,
Capt. & Mrs. Weston, neither of which have we met yet but hope to tomorrow evening, all well. We have a Capt. who has sold his own ship to
Nils Miller. He is living with us, a nice fellow of Windsor, N.S., he is just
awaiting his papers from home. His wife has gone on. Did Jane tell you of
him during your long passage down?

---

36 Evidently the *N.B. Lewis* was moored at Brits wharf in Shanghai.

N.B. Lewis Esq.   Hongkong
Yarmouth   Nova Scotia   Sept. 27th '90

Dear Sir:

As the mail leaves today I will pen you a few lines to inform you that things in general are working along slowly. Owing to a few days bad weather we have been unable to load cargo, but think we will be filled up and ready for sea by 31st.

Markets are dull here at present. Late arrivals are going to Portland Oregon and Calcutta. I am well and trust these few lines may find you the same.

From Your Obedient Servant
B.F. Gullison

Ship N.B. Lewis and Owners in A/C *with B.F. Gullison Master*[37]

Dr.	$Cts.	$Cts.
1890		
Oct. 3 The cash Light dues	33.15	
To cash Rating Chro.	8.00	
To cash Medicines 1.45, 1.00	2.45	
To cash Hospital	23.00	
To cash Painting Cabins	28.00	
To cash Blacksmith	4.39	
To cash Sampan	22.50	
To cash Doctor tending ship	20.00	
To cash Wing Ly-Loong Comprador	234.69	
To cash Towing Outwards	28.00	
Stevedore Loading	258.00	
To cash Cable to Owners	9.40	
To cash Hotel and Ricksha	31.00	
To B.F. Gullison Master	247.47	
	$1052.05	
Cr.		
By Cash Shanghai £200 Stg.		
On demand note Hongkong 3/9/1/8		$1052.05
E. & O.E.		
Hongkong October 3rd 1890		

---

37 Amounts shown may be in 'Mexican' dollars.

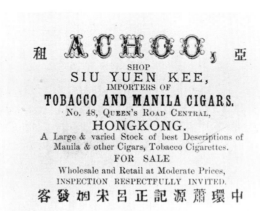

FIG. 61. Business card of Achoo, importer of tobacco, Hong Kong.

FIG. 62. Mary, washerwoman, Hong Kong.

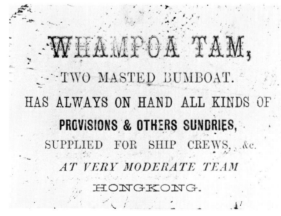

FIG. 63. Whampoa Tam, provisioner, Hong Kong.

List of Ships in the Port of Hong Kong, October 1890

Bark *Constance* (Saint John, N.B.)	Captain Tingley
Ship *Mary L. Stone*[38] (New York, N.Y.)	Captain Sam Park
Ship *Luzon* (New York, N.Y.)	Captain Jerry Park
Ship *George Skolfield*[39] (Brunswick, Me.)	Captain Dunning
Ship *Richard Parsons* (Camden, Me.)	Captain Freeman
Ship *Sintraum* (Freeport, Me.)	Captain Woodstock [Woodside]
Bark *Annie Stafford* (Saint John, N.B.)	Captain Robinson
Bark *Lancefield* (Moncton, N.B.)	Captain Burns
Bark *Asyeria* [Assyeria] (Saint John, N.B.)	Captain Lany
Ship *N.B. Lewis* (Yarmouth, N.S.)	Captain Gullison

Sept. 5th 1890

I agree to pay Pilot A. Loo the sum of twenty dollars $20.00 for piloting ship from sea to Hongkong.

Should I prefer his Comprador after arrival the sum of $10.00 is to be paid to said A. Loo as Pilotage instead of $20.00.

B.F. Gullison,
Master *N.B. Lewis*

N.B. Lewis Esq.   Hongkong Oct. 4th 1890

Dear Sir:

We finished loading last night, squared up my business today and will sail in the morning weather permitting. The typhoon signal has been up now four days and the weather looking kind of seedy. But according to the report this afternoon it has passed s.w. of Hongkong so I think I will be quite safe leaving in the morning.

We have onboard 2550 ton general cargo drawing 16.3 on even keel very light draft but I think will be stiff enough as I have a good set of ballast about 500 ton. Have used the £200 Stg. reserved for expenses here, has small balance left but charged myself for it in disbursement a/c which I trust you will receive and find in order. Hoping to make a good voyage home, I remain, kind Sir, Yours Most Respectfully,

B.F. Gullison

---

38 See Frederick C. Matthews, *American Merchant Ships, 1850-1900*. Salem, Mass., Marine Research Society, 1930, p. 207.
39 Ibid., p. 127.

B.F. Gullison Esq., Ship *N.B. Lewis*   Hongkong
                                               Oct. 8th '90

Dear Friend:

I took the $7.00 you gave me and tried to buy a P.O. order on New York but found they only issue them on U.K. so I bought one on London and the proper authorities at the P.O. in New York will be notified by the P.O. in London to pay you £1-4-4 which was what the amount you gave me called for. Enclosed I send you the receipt I got. By rights I should keep it, but will send it to you so you won't forget you got an order there. Hoping this will be satisfactory to you and that you will have a quick and safe passage.

> I remain yours sincerely
> *Chas. S. Robinson*
> Bark *Annie Stafford*

Capt. B.F. Gullison   REUTER BROCKELMAN & CO.
Brit. Ship *N.B. Lewis*   Hongkong 30th October 1890

Dear Capt. Gullison:

According to your wishes, I have much pleasure to inform you that I have succeeded in sending the telegram which you requested me to send on the following day and for which I beg to enclose a receipt for the same.

Hoping that the telegram has arrived safely to your owner and everything is O.K. should the telegram not be yet received, please let me know by return mail in order that I may enquire the cause of it and to refund the money.

Hoping that you are enjoying in perfect health and has safely arrived,

> I remain
> Yours faithfully
> *F.N. Soares*

DIARY HONG KONG TOWARDS NEW YORK 1890

Oct. 4th 1890
Sailed from HongKong 6 a.m.; Wind NE; discharged pilot noon. Taitami Channel, wind increasing & hauling Easterly, draft of water 16.3 fore & aft. Bar. 29.70 T 83.

Oct. 5th (Sunday)
Lat 19.00   Long 114.30 E
Wind E & ENE; strong breeze, shortened down to reefed topsails & foresail.

Oct. 6th

Lat 18.5 N　Long 114.10 E

Wind East strong breeze under lower topsails & reefed foresail; high & confused sea, bar. very unsteady; 4 p.m. put her head to the Northward Parcles Islands & reefs too handy Bar. 29.60 T 82.

Oct. 7th

Lat 18.19 N　Long 113.49 E

Fresh from ENE; under reefed topsails & foresail. Sea does not seem to decrease very much & weather not looking altogether right. Bar. 29.84 T 82.

Oct. 8th

Lat 16.27 N　Long 113.47

This day has been quite fine after the strong blow; experienced a current here 1 1/2 per hour setting wsw; wind light easterly; day ends light air ENE; water measured; steward 6 1/2 buckets 2 b. forward.[40] Bar. 29.80 T 80.

Oct. 9th

Lat 14.59 N　Long 113.41 E

Fine weather throughout the day; wind light from NE Bar. 29.80 T 83.

Oct. 10th

Lat 14.06 N　Long 112.30 E

Fine weather predominates, wind moderate & steady from NE Bar. 29.80 T 83.

Oct. 11th

Lat 12.45 N　Long 110.52 E

Wind quite steady in force & direction, weather keeping fine. Wind NE & NNE; northerly current setting N 1 mile per hour. Bar. 29.86 T 83.

Oct. 12th (Sunday)

Lat 9.50 N　Long 109.24 E

Wind steady from the NNE; fair weather. Current setting south during 25' the day. Bar. 29.84 T 83.

Oct. 13th

Lat 7.50 N　Long 107.42

Current set ship sw 1/2 s 45' during the day; fine weather, wind light and variable from NE to North NW Bar. 29.82 Ther. 84.

40　The water was low in tanks and thus rationed. The steward is in crew list as both cook and steward.

Oct. 14th
Lat 7.11 N   Long 107.00 E
Wind light & variable from North NE & ENE attended by fine weather very hot. Bar. 29.80 T 85.

Oct. 15th
Lat 6.25 N   Long 106.24 E
Wind light from N attended by fine weather Bar. 29.84 Ther. 87.

Oct. 16th
Lat 5.24 N   Long 105.58 E
Wind wsw; fine weather through the day; mate taken sick tonight Bar. 29.84 T 86.

Oct. 17th
Lat 4.54 N   Long 105.58 E
Wind light & variable; passed three large steamers bound NE; Hoisted our numbers & was answered; mate getting better. Bar. 29.82 Ther. 85.

Oct. 18th
Lat 4.28 N   Long 106.19 E
Wind variable & squally; one very heavy squall from sw; mate on duty; Victor's[41] broken arm doing nicely dressed today. 1 bbl. flour opened (18 days).

Oct. 19th (Sunday)
Lat 3.00   Long 106.50
Wind West & wsw; first part light, middle part very heavy squalls from w.

Oct. 20th
Lat 1.54 N   Long 106.50 E
Very heavy squalls today, wind veering from sw to NW attended by much rain.

Oct. 21st
Lat 1.36 N   Long 106.59 E
Very heavy squalls from sw to NW; jammed against St. Esprit Group but trust the Good Lord will change the wind soon; *squalls very bad*. Bar. 29.82 T 82.

41 The crew wages book for this voyage shows one man named Victor. His last name was Andersen. He joined the ship in New York on January 28, 1890, as an A.B. at $18.00 per month. The record shows him to be a careful man with money. The only purchase he made from the slop chest during the entire voyage was a knife at 30 cents and a hat at 35 cents. He went ashore in Shanghai and bought himself a pair of boots for $6.75 and a suit for $15.00. He was also charged for a bumboat (water taxi) at $5.00 and received one dollar in cash for shore expenses. When he joined the ship he was charged with an advance of $50.00 (perhaps paid to a crimp) but was able to leave the ship in New York January 31, 1891, with $142.76 in his pocket.

Oct. 22nd
Lat 1.32 N   Long 106.59 E
Very heavy squalls; how I would like to be home to have a *good night's rest.*

Oct. 23rd
Lat 1.40 N   Long 107.00 E
Squalls not so heavy but current very strong to SE Bar. 29.92 T 84.

Oct. 24th
Lat 1.30 N   Long 106.18 E
Weather looking more settled but the SE current seems to run stronger; very near two knots this morning; this is a jammer, no wonder my hair comes out. Bar. 29.90 T 84.

Oct. 25th
Lat 1.11 N   Long 106.18 E
First part wind light & variable, light squalls; later part *very heavy.* Sumatra squall; reduced sail to lower topsails & foresail. I think the bark *Lancefield* has lost some sail. Bar. 29.84 T 82.

Oct. 26th (Sunday)
Lat 0.40 N   Long 106.33 E
Light variable airs throughout the day; strong current setting ESE about 1 to 1 1/2 knots; close into St. Esprit Group Bar. 29.82 T 88.

Oct. 27th
Lat 0.20 N   Long 106.30
Light northerly airs attended by fine weather throughout the day. Bark Lancefield to the East of us about 1 1/2 miles. Bar. 29.84 T 87.

Oct. 28th
Lat 00.42 S   Long 106.42 E
Wind light from SW attended by smooth water & fine weather. Current setting ESE 1 knot per hour Bar. 29.84 T 87.

Oct. 29th
Lat 1.13 S   Long 107.20 E
Moderate breeze from South & SW; Lancefield has taken Caramatta strait & we have got to beat & bang around here I suppose. Bar. 29.90 T 84.

Oct. 30th
Lat 1.17 S   Long 107.20 E
First part light breeze from SW; later part squally veering all points, water smooth as glass. It seems almost impossible to get south & I do not care for Caramatta strait. Bar. 29.90 T 84.

Oct. 31st

Lat 1.43 s   Long 107.12 E

Light baffling winds & some heavy squalls from SE; had to let go anchor close to Newland Reef; light airs & current setting us on. Bar. 29.90 Ther. 85 F.

Nov. 1st

Lat 2.11 s   Long 107.12

Weighed anchor this morning at 3 a.m.; wind hauling NE very heavy squalls from SE hauling the wind to NE; 8 p.m. let go anchor entrance of Macclesfield Channel; Jilka s by E 1/2 E 10 miles, 18 fathom.[42]

Nov. 2nd (Sunday)

Lat 3.00 s   Long 107.00 E

Passed through Macclesfield Channel today, light airs from NE Southerly current 1 knot which assisted us on our way; several natives came off from the islands & traded with us. Bar. 29.84 T 87.

Nov. 3rd

Lat 3.58 s   Long 106.24 E

Light air from NW & W attended by fine weather.

Nov. 4th

Lat 4.40 s   Long 106.22 E

Wind light & variable principally from the Eastern & NE 11 p.m. anchored North Watcher bearing s by E dis. 20 miles. Dirty looking weather Bar. 29.84 T 87.

Nov. 5th

Lat 4.58 s   Long 106.22

First part wind North, later hauling NE & E with a squall wind & rain 4 p.m. North Watcher bearing East 6 miles.

J.F. Whitney & Co.   Anjer Java Nov. '90

Gentlemen:

Would you oblige me by paying my small premium to the New York life insurance Co. which will be due before my arrival and charge the same to Ship *N.B. Lewis* and Owners.

I insured through Mathew Clark, Agent, 346 Broadway N.Y. room 24.

We have been making very poor time so far, calms, strong currents, and heavy squalls to contend with, which will help to make a long voyage home

---

42 With squally weather, changing winds, islands all around and heavy currents. Captain Gullison anchored the ship through the hours of darkness in 18 fathoms (108 feet) of water.

but I shall not murmur if it is done in safety. Please remember me to my friends at the office.

> From yours very respectfully
> *B.F. Gullison*

N.B. Lewis Esq.   Anjer November 1890
Yarmouth, Nova Scotia

Dear Sir:

This epistle will inform you that we are all well and right side up with care onboard the good ship *N.B. Lewis*. Although we have had a very hard sight down here to Anjer, head winds, strong currents, heavy squalls and calms to contend with. I assure you *good sir* it is enough to make one turn grey all over, let alone his hair and I shall feel greatly relieved when I get Java Head bearing East.[43]

I trust you have received everything in order from Shanghai and Hongkong and that everything will be found to your satisfiction.

Hoping to make better time from Anjer home, I remain

> Yours Obediently
> *B.F. Gullison*

To show that a difficult voyage among these islands in the Far East was not unique to the *N.B. Lewis* there is inserted here an interesting story told by Basil Lubbock in his book *The Down Easters*. It illustrates, at the same time, the difficulties and dangers the sailing ships encountered among the islands, the sailing qualities of the iron and steel vessels being built in Great Britain and the wide-ranging activities of the Yarmouth ships. The two Nova Scotiamen mentioned, *Antoinette* and *Hectanooga*, were built by Dennis & Doane, in 1874 and

---

43 No wonder Captain Gullison felt this way. Reading the day to day account of the ship's voyage through the China seas from August 1 to November 8 (except for the stay in Hong Kong harbour) it is easy to understand how tired of it all he was.

He had been 'beating and banging' about these seas for over two months. Day after day he made such little progress that he did not make his usual notation of distance sailed. He had to contend with light airs, constant wind changes, sudden gusts of wind and rain, and strong ocean currents flowing against him or across his course. Much of the time he was near land among reefs and small islands and the oppressive heat made sleep difficult or impossible. Several nights he dropped his anchor to prevent the ship running aground in the darkness.

Not only was the Captain fatigued; the ship also showed signs of hard usage. As soon as he was well into the Indian Ocean with fine weather and a steady breeze he bent No. 2 crossjack, spanker, mizzen lower topsail, main lower topsail, foresail and jib. For the next few days sailors were put to work overhauling the sails taken down. At the same time the windlass was overhauled and cleaned and various jobs were performed to restore the vessel to 'ship-shape' condition.

1875 respectively, on the Bay of Fundy shore about four miles south of the shipyard where the *N.B. Lewis* was built.

The story is based on a description of the incident by Mr. A.L. Putnam, a passenger on the Boston-built ship the *Sachem*, on a voyage from United States to the Far East in 1885.

After a good passage in which the *Sachem* pleased the young Putnam (he was scarcely more than a kid) by her prowess in running the Easting down, she arrived at the southern end of the Ombai Passage, between Ombai and Timor Islands, which is one of the usual routes into the Pacific.

Previous to this, whilst running before the westerlies, he records the ease with which the *Sachem* ran by a big Scottish four-mast barque which, he says, looked like a submerged reef with masts and sails sticking out of the froth and foam, whilst thousands of Cape pigeons and mollyhawks circled and darted around her. He was therefore surprised when the doughty flyer failed to beat her way through the Strait. But this was not surprising, for she found a strong southerly current between the islands, with no wind at all except for a few hours every afternoon, when it blew fresh to strong from the north, a dead muzzler for all vessels bound up to China. But for these few hours it was either dead calm or with sudden flurries, willy-waws and rain squalls darkening the sky and ruffling the water.

So here the *Sachem* stuck, along with a number of other vessels awaiting a slant, until at last there were from 20 to 30 ships held up, including the American ships, *Tam o' Shanter*, *Timour* (an 1866 Newburyport ship of 962 tons), *Joseph B. Thomas* (Sam Watts' 1881 ship), and the *Gloaming*, and the Nova Scotians, *Antoinette* and *Hectonoga*.

It was a case of a dead beat to windward every afternoon until the wind fell with the sun; and in these contests of weatherliness the *Sachem* generally found herself in the windward berth at the end of the day. Not a ship succeeded in getting through the Ombai Straits for 16 days.

On the afternoon of the 15th day a strange ship appeared at the tail end of the fleet − a small rakish ship, showing very little freeboard, and with the brown hemp sails of a Britisher. Young Putnam drew the second mate's attention to the newcomer, whose hull could be plainly seen after she had made a couple of tacks. The second mate of the *Sachem* was an Englishman. After taking a good look at the stranger, he remarked impressively: 'I don't know her name, but I know her type, and I can tell you that this bunch of Yankees, Blue-noses, and stockfish-eating Souwegians will now have a chance to see a ship sail and be shown how to get through the Ombai Passage.'

'Sure enough,' writes Putnam, 'in a couple of tacks the stranger came about at the same time as we did, but about a mile to leeward'.

It was now 6 bells in the afternoon, and the wind was blowing a good whole-sail breeze, but, as usual, a dead muzzler for the Northbound fleet. In twenty minutes from the time when the two ships came on to the same tack, the British ship was two miles ahead of the *Sachem* and a mile to windward. In passing, the two ships exchanged signals, and the clipper gave her name as the *Northampton* of London, bound from

London to Shanghai with scrap-iron. (The *Northampton* was a composite ship of 1174 tons, built by Connell of Glasgow in 1866 for the Merchant Shipping Company.)

When the wind fell in the late afternoon the Britisher was a good 10 miles to windward of the *Sachem*, which in her turn was away to windward of the rest of the fleet. And then it was that Barclay, the skipper of the *Northampton*, did what Putnam calls his 'real goat getting trick' – though there was not a ripple on the water, he squared away and ran to leeward to visit and gossip. The *Sachem*, with her yards braced sharp up on the backstays, was lying like a log without steerage way, when the *Northampton* dropped down and backed her mainyard right under the former's counter. Putnam, in commenting on this proceeding, writes: 'The backing of that mainyard seemed a positive insult as far as we were concerned, but the *Northampton* had to do it to stop her way.' He also remembers the British captain singing out across the water: 'If I don't get through here to-morrow I'm going to hunt another hole.' So it seems that this phrase did not originate in the late War.

After a bit of a game the *Northampton*, which, by the way, was so deeply loaded with her heavy scrap-iron cargo that her maindeck was nearly awash, filled away on her mainyard and went off to visit the next ship of the fleet. To the people of the *Sachem* such ghost-like sailing seemed like witchcraft, as they could not detect the slightest whisper of a draught aloft. Nevertheless when darkness fell the *Northampton* was hull down to leeward where her ship visiting had taken her.

That night there was a furious tropical squall, which blew some of the *Sachem's* sails away, and she was in a pretty mess for about an hour. But this left a wind which did not let go until daylight and was sufficiently to one side to allow long and short tacks up the Strait. While all hands on the *Sachem* were clearing up the decks, the ship being on the long port leg, a pair of side-lights were picked up right astern, then the port light faded out and only the green could be seen. Out on their weather beam the *Sachem's* crew caught a glimpse of a painted port ship with her royals furled, and they were able to identify the *Northampton*, going 2 feet to their one.

Putnam declares that there was the sound of a gigantic hiss as the clipper surged by to windward, then she faded into the night like a ghost and was gone for ever from their sight. It was blowing half a gale, and the *Northampton* seemed to be travelling like an express train.

[This sea picture is of special interest as showing the difference in sailing between a crack Clyde clipper and a fleet of sturdy Down Easters and Nova-scotiamen.]

Nov. 6th

Lat 6.00 s   Long 106.55 f

Passed Anjer first part, light air from West, hauling NE, heavy squall; later heavy squalls from SE with a disagreeable looking sky. Day ends bad weather (squally) hauling the wind to all points. Bar. 29.85 T. 85.

Nov. 7th

Lat 6.23 s   Long 105.30 E

Squally weather beating & banging around in Sunda strait. Bar. 29.84 T. 86.

Nov. 8th

Lat 6.10 s   Long 105.01 E

Wind variable from sw to w with squalls & dark stormy looking weather; sea high from sw; departure from Java Head 11 p.m. SE by E 20 miles Bar. 29.89 T. 84.

Nov. 9th (Sunday)

Lat 7.14 s   Long 104 E

Wind hauling to NW in a very heavy squall; later light breeze, Southerly swell running high yet; signalized an Italian bark steering E.

Nov. 10th

Lat 8.44 s   Long 101.59 E

Wind hauling around NE, E, SE, & South with light rain & squalls sea getting quite smooth again.

Nov. 11th

Lat 9.45 s   Long 98.47 E

Course wsw Dis. 200 miles, wind steady from South & SSE attended by fine weather bent No. 2 crossjack, spanker, mizzen Lower topsail, main lower topsail, foresail & jib; day ends fine weather. Bar. 29.92 T. 82.

Nov. 12th

Lat 10.39 s   Long 95.50 E Course wsw dis. 180

Wind veering South, SE & East, light squalls. People are employed overhauling sails etc.; put anchors on bow making ready to overhaul windlass Bar. 29.92 T. 83.

Nov. 13th

Lat 11.44 s   Long 93.34 E Course sw by w 3/4 w Dis. 150

Wind moderate with light rain squalls, shifting the wind from two to four points, generally SE Heavy sea heaving in; people employed at sails, cleaning windlass & various jobs. Bar. 30.00 T. 80.

Nov. 14th
Lat 13.25 s   Long 90.1 E Course sw by w 1/2 w dis. 235 miles.
Wind blowing fresh from SE; heavy beam sea causing ship to roll heavy at
times. People employed at sails & windlass. Bar. 29.98 T. 81.

Nov. 15th
Lat 15.40 s   Long 86.07 E Course sw by w 1/4 w dis. 278 miles.
Good work, fresh breeze throughout, the royals furled, heavy sea running,
sky dark & unsettled looking. Bar. 30.00 T. 81 1 bbl. beef.

Nov. 16th (Sunday)
Lat 17.39 s   Long 82.16 E Course sw by w 1/2 w dis 252 miles.
Wind steady ESE & SE; sea gradually decreasing, later part weather looking
finer, wind moderating Bar. 30.04 T. 78.

Nov. 17th
Lat 18.39 s   Long 78.53 E Course w by s 3/4 s Dis. 203.
Wind hauling Easterly, unsettled looking Bar. 30.00 T. 74.

Nov. 18th
Lat 19.19 s   Long 76.03 E by D.R.
Light rain & overcast sky, very unsettled looking, heavy thunder & lightening at times. Wind ENE; think there must be hurricane to the North of us
although we have not the sea & Bar. quite high & steady. Bar. 30.00 T.
74.

Nov. 19th
Lat 20.19 s   Long 74.14 E
Wind hauling NE, North & NW & West, SE sea running also a westerly swell
signalized Holland bark bound West 15 days 1 bbl. flour opened tonight.
Rove off starboard main upper topsail brace Bar. 30.00 T. 79.

Nov. 20th
Lat 20.58 s   Long 72.46 E Course w 1/2 s Dis. 85 miles.
Wind sw first part, overcast sky & light rain squalls; later part looking
finer, Holland bark in sight astern; men employed repairing sail & cleaning
ship, carpenter caulking. Bar. 30.10 T. 77.

Nov. 21st
Lat 21.15 s   Long 70.45 E Course w 1/2 s Dist. 117
Fine weather throughout the day; wind s & ssw; people employed repair-
ing sail & cleaning ship. Bar. 30.10 Ther. 77.

Nov. 22nd
Lat 22.03 s   Long 69.00 E Course wsw Dis. 111
Wind light from South & SSE attended by fine weather; people employed
repairing sail & overhauling rigging, carpenter caulking. Bar. 30.14 T. 77.

Nov. 23rd (Sunday)
Lat 22.15 s   Long 67.20 E Course w 1/2 s Dis. 87
Fine weather throughout the day; wind SE; heavy westerly swell NE current today Bar. 30.14 T. 78.

Nov. 24th
Lat 23.23 s   Long 65.04 E Course sw by w 3/4 w Dis. 151
Wind moderate veering from SSE to ESE attended by fine weather. Employed repairing sail, reaving off new lanyards in main rigging. Painting & various jobs. Bar. 30.20 T. 77.

Nov. 25th
Lat 24.29 s   Long 61.38 E Course w by s 3/4 s Dis. 205 miles.
Fresh breeze from the s throughout the day. Bar. 30.20 T. 75.

Nov. 26th
Lat 25.48 s   Long 57.57 E Course wsw Dis. 220 miles.
Wind veering from SSE to ESE fresh breeze with occasional squalls. Day ends fine, employed painting, sailmaking & rigging work. Bar. 30.18 T. 77.

Nov. 27th
Lat 26.45 s   Long 54.40 E Course w by s 3/4 s Dis. 190.
Fine weather throughout the day, employed painting, sail making & rigging work; weather quite chilly today. Bar. 30.20 T. 75.

Nov. 28th
Lat 27.47 s   Long 51.41 E Course wsw Dis. 170.
Wind ESE & E attended by fine weather; employed at rigging & sails bent No. 1 fore lower topsail, upper topsail & mizzen lower topsail.

Nov. 29th
Lat 28.39 s   Long 48.41 E Course wsw Dis. 170.
Wind E, steady breeze throughout the day; fine weather Bar. 30.00 Ther. 76.

Nov. 30th
Lat 29.30 s   Long 45.23 E Course w by s 1/4 s Dis. 182.
First part steady from ENE, middle hauling N & NW, later sw attended by . rain & overcast sky with occasional lightening. Later blowing hard from sw.

Dec. 1st
Lat 28.37 A   Long 42.57 E Course w by N 3/4 N Dis. 132.
Wind strong from sw & wsw with increasing sea. Later moderating gradually. Employed at rigging & sails steward 5 buckets casks, steward 1 bucket tank, sailors 2 buckets tank Bar. 30.14 T. 73.

Dec. 2nd

Lat 28.5 s   Long 39.32 E Course w by N 189 miles.

Wind steady in force & direction; heavy sea running later part equally employed sails & rigging. Bar. 30.22 T. 72.

Dec. 3rd

Lat 29.16 s   Long 37.13 E Course sw by w Dis. 142 (true course).

First part fresh breeze & squally; last part moderate from SSE Bent No 1 fore lower topsail; 3 ft. 1 in. main tank[44]; 1 bbl. flour opened tonight (14 days) (had Happy dreams) Bar. 30.22 T. 72.

Dec. 4th

Lat 30.53 s   Long 35.12 E Course sw Dis. 147.

Wind moderate & variable from SE to NE; sea quite smooth, nothing in sight. People variously employed. Bar. 30.10 Ther. 75.

Dec. 5th

Lat 32.32 s   Long 32.26 E Course sw by w Dis. 176.

Wind NE & hazy throughout. Bar. 29.82 T. 75.

Dec. 6th

Lat 32.23 s   Long 30.49 E Course w 1/2 s Dis. 95.

Strong sw ly throughout the day, under topsails & courses; high sea, Shackled cables to anchors, repaired No. 1 spanker Bar. 30.20 T. 70.

Dec. 7th (Sunday)

Lat 33.28 s   Long 29.12 E

Wind veering to NE first part, fine; later, fresh increasing gale sw swell about played out NE sea increasing; (No current here) Sky hazy. B. 30 T. 75.

Dec. 8th

Lat 35.8 s   Long 26.42 E Course sw 1/2 w Dis. 165

Wind E by N mag. or NE true; fresh gale, reduced sail & reefed topsails during the night heavy thunder & lightening from all points, very disagreeable looking but the fair wind covers all obstacles; current here setting w by s 2 knots Bar. 30 T. 75.

Dec. 9th

Lat 35.48 s   Long 20.49 E Course w 1/2 s

Dis. 300 miles[45]; current wsw 50' during the day; day began with easterly wind, overcast sky threatening weather during day. Wind increasing with light rain; heavy black clouds rolling up from all directions with continual

44 Captain Gullison is watching the water supply very carefully.

45 300 miles in 24 hours was the best day's run recorded for the *N.B. Lewis*. The course was close to the southern coast of Africa but the Captain does not mention sighting land.

lightening from SE and heavy thunder in the NW and lightening too from all quarters; reduced sail to reefed; 8 p.m. came out in a very heavy squall from SE clearing up the sky and looking finer. Later part fine weather.

Dec. 10th
Lat 35.24 S   Long 17.52 E Course w 3/4 N Dis. 148.
Fine weather throughout the day. 67 days from Hongkong; 31 days from Java Head; very good work from the Head. Bar. 30.10 T. 75.

Dec. 11th
Lat 34.18 S   Long 15.57 Course NW 3/4 w Dis. 120.
Fine weather throughout the day. Cut out main royal, employed repairing & making sail, also rigging work Bar. 30.10 T. 75.

Dec. 12th
Lat 32.23 S   Long 13.03 Course NW 3/4 w Dis. 175.
Wind w & wsw moderate breeze & fine weather, people variously emp-loyed.

Dec. 13th
Lat 31.12 S   Long 11.12 Course NW 1/2 w Dis. 125.
Fine weather; employed cleaning & sailmaking.

Dec. 14th (Sunday)
Lat 29.32 S   Long 10.2 E Course NW by N 1/2 N Dis. 115.
Wind variable between sw, westerly & NW attended by fine weather. Sighted white bark ahead steering north.

Dec. 15th
Lat 26.59 S   Long 9.9 E Course N by w 3/4 w Dis. 160
Fine weather, all hands employed painting.

Dec. 16th
Lat 25 S   Long 7.31 E Course NW by N 145.
Fine weather, all hands employed painting Bar. 30.10 T. 74.

Dec. 17th
Lat 23.38 S   Long 5.24 E Course NW by w Dis. 145.
Fine weather, employed painting.

Dec. 18th
Lat 22.03 S   Long 3.09 E Course NW 3/4 w Dis. 155.
Wind SSE steady breeze all day, have not touched a brace. People emp-loyed painting. 1 bbl flour 14 days, opened tank flour.

Dec. 19th
Lat 20.33 S   Long 1.00 E Course NW 3/4 w Dis. 150.
Fine beautiful weather, employed painting.

Dec. 20th

Lat 19.17 s   Long 0.35 w Course NW by w Dis. 122.

Wind steady from SSE with fine weather; heaving SW swell heaving in; employed painting, & sailmaking; day ends beautiful fine weather. Main tank sounded 4 ft. 4 in. out; 1 ft. 3 in. in eleven days only used as drinking water.

Dec. 21st (Sunday)

Lat 18.2 s   Long 2.29 w Course NW by w Dis. 130.

Fine; no work transacted as it is Sabbath; nothing in sight.

Dec. 22nd

Lat 17.02 s   Long 3.58 w

Some clouds & rain; employed painting & sailmaking Bar. 30 T. 75.

Dec. 23rd

Lat 15.52 s   Long 5.40 w

Sighted St. Helena this morning 6 a.m. Noon boatman from the island came on board, sent report ashore by him also made a change for potatoes, fish & setra 47 days from Anjer 80 from Hongkong Bar. 30.6 T. 76.

Dec. 24th

Lat 14.41   Long 7.51 w

Light rain squalls & overcast sky & a fine breeze blowing from SE Well, this is Xmas eve; how my heart yearns for *home Dear Home* & loved ones & what a comfort it must be to those that enjoy this blessing. (Killed one of our little pigs.[46]) Bar. 30 T. 75.

Dec. 25th Christmas Day

Lat 13.37 s   Long 10.12 w Course NW by w 1/4 w Dis. 159.

Cloudy weather & a moderate breeze blowing. No work transacted. This Xmas of 1890 has been spent very lonely: how I would like to be at my home. Bar. 30.00 Ther. 75.

Dec. 26th

Lat 12.15 s   Long 12.15 w Course NW by w 1/4 w Dis. 135.

Sky cleared from the dark clouds we have had these few days; beautiful weather, employed painting & sailmaking. I commenced to varnish the cabin today. Bar. 30.00 T. 77.

---

46 'One of our little pigs'. At (at least) four months of age, the porker would have made a sumptuous Christmas repast for a crew of 19. Ideal butchering weight of 180 pounds for bacon hogs is attained (with proper diet) at 5 to 6 months — so this 'little' pig might be safely assumed to weigh at least 100 lb. And even with fresh garden stuff from St. Helena and maybe a little clandestine grog, it was a sad day for the Captain, with his thoughts of home. (Evidently they consumed the pig in two days — see log for Dec. 27.)

Dec. 27th

Lat 11.09 s   Long 13.58 w

Fine weather predominating. Finished main royal & bent it; sets fine. People employed painting & sailmaking; carpenter caulking the bridge. 1 bbl. pork 30 days. Bar. 29.95 T. 78°.

Dec. 28th (Sunday)

Lat 10.95 s   Long 15.49 w Course NW by w 1/4 w Dis. 120

Wind light & steady; no work transacted *as it is Sabbath* (*Very lonesome & homesick*) (*What a long day*). Bar. 30.00 T. 79.

Dec. 29th

Lat 8.56 s   Long 17.41 w Course NW by w Dis. 130 miles.

Fine weather. Later part wind increasing, making 7 1/2 & 8 dead aft. Sent mainsail down & repairing the same: day ends fresh breeze. (5 feet out main tank) Bar. 29.94 T. 80.

Dec. 30th

Lat 7.36 s   Long 19.48 w Course NW by w Dis. 138

Fine weather; painting & repairing sail & sectra; carpenter repairing windlass. 1 bbl. beef 21 days Bar. 30.00 Ther. 82.

Dec. 31st

Lat 6.27 s   Long 21.53 w

Course NW by w 1/4 w Dis. 145. 8 a.m. signalized ship *Ellenbank* of Maryport, 1426 tons from Pisagua bound for Falmouth 63 days [Maryport on Solway Firth, Pisagua in Chile] Commenced main lower topsail.

Jan. 1st 1891

Lat 5.39 s   Long 23.39 w Course NW by w 3/4 w Dis. 110.

Fine weather − 1 bbl. flour opened tonight last. 13 days.[47]

Jan. 2nd

Lat 4.30 s   Long 25.43 w Course NW by w 1/4 w Dis. 138.

Cloudy weather wind SE quite steady. Painting around decks, about squared up. Bar. 29.90 T. 83.

Jan. 3rd

Lat 3.15 s   Long 27.55 w

Light rain squalls, bent No. 1 fore upper topsail. Signalized ship *Conmoren* Swedish, exchanged longitudes he 28.11 me 27.55 mean of Adams & Riggs 28.15 by Riggs without correction.[48]

47 Evidently this was the last barrel of flour. Previous barrel lasted 13 days. The ship is 26 days from New York so there must have been short rations on bread.

48 Comparison between the two ships shows a possible total east-west error of approximately 35 miles in their two charts. The Riggs chronometer appears to be more accurate than the Adams.

Jan. 4th (Sunday)

Lat 1.47 s   Long 29.34 w Course NW 1/4 W Dis. 134.

Wind SE moderate breeze, westerly current 1 knot. Passed several sail steering South. Oh what a lonesome day, 92 days from Hongkong, all well on board thank the GIVER OF ALL GOOD.

Jan. 5th

Lat 00.09 s   Long 30.56 w Course NW 1/2 N Dis. 129.

People employed variously. Still to work at main lower topsail; Westerly current here 1/2 knot; signalized ship *Bangalore* 1699 tons. From B.L.G.H. Richmond for B.L.J.D. Calcutta. Bar. 29.84 T. 84.

Jan. 6th

Lat 00.14 N   Long 32.02 w Course NW 1/2 N Dis. 129.

Wind SE Fine weather, people employed variously, 18 in water in deck tank. Westerly current 1 knot.

Jan. 7th

Lat 2.52 N   Long 32.51 WNW by 1/2 N Dis. 110.

Variable wind & weather, rain squalls at times; caught 200 gals water.

Jan. 8th

Lat 4.6 N   Long 34.45 w Course NW 3/4 W Dis. 132.

Steady fresh breeze from NE (trades here) day ends squally 6 ft. 3 in out, 12 ft. 7 in. in tank, water reduced today; 9 gals. forward 6 gals. aft per day.[49] Main lower topsail finished (good job)

Jan. 9th

Lat 6.17 N   Long 37.21 w Course NW 1/2 W Dis. 202.

Wind steady from NE, squally; at times balling off 10 1/2 & 11 knots. Commenced painting outside, repairing rail & various jobs. Bar. 29.90 T. 82.

Jan. 10th

Lat 8.56 s   Long 40.32 w Course NW 1/2 W Dis. 248.

Strong steady breeze from NE, going good work, had to take the royals in last night − *strong trades* (How lonesome I am tonight).

Jan. 11th (Sunday)

Lat 11.50 N   Long 44.00 w Course NW 1/4 W Dis. 266 (good work).

Wind steady from NE (fine trades).

---

49 Since about Christmas Captain Gullison appears to have been particularly concerned about the supply of fresh water. Today he cuts the ration approximately in half.

Jan. 12th
Lat 14.11 N   Long 47.23 WNW 3/4 W Dis. 250.
Wind NE steady people employed painting outside & tarring down Bent No. 1 foresail.

Jan. 13th
Lat 15.5   Long 49.26 W Course WNW Dis. 115.
First part wind moderating & canting east'ly. Middle backing to NNW & NW. with heavy dark passing clouds & light squalls. The tale end of a norther I presume. Heavy head sea throughout the day. Bar. 29.92 T. 78.

Jan. 14th
Lat 16.39 N   Long 51.53 W Course NW by W 1/4 W Dis. 180 miles.
Squally weather, wind fresh from NNE with a heavy sea; tried to paint some outside but the sea has played mischief with it; bent No. 1 fore T'G.

Jan. 15th
Lat 18.56 N   Long 55.02 W Course NW 1/2 W Dis. 222
(Tank sounded 6 ft. 9 1/2 in. out). Fresh breeze & squally; finished taring down, painting outside or trying to. Bent No. 1 main upper topsail.

Jan. 16th
Lat 21.03 N   Long 57.55 W Course NW 1/2 W Dis. 205.
Squally weather, wind NE bent No. 1 (new) main lower & fore lower topsail & crossjack, spanker; did a little painting on main rail this morning, half the day employed bending sail, sea remaining quite smooth.

Jan. 17th
Lat 23.28 N   Long 61.07 W Course NW 1/2 W Dis. 226 miles.
Wind NE by N fresh breeze & squally, NE sea increasing, head sea about played out; day ends looking finer. *Poor old lonesome Frank Gullison*; may God bless my loved ones at home.

Jan. 18th (Sunday)
Lat 25.37 N   Long 64.12 W Course NW 1/2 W Dis. 212 miles.
Fine weather: how lonely the Sabbath seems. (LOST NE TRADES).

Jan. 19th
Lat 27.31   Long 66.48 W Course NW 180 miles.
First part fine, last part wind hauling west with rain. Took in top gallant sails. Bar. 30.00 T. 71.

Jan. 20th
Lat 29.26 N   Long 66.10 W Course N by E 1/2 E Dis. 120.
First part wind increasing from the west, middle part reefed topsails blowing fresh, last part moderating, set top gallant sail, 1 bbl. beef 21 days.

Jan. 21st
Lat 28.52 N   Long 67.27 W Course WSW Dis. 75
Wind first part moderating, noon calm; killed Dennis this morning.[50]
Length from main truck to deck 129.3.
   "   "   miz. " " "   113.6
   "   "   main T.G. mast   47.0
Bar. 30.40 Ther. 70.

Jan. 22nd
Lat 30.15 N   Long 69.22 W Course NW 1/2 W Dis. 126
First part wind light from north, middle part from NE, later part fresh
from SE making 10 knots, experienced a SW 'ly current here 1/2 knot day
ends blowing fresh from SE (main tank sounded 8 ft. 2 in. out).

Jan. 23rd
Lat 32.48 N   Long 71.28 W Course NW 3/4 N Dis. 190
First part wind SE'ly fresh, under all sail making 11 knots, middle wind
increasing, shortened down to reefed topsails, wind coming out from West
(very mild) Bar. 30.30 T. 71.

Jan. 24th
Lat 33.43 N   Long 72.16 W Course NW 3/4 N Dis. 70
Light southerly airs, people employed stoning deck.

Jan. 25th (Sunday)
Lat 35.55 N   Long 72.45 W Course N by W Dis. 132
First part wind increasing; middle part shortened down to Lower Topsails,
wind south, threatening weather; 4 a.m. hove to under whole main topsail;
blowing a hurricane; 5 a.m. hauled to SW with same force, 7 a.m. a heavy
sea boarded us in the port fore rigging carrying away main sail & ten
stanchions also damaging the forward house Bar. 30.00 Ther. 65.

Jan. 26th
Lat 36.16 N   Long 72.28 W
Wind moderating and backing to South at midnight; later hauling Westerly; fresh breeze; sent down royal & top gallant yards; forward to secure
sail Bar. 30.20 Temp. 62.

Jan. 27th
Lat 38.35 N   Long 71.38 W Dis. 134
Wind light & westerly throughout the day attended by fine weather. Bar.
30.30 Temp. 59.

50 Dennis – probably another pig.

Jan. 28th
Lat 40.15 N   Long 73.02 W
First part wind sw; fresh breeze; middle hauling westerly & moderating.
Later part North & NE light & hazy. 6 p.m. Fire Island being North dis. 8
miles, received pilot on board from No. 13 boat; day ends light rain &
Easterly looking. Bar. 30.40.

News item from *Yarmouth Herald*
New York January 29,1891

Ship *N.B. Lewis*, Gullison, from Hong Kong 117 days on January 25th during a heavy
south west gale, ship hove to, shipped a heavy sea forward breaking railing and ten
stanchions forward and doing other damage.

The following is a copy of a letter mailed Saturday night[51] by steamer
Yarmouth to Captain Gullison at New York.

Capt. Gullison   Feb. 4/91

Dear Sir:
I was glad to hear of your safe arrival. Sorry to hear of your losing stanchions etc., but might of been a lot worse. You rather got the start of me. I
was not just looking for you. Was going to write you today. Should think
there would be no damage to cargo. Suppose you protect yourself by Protest. While I think about it, you had better give officer say $10.00. I think
this amount would of greased things last time and saved $100.00. They
look for it.[52] Everything from Shanghai and Hong Kong came to hand
satisfactory; also letter from Anjer. Well, things are dull enough now in
freighting. Mr. Hagar[53] has probable written you in reference to our charter. I think it fair business for the times. Cargo consists of 17 Locomotives
weighing 1003 tons, measurement 2200. tons.[54] Pieces 394 in number. The
boilers are the largest. We may probable have to cut the lower forward
main hatch beam. I have a memorandum of every piece they load and discharge. Vessels crew to assist stevedores in pieces not over 1 1/2 tons. I
suppose what they would take out by hand. Free literage − no
address − commission 2 1/2% chartering commission. Ship has privilege of
taking ballast or coal for stiffening. $11000 U.S. gold. This will bring to Rio
in the winter about July. I think it will be as well to tow around to Phil. as
soon as ready providing there is no ice which there will not likely be when

51 Saturday night would certainly be January 31, 1891.
52 'They look for it.' A wry commentary on the state of nautical officialdom in 1891.
53 Philadelphia agent.
54 Weighing 1003 tons, measurements 2200 tons. The locomotives weighed 59 tons each, but
    together with their crating they would occupy 220,000 cubic feet of cargo space.

ship is ready. I think they offered to tow *Euphemia* to Phil. for $200.00. We could get wharfage cheap there and as the ships class expires in July it will be a good opportunity to reclass. In making repairs to stanchions it will be that much opening up towards classing. We shall have at least one month to wait before entering on charter. This would give ample time and enable us to pick a number one man for carpenter. Time begins the 10th April according to charter party. As there is only about 1000 tons of cargo in weight I should think we might keep in the most or all of our ballast. It would be a big saving in Rio to have it, both in *time* and expense. Your father and Eugenie was down today and if you wish and would like to come home [one of them] will give you a spell while vessel is getting ready. We will do no repairs in New York.

Yours
N.B. Lewis

P.S. I wrote you after dinner today on receipt of your telegram. Letters sent Saturday will probably turn up at Dead Letter office.   N.B.L.

Yarmouth Feb. 4/91

Capt. Gullison:

Your message just received. I am quite surprised that you have got no letter from me. I wrote on Sat. fully and sent them by Capt. William Cook to mail. You should have had them on Monday. Your father wrote as well and suppose you have not got that. In reference to towing to Philadelphia, I think it will be as well. They offered to tow *Euphemia* around for $200. If no ice had better move around as soon as ready. Regarding stores, I think for Rio voyage and back to U.S. or Bristol Channel will be the round. We will make our repairs in Phil. and probable reclass at same time as putting in stanchions will open her up and save some in cutting. I hope you think well of the business. It seemed to me about the best thing in view. I will communicate with Mrs. Gullison. Your father or Eugenie would come on for a while if you wanted to come home but perhaps you would rather remain and look after things yourself. I thought perhaps to run on to Phil. when ship gets ready for class. I wrote full particulars on Sat. It seems strange the letters miscarried. In haste.

Yours
N.B. Lewis

P.S. As regards the stores do as you think best. If [we] get of [from] Rankin[55] must wait until vessel loaded and risk them around. Had letter from Kelly; wanted to supply stores; suppose for six months would be very large list. Write me by return mail how getting on and what probable ex-

---

55 Rankin was a Yarmouth man in business in New York.

penses New York not including stores and outward tonnage. Letters of Monday at hand this morning. Don't start to go around until chance good and no ice reported. Better give the officers say $10.00, will help things out better. Write me how many stanchions broke and where they start from and also how much rail.   N.B.L.

N.B. Lewis Esq.   New York Feb. 6th '91

Dear Sir:

Your letter of Feb. 4th to hand this morning also a copy of your first letter sent which has got mislaid somewhere; they are trying to find it at the General P.O. now.

We are discharging slowly. Yesterday was a fine beautiful day. Stevedore could only work until 2 p.m. on a/c of wharf being blocked up; our Tallymen stood there until 11:15 last night delivering merchandise. Three ships discharging here and all in the same warehouse makes slow work. We will try and be ready to tow around by the 15th inst. weather permitting. Rainy today no work done. Our broken stanchions commence abreast after part forward house on port side, extending forward to break of forecastle head; twelve in number which will have to come out; probably one or two more when closely examined. Length of Main sail will be about 62 feet. I find that since we discharged between decks that one of the deck beams is split, also some of the chain bolts started. The beam can be fixed with screw bolts I think. Scarfs [joints] in water ways started. Forward house will have to have a general refastening and caulked. I think I can get towed around under $200.00. Have had a number of offers; $190.00 is the lowest yet from dock to dock.

Our cargo is considerably damaged by sea water, along the waterway seam is the only place. It seems impossible to keep Okum in it although it was caulked in Shanghai. This cargo has been very hard on our decks, Sir, it may be fixed without taking a streak of plank out. I would like to get fidded[56] Royalmasts on her this time, fore and main, the cost will not be so very much and it will save this every voyage expense of sending them up and down in port. Please let me know what you think of it. Our expenses here will be about $3800.00; crew wages for the year amounted to $2345.95. I thank you very much for your kind offer and glad to know everything came in order and satisfactory to you. I am very sorry this damage has happened sir, but it was beyond control. I feel as if I had

---

56 A fidded mast is one which can be lowered down along the fore side of the mast immediately below and is supported in position by a fid or short bar of wood or iron passing through the heel of the mast and resting on the trestle trees on either side.

something more to say but cannot think now. This letter will be too late
for the boat. Will go around I suppose.[57] I will write again by next boat.

Yours obediently
B.F. Gullison

N.B. Lewis Esq.   Yarmouth, N.S.   New York Feb. 12/91

Dear Sir:

I received your message in which you said Father would be on.[58] I thank
you *"very much kind Sir"*.

I think we will be discharged by Saturday night if the weather keeps
fine, cargo coming out in splendid order now.

I have arranged for tug, Pilot and crew for going around $2.50 is the
best they can do at Phil. for wharfage at Cattralls.

Paying my mate off Saturday. He and his wife are going home.

Yours Obediently,
Frank Gullison

OFFICE OF A.N. RANKIN
Ships Stores and Chandlery
26 South Street

Capt. B.F. Gullison   New York March 11th 1891

Dear Sir:

I write you these few lines asking how the ship is getting on loading and
whether any thought has been given to stores yet.

In talking the matter over with your son when in New York, I told him
we would like very much to put the supplies aboard again for him, and
would sell them at the same prices delivered in Phil. as in New York, we to
pay expenses and as I am very desirous of making as good a showing this,
my first, year as a partner in the business I sincerely hope we will be
favorably considered in regard to *N.B. Lewis* order. I will, if given the
order, be very particular in packing the goods so as to have them delivered in good order and try to have everything so as to give entire satisfaction.

---

57 Letter will miss boat from Boston to Yarmouth and thus will have to go around by railway.
58 Arrangements have been made for Frank Gullison to go home to Nova Scotia while his father
    takes over the *N.B. Lewis* to load locomotives at Philadelphia for Rio de Janeiro. Captain
    Eugene Gullison commanded the ship for this trip. (See letter dated January 31, 1892.) As far
    as is known Frank Gullison now returned to Nova Scotia for the first time since he took
    command of the *N.B. Lewis* in September, 1885. Capt. Ben Gullison was in Philadelphia from
    February 16 to April 2, 1891.

Do you expect your son on soon and do you think he will stop in New York on the way through? If he does not, will you say to him if he can favor me it will be appreciated. Things have not been very lively since I started in on the new arrangement; not because we did not succeed in holding our business but because there was very little business to hold. I have just finished the ship *Habitant* which sailed last evening for Melbourne and the ship *Lydia* sails about Friday. Capt. Geo. Rogers[59] is going master of the last named, Capt. Perry having gone home.

Hoping this will find you well
I am yours respectfully
Chas. D. Durkee

---

59 Captain Rogers and Captain Perry were both Yarmouth men.

After the *N.B. Lewis* arrived at New York January 28, 1891, from Shanghai and Hong Kong, Captain Gullison returned to his home in Nova Scotia for his first visit in six years. In the undated letter of Nathan Lewis, probably sent about the end of January, Captain Gullison was informed that the ship was chartered to take seventeen locomotives from Philadelphia to Rio de Janiero. Total weight of the cargo was 1003 tons and the freight to be paid was $11,000 U.S. gold. From other information it would appear that Frank's father, Captain Ben Gullison, went to Philadelphia to superintend the loading and his brother Eugene sailed with the ship as master.

The *N.B. Lewis* was back in Philadelphia in the fall of 1891 and Captain Frank returned to his ship. He loaded 8700 barrels of oil at three shillings a barrel and sailed for le Havre, France.

Capt. Gullison   Yarmouth November 28/'91

Dear Sir:

Have nothing to write about only in reference to mate. I went down to see Mr. Allen; he would not go. I don't know of any here. You will have to do the best you can for one. Hope they will soon load you up and get away before ice. Suppose Eugenie will be along home soon. Hope you will be able to get a good mate without much trouble.

Yours

N.B. Lewis

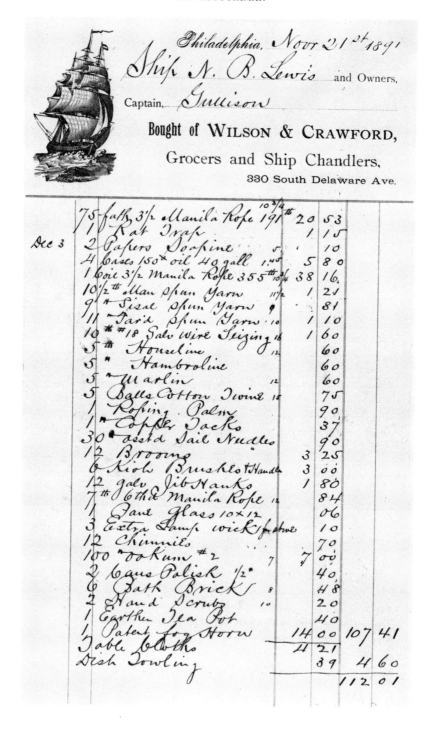

FIG. 64. Invoice of Wilson & Crawford, Philadelphia, for cordage, etc., 1891.

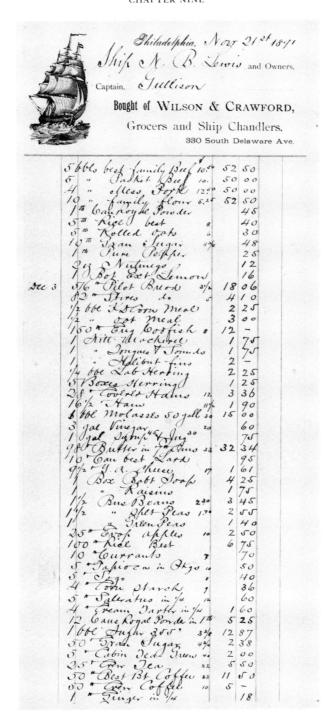

FIG. 65. Invoice of Wilson & Crawford for ship's stores.

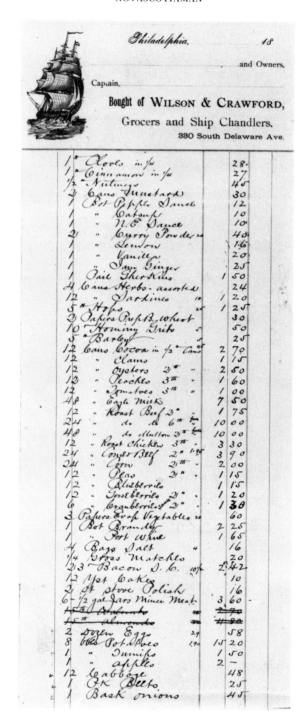

FIG. 66. Invoice of Wilson & Crawford for ship's stores (cont'd.).

Capt. Gullison   Yarmouth December 9, 1891

Dear Sir:

Your several favours at hand. Notice you expect they will keep you your days. Hope weather will keep mild till you get away. I am sending Mr. Andrews; he has been mate some time but had just now got his certificate. I think he is a good man. I could not start him less than $45.00. I thought if we had to pay $42.00 for a man without a certificate we would run a risk, if any trouble, and if went to England would have to ship some one else. Suppose will metal[1] and boot top[2] in Havre. Will write you fully there. The way things look now may have to come back this side again. Eugene[3] is down today. Have not decided yet in reference to new vessel. Hope you will soon get loaded up. If should ice before, you must be careful.

> Yours
> *N.B. Lewis*

Capt. Gullison   Yarmouth December 19, 1891

Dear Sir:

Was glad to hear of you getting safely away from Delaware [Bay]. You must have kept her going all night as I see you passed out at 7:30 a.m. Bills was as small as could expect with about $1500. to pay off crew. Don't think we could have closed any better than to take present freight. Notice the trouble you had with shipping crew. They are a set of scoundrels. I am writing Messers W.F. Hagar & Co. whether the city is run by officials or by the mob. It seems an outrage to let these fellows do as they like. We are having fine West winds and you will probable be getting a good run. Expect she will be slow on a/c of metal. On your arrival, you will see what is the best you can do on metal. Write over to H. Muntz and Co. West Bromwitch England and see what they will deliver a sheet of metal for in Havre and discounts for cash. Mr. Spinney[4] quoted me 6d new. old 4d, nails 8d 2 1/2% off and 1% and he would deduct 1% here. You may be able to do as well on French metal. I shall leave the whole matter with you. Try the market all around and do the best you can in price and discounts. I doubt whether English metal would be subject to duty in Havre. I think you said French metal was good quality. You will be able to find out about

---

1   *N.B. Lewis* was covered with copper sheets (metalled) in le Havre in February, 1888, and now about four years later it is expected she will have to be re-coppered.
2   Boot top: see note p. 125.
3   Eugene is now at home in Yarmouth County.
4   Mr. E.K. Spinney was a local merchant in Yarmouth, dealing in general hardware and ship's chandlery.

this. Don't think there is much, if any difference between Muntz and Vivian. It will be as well to boot top as this has been on as long as they will let it go.

Yours
N.B. Lewis

Capt. Gullison   Yarmouth December 31/'91

Dear Sir:

I wrote you last week in reference to metalling and I see the Romanoff[5] paid 5 3/4 for metal. You will be able to ascertain and get best prices for metal. I wrote you to boot top. Better keep sufficient freights to pay bills and metalling. It looks now as if coal freights were not worth going over to the [Bristol] Channel for. You will see what you can do re empties[6] out to New York or Philadelphia. It is more than probable we shall have to come back this side. 2/6 Havre is the best now for oil. I suppose you have heard of the death of Capt. Baker of the *Maggie Thomson*[7] at Bahia. Eugene expects to take the *Euphemia* when she gets out. We shall hold up the new one for a while and see how things work out. Hoping to soon hear of your safe arrival by cable Nett bills [New York] were $4812.00.

Yours
N.B. Lewis

Capt. Gullison   Yarmouth Jan. 23/'92

Dear Sir:

Cable just at hand announcing arrival. Expect you have had a lot of East winds as I notice it has been cold for some time in England. I have written you twice before in reference to metalling etc. which you will understand all about as regards future business. I don't know what to say as things look dull both sides. Nothing in coal and very little prospect here on this side. Mr. Frank[8] thinks you could get emptys at 8d and ballast free. You might see what you could do. Perhaps by the time you get this side, might get something to go East as the ship will be in order to go.

We are having a very mild winter, no ice or snow and plenty of grip and sickness. I wrote you to reserve enough of freight to pay metalling and hoping this will find you all well.

I am yours truly
N.B. Lewis

---

5   *Romanoff* was a Yarmouth ship.
6   Empty oil barrels.
7   *Maggie Thomson*, Barkentine, 554 tons, partially owned by N.B. Lewis, launched 1889.
8   Mr. Frank (Franque) is agent at le Havre.

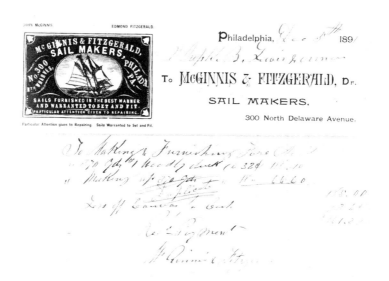

FIG. 67. Invoice of McInnis & Fitzgerald for sails, Philadelphia, 1891.

FIG. 68. Invoice, St. Albans Hotel, room and board for four days, $5.00.

FIG. 69. Bill of lading, Bosshardt & Wilson Co., Philadelphia, covering 2,000 barrels of crude petroleum, 1891.

N.B. Lewis Esq.   Havre January 23/92

Dear Sir:

We arrived here at Havre last evening and tried to get in dock but was just too late so we have to wait here until this afternoon. Too bad after making such a long passage.

   Well, good Sir, I think this passage has been the hardest I ever experienced. I got a good run to Lat-25 N Long 30.00 w of 15 days my hopes were high and I expected to make the passage in 21 days but alas however hopes only seemed to be lowered again for after this we had nothing but a succession of bad Easterly gales and a miserable lot of rain.

   (Balance of this letter could not be deciphered.)

The following excerpts from the log for December 29th through January 5th provide an account of the type of weather encountered in the North Atlantic at this season of the year:

Dec. 29th
Lat 46.07 N   Long 34.20 w
First part wind increasing, furled Upper topsails & reefed foresale rainy & disagreeable. Later Bar. still falling high sea running furled fore lower topsail under reefed foresail & main L topsail Bar. 29.80 T. 66.

Dec. 30th
Lat 47.13 No.   Long 31.56 w
Wind increasing to a hurricane; furled main lower topsail; running before it under reefed foresail; mid pooped & sea doing damage around deck; carrying away binicle & laying up two men. Wind jumping from West to NE with great force — high wsw sea running.

Dec. 31st
Lat 46.25 N   Long 29.17 w
Day begins moderating gradually; two seamen doing well bathing their wounds with crude oil. Wind NE & ENE; squally under TG sails Bar. high at 30.50.

Jan. 1st 1892
Lat 44.51 N   Long 26.35 w
Wind increasing; reefed topsails & courses; later veered ship and hove to under main lower topsail, making good weather. Another *sailor laid up*; day ends stormy. Bar. 30.20.

Jan. 2nd
Lat 45.09 N   Long 2738
Hove to; wind blowing a gale (east) high sea, doing some heavy rolling but not shipping much water. Bar. 30.10.

Jan. 3rd Sunday
Lat 46.16 N   Long 28.02 W
Wind moderating but remaining about in the same quarter East & E by S
Weather looking finer; sea going down; squally. Bar. 3.50.

Jan. 4th
Lat 47.38 N   Long 27.48 W. Course N by W Dis. 75
Wind ESE squally & baffeling under reefed topsails; doing nothing. Passed
ss heading East; Seaman Williams turned to. Bar. ranging very high.

Jan. 5th
Lat 48.32 N   Long 26.56 W Course N by N 1/2 W Dis. 60
Light wind throughout the day from ESE and SE; Sky overcast, nothing in
sight; (Anderson turned to.) Bar. 30.70.

Capt. Gullison   Ship *N.B. Lewis*   HENRY LOVITT
                                                     16 New Quay
                                                     Liverpool 25th Jany. 1892

Dear Friend:
I see your safe arrival in Havre and beg to solicit your patronage for sails
and other supplies. I have a full draft of the ship[9] and can make you No.
1 Yarmouth Cotton delivered for 1/6, fulling 1/2 c per number. I have a
large stock on hand and must sell somehow. I hope to be favoured with
your order. No doubt you have heard of the death of James Lovitt Mayor
of Yarmouth. It has caused a great gloom over the town. Several deaths
there lately. Hope you will keep clear of the lothesome disease. I am just
recovering from a dose. Hoping to hear from you soon.

                              Yours truly
                              H. Lovitt

J.F. Whitney & Co.   Havre
No. 16 State Street   New York   Jany 29th '92

Gentlemen:
Enclosed please accept cheque to the amount of thirty four dollars and
thirty cents $34.30 for value received on 'Life Insurance' with many thanks
for your kindness.

   We arrived here on the 22nd inst. after a very rough passage of 37 days.
Nothing doing on this side except to go out in ballast and 'empty barrels'.

   Please remember me to George Hay and others in the office, from yours
very

                              Respectfully,
                              B.F. Gullison

---

9   Plan of ship's sails.

Messers Arkell Brothers   Cardiff   Havre Jany 31st '92

Gentlemen:

Yours of Jany, *no date*, to hand contents noted.

In reply I can only say that I expect to go out to Philadelphia from here therefore I will not require any slops this time; I did not join my ship last time. I wrote you from home. My brother took her for the voyage so I did not have any chance to look over my vouchers until this present passage. I cannot find anything to show *that I have* or *have not* paid the bill of £1-6-6. I certainly think Mr. Arkell the amount has been paid, however, I will forward said amount with interest to you on receiving reply.

Yours very respectfully,
B.F. Gullison

HENRY LOVITT   16 New Quay
Liverpool 30 January 1892

Dear Capt. Gullison:

Your favour to hand this a.m. Pleased to hear from you. Should you go South you will require to replenish. If so, give me a chance. Sails I can beat the nation and I have your draft. I give you prices for wire at foot [of letter]. You will understand there are three qualities of steel wire. The one I am quoting you is the best steel hawser. I am sure you cannot better it. Awful dull here, hope you will give me all the patronage you can. Kind regards

Yours truly
H. Lovitt

3 in. Best Steel Hawser 36/6¢ will weigh about 7 1/2 ¢
  Winch to hold 100 fathom £3 15/
1 1/2 in. Best Steel wire for gear 58/¢
2 in. Best Steel wire for gear 48/¢
  Less 2 1/2% delivered in Havre

P.S. I quote you Manilla Rope delivered for 38/
Cotton Canvas 14 No. 1 fulling 1/2 less 5%
Try and make up a small order   H.L.

Henry Lovitt Esq.   Liverpool England   Havre February 3rd '92

Dear Friend:

Your favor to hand; note your prices on *best steel wire* and Manilla rope delivered to Havre.

Please send me the following: 75 Fathom best steel flexible wire Hawser 3 1/2 in. 25 Fathom best Manilla Shroud[10] laid 12 in. for spring. 1 winch for holding wire Hawser. also 100 Fathom steel Flexible wire for gear 2 in.

1 Coil Manilla rope 2 1/2 inch
1 do   "   "   2 3/4 inch

Please be particular about this Hawser as I want a good article. Suppose 3 1/2 inch will come little less,

Yours very Respectfully
B.F. Gullison

Capt. Gullison   Ship *N.B. Lewis*

HENRY LOVITT 16 New Quay
Liverpool Feb. 5th 1892

Dear Sir:

Yours of the 3rd inst. to hand this morning and contents noted.

I shall certainly pay particular attention as to the quality of the hawser and Manilla Spring[11] having both fitted complete and all in order.

Mr. Lovitt out of town today. Will send papers by tomorrow's mail.

Yours truly
Henry Lovitt per J.B.

N.B. Lewis Esq.,   Havre February 4th 1892

Dear Sir:

Since my letter to you dated January 23rd I have been quite busy; I know I should have written before, but have put it off hoping to collect more freight [money] and send at same time; Merchants refused to give me any until cargo was totally discharged. It is not business to allow such work but they are supposed to be as good as the bank here and by Franque advice I concluded to let it go as I am trying to get empties[12] out to Phil. from these parties @ 7d. They will not give me decided answer until the 8th inst. Will cable you the offer soon as possible. You instructed me to correspond with metal people in England but as they have agents here I have dealt with them instead. I have prices of Muntz & Co., P.H. Muntz, Greenfield, French and Vivian & Son. Have done the best with the last named; new metal 5 3/4, nails 7 3/4, less 2 1/2%, 1% and 1%. Old metal 3 3/4 less 2 1/2% and 5% for draft, trust this will be satisfactory.

Have cabled with Jones Code. Ship carpenter to take ship from her discharging berth find all labor and tugboat; pay dry dock expenses; find all

---

10 Shroud—a rope or wire stay to support mast or bowsprit.
11 Spring—a line used to moor a vessel.
12 Empty oil barrels.

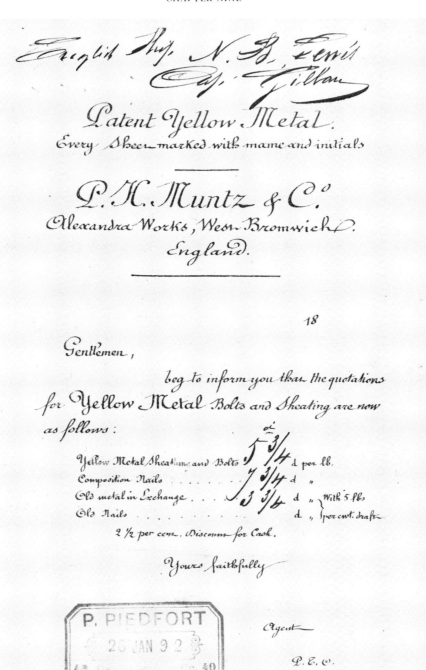

FIG. 70. Quotation on copper sheeting, by P.H. Muntz & Co., Jan. 26, 1892.

materials and haul out of dock for the sum of £1.90 Nett for each and every sheet put on, F10.50C [10 francs, 50 centimes] for every square meter finding everything.

We expect to have cargo discharged tomorrow night, lots of empty bbls. I have ordered a new wire hawser and 25 fathoms #12 Manilla for spring, 100 fathoms steel wire for foot ropes and running gear and two coils of Manilla, from Liverpool, have got considerable blacksmith work to do too, *trying to economize* with it all Mr. Lewis, there are so many things to get, and keep in repair, and *money* will *go* you know. Enclosed please accept £800.0.0 Stg. first bill of exchange; trust you will receive the amount in order. Weather here is very stormy. Several ships waiting here a week for a chance to go to Liverpool and Cardiff. Hoping these lines will find you in good health,

I remain Your Obedient Servant   *B.F. Gullison*

HENRY LOVITT   16 New Quay
Liverpool 8th February 1892

Dear Capt. Gullison:

Your wire hawser etc. sailed today. Not being able to get the B/L will forward it tomorrow with the invoice. You will please deduct expenses off invoice before remitting. I have been to London on business and have not much time tonight to write you. Hope you got the papers all right − no person here − business dull, will write you again tomorrow.

Yours truly
H. Lovitt

HENRY LOVITT   16 New Quay
Liverpool 10 February 1892

Dear Capt. Gullison:

I neglected to enclose the letter in with the invoice and B/L. Whoever looks after getting them put through the Customs see they go on board '*in transit*' to save duty. Nothing new here. I see by the Yarmouth paper Capt. T.J. Perry of Arcadia is dead, also old Capt. Horace Baker. La grippe has fixed a lot of the old people. I am pleased to say it is subsiding here. Kind regards.

Yours truly
H. Lovitt

N.B. Lewis Esq.,   Havre February 12th 1892

Yours of the 23rd ult. to hand yesterday. Glad to hear from you. We came out of dry dock yesterday and towed up to loading berth today to finish repairs and loading chalk ballast. I have taken 250 ton put on board free and trimmed to be discharged at Phil. at ship's expense. I signed charter on empties yesterday, realized 6 1/2d[13] instead of 6d as cabled you. Expect to take about 7000, hope to get away by the last of the month. Oil bbls. came out right, one stove completely which I expect I will have to pay for. About 100 empties in. I call it *very bad storage* and do not think Mr. Gallegar *knows* the ship stevedoring.

   Mr. Franque forwarded to you 2nd bill of exch. to the amt. of £800-0-0 stg.

   Loanda arrived from Philadelphia today 17 days passage. Trusting these will find you well, I remain, yours obediently

                                                   B.F. Gullison

---

Henry Lovitt Esq.   Liverpool, England   Havre Feb. 17th 1892

Dear Sir:

I neglected to answer your lost letter in hopes to receive hawser and a/c from customs before this, but they have arrived this morning all O.K. and I take pleasure in remitting you the amount of invoice £38-8-6 less F10.65c [10.65 francs]. Please endorse and send to me soon as possible and oblidge

                                       Yours Very Respectfully
                                       B.F. Gullison

P.S. '*Many thanks for papers*'. Henry I want a *good carpenter* and cabin boy. Some account. There's lots to be got. Wages £5-10 and £2-0-0. Wire me if you can recommend any.

N.B. Lewis Esq.   Yarmouth, N.S.   Havre Feb. 18th 1892

Dear Sir:

I finished repairs yesterday and commenced taking in chalk today and will finish Saturday night. Expect to commence on bbls. 22nd; they have 10 days to load and do not think they will use all. Will get away as soon as possible. We had a very heavy gale of wind last night from SW, this morning more moderate NW. The general run wooden ships here are going across. Iron steamships for coal which is very low; in fact everything

---

13 d – pence.

according to freight circular. See *Stalwart* has 20s, 21s, 22s to Java, very low. I don't see how we can pay for repairs on such freight.

> From Your Obedient Servant
> *B.F. Gullison*

Captain Gullison   Havre

HENRY LOVITT   16 New Quay
Liverpool 19th February 1892

Dear Sir:

I am in receipt of your covering cheque for 38 pounds in payment of enclosed discharged a/c with thanks. I return you Customs Receipts as well. I have been housed for a few days with a severe cold, feeling better today. Carpenter—up to the time of writing I have not found a suitable man. Will wire you soon as I do. I propose should one suitable turn up to send him by the boat; less expense and trouble to you – if in time should I wire you tomorrow, please reply the way I shall send him. Hope to see you in Liverpool next voyage.

> Kind regards
> *H. Lovitt*

Capt. Gullison   Havre

HENRY LOVITT   16 New Quay
22 Feb. 1892

Dear Friend:

I wired you this p.m. and now await your confirmation. There is only two carpenters in Liverpool and they want 6 pounds advance paid here. Fortunately I had a fellow in an outport says he will go. Doubtless he will want half-pay if so make on me. Hope any time this week will be in time as he is in Ireland and has to come to Liverpool to get to Havre. I will carry out your orders as to telegram when received.

> Yours truly,
> *H. Lovitt*

P.S. Wire just received, crossed mine.
Will send suitable man Wednesday.   H.L.

N.B. Lewis Esq.,

Havre March 2nd 1892

Dear Sir:

We finished loading empties tonight have on board 6975 @ 6 1/2 and 350 ton chalk put on board free. I tried to square up a/c tonight but they are so terrible slow here I did not succeed but hope to by tomorrow's tide as we have a beautiful Easterly wind blowing now. You will see by bill 7100 bbls. charged. We expected to stow them but could not, the difference which is about F 12.50. I will credit ship with my personal a/c along with a few others both Dr. & Cr. Franque a/c will show cash drawn. I did not square up my personal a/c here, thought it better to wait until arrival at Philadelphia.

My steward is drunk tonight and has been for two days giving me much trouble.

B.F. Gullison

Capt. Gullison   Yarmouth April 2/92

Dear Sir:

Will drop you a line and hope to soon hear of your safe arrival at Philadelphia. Hope you may find something to do on arrival. Things seem to look bad. Was pleased with a/c Havre. Think you done well and deserve the HAT.[14] Eugene goes tonight to take *Euphemia*.[15] She goes to River Platte 8 1/2 [16]; don't seem a big rate. We have sold *Otago* and hope she will make company some money which she will do with a reasonable chance. Hoping you will soon report all right in good health.

I am yours truly
N.B. Lewis

V. Franque   Ship Broker   Philadelphia
Havre France   April 9th 1892

Dear Sir:

Will you please forward to me, Ship *N.B. Lewis* classification which I gave to surveyor, to be endorsed. He said he would leave it at your office and I supposed it came onboard with the rest of the papers.

'But it has got mislayed.'

Please give this affect and oblidge yours very,

Respectfully
B.F. Gullison

Capt. Gullison   Yarmouth April 9/92

Dear Sir:

Was glad to hear of your arrival. Sorry business is in such an unsatisfactory state. Messers Hagar telegraphed, might do 1/9 London.[17] Expect this is as good as anything else. Means £1000 freight. Possible might pay port

---

14 'Deserve the HAT' – expression used when captain deserves extra compensation – see letter from Soley dated August 3, 1888.
15 After the *Otago* was sold Eugene was given command of the *Euphemia*.
16 This is probably $8.50 per thousand board feet on lumber.
17 This may be a low rate on oil in barrels.

charges and expences both ports. Would this be better than waiting? I have written Messers Hagar & Co. to consult with you and business coming up that you can see. Any chance of doing anything let me know at once or if it should be liable to be taken and if [you] have not time to telegraph, you can close if to a good port. Perhaps with the London business quoted might get something back. Chalk and emptys and things would be better shape later in the season for business. Suppose it will take you a week to get your chalk and emptys out. Believe Eugene will tow up to Boston Monday next. I don't think I ever saw things as bad in freighting before but believe there will be an improvement before long. Hoping this will find you and Mrs. Gullison in good health.

I am yours truly,
N.B. Lewis

N.B. Lewis Esq.   Yarmouth, N.S.   Philadelphia April 13th 1892

Dear Sir:

Yours to hand of 9th inst. note what you say concerning freight. I do not think we would pay expenses on 1/9 to London. They wired from New York to know if we would accept it as they had ships there that would tow around, we refused, and since have been offered 3/4 more but declined answering 8 1/2[18] offered Boston to Buenos Ayres. Lay days commence about middle of May, 10 1/4[19] Montreal to B. Ayres. Such expenses as towages, shifting ports, sailors, ballast and sectra takes the cream off.

About £2000 expected to Chili's two ports[20] we have a few days to work on yet hope something better will turn up. I wired you tonight about mate, 'Patten preferred'.[21] Bbls. out tonight. We expect to tow up to Richmond first thing in the morning to discharge chalk.

I will send you by this mail Phila. vouchers which Mr. Franque should have sent direct to you.

Hoping you will be able to procure Patten for me, in fact I want a steward and carpenter. Perhaps by the time I want them something will be found, trusting these few lines will find you in good health,

I remain Yours Obediently
Frank Gullison

---

18 $8.50 per thousand on lumber from Boston.
19 $10.25 per thousand on lumber from Montreal.
20 This appears to be a freight offering to Chile.
21 Captain Gullison would like to have Patten as a first mate.

Henry Lovitt Esq.   Philadelphia
16 New Quay   Liverpool   April 14th 1892

Dear Friend Lovitt:

I arrived here on the 8th inst. after a hard passage of thirty-five days. I received a letter from Franque, Ship Broker, at Havre concerning freight on goods you sent to me there.

   Will you please settle with Cunard Co. if all right and oblidge, your very respectfully.

                                         B.F. Gullison

P.S. Enclosed you will find Franque's letter explaining all.
Hope you are well.   B.G.

Capt. Gullison   Yarmouth April 16/92

Dear Sir:

Suppose you are getting about discharged. Hope they will be able to work up the River Platte business. This looks about the best thing I can see. There is nothing in it but it should put you in good position to go East. Might receive back business from Ceylon, Java or Manilla or Singapore but this only anticipating. Ship is now in good order and it seems too bad to run her across her 1/10[22] with no prospect of any business the other side. She could not pay her bills. I telegraphed you in reference to mate. Mr. Patten takes the *Hugh Cann* and his brother goes with him mate. I can't seem to get hold of any one yet [for mate]. It is uncertain about getting mate here. If I find one will telegraph you. In meantime, if you can get one you had better secure him. Vouchers Havre at hand this morning. If we should go to Boston and River [de la Plata], expect it would be as well to tow if could be done reasonable. I think they towed *Otago* from Glouces-ter to Philadelphia, made her shifts[23] and to sea for about $390.00. Will be able to see about this if we secure the business.

                                         Yours
                                         N.B. Lewis

N.B. Lewis Esq.   Yarmouth, N.S.   Philadelphia April 18th 1892

Dear Sir:

Received yours of the 16th this morning contents noted. Mr. Hagar wired you Sat. that we had placed on the River freight.[24] It is about the best

22 It was previously estimated that the 1/9 rate would amount to about £1000.
23 Shifts—probably towage of ship around the harbour.
24 i.e., Accepted a charter on cargo of lumber from Boston to the River de la Plata.

going and gives us a port to work future business. I see by Mr. Hagar's books that *Otago* paid $490.00 [for towing] think it will be better to tow around if we can come near those figures. I have wrote to Eugene[25] about ballast. About how much did *Euphemia* take? Don't you think we had better give ... [indecipherable?] It will not take up as much room and be a great saving at Buenos Ayres. Will I store[26] for 6 months or one year? Do you think we can do better in Boston on stores or will I get them here?

Hope you will be able to get me a good mate. Expect to have chalk out tomorrow.

Yours Obediently
Frank Gullison

N.B. Lewis Esq.   Yarmouth N.S.   Philadelphia April 20th 1892

Dear Sir:

Your telegraph to hand instructing me to sell wood. I have finished discharging chalk today and moved to Cathrall wharf where I shall take in about 200 ton ballast @ 95¢. He takes the wood out and piles it on the wharf and allows me $1.50 per cord. One of my sailors died in the hospital. He is in debt to ship; will have to pay funeral expenses, which will amount to about $15.00.

As yet our lowest bid to tow to Boston is $550.00. Please let me know what you think.

Yours Obediently
Frank Gullison

N.B. Lewis Esq.   Yarmouth N.S.   Philadelphia April 27th '92

Dear Sir:

I understand by your letter of the 19th inst. that you thought it would be cheaper to tow up to Boston which is really the case, also you thought it would be practical to get there soon as possible; this I have been trying to do and made arrangements accordingly and expect to leave Thursday.

Yesterday morning I received instructions by wire through Mr. Hagar 'make figures to compare sailing and towing plenty time'. I hardly knew what to do but after consulting Mr. Hagar thought it better to let things stand as they are and trust it will be all right. We will have to pay $3.00 per day wharfage here after 28th inst.

---

25 Eugene is at Boston with ship *Euphemia* loading lumber.
26 Buy ship's stores.

Difference between sailing and towing according to my calculation:

Sail		Steamer	
To Capes of Delaware sail or tow	$175.00	From Dock to Dock including tug's hawser	
12 A.B.s @ $ 20.00	240.00		$550.00 & 5% off
Extra Ballast	95.00	Say Nett	525.00
Towage in Boston taking out ballast	75.00	6 A.B.s @ $12.00	$72.00
time victualing	nil		
	$585.00		$597.00

I had a great pile of old rubbish to discharge here out of 45 cords of wood taken onboard.

What a lot of rogues they are.

Trying to get away tomorrow.

Yours Obediently

B.F. Gullison

EXCERPT FROM LOG SHIP *N.B. LEWIS*

Cleared from Philadelphia for Boston April 29th 1892.

April 29th
Weighed anchor and proceeded down river 2 a.m. in tow by *S.S. Shawmut*. Rainy weather, wind variable. From dock to dock $525.00 net.

April 30th
In tow, 8 a.m. made Fire Island Lighthouse; noon Shincook; 6 p.m. Montauk lighthouse bearing NW by N 4 miles; wind throughout the day NW & no smooth water.

May 1st Sunday
Day begins with light air and fine weather. Midnight passing through Vineyard Sound; Noon passed Highlands Cape Cod, received pilot on board. 64 hours from Phil. to Boston; dropped anchor at 6 p.m.

Capt. Gullison

Yarmouth N.S.,
April 29/'92

Dear Sir:

Telegram at hand announcing sailing from Philadelphia. Suppose we may look for you up to Boston. Expect take the ordinary chance sailing we would save by towing as sometimes with East winds might be fortnight getting around. Of course, if was sure to get fair wind might save something but would not be much after paying River and Harbour towage, extra ballast and crew. I have a memo. of the general cargo. I think with the bale twine it should make good stowage and those agricultural machines should be not very heavy. Suppose they will give you the heavy stuff in the bottom. Expect stevedore will perhaps want more than [that] for lumber. The River lumber will generally measure 12 boards in height and about 14 inches in thickness so if she makes good stowage, which I think she should with the bale stuff, it should, I think, be better than all lumber. I may take a run over for a day or two after you get to work.

> Yours
> *N.B. Lewis*

P.S. Suppose J.G. Hall & Co. will look after your business in any way you may want to use them. Of course, you will make your own bargains and arrangements.

N.B. Lewis, Esq. Boston, May 1st, 1892
Yarmouth N.S.

Dear Sir:

We arrived here tonight at 6 p.m. Sixty four 64 hours from Philadelphia; good chance. Our expenses there were $2071.53. Suppose Mr. Hagar has informed you and sent vouchers. I am going to try to berth ship tomorrow. Is there any sight of a mate yet Mr. Lewis? How many months provisions will I get here? What amount has Mate McAndrews wife drawn from you Sir?

> Yours Obedient Servant
> *B.F. Gullison*

Capt. Gullison Yarmouth N.S. May 3/92

Dear Sir:

Yours from Boston at hand this morning. Glad to have you safely around. As regards mate, I have not been able to hear of one yet that would be worth the getting but hope that we shall be able to get one, either here or in Boston, soon. As to storing, will decide soon. Think perhaps it would be as well to buy heavy stores like meat for year. I expect in the matter of flour etc. it would be as well not to buy a full year's stock but get it as we go along. This is merely my suggestion. You understand more about it than I do. If any inducement to go East we shall probable go there for home business. McAndrews wife has had 3 months @ 25.00 full amount $75.00. McAndrews had, when he went on, $20.00 to pay passage and expences. Any money left he would account to you for. Hoping you will get good dispatch in Boston and will make good stowage. How much ballast have you in? Hoping either you in Boston or we here will be able to find a good man for mate. There don't seem to be any men for mates tonight.

> Yours truly
> *N.B. Lewis*

Capt. Gullison   Yarmouth N.S. May 3/92

Enclosed please find cheques $72.78 and $71.70. ($144.48 whole amount). Messers John G. Hall and Co. will endorse them for you. Will send more money as you want for disbursements. Happen to have these cheques of Messers Hagar & Co. on hand for advances made by us to crew of Baldwin[27] so send them to you.

> *N.B. Lewis*

N.B. Lewis, Esq.   Yarmouth N.S.   Boston May 5th 1892

Dear Sir:
Yours to hand.

We expect to lay here in the harbour until Monday or Tuesday next; will then take the *Bonanza's* berth. We have about 400 ton ballast onboard drawing now 12.5 feet, 13.5 feet. Will have to trim about 2 1/2 by the stern. Note what you say about stores that you will decide soon.

> Yours Very Respectfully
> *B.F. Gullison*

Wm. Hudson   Philadelphia   Boston May 5th 1892

Dear Sir:
Your letter of 30th ulto. to hand. I do not understand it at all and would ask you to please send me a bill concerning any business with you.

I have had to pay $7.00 here instead of $5.00 as you stated in Memo which actually makes my bill as follows:

27 The *Baldwin* was a barkentine, 561 tons, built at Meteghan for W.H. Hagar and Co. of Philadelphia. Capt. George Wetmore of Yarmouth superintended the building and became the master. H. & N.B. Lewis acted as agents for Hagars. A later letter shows that Captain Frank Gullison had bought an interest in this vessel. *Bonanza*, George L. O'Brien, Master, was lost in 1893 on a voyage from Buenos Aires for Falmouth, England, with a cargo of grain. The crew were rescued.

$44.00 Phil & $47.00 here total $91.00
My agreement with you was
$12.00 per man would be $72.00
Shipping here   6.00
Steward   2.00
                                    _____

                         Total $80.00
Please explain this and oblidge.

                                        Yours
                                        B.F. Gullison

Messers John Dunn Son & Co.   Boston May 11th 1892
New York

Gentlemen:
In reference to the Charter party ....
   I beg to inform you that I am now ready to receive cargo hoping you
will favor me with a quick dispatch here I remain,

                                        Yours Faithfully
                                        B.F. Gullison
                                        Commanding Br Ship *N.B. Lewis*

Captain Anslay Perry   Beaver River   Boston May 12th 1892

Dear Sir:
Do you want a berth as chief mate onboard ship *N.B. Lewis*? Captain
O'Brien[28] was speaking about you here and thought you would take the
chance and that is my reason for asking.
   Wages $40.00
   Waiting your reply I remain

                                        Yours Respectfully
                                        B.F. Gullison

Capt. Gullison   Yarmouth May 13/92

Dear Sir:
Have none of your favors to reply to. Suppose you have not yet got into
your loading berth. Have not got any mate yet. There is what seems like
good man for mate; just passed. He has been with Capt. Weston for two
years in the steamboat. Has just passed for 2nd mate. His name is Robert

28 Evidently Captain O'Brien, a native of Yarmouth County, was also in Boston as master of the
    ship *Bonanza*.

Whittaker. Makes his home with Capt. Weston. I think he is a nice young fellow and if you have none shipped will suit you. He would like to know by return steamer. If you don't want him perhaps Eugene would want him. Hope to soon hear of your getting loaded. Seem to be loading all vessels quite quickly. They may soon load you up. When they get at you let me know about the young man for 2nd mate and if you want him what the wages would be out of Boston. Hoping this will find you all well. I may run over for a day or two later on.

Yours
N.B. Lewis

W.H. Hudson & Co. Boston May 13th 1892

Gentlemen:
I wrote you some time ago in answer to your letter of 30th ulto. and asked for an explanation concerning my business with you. Have you received it? If not I will write it over.

I do not like such a crooked way of doing business.

Yours in haste,
B.F. Gullison

N.B. Lewis Esq. Yarmouth N.S. Boston May 16th 1892

Dear Sir:
Yours of the 13th to hand, *glad to hear* you have 2nd mate for me, wages out of this port is from $26.00 to $30.00 per month.

I wrote you in reply to yours of 3rd inst. acknowledging receipt of Cheques also Friday 13th concerning loading.

They are talking now of putting *Euphemia* in *Bonanza's* berth instead of us to finish her cargo, if so, I will likely remain out here (in the harbour) another week.

If this man is ready I might take him on and discharge "Andrews".

I have not heard from Perry yet.

Yours Faithfully
B.F. Gullison

Capt. Edward Goudey Port Maitland Boston May 16th '92

Dear Bro Goudey:
I wrote you from Phila. concerning my travelling password and card. You will see my time was up March 31st '92 but have received no answer to

321

date. I would like to visit our order here but under present circumstances I feel I am deprived.

We expect to load here for Buenos Ayres $8 1/2 lumber and 10 cubic foot general cargo.

Will be here one month yet.

Yours Fra I.O.O.F.
[Independent Order of Oddfellows]
Frank Gullison

Mr. Alfred Perry   Boston
Salmon River   Digby Co., N.S.   May 16th 1892

Dear Sir & Bro in F.L.T.[29]

I wrote you some time ago asking if you knew of any carpenter I could get to go voyage to Buenos Ayres. I have not received any answer and thought perhaps it got mislaid. I will be very much oblidged to you if you could get me one and will pay you for all trouble. Wages from $26. to $30. per month. Please write me a few lines in answer to this and oblidge yours

very Respectfully,
Frank Gullison

Capt. Gullison   Yarmouth May 17/92

Dear Sir:

Yours of yesterday at hand. Notice you are still laying in the stream. Mr. Whittaker the mate has just been in and will go by tomorrow boat. Wages will be $27.00 per month. I think by the looks of him he will make you a good man.

Steamboat stock[30] sold last sales for $83.00 but I don't see why it should not be a good investment and pay good interest. Last year's putting on the other boat could hardly be taken as a criterion. I would not sell mine for 100 cents to the dollar but I may be wrong. Electric car stock[31] is some-

---

29 F.L.T. – friendship, love, truth.
30 Steamboat stock—Probably a reference to the Yarmouth Steamship Company which was organized by Yarmouth businessmen in 1887 and operated the steamers *Yarmouth* and *Boston* between these ports. The company was later sold to the Dominion Atlantic Railway Company.
31 Electric Car stock—The Yarmouth Street Railway Company was incorporated in 1887 but work was not started on laying tracks until 1892. The contractors were Edison Electric Company of Toronto. The track stretched from the southern end of Main street to the north end of Lake Milo, a distance of about four miles. It was the first streetcar system in the Maritime Provinces and was said to be the shortest in the world when it was built. The line commenced operations on the evening of August 6, 1892, and carried 600 passengers during the evening. The next day, Saturday, 1600 passengers were carried in the afternoon and another 1600 at night. Despite these figures the company cannot be said to have been a financial success and we may hope Frank did not invest money in it. The last trip of the street cars was on October 25, 1928.

what of a problem. Some of our moneyed men who have money laying at 3% have gone into it heavy. I have taken small lot. In time think should be fair stock if town lasts. Should think with this 2nd mate you could let Mr. Andrews go. Hope you may be able to get Mr. Perry.

Yours
N.B. Lewis

P.S. Suppose Eugene will soon get loaded up. Hope they will soon get at Lewis. Will probable send a line by 2nd mate tomorrow. N.B.L.

W.H. Hudson & Son   Philadelphia   Boston May 19th 1892

Gentlemen:
Yours of the 16th to hand this morning note you did not receive my first letter to you so I will send you a 'copy'.

N.B. Lewis Esq.   Yarmouth N.S.   Boston May 19th 1892

Dear Sir:
Your letter of 17th received note what you say about 2nd mate. He has not arrived yet. Paid Mr. Andrews off yesterday, used up about all the money on hand. Will you please send me cheque for $100.00.

I want to square up with the ship soon, may I draw on you for the amount as I expect to use the most of it here. Many thanks for information concerning stock. Where do you expect to send ship from the River [de la Plata].

Harbour Master was onboard last night and says we have got to shift. Obstructing the river.[32]

Yours Obediently
B.F. Gullison

Capt. Gullison   Yarmouth May 20/92

Dear Sir:
Yours of the 19th at hand. I was intending to send you some money today. Enclosed find draft Brooks & Co. on Lawrence Turner & Co. New York 3 days sight for $456.90 endorsed payable to your order. This will keep things along for a while. When you want more let me know. It will make no difference where I pay you but wages a/c only, if here, will save exchange both ends. Banks always want a shave on draft also something for remitting. This draft I am enclosing is sent in payment consignment fish to Cuba. Hoping they will soon get you to work loading. The weather

---

32 The ship was anchored near the mouth of the Charles River.

here is very cold - almost winter. Suppose Eugene will soon be getting away. Suppose you will have to get Messers John G. Hall & Co. to endorse draft for you. How are you getting along with mate? Have you found one yet? Suppose 2nd mate is on hand by this time.

Yours truly
N.B. Lewis

W.F. Hagar & Co. Philadelphia   Boston May 20th 1892

Dear Sir:

We expect to go in *Euphemia* berth Monday, Have been laying in stream since I arrived, last night during a heavy s.e. wind I dragged both anchors and came near running Charleston bridge down and doing lots of damage but owing to the prompt arrival of tugs I escaped without any serious damage.

   I see by memo of cargo that we have considerable twine. Will you inform Messers D. Son & Co. that I would like to have the whole amount of twine at once to work in with cases as broken stowage.[33]

Yours Faithfully
B.F. Gullison

N.B. Lewis Esq. Yarmouth n.s.   Boston May 23rd '92

Dear Sir:

We had a heavy gale from the s.e. on the night of the 19th inst. during which I dragged my anchors and came near doing great damage to shipping and Charleston bridge but owing to the assistance of tugs at daylight we managed to keep her clear of the bridge. I expected to see her do thousands of dollars worth of damage after we started but we came out all right only costing us $59.00 for tugs and men to put her to Constitution Wharf paying $4.00 per day. When I look back and think what it might have cost us inside of 20 minutes it makes me shudder. Second mate came onboard 19th. This disagreeable weather has put things back. I suppose *Euphemia* will finish loading today. When she sails we will take her berth. Your letter of 20th to hand Saturday containing cheque to the amount of $456.90. My wages does not amount to very much so I think I will draw it here and pay my debts with your permission.

Yours Obediently
B.F. Gullison

---

33 Broken stowage – small items to be stored among spaces in general cargo.

A.J. Hudson Esq.   Boston
212 Walnut Street   Philadelphia   May 24th 1892

Dear Sir:

Enclosed please accept order on W.F. Hagar for towage on Ship *N.B. Lewis*. I expect you began to think I had left but I have been detained docking. Just got to berth this morning. Your services have been very satisfactory.

> Wishing you well
> I remain Yours Respectfully
> *Frank Gullison*

W.F. Hagar & Co.   May 24th 1892
Walnut Street Philadelphia   B.F. Gullison
                                          Ship *N.B. Lewis*   Boston

Dear Sir:

Please pay to the bearer J.G. Hudson the sum of $525.00 Five Hundred & twenty-five dollars for towage from Philadelphia to Boston & oblidge.

> *B.F. Gullison*

W.F. Hagar & Co.   Boston
Walnut Street   Philadelphia   May 24th 1892

Dear Sir:

I have forwarded to James McCaully an order on your good self to the amount of $525.00 for towage which you will please accept and oblidge. I see by my account you have on hand $55.00.

I wrote you on 20th concerning *twine* would like to have it soon as possible for broken stowage. Just got in berth today and *Euphemia* went in stream. We have had very disagreeable weather lately. 'Bonanza' sailed today, *hope* they will *load* us up *soon*.

> Yours Faithfully
> *B.F. Gullison*

N.B. Lewis Esq.   Yarmouth N.S.   Boston May 24th 1892

Dear Sir:

We docked last night in *Euphemia* berth and will commence cargo today. Think they will load us right away.

I have a mate, Farnum Patten son of Thomas Patten at Hebron. He has a Masters certificate thought I had better ship him and make him work.

Wages $40.00. Do you know of any good able Frenchman[34] down home for Carpenter they seem to be scarce article here.

Your Obedient Servant,

B.F. Gullison

Capt. Gullison   Yarmouth May 25th '92

Dear Sir:

Glad to hear you are getting at work, also that you have succeeded in getting mate. Hope you have prospect of good dispatch. You were lucky not getting in contact with Charleston Bridge. Expect they would have taken the ship for damages. See Eugene is loaded. Expect sailors are scarce. Try to get heavy stuff in bottom as much possible. See Eugene has about M 135[35] on deck. Not a heavy deck load but the way freights are don't pay to carry large deck load. I am in hopes to come over to Boston for a day or so. Have the *Harry*[36] in now and going on the slip to metal next week. Shall have to be around till get her fixed up. Capt. Henry is confined to the house for last three weeks and don't look as if we would get out for quite a while. Hoping this will find you all well. When you want money let me know.

Yours N.B. Lewis

Capt. Benjamin Gullison
                                                 Boston May 26th '92

Dear Father:

I think you will find the enclosed document all right. Please have the interest added on to the Principal. I think no doubt but what we will take Bowman this voyage and we would like to settle for his board and square up things in general before leaving but still would like for you to look after my place and business. Has Mr. Phillips set out any trees yet? We commenced loading today. *Euphemia* is loaded and about ready to sail. Eugene & Josie[37] are stopping onboard of us at present and we are having a very pleasant time. Eugene has not been very well lately. Has had an operation for the piles; pulled him down considerable. Love to Dear Mother and all the family. Glad to hear she is improving. Eugene asked

---

34 As stated in the introduction, the shipyards along the Bay of Fundy coast employed a large number of French Acadians. They had the reputation of being good workers and many were skilled carpenters.

35 M 135—135,000 feet of lumber.

36 Brigantine *Harry*. See Introduction and Epilogue.

37 Eugene and his wife Josie are visiting Frank and his wife before they sail for South America.

me to enclose his Power of Attorney to you. Write me a few lines and let me know how you are getting along.

From Your son
Frank G.

A.J. Hudson   Boston
212 Walnut Street   Philadelphia   May 31st 1892

Dear Sir:

Since I wrote you last I have received a bill from this Commercial tow boat Company to the amount of $18.00. They say their agreement with me was to dock the ship providing she went directly to berth. They also give me to understand that they had to dock the ship. Now they have the imposition to tender me with the docking. Will you please have this rectified. Knowing you will give this attention,

I remain Yours Respectfully
B.F. Gullison

Capt. Gullison   Yarmouth May 27/92

Dear Sir:

Enclosed please find draft on Messers Lawrence Turner & Co. New York for $602.79 which use in disbursements on ship. See Eugene is kept for crew. Hope he has got men by this time. Weather is very rough and strong winds from s.w.

Yours
N.B. Lewis

Capt. Gullison   Yarmouth June 1st '92

Dear Sir:

Have nothing from you of late. Expect this wet weather is making slow work. Hope weather will improve soon. As regards stores, I think it would be as well to get 12 months salt provisions and other stores for 6 mos. Think most any other stuff except salt provisions can generally be got about as cheap as you go along. Of course we may have to come back this way and if so would not want too much perishable stuff. You no doubt have a better idea of this, than I have. I hope you will get some good weather. I sent you a draft on New York for $602.00.

Yours
N.B. Lewis

N.B. Lewis   Yarmouth N.S.   Boston June 2nd 1892

Dear Sir:

Yours of the 27th ulto. to hand with enclosed draft to the amount of
$602.79 for disbursements.

   Note what you say about stowing heavy cargo in bottom. Will I store
ship for six months or one year?

Yours Obediently

B.F. Gullison

John G. Hall Co.   June 4, 1892
64 Chatham Street   Boston   B.F. Gullison
                                              Ship *N.B. Lewis*

Dear Sir:

Please pay to bearer J. Waters, Stevedore, or order the sum of $125.00
one hundred twenty-five dollars and charge the same to Ship *N.B. Lewis*.

Yours

B.F. Gullison

Captain E. Goudey   Boston June 3rd 1892
Port Maitland N.S.

Dear Ed:

Yours of the 1st to hand and everything perfectly well and I thank you
very much for your kindness in providing the stated amount of $1.00 in
the view you have taken. My letter of the 28th ulto to the Society was as
follows: I herewith enclose to you the sum of $3.00 for T.C. for one year
in advance.

B.F. Gullison

To the Secretary of Orion Lodge   Boston
No. 58 of the I.O.O.F.   June 10th '92
Port Maitland

I have been waiting for my T. C. [Travel Card] about long enough and I
would kindly ask you once more to forward the same immediately.

   Time to begin from expiration of last card, *not* from date of my last letter. *I expect it* and if I have to be deprived of this much longer The
Lodge had better take steps to have my name erased from the books and
refund me the money. Either will be immaterial with me at present.

Yours in F.L.T.

B.F. Gullison

N.B. Lewis Esq.   Yarmouth N.S.   Boston June 10th '92

Dear Sir:

I forgot in my last letter to ask you to please send me some fish: *Cod, Mackerel* and *Herring*.

You will know about the quantity.

Loading is *slow*, rainy all day yesterday, trying to get all the heavy weight in the bottom as much as possible.

> Yours Very Respectfully
> *B.F. Gullison*

P.S. Father spent Monday & Tuesday with us.

Bro Perry:

Yours of 13th inst. received today and contents noted. I went to the General Post Office soon afterwards and found your letter which arrived here June 3rd with enclosed T.C.

The whole trouble was in the address. In most of the civilized cities letters with ships names are delivered onboard but not the case here, however, I have received it now and perhaps I may have a chance to visit a Lodge before leaving.

We expect to sail from here about 25th inst.

> Yours Very Truly,
> *B.F. Gullison*

N.B. Lewis Esq.

I expected to receive a few lines from your good self on yesterday's boat but got disappointed, I thought perhaps you might send the fish. I have about all my stores onboard, bending sails today and getting ready for sea, hope to finish loading by 21st.

We begin to take a list to starboard and I don't know the cause. The cargo is stowed equally and heavy weight as much as possible in the bottom *it cannot be that*. We are loading no cargo today, it being a holiday. I don't expect you will come over now, it is getting so late. How is Captain Henry's health? Hope he is improving.

Fred B. Taylor[38] was offered today $8.00 on lumber and to load at New York for the River (Buenos Ayres).

I will have to use the most of my wages here for fitting out the voyage so with your permission will draw on J.G. Hall and Co. as I require it.

> Yours Most Respectfully
> *B.F. Gullison*

---

38 *Fred B. Taylor* was a Yarmouth ship.

N.B. Lewis Esq.

Please pay to bearer Thomas D. Patten or order the sum of $20.00 twenty
dollars for each and every month beginning from July 15th, being one
half the monthly allotment of his son Chief Mate F.H. Patten of Ship *N.B.
Lewis*.

B.F. *Gullison*, Master

Boston June 1892

LIST OF STORES SHIP *N.B. LEWIS* JUNE 15, 1892

1 bbl. molasses	1 tin bean coffee
1 tub butter	1 case crew coffee
1/2 bbl. bacon	2 boxes raisins
16 tins of butter	1 tin currants
1 bbl. hams	1 tin barley
2 cs. evap. apples	1 tin mustard
1/2 bbl. beans	1 box cr. tarter
2 tins evap. potatoes	6 tins ginger
1 gal. syrup	2 tins allspice
3 doz. soup & boulli	6 tins marjaram & others
2 cases mutton	2 tins cassia
1 doz pie peaches	2 bbls sugar
10 ga. vinegar	1 bag white sugar
2 doz c. beef	6 tins pepper
6 boxes smoked herring	1 tin buckwheat
1 box babbest soap	3 tins Oatmeal
3 boxes soap	1 hf. bbl. Oatmeal
50 lbs. graham	3 tins cornmeal
1 tin graham	4 boxes cocoa
2 doz pumpkin	2 cases lime juice
2 doz blueberries	1 doz jams
2 doz blackberries	1 bbl. Dr. apples
3 doz clams	4 tins lard
3 doz oysters	1 case Eagle milk
30 gal. B. oil	1 box macaroni
6 caddies tea	1 bbl. sp. peas
1 tin crew tea	1 bbl. whole peas
1 paper crew tea	12 papers vap. vegs.
6 bottles pickles	1/2 side bellows leather
1 tub pickles	50 lbs. soda (sal)
2 cases R. Beef	3 lamp burners medium
2 cases Finnan haddy	2 doz medium lamp wicks
2 cases tomatoes	2 doz medium lamp chimneys

2 tins rice
2 cases corn
3 cases peas
2 cases string beans
1 tin tapioca
1 tin sago
10 lbs. saleratus
2 lbs. baking powder
6 bottles curry
2 tins cloves
1 tin hominy
6 tins pearline
12 cornstarch
10 stove polish
3 bottles W. Sauce
6 bottles tamands
6 cans Korn oil
1 bbl. tar
10 lbs. hemp twine
6 sheets emery paper
18 sheets sand paper
1 16 in grindstone
1 sheet pump leather
1 gr. safety matches
6 bbls. pork
1 doz. corn brooms
20 lbs. 2 1/2 in. fin. nails
2 lbs. copper tacks
100 pounds Houslines [?]
80 lbs. marlin
1/2 gal. [?]
2 scrapers

25 lbs. bulk paint
50 lbs. white lead 2nd quality
3 doz. candles
30 gal. pine oil
2 gal. turps
2 gals. machine oil
10 gals. oil
300 lbs. white lead
100 lbs. zinc
25 lbs. red lead
50 lbs. green paint
1 lb. chrome yellow
50 lbs. putty
100 lbs. mast colour
75 lbs. oxide iron
1 gal. copal varnish
1 log book
50 lbs. 4 in. nails
50 lbs. 8 in. spikes
1 bbl. lime
2 W.W. brushes
6 coir [?] brooms
20 lamp black
6 doz. eggs
8 bags potatoes
1 bag onions
1 case soup & boulli
1 tin graham
1/4 bbl. graham
2 doz. pumpkin
3 doz. oysters
3 tins cheap white lead

N.B. Lewis Esq.   June 25th 1892

Dear Sir:

I squared up my a/c tonight but was unable to get my papers from the Argentine Consulate owing to a mistake in the manifest which cannot be rectified before tomorrow morning. We have a difference in the lumber but certainly merchants claim they have the number on board. They did not want Bill of Lading signed in dispute so they concluded to be account-able through J.G. Hall & Co. for short delivery in B. Ayres. According to my reckoning we have about $9915.34 freight. I believe *Euphemia* was

$9857.77. Our general cargo amounts to 1661 ton measurement. Lumber under decks 28,3721 Ft. @ 8 1/2 and 151,569 @ 35 on deck. Our expenses here $3959.25. So you see ship will have to call on your good self to the amount of $256.37 to bal. a/c. You will see my personal cash a/c here is $300.00 so I will give Father an order on you for $99.78 which will square my account with ship and owners. Sailors are all onboard tonight and I hope to have a favourable chance Monday. Draft water F 20.5 & 19.2. I hope you have arrived home safe and your cold much better.

> Your Obedient Servant
> *B.F. Gullison*

> Boston June 25th, '92

Dear Father:

I squared up a/c today amt. of freight $9915.34 $137.45 more than *Euphemia*. Expenses here $3959.00. I expect to sail Monday. Sailors on-board and hope to have favourable chance. I will send you a draft to the amount of $150.00 will you please get Mr. Lewis to cash it and save discount also an order on Mr. Lewis to the amount of $99.78 which balance my wages a/c. I see the *Baldwin*[39] has given us 7% on stock which will be $21.00 more total $270.78. Will you please place this in the Exchange bank. Try and sell my carriage if possible, do as you think best with the grass. Sell it on the spot or barn it. Bowman and wife send love not forgetting your son Frank. May the good Lord guide, guard and protect us and spare us to meet again is our prayer

> Your Loving Son
> *Frank G.*

N.B. Lewis, Esq.   Ship *N.B. Lewis*
Yarmouth, N.S.   Boston   June 25th, 1892

Dear Sir:

Please pay to Benj. Gullison or order the sum of $99.78. Ninety-nine dollars & seventy eight cents to balance wages a/c.

> *B.F. Gullison*

---

39 Frank must have invested $300 in the *Baldwin*.

EXCERPTS FROM LOG SHIP *N.B. LEWIS* VOYAGE BOSTON TO
BUENOS AIRES

June 28th 1892
8 a.m. tug & pilot came alongside: weighed anchor & proceeded on our
voyage: 10.30 pilot & tug left ship; set all sail, wind light from ssw; 6 p.m.
strong breeze sw bar 29.80.

June 29th
Lat 42.10 N Long 66.27 w
Wind moderating Bar. rising, noon, took anchors on board; thick fog bar
30.20.

June 30th
Lat 41.43 N Long 61.57 w
Wind ssw & sw; fog cleared away at noon; seamen employed airing & re-
pairing sail. Bar. 30.40 stady.

July 1st
Lat 41.03 N Long 57.51 w
Wind sw fine beautiful weather throughout the day. Seamen employed
repairing sail Bar. 30.50.

July 27th
Lat 8.05 N Long 22.40 w Course SE dis 152
Wind ssw & sw; one bark in sight to leeward; 4 p.m. sailor Jack fell overboard, hove the life buoys which he soon got hold of; first boat we
launched got capsized; got one of the after boats out & picked the man up
& he helped to pick up the other boat and row to the ship; filled away
main yard & made sail. Day ends squally.

July 28th
Lat 7.00 N Long 21.03 w by DR
No observation first part, wind sw; later squally from West. Course & distance by dead reckoning SE by E dis 152. Expect I will have to tack by appearance of things; would like to be farther west with these monsoons B
30.00 T 83 (I bbl beef).

July 29th
Lat 6.08 Long 19.54
8 a.m. tacked & stood West, very strong breeze from ssw. Royals & crossjack furled, split outer jib; sounded tank, main 12 ft. 18 in. in deck tank:
commenced measuring water this day: 4 qts. per man.

Sept. 3rd 1892
This has been a calm day anchored between Flores & English bank light-
ship. 6 p.m. weighed anchor and proceeded, light breeze from the East &
I hope it will last.

Sept. 4th Sunday
Anchored. Indio Lightship bearing NW 15 miles; calm throughout the day, nothing doing.

Sept. 5th
10 a.m. breeze sprung up from the South; weighed anchor & proceeded on our voyage. 3 p.m. passed Indio Lightship, fine breeze from SE Midnight anchored at Buenos Ayres.

Sept. 6th
6 a.m. weighed and came farther in the roads. Dropped anchor. Doctor came on board. I then went ashore & reported passage. 69 days.

N.B. Lewis Esq.   Buenos Ayres Sept. 14/1892

Dear Sir:

We arrived here on the 5th inst. after a long passage of 69 days; had reverse winds & calms off Abrolhos Isles; eight days & seven days from
Lobas Isle to port on account of not having sufficient water, so you see it
took the cream off my passage. However we are safe at our discharging
berth and have deck load off and one days work between decks; will have
to haul off tomorrow for a steamer.

Your favor of July 20th to hand on arrival, contents noted and shall
have attention. Note at the bottom you say *cable arrival* which I did using
address & Gullison. Suppose you will judge my time here and send orders
accordingly. As far as I can find out the markets are dull. Several ships
have loaded grain here and La Plata @ 13/0 and 10/6 per ton. If I can
close @ 13/0 will cable. We are all well onboard, climate cool & healthy.
Merchants seem to be anxious for our cargo. I did not send first letter that
I wrote on arrival as I was too late for the mail. My carpenter is now laid
up with a broken arm. Have considerable work on hand and will have to
get help to finish it. Mizzen Top Gallant yard to splice and Main & Miz.
Crosstrees to replace. Crew have all left but two. I hope something will
turn up in way of freights before I leave. See *Euphemia* has gone North
again; he has made good time since he left Boston. Suppose you will be
sending me further East. If we could only do something to make a *small
dividend*[1] I know it would be pleasing to all concerned. I did damage to a
Bark coming in the 'Boca'[2] to the amount of £2 with two tug boats and a

---

1   Freights are so low that the ship can hardly make expenses.
2   Boca – dock area in Buenos Aires.

pilot onboard; still the ship is liable according to their regulations. I found our merchants square people so far but can recommend them more highly when I come to settle up. Trusting these hasty lines will find you in good health.

Yours Respectfully
B.F. Gullison

WILLIAMS & CO.
Ship Brokers Steam Ship Agents
Buenos Ayres and Montevideo

Capt. Gullison   Ship *N.B. Lewis*   Buenos Ayres Sept. 1892

Dear Sir:

I will send this by my pilot trusting it may come to hand. We have had a tedious time getting down (the river), head wind most all the way. I had quite a time getting my bills paid that morning and had just ten minutes to spare or pay one day more wharfage. The merchants paid the wharfage and cleared the vessel.

Will you kindly drop me a line to Pernambuco to care of Boswell Williams & Co. letting me know what money I left you in Gold. What is the value in American Currency? Also enclose the third of exchange. I can't square my books without it. Rather a loose way of doing business but I am afraid of my charter being cancelled and I know you will do the buying paper just as well as myself and better but I was sorry to trouble you so much.

Mrs. Card wishes to be remembered to your family and believe me to be yours

faithfully
Henry H. Card

Dear Gullison:

You will find a letter to Dr. Haley enclosed if you have not sent the draft will you enclose it in the letter to him otherwise tear it up.   H.H.C.

Allen Haley Esq.   Buenos Ayres
Windsor   Hants Co., N.S.   Sept. 28th '92

Dear Sir:

I herewith enclose first bill of exchange on the London & River Platte bank to the amount of £84-12-10 Stg.

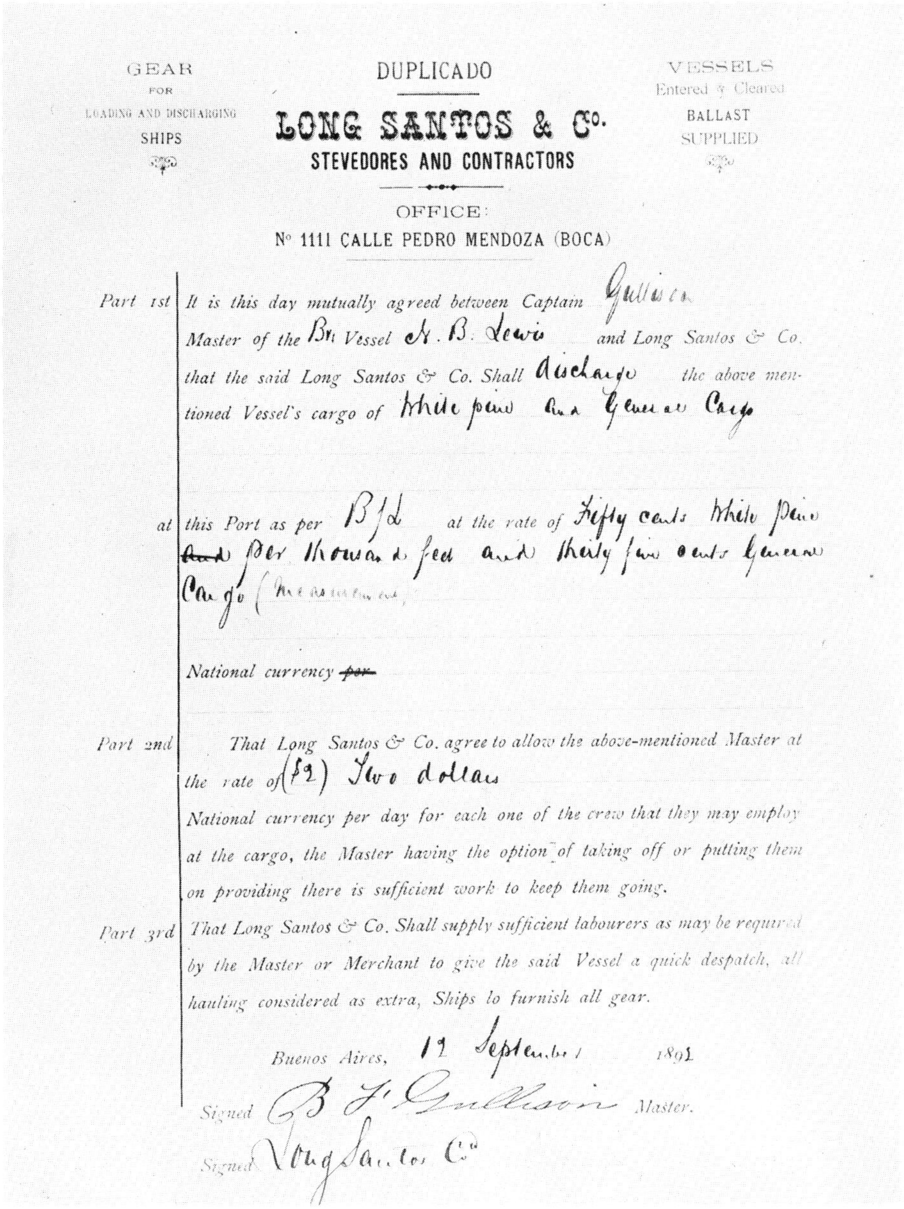

GEAR
FOR
LOADING AND DISCHARGING
SHIPS

DUPLICADO

LONG SANTOS & Cº.
STEVEDORES AND CONTRACTORS

OFFICE:
Nº 1111 CALLE PEDRO MENDOZA (BOCA)

VESSELS
Entered & Cleared
BALLAST
SUPPLIED

Part 1st | It is this day mutually agreed between Captain *Gullison*
Master of the *Brn* Vessel *A. B. Lewis* and Long Santos & Co.
that the said Long Santos & Co. Shall *discharge* the above mentioned Vessel's cargo of *White pine and General Cargo*

at | this Port as per *B/d* at the rate of *Fifty cents White pine*
and per thousand feet and thirty five cents General
Cargo (Measurement)

National currency ~~per~~

Part 2nd | That Long Santos & Co. agree to allow the above-mentioned Master at
the rate of ($2) *Two dollars*
National currency per day for each one of the crew that they may employ
at the cargo, the Master having the option of taking off or putting them
on providing there is sufficient work to keep them going.

Part 3rd | That Long Santos & Co. Shall supply sufficient labourers as may be required
by the Master or Merchant to give the said Vessel a quick despatch, all
hauling considered as extra, Ships to furnish all gear.

Buenos Aires, *12 September* 1892

Signed *B. F. Gullison* Master.

Signed *Long Santos Cº*

FIG. 71. Agreement regarding discharge of cargo at Buenos Aires, Sept. 12, 1892.

This sum Captain Card of the Bkt. *Glenroso* left in my care to forward to you and I hope you will receive the same in order.

Second bill I will send to Capt. Card at New York c/o J.F. Whitney,

Yours Truly,
B.F. Gullison Master

W.D. Lovitt Esq.   Yarmouth N.S.   Buenos Ayres Sept. 28th '92

Dear Sir:

I herewith enclose first bill of exchange to the amt. of £63:15:1 Stg. at 5 D/S on the London and River Plate Bank. Hope you will receive the same *in order*.

This amount Captain Fancy left in my care to forward to you. He sailed Monday morning 26th inst. for Rio Janeiro.

Yours Respectfully
Frank Gullison

The Union Bank of London Ltd.   Buenos Ayres
London E.C.   Sept. 28th '92

Gentlemen:

I herewith enclose the first bill of exchange to the amount £1184:7:6 Stg. at 5 D/S days on the London and River Plate Bank. Which you will please place to the credit of the Bank of Yarmouth Nova Scotia for freight per Ship *N.B. Lewis* payable to N.B. Lewis Esq. Yarmouth, Nova Scotia.

'And advise them accordingly'.

Yours truly
B.F. Gullison Master
Br. Ship *N.B. Lewis*

N.B. Lewis Esq.   Yarmouth N.S.

Dear Sir:

I have forwarded to the Union Bk. of London Ltd. this day the first bill of exchange to the amount £1184:7:6 Stg. at 5 D/S on the London & River Plate Bank will enclose to you copy of same.

We will be discharged by Saturday if we continue work. Cargo coming out in good order, so far nothing offering in the way of freights for a ship of our tonnage. Expecting cable from you any day.

Yours Very Respectfully,
B.F. Gullison

HOTEL DEL NORTE
DE
P. FERNANDEZ Y
N. JAUSTEN
390·Paseo de Julio·392
BUENOS AIRES
GRAN COMODIDAD PARA FAMILIAS
ENGLISH ROOM
CERCA DEL FERRO CARRIL CENTRAL EN LA PRINCIPAL PLAZA
MAISON FRANÇAISE

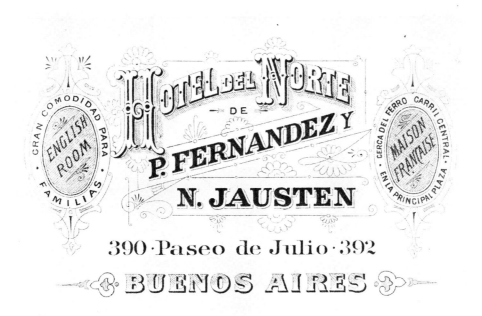

FIG. 72. Business card of Hotel del Norte, Buenos Aires.

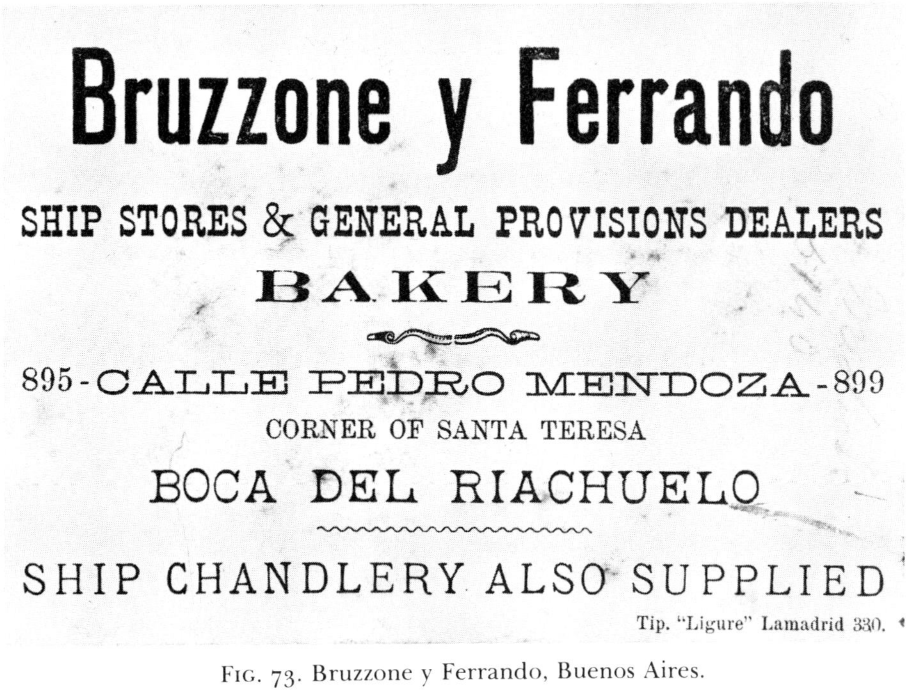

Bruzzone y Ferrando
SHIP STORES & GENERAL PROVISIONS DEALERS
BAKERY
895-CALLE PEDRO MENDOZA-899
CORNER OF SANTA TERESA
BOCA DEL RIACHUELO
SHIP CHANDLERY ALSO SUPPLIED
Tip. "Ligure" Lamadrid 330.

FIG. 73. Bruzzone y Ferrando, Buenos Aires.

Mr. P.J. Walker   Buenos Ayres Oct. 1st '92

Sir:

Not until a few days ago did I notice in that valuable book called *The Chart & Compass*, the abuse you have given Ship Masters in general.

I, for my own part, think it a *gross insult*, not only the paragraph you have written, but the impudence you had in handing me same, so clearly marked and also giving invitations to your Mission. If this is how you expect to gain friendship and improve the Mission board home, I would say you are on the wrong course as a Missionary of the Gospel and would advise you to tack ship and apologize for your insinuating remarks. Your book and papers I will return.

                                        B.F. Gullison

N.B. Lewis Esq.   Buenos Ayres Oct. 1/92

Dear Sir:

Your favor to hand dated Aug. 12th contents noted also cable stating Barbadoes[3] Orders. I have been discharged since 28th inst. waiting your instructions to the cable I sent you on that date which received today as stated above; I hardly expected you would accept the offer we cabled you but thought better to let you know how the Market was. Several ships have closed at these rates. Our cargo came out *all right*.

I forwarded 1st Bill of Exch. to Union Bank London last mail to the amount of $6000.[4] Have squared up with Drysdale & Co. and placed balance of freight in bank until I settle my bills and the quick mail leaves.

                                        Yours Obediently
                                        Frank Gullison

Please excuse Blots and mistakes made in *my hurry*.

Capt. Card   Bkt. *Glenrosa*   Buenos Aires
Pernambuco   Oct. 1st '92

Dear Sir:

Your favor from Pilot today contents noted. I wrote to Dr. Haley on the 28th ulto. and sent 1st exch. on London and River Plate Bk. to the amt. of £84-12-10 Stg. three day sight @ 47 & 3/8.[5] I also wrote to you in care J.F. Whitney and sent enclosed 2nd to said amount giving particulars. I will

3   The ship is sent to Barbados 'for orders', and in the meantime owners will be seeking a cargo.
4   £1184:7:6 is not quite $6000 Canadian (about $5762.66; it may therefore be Argentine dollars—pesos).
5   i.e., 47 3/8 pence per dollar or 5.06 2/3 to pound sterling.

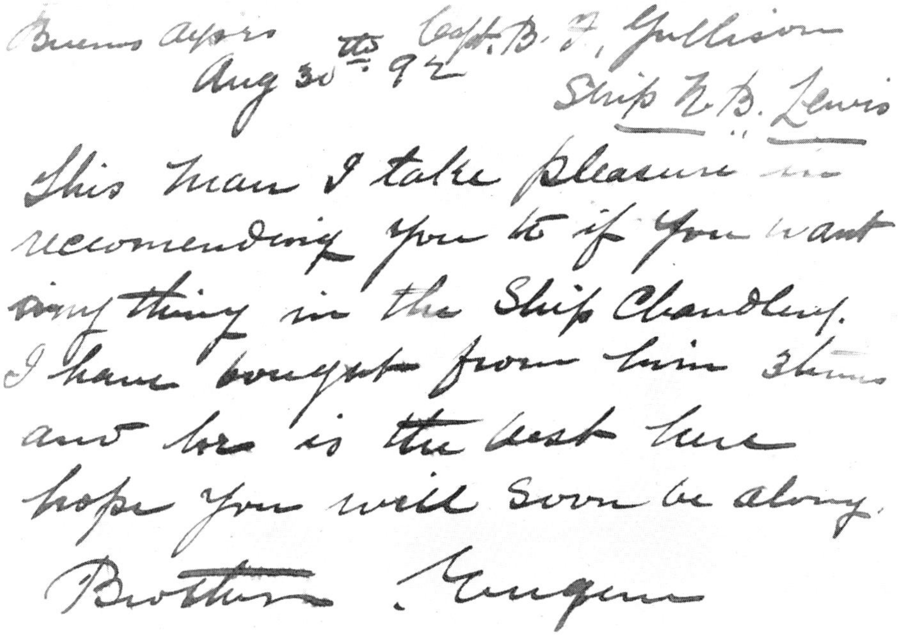

Buenos Ayres
Aug 30ths 92
Capt. B. F. Gullison
Ship N. B. Lewis

This man I take pleasure in
recomending you to if you want
anything in the Ship Chandlery.
I have bought from him 3 times
and he is the best here
hope you will soon be along.
Brother Eugene

FIG. 74. Reverse of Bruzzone y Ferrando card with a note to Capt. Frank Gullison from his brother Eugene.

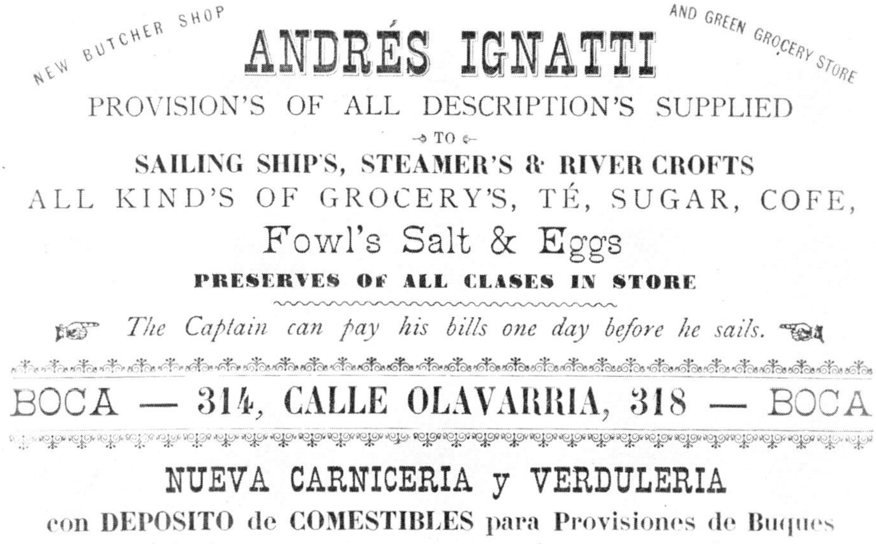

NEW BUTCHER SHOP
ANDRÉS IGNATTI
AND GREEN GROCERY STORE
PROVISION'S OF ALL DESCRIPTION'S SUPPLIED
TO
SAILING SHIP'S, STEAMER'S & RIVER CROFTS
ALL KIND'S OF GROCERY'S, TÉ, SUGAR, COFE,
Fowl's Salt & Eggs
PRESERVES OF ALL CLASES IN STORE
The Captain can pay his bills one day before he sails.
BOCA — 314, CALLE OLAVARRIA, 318 — BOCA
NUEVA CARNICERIA y VERDULERIA
con DEPOSITO de COMESTIBLES para Provisiones de Buques
Á PRECIOS MÓDICOS
Tip. Ligure Lamadrid 330

FIG. 75. Andres Ignatti, Buenos Aires.

now send you 3rd as you requested with regular receipt, the amount you left in my care was: 73 Sovereigns ($5.00).

	Wife wishes to be remembered to your family and self from your friend
	Frank Gullison
365.00	Ship *N.B. Lewis*
32.55	
10.00	
6.10	
15.15	
	Frank Gullison
$428.80	Ship *N.B. Lewis*

Gold @ 47 3/8 £84-12-10 as per bills of exchange.

Dear Friend Card: I hope you will find everything O.K. We are discharged & bound for 'Barbadoes' (orders).

P.S. I will tear up letter as you request.

N.B. Lewis Esq.   Yarmouth   Buenos Ayres
Nova Scotia   Oct. 4th 1892

Dear Sir:

I have settled up my a/c today. Expenses here $1507.35. Arg. and about $1454.00 Amer. Gold. I have remitted to the Union Bank of London Ltd., £1184:7:6 Sept. 28th £572:8:11 Stg. today and advised them to place the same to the cr. of the Bank of Yarmouth N.S. payable to N.B. Lewis Esq. & advise accordingly. Whole amount remitted £1756:16:5 Stg. I got good rates 47 3/8 D/s. I hope everything will turn up all right Good Sir and that you will be able to find good business from 'Barbadoes'. We sail tomorrow if all goes well. Bills are somewhat high compared to Eugene's; crew and advances makes considerable difference. Please let me know what amount Eugene remitted home to Capt. Henry [Lewis].

Yours truly,
B.F. Gullison

The Union Bank of London Ltd.   Buenos Ayres
London E.C.   Oct. 5th '92

Gentlemen:

I herewith enclose 1st bill of exchange to the amount £572.811. Stg. at 3 D/S on London & River Plate Bk. Please place to the cr. of the Bank of

T. O'Connor Duke

Médico-Cirujano

BOCA   Almirante Brown 248

FIG. 76. Business card of T. O'Connor Duke, doctor, Buenos Aires.

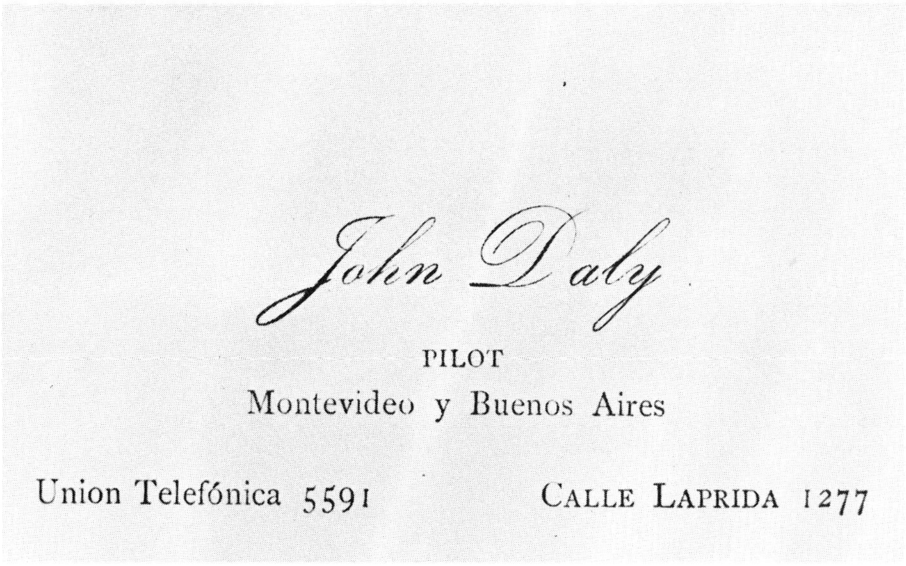

John Daly

PILOT

Montevideo y Buenos Aires

Union Telefónica 5591   CALLE LAPRIDA 1277

FIG. 77. John Daly, pilot, Buenos Aires.

FIG. 78. Dock scene, Muelle de la Boca, Buenos Aires.

Yarmouth N.S. for freight per ship *N.B. Lewis* payable to N.B. Lewis Esq.
of Yarmouth Nova Scotia and advise him accordingly.

> Yours,
> Respectfully
> *B.F. Gullison*
> Commanding Br. Ship
> *N.B. Lewis*

P.S. Whole amt. remitted you £1756:16:5
[NOTE — A duplicate of this letter containing the second bill of Exchange
was sent the same date.]

After discharging cargo the *N.B. Lewis* departed from Buenos Aires October
5th 1892 bound for Barbados for orders. The ship arrived off that island on
November 15th and then continued to Pascagoula as shown by the following
log entries:

Tuesday Nov. 15th/92
Lat 13.00 N   Long 59.10 W
Noon, South Point, W, by N. Ragged Point, North, on Barbados Island.
Pilotage $7.00, fruit $3.50. At 3 p.m. pilot came on board and orders came
off by DaCosta waterman for Pascagoula Miss. We did not have to anchor
at all. What a beautiful island this is. 41 days from Buenos Aires. Barometer 30.00 Thermometer 85 Farenheit.

Monday 28th Nov. /92
Lat 30.01 N   Long 87.27 W
Wind SW & West with fine weather, middle part commences squally, noon
sighted land & tacked Southward.

Tuesday 29th
Midnight standing off and on Sand Island Light. 7 a.m. sighted pilot &
tugboat. Came alongside, towed in to anchor. $45.00 towage, pilotage
$4.00 per foot. 2 p.m. went ashore and reported.

Capt. Gullison   Yarmouth Nov. 16/92

Dear Sir:
I hope ere this you have got your orders at Barbadoes for Pascagoula.
This is not much of a business but it seemed to be the best and in fact the
only thing offering. You will have to be guided in this business by your
own judgement and do the best you can under the circumstances. Would
suggest your taking out all ballast except what you might want to trim

with, as your cargo is deals and boards. Suppose you could pile the heavier aft and make some of the trim that way. Expect there should be no trouble loading in hatch and side ports. You will draw on W.F. Hagar & Co. at sight for funds to disburse. You will see by the charter that you are under the $2.00. This is a hard one but could not be avoided. Hope you will be able to keep some of your crew, by the ship. I have received from your bank your first remittance from B. Ayres. Find this the best and cheapest way. Suppose 'wind up'[6] will soon be along. Takes from 40 to 50 days to get around.[7] Will write again soon. Don't know as I can say any more. Do the best you can with those timber people as they are usually a queer lot. I have written Mr. Hagar to write you and send charter and any other information he can give you. Wire arrival.

Yours
N.B. Lewis

P.S. I am sending this to Messers W. Derry & Co., Moss Point. The *Euphemia* is loading for Southampton at Philadelphia. Rate is two shillings for oil. Had to take out waterways on one side and new rudder stock. Would have brought Lewis North but there is nothing to get and winter and ice to contend with. Hope we may have some better business soon. Can't be worse for sure.   N.B.L.

Capt. Gullison   Yarmouth November 19/'92

Dear Sir:

I write you a few days since fully in care of Derry & Co., Moss Point. I got your 'wind up' yesterday which was very satisfactory. The business was very good for the time and had something left. As it is, it about squares her up. With Philadelphia disbursements behind about $1000, and draft from Havre over $500. This spring bills Phil. $2070. together with Boston bills insurance on freight and advances etc. makes quite a bill. I think we are fortunate these times getting things square. You spoke about Eugene's remittance. It was about 20 pounds more than yours. I think your crew bill at River would be much larger than his as he brought his crew about all back. Cost him about $1500. to pay off in Phil. I have paid Mrs. Patten allowance right along; there is one due today. Suppose they will be in for it anytime. I have written you to draw on W.F. Hagar at sight for disbursements. Hope you will be able to get fair dispatch and not find it too bad loading and we

6   Final settlement.
7   Time for remittance to reach Yarmouth via London from Buenos Aires.

shall be able to save a little of this business. There don't seem anything North. *Equator* at New York can't get even 25 for oil.

Yours
N.B. Lewis

P.S. Had letters from DeCosta Barbadoes dated 4th acknowledging receipt of orders.   Yours N.B.L.

N.B. Lewis Esq.   Moss Point [or Pascagoula]
December 1st 1892

Dear Sir:

We arrived here on 28th ulto. making a passage of 54 days, all well. No one here seemed to know anything about the ship. On arrival I went to the Post Office and received a letter from you giving Derry & Co. as my merchants. After travelling six miles through woods & saw-mills I managed to find these people; they handed me a letter from W.F. Hagar & Co. with C.P. [Charter Party] enclosed. I found by this that Hunter Been and Co. were my merchants. After driving four miles more I managed to find these people and by their appearance and actions I do not think I will hitch with them, in fact they have everything in their own hands and will make about $1000. clear profit on the $2.00 ton and it is going to be hard for me to have to submit to their detention. I have just managed to get a ballast lighter alongside today, and now they want me after loading the lighter to man her and sail 1/2 mile and discharge it again; the Lord only knows when we will get it discharged. According to my charter I have only to discharge it clear of ships side but they say it is custom of port for the ship to discharge the lighter also. I shall have to do it though, I suppose, to try and get along with my work but shall try very hard to make them pay for it in settling a/c. What is your opinion, Sir? Then again we are laying eight miles from Pascagoula which makes it very inconvenient. I have had trouble onboard with five of my Bayres[8] cut-throats this morning, don't know how the affair will end. Sheriff goes onboard in the morning to take them onshore. In a great hurry.

Yours very Respectfully
Frank Gullison

Capt. Gullison   Yarmouth Dec. 2/92

Dear Sir:

Yours of the 13th and 15th came to hand; contents noted. Was glad to hear you had got clear of ballast and was to work loading. These timber folks are

---

8   Bayres – This may be crew shipped at Buenos Aires.

a hard lot. They want all to start with and the balance when you get through; that is if you give them their way. In reference to insurance, I have $1500. on your part and usually insure freight to cover Dis. have increased now on freight $1500.00. In reference to insurance on your stuff you told me to insure $200.00 on it for one year from June 29/91. You must have forgotten. I think there will be no trouble to fix this with Knight. George[9] says he will write Mr. Knight. I am sending Messers J.F. Whitney & Co. today draft for your insurance. Hoping you are getting along well with your loading. Mr. Hagar writes me you had two lighters in on the 15th. Things are looking very dull. Nothing doing North. They are offering 16/6[10] coal Cardiff to Rio. Hoping this will find you and family well and wishing you the compliments of the season

> I am yours truly
> *N.B. Lewis*

W.F. Hagar & Co.   Pascagoula Dec. 4th '92

Gentlemen:

Your letter and C/P enclosed received on arrival here on 28th ulto. See you have got me iron bound this time. Seems hard lines having to pay 2 1/2% on Disb. that is money we actually supply ourselves. If I understand it right, that is what we have to do. How about insurance on freight? Hunter Been & Co. tell me cargo is ready for shipment. Our ballast of 450 ton will not be out before the 10th inst. Very poor facilities for doing business here, Mr. Hagar; we are laying 12 miles from Pascagoula, 14 miles to Scranton 18 to Moss Point so it makes it very inconvenient besides I am having trouble with my crew which is going to swell expenses here; however, I shall try to work everything to best advantage. Please send me cheque for $1000.00 (one thousand).

> Yours
> *Frank Gullison*

Messers Hunter Been & Co.   Pascagoula Dec. '92
Pascagoula   Miss.

Gentlemen:

I beg to inform you that the Br. Ship *N.B. Lewis* now under charter to you is this day ready to receive cargo.

> Yours Respectfully
> *B.F. Gullison Master*

---

9 George is a son of Captain Henry in the insurance business.
10 Compare this rate with 21/6 paid the *N.B. Lewis* in 1888.

Capt. Gullison   Yarmouth Dec. 7/'92

Dear Sir:

Yours of the 2nd at hand. Sorry to hear that you are having trouble with your merchants. They should certainly give you every facility that your C/P calls for,[11] as the $2.00 clause is a swindle, but what is one going to do these days. There is not anything North for a ship to do. This seemed to be the only thing to get. I knew from the past that it was hard for these timber people to do what is right and according to their agreement but did not expect them to take any stand that the C/P did not call for. You will have to do the best you can. I could not do anything for you if I was on the spot. Try to have patience with the situation and do the best which is all anyone can do. Hoping things will turn out more favorable. I have written Mr. Hagar in reference to this trouble. Have been expecting notice of draft but none reported yet. Let me know often by letter how you are getting along. In submitting to the imposition about ballast suppose you will protest against it. Sorry to see your crew is making trouble also.

Yours truly
N.B. Lewis

Capt. Frank Gullison   H.C. KNIGHT INSURANCE
Pascagoula   N.E. Corner Walnut
                                    and Third Sts.
                                    Philadelphia Dec. 10th 1892

Dear Sir:

Enclosed find renewal of policy expiring on your personal effects which I trust you will find all in order. I have renewed this in accordance with your instructions, at the time I took it out, to keep it renewed. I am pleased to note your safe arrival at Pascagoula and trust that you will have good dispatch in loading and a safe trip across. The *Euphemia* loaded here last month for Southampton, Capt. Eugene was looking first rate.

Suppose you have heard the *Hugh Cann* has been turned over to Walter F. Hagar and Co. She is now in Dublin but don't know which way she will go from there. *Baldwin* sailed yesterday from Rio for Barbadoes, and the *Otago* was ordered to Phila. and suppose they have something for her but don't know what. Wishing you every success, I remain,

Yours faithfully,
H.C. Knight

[Note invoice included as follows:

North America $2.00. Personal Effects Ship *N.B. Lewis* 6% $12.00.[12]]

---

11 C/P: charter party.

12 It would appear that Walter F. Hagar & Co. have bought the *Hugh Cann* and *Otago*. The *Baldwin* was built for this firm at Meteghan, Nova Scotia. Under U.S. regulations American owners could do better than foreign owners. The insurance rate was 6%.

N.B. Lewis Esq.   Yarmouth N.S.   Pascagoula Dec. 14th '92

Dear Sir:

Will you please pay to H.C. Knight insurance agent at Phila. the sum of $12.00 as per policy.

   Also pay J.F. Whitney New York $34.30 for yearly Penn Life Ins. and charge the same to my a/c and oblidge

> Yours faithfully
> *B.F. Gullison*

P.S. Enclosed please accept policy and hand to Father at your pleasure. What will my Insur. amt. to on ship *N.B.L.* this last year, the same as usual; or do you reduce it as she depreciates in value?

   I am sorry to trouble you so much but you will understand why it is.   B.F.G.

H.C. Knight Esq.   Philadelphia   Pascagoula Dec. 14th '92

Dear Sir:

Yours to hand of the 10th inst. contents noted.

   I have wrote to Mr. Lewis to pay you $12.00 as per policy. Do you give receipt for this Premium if so send it to Mr. Lewis or does the Policy cover that.

   Many thanks for your information concerning shipping glad to hear from you at any time.

> Yours respectfully
> *Frank Gullison*

J.F. Whitney & Co.   New York   Pascagoula Dec. 14th '92

Gentlemen:

As my Premium on life insurance will soon be due, I have asked Mr. Lewis to settle the same with you. I do not remember receiving any receipts for Prem. paid, don't you think I require the same in case of any dispute arising? Please let me know. You have me iron clad in this. Commenced loading on 12th inst. As you are acquainted with these charters, kindly advise about signing *'bills of lading'*.

   Many thanks for papers; they are very acceptable.

   Wishing you compliments of the Season

> I remain Yours Respectfully
> *B.F. Gullison*

Pascagoula Dec. 31st '92

Dear Father:

Your letter of the 10th inst. received some time ago. Glad to hear you can a/c for the $50.00. Mistakes will happen to the best of folk. I received a letter from Mr. George Lewis a few days ago concerning extra insurance on house. It was a misunderstanding between us, I was under the impression that the extra insurance ran for one year, but understand by his letter it only covered six months, however, I asked him to renew and extend, should my house remain unoccupied. I have also received Policy on Personal effects and will send to you. George will settle and give you receipt. I suppose N.B. Lewis Esq. has settled Premium on New York Life $34.00. Will enclose receipt for '92. Is '91 receipt attached to Policy or in the safe, Father? Now about Mutual of Yarmouth? I paid for one year in advance or deposited with them I think $10.00 when I left home. There should be a little left which no doubt they will give me credit for during the coming year. Will you please attend to this and pay by the year which will save you trouble. I would have asked you to settle all *Prem.* but thought Mr. Lewis and George would understand it better as they were in the business beside save you considerable trouble. I am sorry to bother you so much Father but you have been there before me and know all about such things and I know you will be only too willing to help me. We have about 450,000 lumber onboard now. The weather has been greatly against us of late. I wrote to Ralph and sent it home.[13] Tell him to send me a few lines in return. *Love* to Dear Mother and Family and wishing you all a Happy New Year I remain

Your Loving Son

B.F. Gullison

N.B. Lewis Esq.   Yarmouth, N.S.   Pascagoula Jan 5th '93

Dear Sir:

Yours of the 28th ulto. duly received. I leave soon, merchants think I can arrange to tow outside on to Ship Island at 19F. I am afraid the draft may be 20 Ft. which is too much this time of year. Westerly wind prevailing which tends to drive the water out. However I shall try and do all for the best. We have to date 480,000 Ft. in lower hold. 20,000 between decks drawing 17 ft. even keel, principally dry lumber. Messers John G. Hall will forward you $20.00 rec. from Boston packers on account bad beef.

We are having cold weather lately,

Yours Faithfully

B.F. Gullison

---

13   Frank is asking his father to forward his letter to brother Ralph wherever he is.

J.F. Whitney Esq.   New York   January 9

Gentlemen:

I sent you telegram this morning as follows Ship will draw twenty feet loaded under deck cannot risk 19 feet present water. To load full cargo it will be necessary to move to Ship Island. Merchants refuse expense of three hundred dollars (advise).

  We have on board now about 685,000 ft. drawing 18 feet 6 in. which is quite enough for this place this time of year. Bk. *St. Mary* of New York has been loaded now three weeks waiting for a chance drawing 19 ft. 10 in. also *Blair Drummond* of Glasgow. Merchants has given me to understand here, *unlike the present*, that they would bear expense but this morning they advise contrary. My towage down Ship Island & out again $200.00, Pilotage $122.00, Harbour M. [Master] $5.00. It will no doubt sum up as stated. I think we will take about 850,000 under deck, think it better to tow down even with this expense but perhaps you will be able to do better with Merchants.

> Yours Very Respectfully
> B.F. Gullison
> Ship *N.B. Lewis*

Capt. Gullison   Yarmouth Jan. 18/'93

Dear Sir:

Yours of the 11th at hand yesterday, contents noted, also telegram as follows: Shall I take deckload out side Draft: hold full, 20 feet 3 in.[14] not much chance: Which I suppose referred to taking on deckload outside. I replied don't take deckload, freight would not pay for the risk. There would be good deal of risk and extra expense. Would take all we would get for carrying it. Judging by what they wanted to take you to Ship *Island* should think they would want all the freight on the deckload for expenses so think you are better without it. Suppose by telegram you must be about filled up in hold and now you will have to watch and wait for a chance to get out which I hope you will have soon. Expect these hard North winds are extending right down in the Gulf; if so they will keep tide down. Take every precaution and go carefully and when out and pilot leaves you can send a telegram on shore by him as we shall be very glad to hear you are clear. Hoping this will find you and yours all well. We are having a very cold winter. Suppose the roses are blooming down South.

> Yours etc.
> *N.B. Lewis*

---

14 Ship will draw 20 feet 3 inches without deck load.

N.B. Lewis Esq.   Pascagoula Jany 19th '93

Dear Sir:
This will inform you that we expect to be loaded Saturday night if the weather moderates so we can keep the barges alongside. We are having fearful weather of late most impossible to do anything in shape of loading. I telegraphed you on 15th inst. Ship will draw about twenty feet three inches under deck, will I risk deck load outside? Think poor chance. Received your answer, 'Don't take deck load the freight not equal to the risk', which I think wise as we can hardly get a chance to load inside let alone outside the bar. I had a letter from O'Brien, Ship *Bonanza*, last Sunday. He tells me they have 15 ships there waiting for water. Mobile about the same, still they will be able to get out before us as they have more powerful tugs. Bk. *St. Mary* & *Blair Drummond* here yet. We had a good tide last week but it was so rough in the bar pilots dare not attempt it. I hope we shall be fortunate enough to have a chance when loaded as I am sick and tired of this part of the country.

Yours Obediently
B.F. Gullison

In many of the ports used by the *N.B. Lewis* there was insufficient depth of water in the harbour for a ship of her size and draft. In both Cardiff and Capetown there had been problems because of the shallow water and in Pascagoula it was found the ship could not take a full cargo. To load the *N.B. Lewis* fully she would have to be towed out beyond the bar and the timber taken out by lighter to made a deck load. Both Captain Gullison and Nathan Lewis considered it would not pay to do this. The ship therefore sailed January 31, 1893, with 685,000 feet of lumber in her hold.

In the log of the voyage across the Atlantic to Dordrecht there is an interesting entry for March 7, 1893:

Lat 48.39 N   Long 17.43 Course East 61 miles
Fine weather throughout the day. Wind WNW and NW hauling to NE westerly swell continues. Passed a ship steering west which hoisted their signals but could not distinguish them. Day ends fine. Barometer 30.70 (high).

Although the log of the ship *Euphemia* is not available, there does exist a rough calculation book of Captain Eugene Gullison. It contains this notation for March 7:

Passed ship *N.B. Lewis* this morning at 8 p.m. Signalised, fine, all sail set, wind hauling North and East. Longitude 18.16 Lat 48.07 at 4 p.m. on this day.

The Gullison brothers had thus passed each other without Frank's knowing it.

After his arrival at Dordrecht, Holland, March 22, 1893, Captain Gullison was informed the ship was to be sold if a buyer could be found. It may be assumed that the owners had held a meeting in Yarmouth and decided, in view of the freight rates now being offered, that it would be best to dispose of the vessel. The London agents, John Black & Co., were therefore notified to offer the ship for sale.

N.B. Lewis Esq.   Yarmouth N.S.   Dordrecht March 22nd '93

Dear Sir:

We arrived at our discharging berth yesterday morning *safe* and *sound* and I cabled you 'arrived stop mate allotment what amount.' Received answer 'hundred forty dollars'.[15] We will commence discharging 23rd probably be 14 or 20 days.

Rec. your letter of 24th ulto. on arrival. I have got Messers Wambessie & Co. to help me with my business here. 'The same good house'. We will try and sell but not give away. Anything reasonable will cable you. They have now on hand about 900 ton Chalk for Philadelphia and will fill up on baled loose bedding. The rates I will note before sealing.

That Hunter Been club at Pascagoula I hope never to have dealings with again although Mr. Denny and Dansel are I think fine.

From Yours Faithfully
B.F. Gullison

John Black & Co.   Dordrecht
19 Change Alley   London   March 24th '93

Gentlemen:

Yours of 22nd to hand this morning contents noted. The Ship *N.B. Lewis* is for sale, but we do not propose to give her away. We want £4000 Stg. She is a good ship and has been well taken care of. Your 'Particulars' required I will send you as soon as I go to Rotterdam.

Yours Very Respectfully,
B.F. Gullison

Messers John Black & Co.   Dordrecht March 31st '93

Gentlemen:

Your favor of the 30th to hand. This present cargo is the first in its kind the ship has ever carried, therefore, I cannot give you a definite answer.

15 Before paying off the mate he is finding out from N.B. Lewis what has been paid to his family from the Yarmouth office.

Our present cargo consists of 837,230 Ft. deals with lumber under deck having a space left of 20,000 ft. which we could not fill owing to not having sufficient water on the bar. Now Sir, what she would take on deck 'which is large' and in poop I am not prepared to say. We will have between-decks out tomorrow.

Yours Very Truly,

B.F. Gullison

N.B. Lewis Esq.   Yarmouth, N.S.   Dordrecht April 1st 1893

Dear Sir:

Yours of the 16th ulto. to hand last evening contents noted will have 'between-decks' out Tuesday next and will try and draw £900 and remit you through Union Bk. London as you advise. I have been corresponding with John Black & Co. since I arrived gave them particulars and 4000 Stg. as our price, probably we may get £3500. Ship looks exceedingly well since I have got her painted outside and I shall hate like the deuce to part with her as she is a good ship and *everything in order onboard*, very near two suits of sails. New steel wire hawser and about all of her yards No. 1 and the best of all a good '*class*'. I know I have not done anything of late in remittances but I have tried to do my best and know *you* do not *blame me*. I have obeyed your orders and kept my ship in a condition that I am not ashamed of today and I think she should demand a good price something beyond the common sum. I believe financially it is better to sell, as you say, if we can get £3500 but not under that. Enclosed please accept Power of Attorney, signed as you request.

I remain Dear Sir,

Your Obedient Servant

B.F. Gullison

The Union Bank of London Ltd.   Dordrecht

London E.C.   April 4th 1893

Gentlemen:

I herewith enclose first bill of exchange to the amount £900.0.0 Stg. at 8 D/S on the Rotterdam Bk.

   Which you will please place to the Cr. of the Bank of Yarmouth Nova Scotia for freight Per Ship *N.B. Lewis* payable to N.B. Lewis Esq., Yarmouth Nova Scotia and advise them accordingly.

Yours truly

B.F. Gullison, Master

Br. Ship *N.B. Lewis*

N.B. Lewis Esq.   Yarmouth   Dordrecht April 5th 1893
Nova Scotia

Dear Sir:

I forwarded to you yesterday through the Union Bank of London
£900.0.0 Stg. 8/D bills and hope you will receive the same in order. I have
had no word from John Black & Co. since I last wrote you. Discharging
moving slowly, probably finish about 12th inst. Nothing now to inform you
Sir and hoping these few lines will find you in good health, I remain,

Yours Obediently
B.F. Gullison

P.S. We are having 'steady' Easterly winds ever since I arrived.

Messers John Black & Co.   Dordrecht
5 East India Avenue   London   April 10th '93

Gentlemen:

Would you please inform me whether you have had a chance to dispose of
Ship *N.B. Lewis* and about what time have you got to do the same. I have
an offer for 'New York' 4/0 on cement about 1000 ton. Expect to be discharged 14th inst.
    Please advise and oblige, Yours

Very Respectfully
B.F. Gullison

Messers John Black & Co.
5 East India Avenue   London

Gentlemen:

I received your letter and note contents. Captain Pederson remains here
yet. He has had a gentleman from London with him a Mr. Dason I believe
to inspect our ship, seems to like her *well* but thinks £4000 too high, has
he made you an offer yet?
    We have also had two Gentlemen from Clarkson's house, sounding,
picking and jigging.
    We have been delayed discharging, hope to be out Monday 17th. About
what amt. do you think will be offered for the Ship? I have my wife and
family with me and would like you to advise the cheapest way to go from
here should we sell and oblige,

Yours Very Respectfully
B.F. Gullison

Apl. 15th '93

From
To
B.F. Gullison
John Black & Co.
Ship *N.B. Lewis*
London E.C.

Dear Sir:

Yours of the 14th to hand this morning for my part I do not care for coal at that freight mentioned.

Captain Pederson remains here yet 'talks' encouraging and says he has made you no offer yet wants to see the bottom first. Expect to be out Monday night, please let me know his offer soon as possible that I might arrange future business.

Yours in Haste
Frank Gullison

Messers John Black & Co.   Dordrecht Apl. 18th '93
5 East India Avenue   London

Gentlemen:

Your telegram to hand yesterday, as follows: Lewis cables try £3200. Otherwise accept £3000. Wording also confirmed by letter this morning, note all you say concerning ship. 'I am ready now for anything'. I turned out 500 pieces over bills Lading for quantity. If ship is sold will the chronometer be included? Who makes contract for dry dock, buyers or sellers? Please inform that all may be done *right*.

Yours Respectfully
B.F. Gullison

N.B. Lewis Esq.   Yarmouth N.S.   Dordrecht April 18 '93

Dear Sir:

John Black & Co. cabled me tonight '*Ship Sold*'. I suppose this will mean £3200 Nett.

We finished discharging this morning came out all right suppose we will go into drydock tomorrow or next day 20th. The thoughts of leaving the old Clipper makes me '*feel bad*' however, I think it will be better financially. I feel very *proud* of her. I assure you Mr. Lewis people in general here remark what a fine able-looking ship.

I expect to go from here to New York and then home. Want to leave Saturday if possible.

Enclosed please accept a/c of wages.

Yours Very Respectfully
B.F. Gullison

As can be imagined, Captain Gullison's feelings regarding the sale were mixed. On the one hand he knew business conditions were bad, but on the other hand the *N.B. Lewis* was his beloved ship. It had been his pride to keep her in first class condition for the past seven years and it was hard to part with her. In the end, however, the ship was sold for about £3200 ($15,500 Canadian), and Captain Gullison headed for home with his wife, his son, and perhaps his chronometer.

The buyer was Thomas S. Falck of Stavanger, Norway, and the ship was re-named the *Heidrun* in April or May of 1893. The *Heidrun* was wrecked in 1901. *Lloyd's Weekly Shipping Index,* Feb. 1, 1901, reports from Delfzyl 'the Norwegian ship *Heidrun* went adrift in a terrific gale last night and is now aground on the south bank against the stones. Her bottom is damaged and it will be difficult to get her off.'

The report on February 25 was that 'she will probably now be sold to be broken up, as the re-floating would be difficult'. And on February 26, she was reported sold.

Here ends the saga of a gallant ship.

With the sale of the ship *N.B. Lewis* in 1893 the narrative of this Novascotiaman comes to an end. However, it may be of some interest to follow the fortunes of the Lewis brothers and the Gullison family. Their history illustrates in a small way the social and economic conditions which existed in Western Nova Scotia during the concluding decade of the 19th century and the early years of the 20th.

It was in the period from around 1845 to 1879 that Yarmouth prospered most as a ship owning community. Many of the individuals and firms starting around the middle of the century owned in excess of twenty thousand tons during that period, and Campbell's history lists 31 owners who owned a total of more than ten thousand tons. The same list gives H. & N.B. Lewis a total of 12,115 tons. In many cases, as with Henry and Nathan Lewis, the tonnage given is really the total operated rather than owned.

As stated in the introduction, the first ship built by the Lewis brothers for the ocean freighting trade was the *Mizpah*, 898 tons, launched at Salmon River in 1873. The firm of H. & N.B. Lewis was formed the following year and a reference to the list of vessels and owners on page 372 shows that for ten years a new vessel was built every second year.

In 1875 the brother-in-law (William Rogers) of Henry and Nathan died and they with their sister Chloe (Mrs. Rogers) were appointed administrators of the vessels of which he had been the principal owner. These vessels included the *Republic*, the *R. Hilton* and the *E.H. Duval*. The last named ship was sold almost at once but the others continued to be operated for many years.

It can thus be seen that for ten years there was a steady growth in the operation of H. & N.B. Lewis in the ocean freighting trade. Unfortunately the next decade showed a decline in the business as rapid as the growth had been. By 1894 all the ocean freighters had been either wrecked or sold, and ocean freighting was finished for Henry and Nathan Lewis.

FIG. 79. Beaver River, looking north, around 1900.

FIG. 80. Gullison Brothers' Store, Salmon River, around 1900.

The evidence is that the brothers had seen what was coming and while still operating the fleet of freighters they had been developing a different type of business. During the growth period of the firm the wharf property was improved and extended to cover an area of 60,000 square feet, providing facilities for the fishing industry, and later the importation and sale of hard and soft coal. In 1883 the schooner *Harry Lewis*, 111 tons, was built by Henry and Nathan, as sole owners, for the salt fish trade between Yarmouth and the West Indies. Another schooner, the *Georgina*, was built in 1888 with other owners for fishing on the 'banks'. H. & N.B. Lewis also held interests in other schooners and were general fish buyers and sellers of fishing supplies. In 1890 the *Harry Lewis* was sold in Barbados and the following year the Brigantine *Harry*, 144 tons, was built to replace it in the West Indian trade. Thus as the freighting vessels were disposed of, their owners' attention turned to the purchase of fresh fish and the export of dried cod and importation of West Indian produce. While they maintained the store near the wharves for the sale of fishing supplies and ship chandlery, they also opened a store for the sale of general merchandise on Main Street about a block away from the wharf.

In 1889 Nathan Lewis died and Henry purchased from the heirs Nathan's interest in the business and in the Brigantine *Harry*. The *Harry* was held until 1908 when it was sold to James McKinnon at North Sydney, N.S. With the sale of the *Harry* the fish business and the West Indian trade was discontinued. At about the same time the general store on Main Street was sold and from then until Henry died in 1921 the chief business was marine insurance and the importation and sale of hard and soft coal. Unfortunately Henry's son George died in 1900 at the early age of 33. He had established a prosperous marine insurance business and the other son, Harry, continued with this business during his lifetime.

While records of Frank Gullison's life after retiring from sea are scanty, some details are known.

It would appear that after the *N.B. Lewis* was sold he returned to Nova Scotia for a period and then through Soley & Co. of Liverpool, England, he obtained command of the ship *Ancaios*. There is a letter from Soley & Co., dated December 15, 1905, addressed to Capt. B.F. Gullison, ship *Ancaios*, Capetown, which states 'This will introduce Captain J.E. Ritchie who as previously advised is to relieve you in command of the *Ancaios* upon arrival at the Cape'.

Real estate records show that Captain Benjamin Gullison, Frank's father, was buying and selling various properties after he retired from the sea. About 1895 he bought a store property in Salmon River and the Gullison family – father Ben, and the two sons, Frank and Eugene – began a business under the name of Gullison Brothers. They operated a general store on the corner of the main road and the Salmon River road and owned two schooners, the *Annie* and the *Hattie*. It may be presumed that during the late 1890's and

FIG. 81. Ship *Ancaios*.

early 1900's, Frank and Eugene took turns staying home and operating the store, and going to sea as master of a sailing ship.

A few meagre details of the business are available. These include an account of the first few trips of the *Annie*.

SCHOONER ANNIE

First Trip

Beginning April 7th ending April 11th 1896
Cape St. Mary – Rockland [Maine] – Meteghan, N.S.

Expenses Cape St. Mary

April 7	Customs	3.00
	Edson Ellis stoves	1.75
	Wharfage .75 Invoice .10	.85
	Fish .50 help loading 6.00	6.50
	Hired man .50 paraffin tin .15	.65
	Saw .75 potatoes .50	1.25
	Water cask .50 lamps .50	1.00
	Father's bill 6.00 filling water .26	6.26
	1/2 wharfage on 70 cords wood	1.05
		$22.31

Rockland Expenses

April 9	Telegram home	.45
	Entering and clearing	4.32
	Hired help	5.50
	Blocks and sheaves	1.60
		$11.87
	Cash to seamen first trip	3.00
	Total expenses	37.18

CREDIT

	By 70 cords of wood @ $2.75	$192.50
	1/2 (freight)	96.25
	Disbursements	37.18
	Profit	59.07
	One-third share	19.69

Second Trip

Beginning April 11th ending May 9th

April 11	Expenses Meteghan		27.07
" 28	" Boston		60.72
May 4	" Salmon River		21.96
" 6	" Rockland		11.80
			$121.55
		Wages	96.00
			217.55

CREDIT

April 28	By freight on piling		181.51
	From J.G. Hall & Co.		
May 7	By freight Rockland		91.00
			272.51
		Expenses	217.55
		Profit	56.44
		One-third share	18.81

The total earnings of each of the three partners from April 7 to December 30, 1896, were:

April 9 − one third share	$19.69
May 7 − one third share	18.81
August 14 − one third share	84.67
November 13 − one third share	8.00
November 23 − one third share	28.14
December 30 − one third share	25.05
	$184.36

The profits seem small compared with present day earnings, but they should be considered against the economy of the time when a day labourer might receive one dollar for the work of a twelve hour day.

Another interesting item in the account book shows that John G. Hall & Co., who had long been the agents in Boston for H. & N.B. Lewis, were also acting as agents for Gullison Bros.

FIG. 82. Captain Frank Gullison and his wife. The photograph was taken in Australia about 1905.

Tom Foley of Salmon River, who remembers well the Gullison Brothers and their schooners, says the trade was cordwood to Rockland, Maine, and piling to Boston and fish and lumber to the West Indies. 'But', he says, 'The "heft" of the business was piling to Boston.'

It has been said that the 'Back Bay' area of Boston was built on Nova Scotian tree trunks driven into the soft bottom of that swampy ground as foundation material for the buildings erected there. It has also been remarked that many a Nova Scotian landed from the Yarmouth steamer on Long Wharf with a hammer and a saw ready to go to work on those same buildings.

The business of Gullison Brothers was at Salmon River; but during the latter part of their lives the father and two sons lived close to the Beaver River church, which was their great interest. Frank was the superintendent of its Sunday school for many years. Thus they passed their final years, the father, Captain Ben and the two sons Frank and Eugene all dying within a few years of each other between 1924 and 1930, aged respectively 88, 69 and 69.

Lewis Family Relationships

The family names included are restricted to those involved in this narrative.

Waitstill Lewis of Westerly, Rhode Island, went to Halifax and later returned to the U.S.A. prior to the American Revolution. His children remained there except for: Waitstill Lewis, son of the above, who settled in Yarmouth, Nova Scotia.

Waitstill Lewis had a son William who had three children who became owners of Yarmouth vessels.

1. Chloe Lewis married William Rogers, owner of a number of vessels. When her husband died in 1875, she became one of the administrators of his estate with her brothers Henry and Nathan.

2. Henry Lewis, 1830–1921, married Esther Holmes, daughter of Captain Kendall Holmes of Hantsport and had six children. Two sons were connected with the firm of H. & N.B. Lewis: Harry, born 1870, died 1940; and George, born 1866, died 1899.

3. Nathan Lewis married Adaline Cann, daughter of Lyman Cann of Yarmouth. He did not have any children of his own. He adopted a nephew of his wife, Lewis Chipman, who became a lawyer in the law firm of Corning & Chipman (later Chipman & Sanderson). Murray Lewis, who sailed on the maiden voyage of the *N.B. Lewis*, was a son of George M. Lewis, cousin of Henry and Nathan.

Gullison Family Relationships

The family included are restricted to those involved in this narrative.

Captain Benjamin Gullison (1836–1924) had three sons:

1. Benjamin Franklin Gullison (1858–1927)
    Married Idella Corning (1863–1930), daughter of Captain Thomas
    Corning (1824–1904). A brother of Idella, Thomas H. Corning, was the
    mate on the maiden trip of the *N.B. Lewis* in 1880. Frank and Idella were
    married in Beaver River March 3, 1883. They had one son Bowman, born
    February 14, 1885, died September 28, 1913.

2. Eugene Gullison (1861–1930)
    Married Josie Corning daughter of David Corning.
    They had 2 children, Fred who became a doctor in Yarmouth (deceased),
    and Beulah Gullison Perry, resident of U.S.A.

3. Ralph Ernest Gullison (1869–1947)
    Married Anetta Covey of Indian Harbour, N.S.
    Under the Canadian Baptist Foreign Mission he became a missionary in
    India where he lived from 1896 to 1947.
    He had three children: Ralph Ben Gullison, medical missionary in India
    retired to Vancouver; Genevieve Foulkes; and Ray Gullison.

Ralph Ernest Gullison, M.A., D.D., the youngest son of Captain Ben Gullison,
was born March 21, 1869. As a boy of sixteen he must have been considering
'going to sea' like his two older brothers, for he wrote Frank in New York in
1885 asking if he could join his ship on the next voyage from New York to
Shanghai. While advising against it, Frank gave his permission and Ralph

joined the ship as a sailor in January, 1886. He sailed around the world to Shanghai, San Francisco and Dunkirk, and was paid off at the latter port in March, 1887. During the voyage, he had become convinced his brother Frank was right and that the life of a sailor was not for him. He returned to Nova Scotia and went back to school in Yarmouth County. The following year he attended Horton Academy, a boarding school in Wolfville, Nova Scotia, where he prepared to enter Acadia University. He later graduated from this University in Arts and Theology.

He married Miss Anetta Covey of Indian Harbour, St. Margaret's Bay, Halifax County. After serving in the Baptist pastorate in the Kingston-Tremont field he volunteered as a missionary to India under the Board of the Canadian Baptist Foreign Mission. He landed at Bimlipatam on the Eastern coast of India in December, 1896. After an initial period of language study and service in Bobbili he moved to Bimlipatam (now Bheemunipatnam) in 1897; there he and his wife spent forty years.

Reverend and Mrs. Gullison were engaged in evangelistic and educational work, founding and building churches and establishing schools. The large Central Boarding School in Bheemunipatnam, started about 1913, is still serving the northern fields of the mission after more than sixty years. In 1933, he was honoured by Acadia University with the degree of Doctor of Divinity, Honoris Causa. Dr. Gullison served on the Educational Councils of the Indian Government for many years and in 1937 he was honoured by being presented with the 'King's Medal'.

Dr. Ralph Gullison retired from the Mission Service in 1937, living for ten years in Ootacamund in South India until his death in 1947.

APPENDIX C

LIST OF VESSELS OPERATED BY H. & N.B. LEWIS IN THE OCEAN FREIGHTING TRADE

Date Built	Name	Tonnage	Where Built	Owners (and Number of Shares Held)*	Disposal
1868	*W.H. Duval* bark	661	Shelburne	Wm. Rogers, Joseph Goudey, Wm. H. Cook, Edmund H. Duval (of Quebec)	Lewis interest sold 1875. Vessel sold to Quebec 1884.
1871	*Republic* ship	843	Shelburne	Wm. Rogers 32, Benjamin Hilton 16, Wm. H. Cook 4, Joseph A. Corning 4, Wm. Kelley 8. Chloe Rogers (widow of W. Rogers), Henry Lewis and Nathan Lewis became administrators after Sept. 1876 with 32 shares (owned 20 when ship was wrecked).	Wrecked off Dunkirk 1886
1873	*Mizpah* bark	898	Salmon River	Nathan Lewis 14, Henry Lewis 14, Hugh Cann 16, Hugh E. Cann 12, Frances G. Cook 8.	Wrecked at Gabarous, n.s., 1887.
1874	*Otago*	1095	Salmon River	Nathan Lewis 14, H. Lewis 12, Hugh Cann 12, Hugh E. Cann 14, Frances Cook 6, Benjamin Gullison 6.	Sold to Otago Shipping Co. 1892
1874	*B. Hilton* bark	986	Shelburne	Wm. Rogers 36, Ben Hilton 16, Bradford Hilton 4, Wm. T. Kelly 8. Chloe Rogers, H. Lewis and Nathan Lewis became administrators Sept. 1876.	Sold at Antwerp July 1882
1876	*Hugh Cann* bark	1073	Salmon River	Nathan Lewis 16, H. Lewis 8, Hugh Cann 16, Hugh E. Cann 8, Lyman Cann 4, Hugh Kenealy 6, Hebert Cann 4, George Eldridge 4	Sold about 1892
1878	*Equator* ship	1273	Salmon River	Nathan Lewis 12, Henry Lewis 8, Hugh Cann 8, Hugh E. Cann 8, Frances G. Cook 8, Hugh Kenealy 6, George K. Trefry 4, Wm. H. Cook 4, Elizah Phillips 4, Jacob S. Allen 2.	Wrecked on Briar Island n.s.

LIST OF VESSELS OPERATED BY H. & N.B. LEWIS IN THE OCEAN FREIGHTING TRADE (CONTINUED)

Date Built	Name	Tonnage	Where Built	Owners (and Number of Shares Held)*	Disposal
1880	*N.B. Lewis* ship	1325	Salmon River	Nathan Lewis 12, Henry Lewis 16, Hugh E. Cann 12, Hugh D. Cann 12, Benjamin Gullison 4, Elisabeth Cann 4, Hugh Kenealy 4,	Sold at Dordrecht 1893
1882	*Euphemia* ship	1340	Salmon River	Henry Lewis 19, Frances G. Cook 8, Wm. H. Cook 6, Hugh Kenealy 8, Abram Hatfield 4, Sam. Hatfield 4, Nathan Lewis 6, Trefry 4, Smith Horton 2, Thomas J. Perry 2, George K. Trefry 5, George G. Crosby 2.	Sold in 1905 to an Italian firm registered in Genoa
1889	*Maggie Thompson* barkentine	554	Meteghan River	Nathan Lewis 38, George Lewis 4, John C. Blackadar (builder) 4, James Blackadar 4, Eben E. Archibald 4, David Wetmore 4, Edgar Crosby 4, Arch Blackadar 2.	Lost at sea February 1893

*The owners listed are usually the original shareholders. There were various changes in the ownership during the lifetime of the vessels. For instance, it was generally arranged for the captain to have at least four shares. These might be bought from a previous captain or one of the other owners.

Glossary of terms and miscellaneous notes

1. Bill of lading
2. Comprador
3. Coppering a wooden sailing vessel
4. Crimps and sailors
5. Currency
6. Freight payments
7. Insurance of vessels
8. Manifest
9. Registration of vessels
10. Sails (how named)
11. Slop chest
12. Tonnage (definitions)
13. Valuation of vessels

1. *Bill of Lading*—Shippers provided a bill of lading (B/L) which contained a list of the cargo and terms of shipment. As cargo was received on board, it was checked for amount and condition by the ship's officers.

2. *Comprador*—There were many long-established European and American business houses in the ports of Shanghai and Hong Kong that acted as ship's agents. These firms usually employed a local Chinese to act as a sort of 'headman' to deal with other Chinese firms and with local Chinese labour. These employees were known as compradors, and in due course, many of them established businesses themselves. They learned enough of the English language to deal with the captains and thus began to act as go-betweens for the captain and the local people, providing various services needed by the ships.

'Cheap Jack's' business card (p.255) illustrates the wide range of his activities. The comprador's agent was usually the first to board a ship when it entered the harbour, or as in Hong Kong, meet the ship outside the harbour to offer his services.

3. *Coppering a wooden sailing vessel*—Rough rule for finding what quantity of metal sheeting will cover a vessel:

Take the average height you want to copper the vessel, to which add for very *sharp* vessel 7; *medium* 8 and *very full* 9 feet. Multiply this figure by the length of the keel and divide by two.

Example

Suppose vessel has length of keel	170 feet
" " " average height of	15 1/4 feet
" " is medium - add	8 feet
Total height	23 1/4 feet

Multiply 23 1/4 by 170 equals 3,953
Divide by 2   "   1,971

Vessel would require between 1,900 and 2,000 sheets of copper.

NOTE: sharp, medium and full are descriptive of types of hull. In modern usage the term used would be "coefficient of fineness".

4. *Crimps and Sailors*—In most of the ports frequented by sailing ships were men known as crimps. According to stories of the time, they were much the same type in all ports around the world. Hard, unscrupulous, and often cruel, they usually operated sailors' boarding-houses or had an arrangement with a boarding-house keeper.

When a ship was ready for sea the captain notified a crimp how many sailors he needed and they were usually delivered to him just before the ship sailed. The captain paid an agreed sum for each man delivered. In the larger ports, many of the crimps had agents or 'runners' whose job was to watch for the arrival of vessels and when the sailors came ashore after being paid off, they enticed them to their houses with offers of liquor and women.

Young, ambitious sailors soon learned enough to avoid such pitfalls but there was a class of 'professional' sailor who could not seem to resist the enticements offered. He would accept the offers, have a good spree, and then in a few days would usually wake up from a drunken stupor in the forecastle of a ship outward bound, with pockets empty and sick in body and spirit.

In ports such as San Francisco, where sailors were scarce, the crimp could afford to give credit to a sailor for his 'entertainment' and collect his account from the captain when the sailors were shipped. The sailor would then, during the voyage, obtain his needs from the 'slop chest' (see explanation p. 377) on credit from the captain, who would in turn collect when the sailor was paid off. Thus many sailors saw very little money for years at a time. On the other hand, in well-run ships such as the *N.B. Lewis*, there are many examples of sailors who were careful with their money and kept their savings to send home for their use when they retired from the sea.

5. *Currency*—At this time the English pound was the strongest and most common currency in the world. Most freights were quoted in pounds, shillings and pence. The usual exchange value of the Canadian and U.S. dollar was $4.86 per pound sterling.

6. *Freight payments*—Payments for freight received by the captain of a vessel were usually remitted to the owners by the purchase of a draft on a London bank (also known as a bill of exchange). The London bank would in turn remit the amount to a Yarmouth bank for the account of the owners. Because of the high percentage of ships lost, it was the custom to send a first and second bill of exchange (B/E) on different ships. In the early days, as many as three bills of exchange, all copies of the first, might be mailed to London from the Far East.

   In the United States and England payments were usually made to the ship's agents, who would then remit the net balance to the owners in Yarmouth after deducting any amounts which had been paid by them for expenses.

7. *Insurance*—Insurance was usually arranged by the owners in Yarmouth, in the case of the vessels we have considered, with Yarmouth insurance companies. The risk was also generally divided among the companies. For instance, if the total insurance on the vessel was to be $25,000 it might be divided among the companies concerned into $8,000, $8,000 and $9,000. When a loss occurred insurance claims would be paid by each company on the basis of the ratio of its insurance carried to the total insurance of the vessel.

   There is not any certain information on the rates of insurance paid on the *N.B. Lewis*. Some information is available on other Nova Scotia sailing vessels of the time. A fairly common rate was 11% per year with a return premium of 3% if no loss occurred during the period. A rough estimate of the cost of insurance might be 8% on 75% of the valuation of the vessel in the year the insurance was placed.

8. *Manifest*—If a cargo came from many different shippers, the quantities listed in the various bills of lading were summarized in a manifest.

9. *Registration*—When a vessel was built it was listed at its port of registry and given a number. In Canada, the Registrar of Shipping was usually the Collector of Customs in each port. The numbers of all British ships were on file with the British Board of Trade in London and with Lloyd's insurance office.

10. *Sails*—Generally speaking sails take their names from the mast and stay on which they are carried. Thus the square sail carried on the fore royal mast is the fore royal; on the fore top gallant mast, the fore top gallant; on the fore top mast, the fore topsail. The sails on the lower mast are the exception, for collectively they are termed 'courses', and individually, fore-sail, main-sail and cross-jack, the latter being the lower sail on the mizzen mast. A gaff sail set on the aftermast of a square rigger is the driver or spanker, while gaff sails on any other square rigged mast are known as spencers. Fore and aft sails set on stays are either stay-sails or jibs, according to their position. See: *Masting and Rigging*, by Harold A. Underhill. Brown, Son, and Ferguson; Glasgow, Scotland, 1946.

11. *Slop Chest*—A term for goods such as underwear, socks, oil skins, tobacco, etc., kept on hand in the ship to be sold to the sailors as they might require. Anything obtained by a sailor would be charged to his account and deducted from his wages when he was paid off. In sailing ship days any profit on the slop chest was usually a perquisite of the captain, although he might not deal directly with the sailor in the transactions. A needed article might be obtained through the mate of the watch, or perhaps a steward or cabin boy.

12. *Tonnage*—Registered tonnage of a vessel is based upon the amount of cubic space available for cargo, the formula being 100 cubic feet of usable cargo space equals 1 ton.

   Gross tonnage is a measure of the internal volume of the ship and is equal to the under deck tonnage plus the tonnage of all enclosed spaces above the tonnage deck.

   Net tonnage is a residual tonnage after the various allowances for propelling power, crew spaces and navigational spaces have been deducted from gross tonnage. For further information on 'tonnage' consult Lloyds' *Register of Shipping*.

13. *Valuation of Vessels*—While the value of a vessel depreciated with age there were other factors taken into account when placing a value on a vessel. Some vessels were cared for better than others. Captains and mates meeting in various foreign ports would talk about the Yarmouth vessels they knew and by letters and personal visits this information would become known among shareholders in the town and county. It was a

common custom to buy and sell shares at auction. If an estate was to be settled or if, for any reason, someone wished to sell shares in a vessel, they were put up for auction. The price paid per share thus fixed a value on the vessel. The value of shares rose and fell with freight rates paid. It was a free-trading world, with no income tax to pay but with great risks involved.

*Voyages of N.B. Lewis with Summary of Earnings and Expenses
from Information Available*

The financial information regarding the voyages of the *N.B. Lewis* is not complete enough to provide an accurate statement of the amount earned by the ship during the period it was under the management of H. & N.B. Lewis. For those interested, a summary of the voyages and the information which is available regarding earnings and expenses will be found on the succeeding pages.

It will be noted that for the first five years, from August, 1880, to December, 1885, there is no definite information regarding earnings, etc. However, a rough estimate can be made for these years. The rate on wheat from Philadelphia to Cork − for orders − during August of 1880 was between 5 shillings 10 1/2 pence (5/10 1/2) and six shillings (6/) per quarter. With eight bushels to a quarter the freight from Philadelphia to Waterford, Ireland, on the first freight-carrying voyage of the *N.B. Lewis* would be about $14,500.00.

In December, 1880, the rate had dropped a little to between 5/3 and 5/9. If we assume a rate of 5/6 the freight to Havre would have amounted to about $12,800.00. During 1880 and 1881 the four trips back and forth across the Atlantic might have grossed around $50,000.00. With a new ship the operating costs for the same period might have been $20,000.00.

We can assume that on the next trip from London to San Francisco the *N.B. Lewis* must have carried a load out as well as bringing back a cargo of 2060 tons of wheat. During the next two and a half years there were two voyages from Cardiff to South America with coal, a voyage from South America to India and back to England and then two voyages across the North Atlantic from America to England.

It does appear that by the summer of 1885, when Captain Gullison took

379

command, the ship had probably earned enough to cover her cost and that the shareholders had received back their original investment.

There is no record of the expense and earnings of Capt. Gullison's first voyage in the *N.B. Lewis* from Philadelphia to London and back to New York. However, in his letter of February 10, 1886, to N.B. Lewis it would appear that the net profit of that voyage was $2500, which was the difference between the New York expense and the draft of W.F. Hagar & Co.

Record of Voyages N.B. Lewis First Five Years

Year	Probable Voyage Number	Departure	Arrival	Days at Sea	Port to Port		Days in Port	Cargo
					Captain Ben Gullison			
1880	1st	Aug. 6	Aug. 15	9	Yarmouth	to Philadelphia	9	In ballast
1880		Aug. 24	Sept. 25	32	Philadelphia	" Waterford Ire.	21	80117 bu. corn
1880		Oct. 16	Nov. 11	31	Waterford	" Philadelphia	31	in ballast
1880/81	2nd	Dec. 4	Jan. 7	26	Philadelphia	" Havre	37	76800 bu. grain
1881		Feb. 13	Mar. 11	26	Havre	" Philadelphia	13	
1881	3rd	Mar. 22	Apr. 28	35	Philadelphia	" Hamburg	26	7709 sacks wheat
1881	4th	May 24	June 30	37	Hamburg	" Philadelphia	43	part cargo salt
1881	5th	Aug. 12	Sept. 9	28	Philadelphia	" London	53	
					Captain George Eldridge			
1881	6th	Nov. 1	April 6	156	London	" San Francisco	56	
1882	7th	June 1	Oct. 12	133	San Francisco	" Fleetwood	56	2060 tons wheat
1882					Fleetwood	" Cardiff		
1882/83	8th	Dec. 7	Jan. 11	35	Cardiff	" Rio de Janeiro	65	probably coal
1883		Mar. 17	May 7	51	Rio de Janeiro	" Calcutta		
1883	9th	June 20	Nov. 5	138	Calcutta	" London		
					London	" Cardiff		
1884	10th	Feb. 18	June 9	111	Cardiff	" Valparaiso	27	probably coal
1884/85		Nov. 9	Feb.		Valparaiso	" London		
					Captain Crosby			
1885	11th	June 5	July		New York	" Amsterdam		
1885		Aug. 1	Sept. 10	40	Amsterdam	" Philadelphia	25	possibly oil
					Captain Frank Gullison			
1885	12th	Oct. 5	Nov. 5	31	Philadelphia	" London	13	
1885		Nov. 18	Dec. 31	43	London	" New York		

Summary of Earnings: Ship N.B. Lewis from January 1, 1886 to March 1893

Date		Voyage	Expense	Port	Cargo	Rate	Earnings
Feb.	1886	New York to Shanghai	$6,708.60	New York	49,418 cases oil ballast	.31	$15,319.58
July	1886	Shanghai to San Francisco	2,852.70	Shanghai			
Oct.	1886	San Francisco to Dunkirk	4,123.27	San Francisco	1971 tons wheat ballast	27/6s	13,186.00
Mar.	1887	Dunkirk to Cardiff	5,109.30	Dunkirk			
May	1887	Cardiff to Capetown	4,864.62	Cardiff	2027 tons coal ballast	18/6s	9,123.00
Aug.	1887	Capetown to New Orleans	2,594.00	Capetown			
Dec.	1887	New Orleans to Havre	8,246.47	New Orleans	4460 bales cotton ballast		13,103.75
Feb.	1888	Havre to Penarth	5,790.00	Havre			
Mar.	1888	Penarth to Rio de Janeiro	4,076.00	Penarth	2082 tons coal ballast	21s	10,637.00
June	1888	Rio de Janeiro to Cardiff	2,589.00	Rio de Janeiro			
July	1888	Cardiff to Capetown	4,667.00	Cardiff	2082 tons coal ballast	21/6s	10,890.00
Nov.	1888	Capetown to New York	2,225.00	Capetown			
Jan.	1889	New York to Surabaya	6,368.52	New York	48791 cases oil	.40	19,516.40
July	1889	Surabaya to New York	3,284.55	Surabaya	1853 tons sugar	$8.10	15,009.30

Summary of Earnings: Ship N.B. Lewis from January 1, 1886 to March 1893 (continued)

Date		Voyage	Port	Expense	Cargo	Rate	Earnings
Dec.	1889	New York to Shanghai	New York	12,239.04	50,000 cases oil	.37	18,500.00
June	1890	Shanghai to Hong Kong	Shanghai	3,162.00			
Sept.	1890	Hong Kong to New York	Hong Kong	973.00	mixed cargo		10,000.00
Jan.	1891	New York to Philadelphia	New York	3,800.00	ballast 17		
		Philadelphia to Rio de Janeiro	Philadelphia	unknown	locomotives ballast		11,000.00
		Rio de Janeiro to Philadelphia	Rio de Janeiro	unknown	8700 barrels oil		
Dec.	1891	Philadelphia to Havre	Philadelphia	unknown	6975	3s	6,341.00
Feb.	1892	Havre to Philadelphia	Havre	unknown	M.T. bbls. oil ballast	6 ½ d	919.00
April	1892	Philadelphia to Boston	Philadelphia	unknown			
June	1892	Boston to Buenos Aires	Boston	3,959.25	lumber and mixed cargo		9,915.34
Oct.	1892	Buenos Aires to Pascagoula	Buenos Aires	1,454.00	ballast		
March	1893	Pascagoula to Dordrecht	Pascagoula Dordrecht	3,898.32 unknown	837230 ft. deals		10,000.00 (est.)

NOTE: From the beginning of 1886 to March 1893, when the ship was sold, a rough financial statement of the *N.B. Lewis* might be somewhat similar to this, with figures rounded out to hundreds.

Summary

Rough estimate of earnings ship *N.B. Lewis* 1880-1893

Earnings 1880 to July 1885 not known		
Net earnings estimated at		$ 40,000.
First voyage of Capt. Frank Gullison 1885		
Net earnings estimated at		2,500.
Voyages 1886-1893		
Total estimated earnings		173,500.
	Total	216,000.

Expenses

Port expenses as listed 1886-1893	$108,000.	
Estimated where not given	20,000.	
Estimated expenses at Yarmouth office including insurance	30,000.	
	158,000.	158,000.
Net profit to shareholders		58,000.
Proceeds from sale of vessel about		13,000.
	Total	$ 71,000.

Cost of vessel about $40,000.

Balance after sale of vessel about $31,000.

It would thus appear that a shareholder in the *N.B. Lewis* received back his original investment plus a yearly return on that investment of an annual average of about six per cent.

At that time this would have been an average return on a safe investment such as a mortgage but it could not be considered sufficient return for such a risky investment as a sailing ship.

Crew List Ship N.B. Lewis
Voyage to Shanghai and Hong Kong from New York 1890
(from Seamen's Wages Account Book for the Voyage)

Name	Rank	Wages
Emerson Graves	First mate	$35.00 per month
Alex McQuarrie	2nd mate	25.00
Reynold Clifford	Cook & Steward	40.00
John Wissik	Carpenter	26.00
Thorval Anderson	A.B. (able seaman)	18.00
Carl Beck	A.B. " "	18.00
Victor Anderson	A.B. " "	18.00
William Thorne	A.B. " "	18.00
Stephen Olsen	A.B. " "	18.00
Gustaf Carlsson	A.B. " "	18.00
Thomas Barron	O.S. (ordinary seaman)	14.00
Israel Gulligan	O.S. " "	14.00
Robert Peters	boy	10.00
Frank Desmond	A.B.	18.00
Y.T. Van Hymen	A.B.	18.00
Turi Sepp	A.B.	18.00
Gustav Jansen	A.B.	15.00
John Carlson	A.B.	18.00
Nils Nanson	A.B.	18.00

Captain Gullison's name is not included in the crew list. It is believed that at this time he was being paid at the rate of $75 per month.

*List of vessels mentioned in text and letters arranged under the following headings -
Name; Rig: Ship (S), Bark (B), Steamer (St), Schooner (Sch.); Tonnage; Where Built;
When Built; Builder; Port Registry; Owners.*

Abbie S. Hart	S; 1450; Tusket, N.S.; 1880; J.A. Hatfield; Yarmouth, N.S.; Wm. Law & Co.
Adolphus	S; 1319; Green Cove, N.S.; 1873; Yarmouth, N.S.; A.C. Robbins & Co.
Agenor	S; 1487; East Boston, Mass.; 1870; Curtis; Boston, Mass.; E. Williams & Co.
Annie	Sch.; 71; Salmon River, N.S.; 1895; ------; Yarmouth, N.S.; Ben Gullison
Annie Goudey	B; 1135; Meteghan, N.S.; 1873; ------; Yarmouth, N.S.; L.E. Baker
Annie Stafford	B; 1299; Black River; 1881; McLeod; St. John; J.W. Penry
Antoinette	B; 1118; Yarmouth, N.S.; 1874; ------; St. John; R.C. Elkin
Ancaios	S; 1704; Pt. Glasgow; 1891; Russell & Co.; Liverpool; G.T. Soley & Co.
Assyria	B; 1148; Courtney Bay, N.B.; 1887; O. Pitfield; St. John; Taylor Bros.
Baldwin	Barkentine; 561; Meteghan; 1891; Mark White; Yarmouth, N.S.; W.F. Hagar
Bangalore	S; 1699; Stockton, Eng.; 1886; Richardson Duck & Co.; London; G. Croshaw
Benquella	St.; 990; Southampton; 1862; Day & Summers; Lisbon; W. S. Bailey
Blair Drummond	S; 1450; Greenock, Scot.; 1874; ------; Glasgow; Thomson & Gray
Bonanza	S; 1078; St. Mary's Bay; 1875; E. Everett; Yarmouth, N.S.; R.T. Crosby
S.S. Cheribon	St; 1975; Dumbarton; 1882; W. Denny & Bros; Marseille; CIE Nationale de Navigation
Charles S. Whitney	S; 1651; Spencer's Island, N.S.; 1885; Spencer's Island Co.; Parrsboro; Geo. D. Spicer 1887
Charlie Baker	S; 1063; Brookville, N.S.; 1874; ------; Yarmouth, N.S.; L.E. Baker & Co.
Constance	B; 1592; Harvey Bank, N.B.; 1884; G.S. Turner; St. John; Geo. F. Smith

Cutty Sark	S; 921; Dumbarton, Scot.; 1869; Scott & Linton; London; Willis & Son
Cyprus	B; 1091; Bridgetown, N.S.; 1878; Young; St. John; Troop & Son
Don Enrique	S; 1344; Newburyport, Mass.; 1871; ------; Liverpool; B. Cremor 1890
Ellenbank	B; 1426; Maryport, Eng.; 1885; Ritson & Co.; Liverpool; McDrarmid 1891 Greenshields & Co.
Emilie L. Boyd	B; 1241; Green Cove, N.S.; 1881; E. Raymond; Yarmouth, N.S.; Wm. Law & Co. 1887
Ellen A. Read	S; 1750; Tusket N.S.; 1884; S. Treffry; Yarmouth, N.S.; Wm. Law & Co.
Fanny L. Cann	B; 797; Clyde River, N.S.; 1878; Coffin; Yarmouth, N.S.; Lyman Cann
Fred Taylor	S; 1798; Tusket, N.S.; 1883; Jeffry; Yarmouth, N.S.; Wm. Law & Co. 1885
Frolic	S; 1368; Mystic Ct.; 1869; Greenman, N.Y.; John A. McGaw
Gaelic	St; (Schooner Rigged) 2691; Belfast; 1885; Harland & Woolft, Liverpool; Oceanic Steam Navigation Co., Ltd.
George R. Skolfield	S; 1645; Brunswick, Me.; 1885; G.R. Skolfield; Brunswick; Skolfield Bros. 1890
Glenrosa	B; 504; Cheverie, N.S.; 1890; Roderick Bros.; Windsor; Allen Haley
Gloaming	S; 1499; Maitland, N.S.; 1879; J. Monteith; Maitland; T & E Kenney 1891
Glory of the Seas	S; 2102; East Boston, Mass.; 1869; Donald McKay; Boston; Donald McKay
Habitant	B; 1619; Scott's Bay, N.S.; 1885; J. Steele; Windsor; Sheffield & Wickwire 1891
Hectanooga	B; 1043; Clyde River; 1875; T. Coffin; Yarmouth, N.S.; A.C. Robbins 1891
SS Jason	St; 1412; Newcastle; 1880; A. Leslie & Co.; Liverpool; Ocean Steamship Co.
John Bunyan	S; 1193; Meteghan, N.S.; 1875; B.F. Robichaud; Yarmouth, N.S.; L.E. Baker 1885
Joseph B. Thomas	S; 1851; Thomaston, Me.; 1881; Watts & Co.; Thomaston, Me.; Samuel Watts & Co. 1891
Lancefield	B; 994; Moncton, N.B.; 1881; Crandall & Co.; St. John; Crandall & Co.
Lennie	B; 984; Belliveau's Cove; 1871; Lovitt; Yarmouth, N.S.; W.D. Lovitt 1885
Lillian	B; 618; Harrington Me.; 1873; ------; Harrington Me.; O.P. Rumball
Lizzie C. Troop	S; 1391; St. John; 1873; ------; St. John; Troop & Son 1885
Loanda	B; 1521; Courtney Bay, N.B.; 1881; J. Fraser; Windsor; Bennet Smith & Sons 1891
Luzon	S; 1339; East Boston; 1881; Smith & Townsend; New York; DeGroot & Peck 1890
Lydia	B; 1201; Tusket, N.S.; 1874; ------; Yarmouth; Wm. Law 1891
Mary L. Burrill	B; 1456; Little Brook, N.S.; 1883; A. Blinn; Yarmouth; Wm. Burrill
Mary L. Stone	S; 1420; Bath, Me.; 1874; Gross & Sawyer; New York; DeGroot & Peck 1890

Minnie Burrill	B; 1466; St. Mary's Bay; 1881; Burrill; Yarmouth; Wm. Burrill 1887
Monrovia	B; 532; Setauket, L.I.; 1878; ------; New York; Yates & Porterfield 1885
Morning Light	B; 1310; Meteghan, N.S.; 1878; Germain & Co.; Yarmouth; G. H. Perry
Mary Pendleton	S; 1385; Belfast Me.; 1871; H. McGilvery; Belfast Me.; Pendleton & Co.
Narwhal	S; 1327; Church Point, N.S.; 1879; Lovitt & Co.; Yarmouth; Lovitt & Co. 1887
North American	S; 1584; East Boston, Mass.; 1873; ------; Boston; Henry Hastings
Northampton	See Note Page 280
Petitcodiac	B; 682; Salisbury, N.B.; 1879; McEwen; Moncton; A.L. Wright 1887
Piako	S; 1075; Glasgow; 1876; A. Stephens & Sons; Lyttleton, New Zealand; N.Z. Shipping Co. 1884
SS Prince Arthur	St; 2041; Hull; 1899; Earls Co. Ltd.; Boston; Dominion Atlantic Railway
Queen of the Fleet	B; 941; Dorchester, N.B.; 1876; Palmer; Liverpool, Engl.; George Clark 1885
Richard Parsons	B; 1116; Comden, Me.; 1878; J. Pascal; Comden; Carleton Norwood & Co. 1887
SS Rolff	St; 794; Copenhagen; 1870; ------; Copenhagen; Danish Steam Packet Co.
Romanoff	B; 1049; ------; 1876; Yarmouth; A.F. Stoneman
Rossignol	B; 1510; Tusket; 1872; ------; Yarmouth; A.C. Robbins 1885
Ryerson	B; 1428; Salmon River, N.S.; 1873; J.K. Ryerson; Liverpool, Eng.; Wm. Charland 1885
Sachem	S; 1312; E. Boston; 1876; C. Sampson; Boston; M.F. Pickering & Co. 1891
Sintram	S; 1590; Freeport, Me.; 1877; E.C. Soule; Freeport; E.C. Soule
Sovereign of the Seas	S; 1502; East Boston, Mass.; 1868; Donald McKay; New York; Lawrence Giles & Co.
Stalwart	B; 1545; Barton, N.S.; 1885; J. Urquhart; Yarmouth; Jacob Bingay 1891
Stamboul	S; 1248; H. Gilbert N.S.; 1875; J. Bingay; Yarmouth, N.S.; J.J. Lovitt & Co.
St. Mary	B; 679; Eastport, Me.; 1869; ------; New York; J.W. Elwell & Co. 1891
Tam O'Shanter	S; 1522; Freeport, Me.; 1875; ------; Portland; E.C. Soule 1891
Thiorva	S; 1174; New Glasgow, N.S.; 1876; ------; Pictou; J.W. Carmichael 1887
Timour	S; 962; Newburyport, Mass.; 1865; ------; Boston; Wm. Perkins & Co. 1873
Troop	S; 1526; Dumbarton, Scot.; 1884; A. McMillan & Son; St. John; Troop & Son 1887
Tuskar	B; 1556; Avondale, N.S.; 1883; Wm. Card; Windsor, N.S.; Fred Curry
Vandalia	S; 1422; Harvey, N.B.; 1883; G.S. Turner; London; A.E. Kinnear (1890)
Z. Ring	S; 1371; St. John; 1872; ------; St. John; J.F. Cruickshank 1887

A List of Freight Rates Mentioned in
NOVASCOTIAMAN

Rate on coal from England to Canada 6s to 7s per ton.
Rate on oil. New York to Shanghai 31¢ per case.
Grain rates. San Francisco to Europe around 27/6.
Sugar rates. Manila 4 1/2.
Unchartered rates on oil 2/1. Probably u.s. to Europe in barrels.
Closed at Frisco. Grain 27/6.
Captain Ben does not consider 27/6 enough.
Letter from Black re coal rates.
Letter from Black re commission and brokerages.
Paying 23¢ for case oil to Japan 'nothing in that'.
December 20th, '87. Freight rates on cotton.
1/2 of coal freight is advanced by shippers.
Various coal rates.
Coal rate to Capetown 21 shillings.
Coal and oil freight rates.
Coal and oil freight rates.
Sugar rate 1888 − 27/6. March 1889 − 33/9 (equals $8.10 gold)
Estimate $8,000.00 gross profit on round trip to Java.
Freight rates: barrel oil 1/9 to u.k. and continent; deals 60
        shillings to 62/6; pitch pine £6.5s;
            coal to Rio 29s;
                to Montevideo 31s.;
                to Capetown 28s.;
                to Buenos Aires 34s.

Rate on lumber: Montreal to River Platte $17.50.

Case oil to Shanghai 37¢.

Rate on lumber Boston to Buenos Aires $15.50.

Oil rate to Havre from Philadelphia 2/6.

Rate on empty oil barrels Havre to Phil. 6 1/2d.

Chalk for ballast put on board free.

Rate on lumber to River Platte $8.50.

Rate of 1/9 Phil. to London means £1,000 total freight for voyage (possibly pays port charges and expenses both ports.)

Another estimate 1 shilling 10 pence rate on oil, across Atlantic (doesn't pay expenses.)

Rate on lumber from Boston to Buenos Aires $8.50.

Rate on grain from Buenos Aires and LaPlata 13s to 10/6d.

Rate on oil 2 shillings Philadelphia to Southampton.

Rate on coal. Cardiff to Rio de Janeiro 16/6.

s or / = shillings

d = English pence

27/6 = twenty-seven shillings and six pence

£ = English pound, with average value of four dollars and eighty-six cents in u.s. or Canadian funds

Voyage of N.B. Lewis from Shanghai to San Francisco, 1886

'Trouble with my sailors': The Seaman's Wages Account Book for the voyage shows that on July 21, the day before the *N.B. Lewis* was due to sail, almost half of the crew, including the second officer, were arrested in Shanghai.

The ship was evidently docked across the river from the city because the sailors were charged on an average of three dollars for 'Bumboat' which would be the local Chinese sampan or river-taxi. Captain Gullison's list of advances to the sailors shows that most of them paid a shoemaker from $2.25 to $3.75 for boots and $5.00 to $6.50 to a tailor except the second officer Thomas Ferguson who paid the shoemaker $6.50 and had a tailor bill of $15.75.

The eight men arrested in Shanghai paid an average of $1.50 to $2.70 each for warrants for arrest, fines and police costs. One man, Joseph Gunning, must have been in real trouble for his court costs totalled $11.70.

It is also interesting to note from the records that only two of the eight men arrested – Thomas Ferguson and John Johnson – were still with the ship when it reached Dunkirk. The others must have left the ship at San Francisco as mentioned in letter from *N.B. Lewis* dated October 2, 1886.

The official report of the ship *N.B. Lewis* to the British Consul at San Francisco lists the sailors below as deserted. They apparently left the ship on arrival without a settlement in regard to their pay. Six of these sailors were in trouble in Shanghai – (See letter July 22, 1886). The following information from the crew wages account book shows amount of fine at Shanghai and the amount each sailor owed.

Sailors fined at Shanghai	Fines	Total owed Shanghai
T. Fitzpatrick	$ 2.70	£6-15-11
Wm. Nabb	1.50	£6-15-11
Thomas Springer	2.70	£6-16-1
Charles Cramer		£6-5-8
Joseph Gunning	11.70	£5-19-4
Joseph Lucreet	2.70	£5-11-10
Hans Joseph		£5-4-11
Wm. Westlake		£6-19-10
R. Glover		£5-16-6
Ed. Simons	.70	£5-18-11
Geo. Pike		£6-15-11
Jas. Heel or Heald		£6-14-0

Rate of wages of AB £2-15-0 per month.

The collected letters, etc., of Captain Benjamin Franklin Gullison.

Tissue letter copying book containing copies of Captain Gullison's letters from Jan. 18, 1886, to April 18, 1893.

Folder of hand-written letters to Captain Gullison from Captain Henry Lewis, Nathan B. Lewis, various members of the Gullison family, friends and ships' agents in London, Liverpool and Cardiff.

Logs of the ship *N.B. Lewis*

1880	Voyage Yarmouth to Philadelphia
	Voyage Philadelphia to Waterford, Ireland, and return
	Voyage Philadelphia to Havre, France
	Voyage Philadelphia to Hamburg
1886-87	New York to Shanghai, San Francisco, Dunkirk
1888	Cardiff to Rio de Janiero and return
	Cardiff to Capetown
	Capetown to New York
1890	New York to Shanghai, Hong Kong, and return to New York
1892-93	Philadelphia to Havre and return
	Philadelphia to Boston
	Boston to Buenos Aires
	Buenos Aires to Pascagoula, Miss.
	Pascagoula to Dordrecht, Holland

Various account books kept by Captain Gullison, including seamen's wages account books.

Local History

BREBNER, J.B. *The Neutral Yankees of Nova Scotia.* New York, Columbia University Press, 1937.

BROWN, G.S.A. *History of Yarmouth, Nova Scotia.* Boston, Rand Avery & Co., 1888.

CAMPBELL, REV. J.R. *History of the County of Yarmouth*, N.S. Saint John, N.B., J. & A. McMillan, 1876.

D'ENTREMONT, H. LEANDER. *The Baronnie de Pombcoup and the Acadians.* Yarmouth, N.S., Herald-Telegram Press, 1931.

LAWSON, J. MURRAY. *Record of Yarmouth Shipping.* Saint John, N.B., J. & A. McMillan, 1876.

————. *Record of Yarmouth Shipping.* Appendix. Yarmouth, N.S., Yarmouth Herald, 1884.

————. *Yarmouth Reminiscences.* Yarmouth, N.S. Yarmouth Herald, 1902.

POOLE, EDMUND DUVAL. *Annals of Yarmouth and Barrington, Nova Scotia, in the Revolutionary War.* Yarmouth, N.S., Yarmouth *Herald*, 1899.

RICKER, JACKSON. *Historical Sketches of Blenwood and the Argyles.* Truro, N.S., Truro Publishing Co., 1941.

WILSON, ISAIAH W. *History of the County of Digby.* n.p., n.d.

Yarmouth Herald and Telegram, 1880-1893

Maritime History

BIXBY, WILLIAM. *South Street, New York's Seaport Museum.* N.Y., David McKay, 1972.

CLARK, ARTHUR H. *The Clipper-ship Era.* N.Y. Putnam, 1910.

HUTCHINS, JOHN GREENWOOD BROWN. The American Maritime Industries and Public Policy, 1789-1914. Cambridge, Mass., Harvard University Press, 1941.

LUBBOCK, ALFRED BASIL. *The Down Easters.* Glasgow, Brown, Son & Ferguson Ltd., 1929.

MARVIN, WINTHROP L. *The American Merchant Marine; its History and Romance from 1620 to 1902.* N.Y., Scribners, 1916.

MATTHEWS, FREDERICK C. *American Merchant Ships.* Salem, Mass., Marine Research Society, 1930.

MORISON, W.E. *Maritime History of Massachusetts.* Cambridge, Mass., Houghton Mifflin & Co., 1921.

RANDIER, JEAN. *Men and Ships around Cape Horn, 1616-1939.* N.Y., David McKay, 1969.

SPICER, STANLEY I. *Masters of Sail.* Toronto, Ryerson, 1968.

UNDERHILL, HAROLD A. *Masting and Rigging.* Glasgow, Brown, Son & Ferguson, 1946.

VILLIERS, ALAN. *Men, Ships and the Sea.* Washington, D.C., National Geographic Society, 1973.

WALLACE, FREDERICK WILLIAM. *Wooden Ships and Iron Men.* London, Hodder & Stoughton, 1924.

INDEX

The index includes individuals, vessels and place names other than frequently referred to entries that appear throughout the book.

Petitcodiac, 388
Piako, 238
Pike, George, 392
Pope & Talbot, 107
Port Eads, 149
Portland, Ore., 271
Porter, Rev. Cahoon, 169
Prince Arthur, 74
Prince Lucine, 165
Putnam, A.L., 280

Queen of the Fleet, 142

Rawden, Capt., 220
Rankin, A.N., 293
Raymond, Lydia, 97
Raymond, Norman, 88
Republic, 22
Richard Pearson, 273
Ritchie, Capt., 362
Riggs & Bro., 73
Robinson, Capt., 192
Robinson, Charles S., 274
Rockland, 364
Rogers, Chloe Lewis, 359
Rogers, Capt. George, 296
Rogers, William, 369
Rolff, 233
Romanoff, 224
Rose, Capt., 35
Rossignol, 139
Rotterdam, 38
Ryerson, 142

Sachem, 280
St. Helena, 287
Salmon River, 361
St. Mary, 352
Sarah, 21
Samarang, 213
Sapelo, Ga., 56
Sarnia, 124
Sepp, T., 385
Sennett, James, 109
Septwear, D., 228
Shanghai, 231
Simons, Ed, 392
Sintram, 273
Soares, R.N., 274
Soley, G.T., 207
Spicer, Capt. George, 231

Spinney, E.K., 301
Springer, Thomas, 392
Stalwart, 77
Sunda Straits, 218
Stamboul, 270
Staten Island, 208
Stephen, I.M., 184
Swansea, 112
Stoneman, A.F., 224

Tam O'Shanter, 280
Theoff, Capt., 88
Theresa, 190
Thiorva, 262
Thomas Joliff, 168
Thorne, William, 385
Timour, 280
Timgley, Capt., 273
Trask, Alfred, 68
Trask, Charles, 68
Trefry, Capt., 52
Treharne, druggist, 181
Troop, 260
Tuskar, 168
Tybee, 54
Tylor & Lewis 196

Usher, 16

Vandalia, 126
Van Hymen, 385
Van Leeveren, J.,
Vickery, Capt., 51
Victoria, V.I., 91
Vosbrug, 234

Walker, P.J., 340
Wambessie & Sons, 36
Wardell, D., 259
Westlake, Wm., 392
Wetmore, George, 319
Weston, Capt., 270
White Rose Co., 122
Whitney, Charles, 262
Whittaker, Robert, 321
Wilson & Crawford, 298
Woodstock, Capt., 273

Yang tse Kiang, 266
Yarmouth, 292

Z. Ring, 262